STRESS, COPING, AND DEPRESSION

STRESS, COPING, AND DEPRESSION

Edited by

SHERI L. JOHNSON
ADELE M. HAYES
University of Miami, Coral Gables

TIFFANY M. FIELD
Nova Southeastern University

NEIL SCHNEIDERMAN
PHILIP M. McCABE
University of Miami, Coral Gables

Routledge
Taylor & Francis Group
LONDON AND NEW YORK

First published 2005 by Lawrence Erlbaum Associates, Inc.
Published 2014 by Routledge

2 Park Square, Milton Park, Abingdon, Oxfordshire OX14 4RN
711 Third Avenue, New York, NY 10017

Routledge is an imprint of the Taylor and Francis Group, an informa business

Cover design by Kathryn Houghtaling Lacey

Library of Congress Cataloging-in-Publication Data

Stress, coping, and depression / edited by Sheri L. Johnson ... [et al.].
p. cm.
Includes bibliographical references and indexes.

ISBN 978-0-8058-3440-6 (hbk)
ISBN 978-1-138-00343-9 (pbk)

1. Depression, Mental--Etiology--Congresses. 2. Depression, Mental--Treatment--Congresses. I. Johnson, Sheri L. II. University of Miami Symposia on Stress and Coping (15th)

RC537.S84 2000
616.85'27--dc21

99-047473

Contents

Preface

Because of its prevalence, depression has been described as the common cold of mental illness. To receive a diagnosis of major depression, an individual must experience the following symptoms for a period of 2 weeks or more: sad mood or loss of pleasure, with at least four other symptoms such as sleep disturbance, appetite or weight changes, psychomotor agitation or retardation, fatigue, feelings of worthlessness or guilt, diminished ability to think or concentrate, and recurrent thoughts of death or suicide (American Psychological Association, 1994). As many as 13% of men and 21% of women meet these criteria during their lifetime (Kessler et al., 1994).

The devastating consequences of depression on the individual, family, and society have received increasing recognition. Of the physical and psychiatric disorders defined by the World Health Organization (WHO), depression ranked as the fourth leading cause of disease burden in 1990 and is projected to become the single leading cause of disease burden by 2020 (Murray & Lopez, 1996). There is increasing evidence that depression worsens the course and mortality rates associated with a number of diseases, such as HIV infection, coronary heart disease, cancer, and diabetes (Goodnick, 1997; Maldonado, Fernandez, Garza Trevino, & Levy, 1997; McDaniel, Musselman, & Nemeroff, 1977; Shapiro, Lidagoster, & Glassman, 1977; Stober, Schwartz, McDaniel, & Abrams, 1997). In addition, this disorder takes a toll on marital relations, parenting skills, and general family conflict and cohesion (Keitner, Miller, & Ryan, 1993). In the United States, the direct and indirect costs of depression are estimated to exceed $30 billion per year (Rice & Miller, 1995). The most tragic consequence is that as many as 15% of individuals with recurrent depression commit suicide (Clark & Fawcett, 1992).

As research on depression has evolved, the recurrent nature of this disorder has become increasingly apparent. As many as 76% of individuals who meet criteria for an index episode of depression will experience a recurrence within 10 years (Piccinell & Wilkinson, 1994). The long-term consequences are heightened by evidence of high rates of depression among children of depressed mothers (Hammen, chap. 5, this volume). Thus, many researchers have shifted toward a life-course perspective in an attempt to understand long-term vulnerability for individuals, as well as determinants of family transmission across generations.

Although the consequences of depression are disturbing, new developments in the field are exciting and increase our understanding of the etiology and treatment of depression. To provide a forum to discuss these developments, we chose depression as a focus for our annual University of Miami Stress and Coping conference. Each presenter then contributed a chapter for this volume. We invited presentations and chapters from researchers who were taking novel social, psychological, and biological approaches to depression. We selected authors to cover three important domains: child development, basic adult psychopathology, and treatment. Given the breadth of the depression field, we emphasized particularly innovative and empirically grounded theory and treatment development rather than complete coverage of all related models (for more comprehensive coverage of existing models, see Beckham & Leber, 1995). Our authors supply a range of thought-provoking ideas that we believe are likely to inspire future developments in understanding the etiology and treatment of this debilitating disorder.

CHILD DEVELOPMENT

Our first section, on child development, begins with a chapter by Field (chap. 1, this volume) that focuses on the impact of maternal depression on their infants. Field's studies integrate biological and behavioral characteristics of depressed mothers and their infants. Depressed mothers demonstrate two interaction styles with their infants that are associated with unique neurotransmitter, brain asymmetry, and behavioral patterns in both mothers and their neonatal infants. Field's model of maternal depression emphasizes the prenatal transmission of biological dysregulation, which is then compounded by mother–infant interactions.

Tronick and Weinberg (chap. 2, this volume) present a theoretical model of infant affect regulation that guides their research on gender differences in reactivity to depressive mother–infant interaction. Their work provides evidence that maternal depression differentially impacts the affective behavior of infant sons and daughters.

Marshall and Fox (chap. 3, this volume) then provide a thorough review of hemispheric laterality and depression. Frontal hemispheric asymmetry is a vulnerability factor among depressed adults that can be conceptualized as an indicator of systems that modulate approach and withdrawal behavior. Infants of depressed mothers display frontal asymmetry, thus the authors present a developmental model of links between frontal asymmetry, emotion regulation, and depression.

We conclude this section with a methodological contribution from Johnson and Jacob (chap. 4, this volume) that outlines the use of hierarchical linear modeling (HLM) to understand risk factors among family members of depressed individuals. HLM appears particularly suited to family research because it simultaneously accounts for variables that operate across each child within the family (e.g., exposure to parental depression) and characteristics that are unique to the child (e.g., age and gender). Within these analyses, parental depression, but not maternal depression, appears to be moderated by the number of years parents have been married.

BASIC ADULT PSYCHOPATHOLOGY

Our chapters in the second section move from broad social environmental influences, through personality and information-processing approaches, to an integrated model of biological and cognitive processing involved in the genesis of depressive symptoms. Hammen (chap. 5, this volume) describes her model for integrating life events with developmental forces, with a particular emphasis on the early experiences and attachment styles that shape interpersonal coping skills, and thereby contribute to stress generation. Hammen's work provides a model of how depressed parents may model interpersonal styles and stress generation for their children, thereby promoting the development of depression among offspring.

Other chapters in this section address intrapsychic mechanisms in the genesis of depressive symptoms. Blaney (chap. 6, this volume) provides a review of experimental studies that assess individual differences in stress vulnerability. He highlights a number of methodological and measurement issues that deserve more attention, and then recommends that researchers consider conceptually driven taxonomies of vulnerability and stress.

Gotlib and Neubauer (chap. 7, this volume) review the literature on memory and attention biases associated with depression vulnerability. They also draw from cognitive science to present a more specific model of information-processing impairment in individuals prone to depression. On the basis of an integrative review of findings to date, they discuss important future research goals.

Scott and his colleagues (chap. 8, this volume) review the evidence for mood as a final common pathway into depressive episodes. They present evidence that sad mood is the common outcome across most risk factors for depression and the most common symptom in the prodromal phases of depression. Given this, the authors review cognitive mechanisms that may mediate and moderate the transduction of mood states into full-blown depressive episodes. They place particular emphasis on the quality of affective distress in depression, and they argue that sadness, anxiety, and irritability in depressive episodes are likely to be associated with specific symptom profiles.

Writing in tandem, Winters, Scott, and Beevers (chap. 9, this volume) provide an excellent summary of the neurophysiological systems involved in the processing of emotionally relevant stimuli. Their model suggests that the functional balance across neurotransmitter pathways may explain the different constellation of mood and symptom patterns seen in depression and may parallel individual differences in symptoms described in chapter 8. In short, chapters 8 and 9 provide a set of testable hypotheses for explaining the enormous heterogeneity in depressive symptoms.

TREATMENT

The chapters in this final section describe new applications and innovations in psychotherapy for unipolar and bipolar disorder. DeRubeis and his colleagues (chap. 10, this volume) describe their program of research that aims to better understand the efficacy of cognitive therapy for depression, as well as the therapist and patient behaviors that are associated with symptom reduction. They address the recent controversy concerning the efficacy of cognitive therapy in the treatment of severe depression and describe a multisite study designed to address some of the questions raised by previous research. In another line of research, they offer a novel approach to the study of the change in cognitive therapy for depression. They present a methodology for identifying critical drops in depression symptoms and the therapist and patient processes that are associated with these drops. This approach sheds some interesting light on the process of change in cognitive therapy, and it is likely to provide an innovative methodology for researchers studying the change process across psychotherapies.

The chapters by Antoni (chap. 11, this volume) and by Kilbourn, Saab, and Schneiderman (chap. 12, this volume) describe unique applications of cognitively based psychotherapies and stress-management techniques for the treatment of depression in HIV-infected patients and in post-myocardial infarction patients, respectively. These authors review 10 years of their research in these areas, which provides the foundation for their current programs of treatment and research. In both programs, the authors conduct a thorough assessment of both psychosocial and physiological functioning across the course of therapy. This approach allows for fascinating research on the pathways of change and the relation between psychosocial factors and disease processes.

Hayes and Harris (chap. 13, this volume) describe a therapy that they are developing to address the full range of psychosocial variables that influence the course of depression. The authors review literatures on the psychopathology of depression, the process of change in psychotherapy, and on psychological well-being that form the theoretical foundation of their integrated therapy. Their approach integrates diverse, empirically grounded concepts and interventions, and it focuses on both symptom reduction and the promotion of wellness. This comprehensive treatment is specifically designed to reduce the relapse rates associated with current therapies for depression. The authors are collaborating with Drs. Antoni and Schneiderman to examine the relations between change in psychosocial factors, symptoms, and neuroendocrine and immune functioning. An examination of these relations may begin to clarify the well-documented relations between depression, physical health, and disease. In addition, the authors describe a number of methodological advances in the study of therapy process and outcome.

In the final chapter, George, Friedman, and Miklowitz (chap. 14, this volume) venture into an area long dominated by pharmacological treatments. These authors present a review of the psychosocial factors that influence the course of bipolar disorder and then present their integrated family and individual therapy, which carefully and innovatively addresses these factors. As an adjunct to mood-stabilizing medication, this exciting new therapy holds promise in reducing the high rates of relapse associated with bipolar disorder.

This volume provides the reader with stimulating models of etiology and treatment in depression. The contributing authors offer a variety of novel perspectives on the processes that put adults and their children at risk for depression, on the environmental, psychological, and biological mechanisms involved in the genesis of an episode, and on how to address the psychosocial context of depression. These chapters share several commonalties, including careful attention to empirical literature and an emphasis on integration across domains. We believe these chapters provide a rich and sophisticated understanding of the environmental and intrapsychic risk factors that contribute to the onset and maintenance of depression and are important to consider in its treatment. We hope the volume provides a rich array of hypotheses for future empirical study.

ACKNOWLEDGMENTS

We are thankful for the support of the following individuals: Rod Wellens, Brian Dursam, Ellie Schneiderman, R. Jay Turner, and the graduate students and faculty members of the Department of Psychology at the University of Miami. Without their support, this conference and volume would not have been possible. We are deeply indebted to Sandra Racoobian and Jacqueline Machado for their help with manuscript preparation. This endeavor was also supported by the University of Miami Department of Psychology, the Behavioral Medicine Research Group, and the Touch Research Institute.

REFERENCES

American Psychiatric Association. (1994). *Diagnostic and Statistical Manual of Mental Disorders* (4th ed.). Washington, DC: APA.

Beckham, E. E., & Leber, W. R. (Eds.). (1995). *Handbook of depression* (2nd ed.). New York: Guilford Press.

Clark, D. C., & Fawcett, J. (1992). Review of empirical risk factors for evaluation of the suicidal patient. In B. Bongar (Ed.), *Suicide: Guidelines for assessment, management, and treatment.* New York: Oxford University Press.

Goodnick, P. J. (1997). Diabetes mellitus and depression: Issues in theory and treatment. *Psychiatric Annals, 27*(5), 353-359.

Keitner, G. I., Miller, I., & Ryan, C. E. (1993). The role of the family in major depressive illness. *Psychiatric Annals, 23*(9), 500–507.

Kessler, R. C., McGonagle, K. A., Zhao, S., Nelson, C. B., Hughes, M., Eshleman, S., Witchen, H. O., & Kenderl, K. S. (1994). Lifetime and 12-month prevalence of DSM-III-R psychiatric disorders in the United States: Results from the national comorbidity survey. *Archives of General Psychiatry, 51*, 8–19.

Maldonado, J. L., Fernandez, F., Garza Trevino, E. S., & Levy, J. K., (1997). Depression and its treatment in neurological disease. *Psychiatric Annals, 27*(5), 341–346.

McDaniel, J. S., Musselman, D. J., & Nemeroff, C. B. (1997). Cancer and depression: Theory and treatment. *Psychiatric Annals, 27*(5), 360–364.

Murray, C. J. L., & Lopez, A. D. (1996). *The global burden of disease: A comprehensive assessment of mortality and disability from diseases, injuries, and risk factors in 1990 and projected to 2020.* Boston, MA: Harvard University Press.

Piccinelli, M., & Wilkinson, G. (1994). Outcome of depression in psychiatric settings. *British Journal of Psychiatry, 164*, 197–304.

Rice, D. P., & Miller, L. S. (1995). The economic burden of affective disorders. *British Journal of Psychiatry, 166*, 34-42.

Shapiro, P. A., Lidagoster, L., & Glassman, A. H. (1997). Depression and heart disease. *Psychiatric Annals, 27*(5), 347–352.

Stober, D. R., Schwartz, J. A. J., McDaniel, J. S., & Abrams, R. F. (1997). Depression and HIV disease: Prevalence, correlates and treatment. *Psychiatric Annals, 27*(5), 372–377.

Part I

CHILD DEVELOPMENT

Chapter **1**

Infants of Depressed Mothers

Tiffany M. Field
Touch Research Institutes, University of Miami Medical School and Nova Southeastern University

Maternal depression negatively affects infants as early as the neonatal period, implicating prenatal effects of maternal depression. This is discussed in the first section of this chapter. As early as birth, the infants show a profile of dysregulation in their behavior, physiology, and biochemistry, which probably derives from prenatal exposure to a biochemical imbalance in their mothers. These effects are compounded by the disorganizing influence of the mothers' interaction behavior.

Nondepressed caregivers, such as fathers, may buffer these effects because they provide more optimal stimulation and arousal modulation. The evidence for this and the positive effects of several laboratory interventions are presented in the second section of this chapter. Interventions such as massage and music therapy, which are mood altering for the mothers and arousal reducing for the infants, make the mothers and infants more responsive to interaction coaching and improve their interactions. These interventions may be effective because (a) they induce a better mood state in the mothers (and alter right frontal electroencephalograms, EEGs, a marker of depression) and (b) they reduce sympathetic arousal in the infants. Norepinephrine and cortisol levels, for example, are lower following 1 month of these therapies, and (c) being less sympathetically aroused, both the mothers and infants can be more responsive and more available to interaction coaching; thus, their interactions subsequently improve.

Depressed mothers have two predominant interaction styles, *withdrawn* or *intrusive*, which seem to have differential, negative effects on infants related to inadequate stimulation and arousal modulation. The type of interaction coaching that is effective depends on the interaction style of the mother. These data and a model regarding the different types of maternal depression are presented in the final section of this chapter.

INFANTS OF DEPRESSED MOTHERS

Infants of depressed mothers appear to have a profile of dysregulation as early as the neonatal period. This *dysregulation profile* is characterized by: (a) limited responsivity on the Brazelton, excessive indeterminate sleep, and elevated norepinephrine and cortisol levels at the neonatal period; (b) relative right frontal EEG activation at 1 week, 1 month, and 3 months, and stability in these patterns from 3 months to 3 years; (c) limited responsivity to facial expressions, lower vagal tone, and signs of neurological delay at 6 months; (d) less social referencing at 9 months; and (e) limited play and exploratory behavior, inferior Bayley scores, and delayed growth at 12 months.

Neonatal Period

In our neonatal studies, the newborns of depressed mothers showed inferior performance on the Brazelton orienting items (particularly on the inanimate items), received inferior scores on the depression and robustness factors, and demonstrated more neonatal stress behavior (Abrams, Field, Scafidi, & Prodromidis, 1995; Lundy, Field, & Pickens, 1996). They also showed excessive indeterminate sleep (sleep that is difficult to code), which is disconcerting given that Sigman and Parmelee (1989) found an inverse relation between indeterminate sleep during the neonatal period and IQ scores at 12 years. Newborns were also less attentive and less expressive during a procedure of modeled faces (Lundy et al., 1996). Both the depressed mothers' and their neonatal infants' norepinephrine and cortisol levels were significantly elevated (Lundy et al., 1999). Assessments of EEG asymmetry revealed a pattern that is noted in chronically depressed adults, namely, relative right frontal EEG activation in both the mothers and their infants when the infants were 3 months old (Field, Fox, Pickens, Nawrocki, & Soutullo, 1995), when they were 1 month old (Jones, Field, Fox, Lundy, & Davalos, 1997) and even as early as 1 week of age (Jones, Field, & Fox, 1999). Relative right frontal EEG activation at 1 month also was related to indeterminate sleep patterns and negative affect at the neonatal assessment (Jones, Field, Fox, Lundy, & Davalos, 1997). The relative right frontal EEG activation among depressed mothers is not surprising, but the appearance of this pattern as early as 1 week in their infants was very unexpected, given the supposed plasticity of brain development and the relatively undeveloped frontal cortex during the first several months of life.

The Infancy Period

In our laboratory studies on affect perception and production, we learned that depressed mothers exhibited fewer positive and animated facial expressions and less animated vocal expression (Raag et al., 1997) and that infants of depressed mothers produced more sad and angry faces and showed fewer expressions of interest (Pickens & Field, 1993b). They also showed a preference for sad faces and/or voices (greater time looking at videotaped models looking and sounding sad; Lundy, Field, Cigales, Quadra, & Pickens, 1997), which might relate to sad expressions being more familiar to them. They also displayed less accurate matching of happy facial expressions with happy vocal expressions (Lundy et al., 1996). In addition, the absence of a relation between infant facial expressions and vagal tone in infants of depressed mothers suggested biobehavioral uncoupling that might derive from the infants' excessive vigilance in emotional situations (Pickens & Field, 1993b). Finally, during a mother-holding-doll situation, infants of depressed mothers showed less protest behavior (Hart, Field, Letourneau, & DelValle, 1998).

At 6 months, vagal tone was significantly lower and behavioral responses to facial expressions were slower in the infants of depressed mothers (Field, Pickens, Fox, Nawrocki, & Gonzalez, 1995). Although the significance of lower vagal tone is not entirely understood, higher vagal tone is typically associated with better performance on attention and learning tasks. By 12 months, infants of depressed mothers were more likely to exhibit neurological soft signs, and they showed less exploratory behavior, lower Bayley Mental and Motor Scale (BMMS) scores, and lower weight percentiles (Field et al., 1998).

Preschool Period

In our longitudinal follow up, 75% of the mothers with high scores on the Beck at the neonatal period had elevated Beck scores at the 3-year follow up. Their preschool-age children continued to show interaction problems, and they demonstrated clinical scores on the externalizing and internalizing factors of the Child Behavior Checklist (CBCL; Field, Yando, et al., 1996) and elevated cortisol levels. Additionally, their mothers viewed them as vulnerable (Bendell et al., 1994). Predictors from the 3-month infancy assessment that explained 3-year outcome variance included heart-rate (HR) variability and ratings of the infants' interactions with a stranger

(Bendell et al., 1994). In terms of the stability of EEG patterns, 3-month-old infants with relative right frontal EEG activation continued to demonstrate the same pattern at 3 years (Jones, Field, Fox, Davalos, & Pickens 1997). The 3-year-old children with relative right frontal EEG activation also showed more inhibited behavior in strange object and strange person situations, and they showed nonempathetic behavior during their mothers' display of distress (crying) behavior. Two styles of nonempathetic behavior were noted, including passive–withdrawn and angry–aggressive behavior.

INTERVENTION STUDIES

Comprehensive Intervention

In a comprehensive intervention study, mothers and their infants were followed over the first 6 months to assess the infants' development and to identify potential markers from the first 3 months that predicted chronic depression in the mothers (Field, 1999). Of the depressed mothers we sampled, 70% appeared to have chronic depression that persisted across the first 6 months of the infants' life. The infants of these mothers showed delays in growth and development at 12 months (Field, 1992).

Physiological–biochemical markers that we identified for the mothers' chronic depression included relative right frontal EEG activation, low vagal tone and serotonin (as indexed by the metabolite 5H1AA), and elevated norepinephrine and cortisol levels (Field, 1999). These variables, measured at 3 months, accounted for 51% of the mothers' continuing depression at 6 months (with maternal relative right frontal EEG activation alone explaining 31% of the variance). Because infants, whose mothers remained depressed at 6 months, began to show growth and developmental delays at 1 year, it was important to identify those mothers for intervention purposes. In this study, a simple electrocardiogram (EKG), EEG, and urine analysis (for cortisol, norepinephrine, and serotonin) together could explain more than half the variance in the mothers' continuing depression and could be used to identify those mother–infant dyads needing early intervention. We used these markers to identify a second sample of chronically depressed mothers to receive an intervention. Mothers in the intervention received social, educational, and vocational rehabilitation and mood-induction interventions, including relaxation therapy, music mood induction, massage therapy, and interaction coaching. Additionally, their infants received day care.

Although the intervention mothers continued to have higher depression scores than the nondepressed mothers, their interaction behavior became significantly more positive and their biochemical values and vagal tone normalized or approximated the values of the nondepressed control group. The infants in the intervention group also showed more positive interaction behavior, better growth, fewer pediatric complications, and normalized biochemical values, and by 1 year, they obtained superior BMMS scores. Thus, chronically depressed mothers could be identified and offered a relatively cost-effective intervention. This intervention attenuated the typical delays in growth and development. Finally, although we had limited success modifying depressed mothers' relatively flat facial and vocal expressions (Raag et al., 1997), we were able to increase their touching behavior. This, in turn, improved the mothers' mood state and interaction behavior as well as their infants' interaction behavior, and it was a very effective modulation of negative state during Tronick's still-face situation (Pelaez-Nogueras, Field, Pickens, et al., 1996).

Other Effective Interventions

Natural Buffers of the Depressed Mothers' Negative Effects (Fathers and Nursery School Caregivers). Natural buffers in the environment included nondepressed fathers or boyfriends (Hossain, Field, Pickens, & Gonzalez, 1995) and the nursery school teachers of the infants of depressed mothers (Pelaez-Nogueras, Field, Cigales, Gonzalez, & Clasky, 1995). Infants of depressed mothers received better interaction ratings when interacting with their nondepressed fathers and with their nursery school teachers. Our study on switching mothers, which asked whether depressed infants improved when interacting with nondepressed mothers and whether depressed mothers showed more responsive behavior with infants of nondepressed mothers, yielded very few group differences (Martinez et al., 1996). The infants' depressed behavior generalized to the nondepressed strangers, possibly because interacting with strangers was stressful for the infant (Field et al., 1988). Interestingly, the depressed mothers did not affect the infants of nondepressed mothers negatively, suggesting that those infants might be less vulnerable to unresponsive interaction behavior than the infants of depressed mothers.

Massage Therapy for the Infants. Massage therapy was another effective intervention for the infants of depressed mothers. In contrast to rocking, massage therapy contributed to more organized sleep patterns, more positive interaction behaviors, and greater weight gain (Field, Grizzle, Scafidi, Abrams, & Richardson, 1996).

Mood-Induction Interventions for the Mothers. For the mothers, music therapy (Field, Martinez, et al., 1998) and massage therapy (Field, Grizzle, et al., 1996) sessions were extremely effective short-term interventions. Both types of therapy led to attenuated relative right frontal EEG activation (Field, Grizzle, et al., 1996). These results were surprising, because EEG had been considered unalterable in the adult literature; in this literature, relative right frontal EEG activation has been described as a marker of chronic depression (Henriques & Davidson, 1990). More recent positron emission tomography (PET) data on blood flow, however, suggest that frontal cortex activity might reflect a mood-state difference, whereas activity in the amygdala might function as a trait marker of depression (Drevets et al., 1992).

Interaction Coaching. Coaching, including either imitation or attention-getting instruction, was effective in improving interaction behaviors; mothers became more animated during attention getting and more sensitive to their infants' signals during imitation. Their infants, in turn, became more responsive (Pickens & Field, 1993a).

WITHDRAWN VERSUS INTRUSIVE DEPRESSED MOTHERS

Studies of the interactions, both spontaneous and those during interaction coaching, reveal different styles of maternal behavior that are associated with asynchronous mother–infant interactions (Cohn, Campbell, Matias, & Hopkins, 1990; Field, Healy, Goldstein, & Guthertz, 1990). One style consists of a pattern of disengagement (*withdrawal*). In this type of dyadic interaction, mothers demonstrate affectively restricted behaviors. They turn away from their infants, adopt a slouched-back posture, verbalize in an flat tone of voice, and display little facial expression. In several mothers, these behaviors are seen for 75% of the interaction time.

Although depressed mothers' interaction behavior typically has been described as withdrawn (Field, 1992), some depressed mothers show intrusive interaction behavior (Cohn, Matias, Tronick, Connell, & Lyons-Ruth, 1986; Field et al., 1990). Intrusive mothers are involved with their infants to the point of interfering and may exhibit anger, hostility, and irritability (Lyons-Ruth, Zoll, Connell, & Grunebaum, 1986). Lyons-Ruth et al. (1986) reported that increasing maternal depression was associated with greater covert hostility and more interference with infants' goal-directed activity. Others, however, have associated maternal depression with overt physical intrusiveness (Malphurs, Raag, Field, Pickens, & Pelaez-Nogueras, 1996).

Different Interaction Styles Are Associated With Differential Infant Outcomes and Responses to Interventions

In our initial studies of these profiles, withdrawn styles were much more common than intrusive styles (Field et al., 1990). In data presented by

Cohn et al. (1986, 1990) and in our more recent sample of depressed adolescent mothers, these styles were almost evenly distributed. These styles had differential effects on the infants (Malphurs, Raag, Field, et al., 1996). A recent study of the first year of development of these two groups of infants suggested that at 3 months, the infants of withdrawn mothers had relative right frontal EEG activation (like their mothers) and lower interaction ratings, whereas the infants of intrusive mothers had relative left frontal EEG activation (also like their mothers). At 12 months, the withdrawn mothers had higher Beck Depression scores, and their infants had lower Bayley mental scores compared with intrusive mothers. By toddlerhood, depressed mothers showed the undesirably extreme styles of permissive or authoritarian parenting (Pelaez-Nogueras & Field, 1999).

Data on interaction coaching suggest further implications of withdrawn or intrusive interaction styles. In the intervention study previously described (Pickens & Field, 1993a), when depressed mothers were instructed to imitate their infants, their pacing slowed and their contingent responsivity increased. When instructed to get their infants' attention, they played more games and displayed more positive affect. Building on these findings, we conducted a study to assess whether these techniques were differentially effective for intrusive versus withdrawn depressed mothers (Malphurs, Larrain, et al., 1996). Instructions to "imitate your infant" (or to slow down and be less intrusive) were more effective in optimizing interactions of intrusive mothers, whereas instructions to "keep your infant's attention" were more effective with withdrawn mothers.

The behavior patterns displayed by these mothers are clearly different, but the data are inconsistent on the behavioral differences noted in the infants of intrusive versus withdrawn mothers. Cohn et al. (1986) reported that withdrawn mothers spent approximately 70% of their time disengaged from their infants and responded to their infants only when the infants were distressed. Intrusive mothers showed anger and irritation or roughly handled their infants 40% of the time. The infants of intrusive mothers protested less than 5% of the time, but spent 55% of the time avoiding their mothers. On the other hand, infants of withdrawn mothers protested 30% of the time and watched their mothers less than 5% of the time. Data from Field and her colleagues (1990) indicated, in contrast, that infants of withdrawn mothers were inactive and spent the majority of their time looking around, whereas infants of intrusive mothers fussed a larger proportion of the time.

In summary, knowing the differences between infants of intrusive and withdrawn mothers suggested intervention strategies that corresponded to the mother's interaction profile. For example, Malphurs, Larrain, et al. (1996) showed that specific intervention techniques tailored to the interaction profile of the mother elicited positive responses. Effective coaching behaviors were different when the mother was intrusive versus when the mother was withdrawn.

HEURISTIC MODEL

The model that we had derived from our research on depressed mothers and infants suggested that depressed mothers are emotionally unavailable to their infants and therefore unable to provide adequate stimulation and arousal modulation. In this model, called *psychobiological attunement* (Field, 1985, 1992, 1995), external regulation is required from caregivers for infants to develop adequate self-regulation. A similar model, entitled *mutual regulation,* was developed by Tronick and his colleagues (Tronick & Gianino, 1986).

Our recent data suggest that infants of depressed mothers have an even greater need for external regulation because they are dysregulated as early as the neonatal period. Their sympathetically aroused state (i.e., elevated norepinephrine and cortisol levels) may have contributed to the neonatal profile of disorganized behavior on the Brazelton Scale, excessive indeterminate sleep, and relative right frontal EEG activation. We then speculated that the infants' sympathetic arousal would be further compounded by inadequate stimulation and arousal modulation from their mothers. Whether the mothers had a withdrawn (i.e., understimulating) or intrusive (i.e., overstimulating) interaction style, their stimulation was considered inadequate. Animal data suggest that inadequate stimulation could contribute to the infants' neurotransmitter (i.e., elevated norepinephrine) and neuroendocrine (i.e., elevated cortisol) imbalance (Kraemer, Ebert, Lake, & McKinney, 1984). In turn, the infants may have developed withdrawn behavior (i.e., irritable affect and high activity levels) as stimulus barriers to block the inappropriate stimulation from their mothers, hence avoiding further sympathetic arousal. This profile of dysregulation in biochemistry (i.e., elevated cortisol and norepinephrine), physiology (i.e., low vagal tone and right frontal activation), and sleep–wake behavior (i.e., excessive indeterminate sleep) was thought to contribute to the excessive externalizing and internalizing behaviors noted at the preschool stage and the disproportionate incidence of depression, conduct disorder, and aggression (i.e., inadequate self-regulation) reported in older children of depressed mothers.

More recent data suggest the need to modify this model. In the more evenly balanced sample of intrusive and withdrawn mothers, the data suggest that the infants of depressed intrusive mothers may show better development (at least better interaction behaviors and 1-year BMMS scores). This may result from more verbal stimulation from their intrusive mothers and/or greater approach behavior (i.e., exploratory behavior) shown by the infants themselves. The infants of intrusive mothers may be less dysregulated, which would enable them to modulate their mothers' excessive stimulation. It is also possible that the intrusive mother–infant group only look better by comparison with the withdrawn mother–infant group, which highlights the continuing need for a nondepressed control group. In addition, as suggested by animal-stress models, these infants' accelerated development could relate to stress. We designed research to determine how these two maternal interaction styles differentially affected the development of their infants, how the infants' dysregulation interacted with the maternal behavior effects, and ultimately, what types of intervention these findings would suggest. These data are elaborated on in the following section.

NEONATAL DYSREGULATION

In a recent study (Abrams et al., 1995), we noted that newborns of depressed mothers had inferior Brazelton scores. They also had behavioral, physiological, and biochemical characteristics that were similar to those of their depressed mothers, including flat affect, relative right frontal EEG activation, and elevated norepinephrine and cortisol levels (see Table 1.1). These findings suggest that the infants were affected prenatally by their

TABLE 1.1
Newborns of Mothers Who Were Depressed at the Neonatal Period

Neonatal Measures	*Depressed*	*Nondepressed*	*p Level*
Brazelton			
Habituation	5.1	5.9	.01
Orientation	5.2	5.6	.05
Depression	3.6	2.6	.05
Sleep			
Active	4.0	5.9	.05
Indeterminate	28.8	20.0	.05
Interaction rating Scales			
Mother	2.3	2.6	.001
Infant	2.4	2.6	.05
Biochemical Values			
Mother			
Norepinephrine	50.0	37.0	.05
Epinephrine	7.1	.50	.005
Serotonin (5HIAA)	2285.0	2721.1	.05
Infant			
Norepinephrine	141.3	58.2	.001
Epinephrine	17.2	9.1	.001
Vagal Tone	3.0	4.2	.005
EEG	-0.04	+.03	.05

TABLE 1.2
Newborns of Prenatally Depressed Mothers

	Depressed	*Nondepressed*	*p Level*
Prenatal BDI	29	10	.001
Obstetric Complications	79	129	.001
Brazelton Scores			
Orientation	3.8	5.4	.05
Motor	3.7	4.9	.05
Abnormal Reflex	3.1	1.6	.005
Lester Depression	4.6	1.9	.001
Attentiveness Faces	3.2	4.6	.005
Mother	2.3	2.6	.001
Infant	2.4	2.6	.05
Facial Expressivity	2.1	3.8	.005
EEQ	-0.2	+0.04	.001

mothers' depression (and/or a genetic predisposition that would be difficult to evaluate at this time).

Thus, we recently conducted a study on prenatal depression in last trimester mothers and noted not only elevated depression scores, but also elevated norepinephrine and cortisol levels, lower dopamine levels, and more obstetric complications (Lundy et al., 1999). The newborns had a similar biochemical profile. Ultrasound videotapes suggested lower activity levels and fewer facial expressions in the fetuses of prenatally depressed mothers (Dieter et al., 1999). As newborns, they scored less optimally on the Brazelton orienting, motor, abnormal reflexes, and Lester depression scales. They also showed less attentiveness and fewer facial expressions in response to modeled facial expressions. By 1 week of age, they showed greater relative right frontal EEG activation (see Table 1.2).

Intrusive–Withdrawn Depressed Mother Interaction Styles

Dysregulation noted in newborns of depressed mothers is further complicated by depressed mothers' different interaction styles. In addition to their differential effects on interaction behaviors, physiological differences were noted in infants of intrusive versus withdrawn mothers. As previously described, infants of depressed mothers have typically shown greater relative right frontal EEG activation (Field, Fox, et al., 1995; Jones, Field, Fox, Davalos, et al., 1997). We suggested that this pattern of asymmetry is a marker of physiological dysregulation in infants of depressed mothers. In support of our model of dysregulation, our data suggest that 3-month-old infants with relative right frontal EEG activation also showed dysregulation in behavioral and autonomic (i.e., physiological and biochemical) systems (see Table 1.3). During the neonatal period, infants with relative right frontal EEG activation demonstrated less quiet sleep, more indeterminate sleep, lower Brazelton habituation and range of state scores, and elevated norepinephrine and cortisol levels. At 1 month, these infants spent less time in active awake states and had more abnormal reflexes. At 3 months, the infants and mothers had lower interaction ratings and at 6 months, the infants received inferior ratings on the neurological exam as well as lower vagal tone. At 12 months, the infants had smaller head circumferences and lower BMMS scores.

Theories on approach–withdrawal emotions and corresponding left–right frontal EEG activation, proposed by Fox and Davidson (1984; see also Marshall & Fox, chap. 3, this volume), provide a framework for understanding the asymmetry patterns in infants of intrusive versus withdrawn

TABLE 1.3
Right Frontal Versus Left Frontal EEG Infants

	Group		
Variables	*Right EEG*	*Left EEG*	*p Level*
Neonatal			
Quiet Sleep	20.4	44.6	.01
Indeterminate Sleep	46.1	23.6	.01
Habituation	5.2	6.4	.05
Range of State	3.7	4.2	.05
Infant Norepinephrine	64.9	47.9	.005
1-Month			
Active-Awake	16.8	42.3	.05
Abnormal Reflexes	1.5	.0	.05
3 Months			
Infant Interaction Rating	2.3	2.6	.05
Mother Interaction Rating	2.0	2.3	.05
6 Months			
Neurological (INFANIB)			
Head/Trunk	15.2	18.6	.01
Legs	15.0	17.6	.05
Total	63.4	70.0	.05
Infant Vagal Tone	2.9	3.5	.05
12 Months			
Head Circumference	45.6	47.0	.05
Bayley Motor Scale	111.6	127.0	.05

mothers. Given that infants' EEG asymmetry tends to mimic that of their mothers' (Field, Fox, et al., 1995; Jones, Field, Fox, Davalos, et al., 1997) and that angry intrusive behaviors are approach emotions, one would expect that infants of intrusive mothers might show greater relative left frontal EEG activation patterns. Infants of withdrawn mothers might be expected to show relative right frontal EEG activation.

In a recent study, the impact of these different interaction styles (intrusive–overstimulating and withdrawn–understimulating) was assessed in infants. Mothers were categorized as intrusive or withdrawn based on their face-to-face interaction behavior with their 3-month-old infants (Jones et al., 1999). Behavioral assessments were made at 3, 6, and 12 months. The results indicated that infants of withdrawn mothers showed less optimal interaction behavior and relative right frontal EEG activation at 3 months and lower BMMS scores at 1 year. Infants of intrusive mothers, in contrast, had higher dopamine levels and relative left frontal EEG activation (see Table 1.4).

We then looked retroactively at the neonatal data to determine whether there were any differences between the infants of intrusive and withdrawn mothers as early as the neonatal period. Although the mothers from both groups had been diagnosed as dysthymic and had equivalently high BDI scores, the intrusive mothers had higher dopamine levels. The infants of withdrawn mothers had lower Brazelton orientation and motor scores, higher Lester Depression scores, and lower dopamine levels (see Table 1.5).

TABLE 1.4
Infants of Withdrawn Versus Intrusive Mothers at 3 and 12 Months

	Withdrawn	*Intrusive*	*p Level*
3-Measures			
Interaction Ratings			
Mother	2.2	2.6	.05
Infant	2.0	2.5	.01
EEG			
Mother	-0.03	0.04	.05
Infant	-0.03	0.05	.05
Mother Cortisol	115.8	88.0	.05
Infant Interaction Rating	2.3	2.6	.05
Mother Interaction Rating	2.0	2.3	.05
Infant Dopamine	792.0	1597.2	.005
12 Months			
Mother BDI Scores	2.8	17.8	.05
Infant Bayley Mental Scores	101.0	108.0	.05

TABLE 1.5
Retrospective Data for Newborns of Intrusive–Withdrawn Depressed Mothers

Neonatal Period	*Withdrawn*	*Intrusive*	*p Level*
Mother BDI Score	25.1	25.0	NS
Infant Newborn Head Circumference	32.7	33.9	.05
Infant Brazelton Scores			
Orientation	4.3	6.2	.05
Motor	3.9	4.5	.05
Depression	4.6	3.0	.05
Infant Dopamine	497.9	621.0	.05

By 1 month of age, significantly more infants of withdrawn mothers showed relative right frontal EEG activation in contrast to infants of intrusive mothers, who showed relative left frontal EEG activation (see Table 1.5).

The elevated dopamine in the intrusive mothers and their infants might not be surprising given that dopamine is an activating neurotransmitter. It has been considered a pivotal neurotransmitter in the model of childhood psychiatric disorders developed by Rogeness and colleagues (Rogeness, Javors, & Pliszka, 1992). In this model, derived from a fairly extensive database on multiple childhood disorders, high norepinephrine and high dopamine levels are typically found among normal, extraverted, high-energy children. Children with elevated norepinephrine and dopamine but low serotonin levels, however, often have externalizing problems. High norepinephrine accompanied by low dopamine is associated with anxious, inhibited, depressed behavior. This is congruent with our findings that infants of withdrawn mothers, who themselves show lower activity levels, less responsivity to social stimulation, and greater relative right frontal EEG, also showed lower dopamine levels.

Weiss and colleagues (Weiss, Demetrikopoulos, West, & Bonsall, 1998) developed an animal model (in the rat) linking the noradrenergic and dopaminergic systems in depression. Although numerous observations indicate that norepinephrine is important in the pathogenesis and therapy for depression, basic research implicates dopamine more than norepinephrine in depression-related behavioral responses, including dampened motor activity and hedonic responses (Weiss et al., 1998). In their animal model of stress-induced behavioral depression, they traced depressive symptoms to abnormal activity (hyperresponsivity) of the locus coeruleus neurons, which then release gelanin from the locus coeruleus access terminals, in turn inhibiting (*hyperpolarizing*) dopamine neurons in the ventral tegmentum to mediate depression-related behavioral changes.

Thus, the elevated norepinephrine levels and the depressed dopamine levels suggest that withdrawn mothers relative to intrusive mothers experience more dampening of motor activity and hedonic responses with their depression. Intrusive mothers (and their infants) may experience a stress-induced increase in dopamine, whereas prolonged and repeated stress would more likely lead to decreased dopamine levels (which might explain the pattern seen in the withdrawn mothers and infants). This pattern of elevated norepinephrine and depressed dopamine in infants at the neonatal period also might explain the depressed activity and responses to social stimulation on the Brazelton and their greater relative right frontal EEG activation.

Any early neurotransmitter effects, of course, would be compounded by the mothers' interactive behavior. It is unclear why mothers with depression display withdrawn and intrusive profiles. These two profiles may derive from different neurotransmitter profiles, as already mentioned, or from different temperament or personality styles, such as approach–withdrawal orientation, extroversion–introversion, or externalization–internalization discussed by Eysenck (1967). These mothers may experience different emotions (e.g., anger in the case of the intrusive mothers and sadness in the case of the withdrawn mothers). Alternatively, these mothers may have developed different coping-with-depression styles; these styles have been labeled *anger out* versus *anger in* in the psychotherapy literature or *active coping* versus *passive coping*. These profiles also could be manifestations of different subtypes of pathology, as in the old nomenclature *reactive–endogenous*. They also could reflect different stages of severity, with intrusive behavior happening at an earlier stage of depression and withdrawn behavior occurring later, as learned helplessness, psychomotor retardation, and anhedonia develop. The intrusive style may be seen more often in younger depressed mothers. Our pilot data suggest that these styles are stable, at least across the first year of life (Jones, Field, Fox, Davalos, et al., 1997) and that they are characteristic not only of these mothers' interactions with their infants, but also with their spouses or boyfriends (Hart, Field, Jones, & Yando, 1999).

PSYCHOBIOLOGICAL ATTUNEMENT MODEL RECONSIDERED

These more recent data suggest a reconsideration of our psychobiological attunement model. In that model, we argued that the infant's dysregulation is later compounded by inadequate stimulation and arousal modulation from their mothers. Whether the mothers had withdrawn (i.e., understimulating) or intrusive (i.e., overstimulating) interaction styles, their stimulation was considered inadequate. The more recent data, which show better developmental outcome for the infants of intrusive mothers, raise questions about some of the assumptions of the original model.

The new data suggest that the excessive stimulation by the intrusive mothers, particularly verbal stimulation, may facilitate better cognitive development of their infants. The better cognitive development also might result from pressures for the infant to respond to the mothers, as opposed to the infants of withdrawn mothers, who can be inactive in response to their mother's inactivity. The more actively responding infant might process more stimulation and, in turn, become more exploratory, suggesting a more indirect pathway for the mothers' effects on their infants' development.

The neonatal data also show more optimal Brazelton performance and relative left frontal EEG activation in infants of intrusive mothers when compared to withdrawn mothers. These results suggest that infants of intrusive mothers may be less dysregulated as early as the neonatal period, potentially because their mothers had a more balanced, less disturbed neurotransmitter pattern (i.e., elevated norepinephrine and elevated dopamine), in turn, less negatively affecting fetal development and contributing less to behavioral and biological disturbances in their infants.

The behavioral, physiological, and neurochemical profiles that could be predicted from the data on these withdrawn and intrusive depressed mothers and their infants or children can be seen in Table 1.6. A longitudinal research program to test this model is outlined, including the dimensions to be measured, the measures to be used, and directional predictions for the withdrawn and intrusive mothers and their offspring. In this model, the withdrawn mothers are understimulating and they display flat but anxious affect and a withdrawn–introverted interaction style. Additionally, they display lower vagal tone, relative right frontal EEG activation, and elevated norepinephrine and depressed dopamine levels. The intrusive mothers, in contrast, are overstimulating and they display more angry affect, an approach–extraverted interaction style, higher vagal tone, relative left frontal EEG activation, and elevated norepinephrine and dopamine. Although good mothers (i.e., those who show more optimal interaction behaviors) should be assessed as well, we do not have pilot data on those mothers to make predictions.

Profiles of the fetus and newborn of the withdrawn mothers are characterized by lower fetal activity, less frequent and less variable facial expressions, higher fetal HR, and lower vagal tone. At the neonatal stage, the newborn of the withdrawn mother displays lower Brazelton Scale scores, more indeterminate sleep, lower vagal tone, relative right frontal EEG activation, and elevated norepinephrine but depressed dopamine levels. In contrast, the fetus of the intrusive mother is expected to display higher fetal activity, more frequent and more variable fetal facial expressions, lower fetal HR, and higher vagal tone. At the neonatal stage, they display higher Brazelton scores, less indeterminate sleep, higher vagal tone, relative left frontal EEG activation, and elevated norepinephrine and dopamine levels.

TABLE 1.6
Profile of Depressed Mothers and Their Infants or Children

Dimensions	*Measures*	*Withdrawn*	*Intrusive*
Activity Level	# Behaviors	Understimulated	Overstimulated
Affect	Faces/Voices	Anxious	Angry
Interac. Style	Extravers./Introvers.	Withdrawn/Introverted	Approach/Extraverted
Feelings	POMS Scale	Anxiety	Anger
Physiology	Vagal Tone	Lower VT	Higher VT
	EEG	Right Frontal EEG	Left Frontal EEG
Neurotransmitter Pattern	NE, DA	↑ NE ↓ DA	↑ NE ↑ DA
		Infants or Children	
Parental (last trimester)			
Affect	Fetal Facial Expressions	Less Freq./ Less Variable	More Freq./ More Variable Activity Level
Activity Level	Fetal Activity	Lower	Higher
Physiology	Vagal Tone	Lower	Higher
Neonatal/One Week			
Development	Birth Meas. (wt., lngth, hc., & Ob/Neonatal complications	Normal	Normal
Behavior	Brazelton Scale Scores	Lower	Higher
Sleep	Sleep/Wake Behav.	> Indeter. Sleep	< Indeter. Sleep
Physiology	Vagal Tone	Lower	Higher
	EEG	Right	Left
Neurotransmitter Pattern	NE, DA	↑ NE ↓ DA	↑ NE ↑ DA
Early Infancy			
Activity Level	# Behav.	Low	High
Affect	Faces/Voices	Flat	Pos./Neg. Mix
Interac. Style	Resp. to Faces	Low Atten./ Low Express.	High Atten./ High Express.
Physiology	Vagal Tone	Lower	Higher
Neurotransmitter Pattern	NE, DA	↑ NE ↓ DA	↑ NE ↑ DA
Later Infancy			
Interac. Style	Exploration	Internalizer	Externalizer
Cog. Dev.	Bayley Ment.	Lower Score	Higher Score
Preschool			
Behavior Prob.	CBCL	Internalizer	Externalizer
Inhibition	Novel Room/Stranger	Inhibited	Exploratory
	Mother Leaving Room	Non-Self-Regulated	Self-Regulated
Empathy Paradigm		Non-Emp-Withdrawn	Non-Emp-Angry

In early infancy, the infants of the withdrawn mothers display low activity levels, flat affect, low attentiveness and low expressivity in response to facial expressions, lower vagal tone, relative right frontal EEG activation, and elevated norepinephrine but depressed dopamine levels. In contrast, the infants of intrusive mothers display higher activity levels, a mix of positive and negative facial expressions, high attentiveness and expressivity in response to facial expressions, higher vagal tone, relative left frontal EEG activation, and elevated norepinephrine and dopamine levels.

Later in infancy (at 1 year), the infants of withdrawn mothers are expected to be less exploratory and to have lower BMMS scores. In contrast, the infants of intrusive mothers are expected to be more exploratory and to have higher BMMS scores.

At the preschool stage, the children of the withdrawn mothers are expected to show internalization on the CBCL, as well as to appear less socially responsive, less self-regulated, and more inhibited in a laboratory social interaction paradigm. Additionally, they are expected to show nonempathetic, withdrawn styles on the empathy paradigm. In contrast, the preschool children of the intrusive mother are expected to show more externalization on the CBCL, to be more responsive and self-regulated and less inhibited during the inhibition paradigm, and to appear nonempathetic and angry in the empathy paradigm. Although not shown in this table, we would also index serotonin levels (using the metabolite 5H1AA). If the children of the intrusive mothers had low serotonin levels combined with high norepinephrine and dopamine levels, the Rogeness et al. (1992) model would predict that they would show more aggression and externalization.

In summary, maternal depression effects include a range of negative biological and behavioral effects on the mothers' offspring during the fetal period, the neonatal period, infancy, and early childhood. The maternal depression effects appear to be long lasting, which highlights the importance of early interventions. Several interventions appear to successfully change maternal interaction behavior as well as other outcome variables. Successful interventions include brief mood inductions, intensive day-care-like interventions, and the use of substitute caregivers, such as nursery school teachers and fathers. Because the outcomes and the appropriate interventions appear to depend on the type of maternal depression interaction style, we focused on identifying the differences between intrusive and withdrawn mothers and their differential effects on their infants. This significantly altered our model from viewing both understimulation and overstimulation as undesirable to viewing understimulation as worse than overstimulation.

Because maternal depression effects begin as early as pregnancy, our findings increasingly highlight the importance of starting interventions during pregnancy. Further research is needed not only to identify those mother–infant dyads at risk for undesirable outcomes, but also to find interventions that may be preventive rather than those that target existent problems.

ACKNOWLEDGMENTS

We wish to thank the infants and parents who participated in this study as well as the research assistants who helped with the data collection. This research was supported by a National Institute of Mental Health (NIMH) Research Scientist Award (#MH00331) and an NIMH research grant (#MH46586) from Johnson & Johnson to Tiffany Field.

REFERENCES

Abrams, S. M., Field, T., Scafidi, F., & Prodromidis, M. (1995). Newborns of depressed mothers. *Infant Mental Health Journal, 16*(3), 231–235.

Bendell, D., Field, T., Yando, S., Lang, C., Martinez, A., & Pickens, J. (1994). "Depressed" mothers' perceptions of their preschool children's vulnerability. *Child Psychiatry and Human Development, 24,* 183–190.

Cohn, J. F., Campbell, S. B., Matias, R., & Hopkins, J. (1990). Face-to-face interactions of postpartum depressed and non-depressed mother-infant pairs at two months. *Developmental Psychology, 26,* 15–23.

Cohn, J. F., Matias, R., Tronick, E. Z., Connell, D., & Lyons-Ruth, K. (1986). Face-to-face interactions of depressed mothers and their infants In E. Z. Tronick & T. Field (Eds.), *Maternal depression and infant disturbance* (pp. 31–45). San Francisco: Jossey-Bass.

Dieter, J. N. I., Field, T., Hernandez-Reif, M., Jones, N. A., Lecanuet, J. P., Salman, F. A., (1999). *Prenatal depression and increased fetal activity.* Manuscript submitted for publication.

Drevets, W. C., Videen, T. O., Price, J. L., Preskorn, S. H., Carmichael, S. T., & Raichle, M. E. (1992). A functional anatomical study of unipolar depression. *The Journal of Neuroscience, 12*(9), 3628–3641.

Eysenck, J. J. (1967). *The biological basis of personality.* Springfield, IL: Thomas.

Field, T. (1985). Attachment as psychobiological attunement: Being on the same wavelength. In M. Reite & T. Field (Eds.), *Psychobiology of attachment* (pp. 415–454). New York: Academic Press.

Field, T. (1992). Infants of depressed mothers. *Development and Psychopathology, 4,* 49–66.

Field, T. (1995). Infants of depressed mothers. *Infant Behavior and Development, 18,* 1–13.

Field, T. (1999). Longitudinal follow-up of infants of depressed mothers. *Adolescence.*

Field, T., Bendell-Estroff, D., DelValle, C., Malphurs, J., Yando, R., & Hart, S. (1996). Exploratory behaviors and development in infants of depressed mothers. *Child Psychiatry and Human Development.*

Field, T., Fox, N., Pickens, J., Nawrocki, T., & Soutullo, D. (1995). Right frontal EEG activation in 3- to 6-month infants of "depressed" mothers. *Developmental Psychology, 31,* 358–363.

Field, T., Grizzle, N., Scafidi, F., Abrams, S., & Richardson, S. (1996). Massage and relaxation therapies' effects on depressed adolescent mothers. *Adolescence, 31,* 903–911.

Field, T., Healy, B., Goldstein, S., & Guthertz, M. (1990). Behavioral state matching and synchrony in mother-infant interactions of nondepressed versus depressed dyads. *Developmental Psychology, 26,* 7–14.

Field, T., Healy, B., Goldstein, S., Perry, S., Bendell, D., Schanberg, S., Zimmerman, E. A., & Kuhn, C. (1988). Infants of depressed mothers show "depressed" behavior even with non-depressed adults. *Child Development, 59,* 1569–1579.

Field, T., Martinez, A., Nawrocki, T., Pickens, J., Fox, N., Schanburg, S. (1998). Music shifts frontal EEG in depressed adolescence. *Adolescence, 33,* 109–116.

Field, T., Pickens, J., Fox, N., Nawrocki, T., & Gonzalez, J. (1995). Vagal tone in infants of depressed mothers. *Development and Psychopathology, 7,* 227–231.

Field, T., Yando, R., Lang, C., Pickens, J., Martinez, A., & Bendell, D. (1996). Longitudinal follow-up of children of dysphoric mothers. *Journal of Clinical Child Psychology, 25,* 272–279.

Fox, N., & Davidson, R. (1984). Hemispheric substrates of affect: A developmental model. In N. A. Fox & R. J. Davidson (Eds.), *The psychobiology of affective development* (pp. 111–135). Hillsdale, NJ: Lawrence Erlbaum Associates.

Hart, S., Field, T., Jones, N. A., & Yando, R. (1999). Intrusive and withdrawn behaviors of mothers interacting with their boyfriends. *Journal of Child Psychology and Psychiatry, 40,* 239–246.

Hart, S., Field, T., Letourneau, M., & DelValle, C. (1998). Jealousy protests in infants of depressed mothers. *Social Development, 7,* 54–61.

Henriques, J. B., & Davidson, R. J. (1990). Regional brain electrical asymmetries discriminate between previously depressed and healthy control subjects. *Journal of Abnormal Psychology, 99,* 22–31.

Hossain, Z., Field, T., Pickens, J., & Gonzalez, J. (1995). Infants of "depressed" mothers interact better with their nondepressed fathers. *Infant Mental Health Journal, 15,* 348–357.

Jones, N. A., Field, T., & Fox, N. A. (1999). EEG activation in one-week-old infants of depressed mothers. *Infant Behavior and Development, 21,* 537–541.

Jones, N., Field, T., Fox, N. A., Davalos, M., & Pickens, J. (1997). Brain electrical activity stability in infants/children of depressed mothers. *Child Psychiatry and Human Development, 28,* 112–116.

Jones, N., Field, T., Fox, N. A., Lundy, B., & Davalos, M. (1997). EEG activation in one-month-old infants of depressed mothers. *Development & Psychopathology, 9,* 491–505.

Kraemer, G. W., Ebert, M. H., Lake, C. R., & McKinney, W. T. (1984). Cerebrospinal fluid changes associated with pharmacological alteration of the despair response to social separation in rhesus monkeys. *Psychiatry Research, 11,* 305–315.

Lundy, B., Field, T., Cigales, M., Quadra, A., & Pickens, J. (1997). Vocal and expression matching in infants of mothers with depressive symptoms. *Infant Mental Health Journal, 18,* 265–273.

Lundy, B., Field, T., & Pickens, J. (1996). Newborns of mothers with depressive symptoms are less expressive. *Infant Behavior & Development, 19,* 419–424.

Lundy, B., Jones, N., Field, T., Pietro, P., Nearing, G., Davalos, M., & Cuadra, A. (1999). Prenatal depressive symptoms and neonatal outcome. *Infant Behavior and Development, 22,* 119–131.

Lyons-Ruth, K., Zoll, D. L., Connell, D., & Grunebaum, H. Y. (1986). The depressed mother and her one-year-old infant: Environment, interaction, attachment and infant development. In E. Tronick & T. Field (Eds.), *Maternal depression and infant disturbance* (pp. 61–83). San Francisco: Jossey-Bass.

Malphurs, J., Larrain, C. M., Field, T., Pickens, J., Pelaez-Nogueras, M., Yando, R., & Bendell, D. (1996). Altering withdrawn and intrusive interaction behaviors of depressed mothers. *Infant Mental Health Journal, 17,* 152–160.

Malphurs, J., Raag, T., Field, T., Pickens, J., & Pelaez-Nogueras, M. (1996). Touch by intrusive and withdrawn mothers with depressive symptoms. *Early Development and Parenting, 5,* 111–115.

Martinez, A., Malphurs, J., Field, T., Pickens, J., Yando, R., Bendell, D., DelValle, C., & Messenger, D. (1996). Depressed mothers' and their infants' interactions with non-depressed partners. *Infant Mental Health Journal, 17,* 74–80.

Pelaez-Nogueras, M., & Field, T. (1999). The parenting styles of depressed mothers. *Early Development and Parenting.*

Pelaez-Nogueras, M., Field, T., Cigales, M., Gonzalez, A., & Clasky, S. (1995). Infants of depressed mothers show less "depressed" behavior with their nursery teachers. *Infant Mental Health Journal, 15*, 358–367.

Pelaez-Nogueras, M., Field, T., Pickens, J., Hossain, Z., Gonzalez, J., & Larrain, C. (1996). Depressed mothers' touching increases infants' positive affect and attention in the still-face interactions. *Child Development, 67*, 1780–1792.

Pickens, J., & Field, T. (1993a). Attention-getting vs. imitation effects on depressed mother–infant interactions. *Infant Mental Health Journal, 14*(3), 171–181.

Pickens, J., & Field, T. (1993b). Facial expressivity in infants of "depressed" mothers. *Developmental Psychology, 29*, 986–988.

Raag, T., Malphurs, J., Field, T., Pelaez-Nogueras, M., Martinez, A., Pickens, J., Bendell, D., & Yando, R. (1997). Moderately dysphoric mothers behave more positively with their infants after completing the BDI. *Infant Mental Health Journal, 18*, 394–405.

Rogeness, G. A., Javors, M. A., & Pliszka, S. R. (1992). Neurochemistry and child adolescent psychiatry. *Journal of the American Academy of Child and Adolescent Psychiatry, 31*, 765–781.

Sigman, M., & Parmelee, A. (1989, January). *Longitudinal predictors of cognitive development.* Paper presented at the American Association for the Advancement of Science Meeting, San Francisco, CA.

Tronick, E. Z., & Gianino, A. F. (1986). The transmission of maternal disturbance to the infant. *New Directions in Child Development, 34*, 5–11.

Weiss, J. M., Demetrikopoulos, M. K., West, C. H., & Bonsall, R. W. (1998). Gelanin: A significant role in depression. *Annals of New York Academy of Science, 863*, 364–382.

Chapter 2

Gender Differences and Their Relation to Maternal Depression

E. Z. Tronick
Children's Hospital, Boston, MA

M. Katherine Weinberg
Harvard Medical School

Our research is beginning to uncover gender differences in the socioemotional reactions and behavior of infant sons and daughters of mothers with a history of depression. These findings are arising out of our work on the effects of maternal depression on infant development and our work on gender differences in the behavior of sons and daughters of well mothers (Weinberg & Tronick, 1998; Weinberg, Tronick, Cohn, & Olson, 1999). These two lines of research naturally converged on the question of whether or not infant sons and daughters of depressed mothers might be differentially affected by the socioemotional behavior of their depressed mothers. Gender differences in infant reactions to depressed affect is a critical question to evaluate if we are to understand differences in the forms of psychopathology manifested by boys and girls. Given our findings on the effects of depression and the affective and regulatory differences of boys and girls, we hypothesized that boys would be more vulnerable to the effects of maternal depression than girls would be (Tronick & Weinberg, 1997). To put it differently, boys would be more reactive to maternal depression than would girls. Indeed, these are the differences that we seem to be finding in these studies of the infant sons and daughters of depressed mothers, which were supported by grants from the Prevention and Intervention programs at NIMH.

Maternal depression is a common postpartum problem shown to compromise maternal and infant socio-affective functioning (see Downey & Coyne, 1990; Field, 1995; Weinberg & Tronick, 1997 for reviews). Several studies have found that during social interaction with their infants, depressed mothers, when compared to nondepressed mothers, are more affectively negative and more disengaged. For example, depressed mothers engage in less play, use less motherese, and express more sad affect. However, depressed mothers behave in more specific and heterogeneous ways. Some depressed mothers are intrusive and show angry facial expressions, whereas other depressed mothers express sadness and are withdrawn (Cohn & Tronick, 1989).

In general, infants of depressed mothers have difficulties engaging in sustained social and object engagement and show less ability to regulate affective states. Thus, they look less at their mother and they show less positive affect and more negative affect. Their reactions are specific, however, to their mothers' interactive style; the infants of the intrusive, depressed mothers act in a more avoidant fashion compared to the infants of withdrawn mothers, who are more distressed. At 1 year of age, many of these infants show poorer performance on developmental tests (e.g., the Bayley Scales of Infant Development) and higher levels of insecure attachment to the mother (Lyons-Ruth, Connell, & Grunebaum, 1990; Murray & Cooper, 1997). Thus, exposure to maternal postpartum depression appears to compromise infant social, emotional, and cognitive functioning.

In previous research, Tronick and Weinberg (Tronick & Cohn, 1989; Weinberg et al., 1999) found gender differences in 6-month-old infants of nondepressed mothers. For example, Weinberg and her colleagues found that boys were more emotionally reactive than were girls during face-to-face social interactions with their mothers. Boys were more likely than were girls to show facial expressions of anger, to fuss and cry, to want to be picked up, and to attempt to get away or distance themselves from their mothers by arching their back and turning and twisting in their infant seats. Boys were also more oriented toward their mothers than were girls. Boys were more likely than were girls to display facial expressions of joy and to communicate with their mothers using neutral or positive vocalizations and gestures. By contrast, girls were more object oriented than were boys. They were more likely than were boys to look at and explore objects and to display facial expressions of interest. Furthermore, girls showed more self-regulatory behaviors than did boys.

Our interpretation of these gender differences focused on differences in boys' and girls' self-regulation of affect. Boys' greater emotional reactivity suggested that boys have greater difficulty self-regulating their affective states and that they need to rely more on maternal regulatory input than do girls. To the extent that boys are more dependent than are girls on their mothers to regulate their affective states, they then must communicate their needs more explicitly and frequently than do girls. The boys' greater dependence on external regulation might explain the greater variability and intensity of their expressions and the finding that much of their affective behavior was directed toward their mothers. This interpretation of the differences between boys and girls is based on the *Model of Mutual Regulation (MRM)* developed by Tronick (1989), in which the affective state of the infant is dependent on the capacity to regulate his or her affect and the adult partner's ability to provide regulatory input.

The MRM sees the mother (or any adult interactant) as an exogenous, but functionally integral, component of the infant's capacity for regulation (Hofer, 1981, 1984). The mother's capacity to effectively regulate the infant's affective state is affected by many factors, including her affective state, her representation of the infant, her history of parenting, the state of her other intimate relationships, and during the interaction, by her apprehension of the infant's affective messages. Thus, the infant's capacity to organize his or her affective communications is critical to the quality of the mutual regulation of the interaction.

Weinberg and Tronick (1994) found that infant affective behavior is organized into configurations of face, voice, gesture, and gaze. In one configuration, labeled *Social Engagement*, the infant looks at the mother, positively vocalizes, and smiles. Importantly, crying, looking away, and withdrawal behaviors are less likely to co-occur with the displays making up Social Engagement. In another configuration, *Active Protest*, the infant looks away from the mother, engages in active withdrawal behaviors, cries, and displays a facial expression of anger. In this configuration, smiles, positive gestures, and vocalizations are inhibited. Two other configurations, *Object Engagement* and *Passive Withdrawal*, also involve distinct combinations of expressive modalities. From our perspective, each of these configurations reflect a different state of brain organization that assembles distinctly different configurations of face, voice, and body (Tronick et al., 1998).

Each configuration clearly communicates the infant's affective state and evaluation of the interaction. The Social Engagement configuration conveys the message "I like what we are doing together; let's continue doing it;" the Active Protest configuration tells the caregiver that "I don't like what is happening and I want it to change now;" the Passive Withdrawal configuration communicates messages such as "I don't like what is happening but I don't know what to do;" and the Object Engagement configuration conveys the message, "I want to continue looking at this object and not playing with you." Thus, the configurations serve to regulate the behavior of the infant's partner during the interaction by conveying information to the partner about the infant's immediate intentions and evaluation of the current state of the interaction. Nonetheless, as clearly defined as these configurations are, the interaction is neither always positive nor synchronous.

In our studies of normal mother–infant face-to-face interactions, expressions of positive affect by either the mother or the infant occur about 42%

of the time for the mother and 15% for the infant (Cohn & Tronick, 1987; Tronick & Cohn, 1989). A dramatic instance of normal variation is Tronick and Weinberg's (Tronick & Cohn, 1989; Weinberg et al., 1999) findings of gender differences in affect and interactive coherence. These gender differences reflect normal variants and highlight the range of affective expressiveness, regulatory behavior, and synchrony that occurs during normal interactions.

Tronick (Tronick & Cohn, 1989; Tronick, 1989) has characterized the typical mother–infant interaction as one that moves from coordinated (or synchronous) to miscoordinated states and back again over a wide affective range. The miscoordinated state is referred to as a *normal interactive communicative error* or *misregulation.* The interactive transition from a miscoordinated state to a coordinated state is referred to as an *interactive repair.* The process of reparation is mutually regulated. The partners—infant and adult—signal their evaluation of the state of the interaction through their affective configurations. In turn, in response to their partner's signals, each partner attempts to adjust his or her behavior to maintain a coordinated state or to repair an interactive error. Critically, successful reparations and the experience of coordinated states are associated with positive affective states, whereas unrepaired interactive errors generate negative affective states. Thus, the infant's affective experience is determined by a dyadic regulatory process.

In normal dyads, interactive errors are quickly repaired. In studies of face-to-face interaction at 6 months of age, repairs occur at a rate of once every 3 to 5 seconds, and more than one third of all repairs occur by the next step in the interaction (Tronick & Gianino, 1980). Observations by Beebe (Beebe & Lachmann, 1994) and Isabella and Belsky (1991) replicate these findings and support the hypothesis that the normal interaction is a process of reparation. They found that maternal sensitivity in the mid range, rather than at the low or high end, typify normal interactions. Mid-range sensitivity is characterized by errors and repairs as contrasted to interactions in which the mother is "never sensitive or always sensitive." These researchers also found that mid-level sensitivity was associated with security of attachment.

It is our hypothesis that reparation of interactive errors or miscommunications is the critical process of normal interactions that is related to developmental outcome rather than sensitivity, synchrony, or positive affect per se. That is, *reparation,* its experience and extent, is the social interactive mechanism that affects the infant's development. In interactions characterized by normal rates of reparation, the infant learns which affective, communicative, and coping strategies are effective in producing reparation and when to use them. This experience leads to the elaboration of communicative and coping skills and the development of an implicit procedural understanding of interactive rules and conventions (Tronick, 1998). With the experiential accumulation of successful reparations, and the attendant transformation of negative affect into positive affect, the infant establishes a positive affective core (Emde, Kligman, Reich, & Wade, 1978; Gianino & Tronick, 1988). The infant also learns that he or she has control over social interactions. Specifically, the infant develops a representation of himself or herself as effective, of his or her interactions as positive and reparable, and of the caretaker as reliable and trustworthy. These representations are crucial for the development of a sense of self that has coherence, continuity, and agency and for the development of stable and secure relationships (Tronick, 1980; Tronick, Cohn, & Shea, 1986).

From the perspective of mutual regulation, the functional consequences of reparation suggest that when there is a prolonged failure to repair communicative errors, infants will initially attempt to reestablish the expected interaction and experience negative affect when these reparatory efforts fail. To evaluate this hypothesis, Tronick created a prolonged mismatch with the *Face-to-Face Still-Face paradigm* (Tronick, Als, Adamson, Wise, & Brazelton, 1978). In this paradigm, the mother engages in normal face-to-face interaction until a mismatch is created by having the mother hold a still-face and remain unresponsive to the infant. The mother fails to engage in her normal interactive behavior and regulatory role. Infants almost immediately detect the change and attempt to solicit the mother's attention. Failing to elicit a response, most infants turn away, only to look back at the mother again. This solicitation cycle may be repeated several times. When the infants' attempts fail to repair the interaction, however, infants often lose postural control, withdraw, and self-comfort. Disengagement is profound even with this short disruption of the mutual regulatory process and break of intersubjectivity. The infant's reaction, although much less severe, is reminiscent of the withdrawal of Harlow's isolated monkeys or of the infants in institutions observed by Bowlby and Spitz (Bowlby, 1951, 1980; Spitz, 1965). The still-faced mother is a short-lived, experimentally produced mild form of neglect that precludes the establishment of a shared interaction and the dyadic expansion of consciousness (see Tronick, 1998).

These findings have implications for the infants of depressed mothers, given the effects of depression on maternal affect and caregiving (Murray & Cooper, 1997; Weinberg & Tronick, 1998). We hypothesized that infant boys would be more vulnerable to maternal depressive status than would infant girls because boys appear to require more regulatory support than do girls. Thus, we expected that the interactions of depressed mothers and their sons would have longer and more chronic failures of reparation than would the interactions of mothers and daughters. We also expected that sons of depressed mothers would become more affectively reactive than would daughters of depressed mothers.

In a preliminary study, we examined 23 infants (12 girls and 11 boys) and their mothers. All mothers and infants were recruited from the maternity wards of Boston-area hospitals. The infants and mothers met a set of low-risk criteria to minimize the confounding effects of variables (e.g., poverty and prematurity) known to compromise parenting and infant outcome. Mothers were between the ages of 21 and 39, healthy, living with the infants' fathers, and had at least a high-school education. Infants were healthy, full-term, and clinically normal at delivery as determined by pediatric examination. All infants were first born. Mothers of boys and mothers of girls did not differ on these demographic or medical variables. Thus, this sample of mothers and infants was low risk in social and medical status. This low-risk status allowed us to more effectively assess the effects of depression unconfounded by other high-risk factors.

All mothers met criteria for a lifetime diagnosis of major depression using the Diagnostic Interview Schedule, Version III–Revised (DIS–III–R). The DIS–III–R is a well-established, structured instrument developed by NIMH to assess psychiatric status using both Research Diagnostic Criteria (RDC) and DSM–III–R criteria. All mothers received a clinical diagnosis of major depression prior to having the baby, and approximately 20% of them met diagnostic criteria for depression during the first 6 months postpartum.

At 3 months and 6 months of infant age, mothers and infants were videotaped in Tronick's Face-to-Face Still-Face paradigm (Tronick et al., 1978; Weinberg & Tronick, 1996, 1997). The infants' and mothers' facial expressions and behaviors were coded second-by-second from videotapes. Infants' and mothers' facial expressions were coded with Izard's system for identifying affect expressions by holistic judgments (AFFEX) system. The infants' behavior was coded with Tronick and Weinberg's Infant Regulatory Scoring System (IRSS), which codes six dimensions of infant behavior, including the infants' *direction of gaze, vocalizations, gestures, self-comforting, distancing or withdrawal,* and *autonomic stress indicators.* The mothers' behavior was coded with Tronick and Weinberg's Maternal Regulatory Scoring System (MRSS), which codes six dimensions of maternal behavior, including *direction of gaze, proximity to infant, caregiving activities, types of touch, vocalizations,* and *eliciting behaviors.*

Although the coders were blind to maternal group (i.e., depressed and nondepressed) membership, maintaining coders' blindness to gender is difficult. Mothers refer to the infants by name and often dress them in a manner suggestive of the infants' gender. Asking mothers to modify their normal routines with their infant may produce reactive effects in the mothers. To overcome these problems, we adopted the procedures we used in our previous study of gender differences. Mothers and coders were not told that one objective of the study was to evaluate gender issues, but that the study was concerned with infant interactive and communicative behavior with mothers. Thus, neither mothers nor coders knew that the study was concerned with issues of gender. Furthermore, coding was done by several independent coders. For example, one coder coded infant gaze, whereas another coded infant vocalizations. As noted by Melson and Fogel (1982), the independent multiple coder approach is unlikely to result in consistent bias. Moreover, frequent interrater reliability checks ensured that coders remained unbiased and reliable. Interrater reliability was calculated on 20% of the data. Mean kappas ranged from .77 to .85.

T tests were performed to determine the effect of infant gender on (a) maternal MRSS behavior and AFFEX facial expressions and (b) infant IRSS behavior and AFFEX facial expressions across the episodes of the Face-to-Face Still-Face paradigm. Preliminary analyses of 3-month observations indicate that depressed mothers were nearly twice as likely to express neutral affect to their sons than to their daughters. They also tended to show more facial expressions of anger when interacting with their sons than with their daughters. Analyses of 6-month observations indicate that these mothers continued to show significantly more facial expressions of anger directed toward their sons than their daughters.

No significant gender differences were apparent in the infants' behavior at 3 months of age. At 6 months of age, however, boys as compared to girls appeared more vulnerable to their mothers' depressive status. Male infants, as compared to female infants, were two times less likely to express facial expressions of joy. They were also more likely to gesture, suggesting that they were more agitated or that they were attempting to communicate their needs to their mother. In addition, male infants, as compared to female infants, were three times less likely to use self-comforting strategies such as sucking on a thumb to self-regulate emotional states.

The data indicate that mothers with a history of major depression were more affectively negative with their sons than their daughters. In addition, male infants, as compared to female infants, were less emotionally positive and less likely to use self-comforting strategies to regulate affective states on their own. Thus, maternal depression seemed to have a differential effect on the early interactive behavior of sons and daughters; the sons of depressed mothers appeared more disrupted and dysregulated by maternal behavior than did the daughters of depressed mothers.

The research on gender differences in children of nondepressed mothers and the MRM suggest an interpretation of these findings (Tronick & Cohn, 1989; Weinberg et al., 1999). Boys, compared to girls, are more demanding social partners, have more difficult times regulating their affective states, and may need more of their mothers' support to help them regulate affect. This increased demandingness would affect the infant boys' interactive partner.

In this study, mothers with a history of depression appeared to have difficulties giving their sons the regulatory scaffolding that they needed. For example, mothers displayed more angry and neutral facial expressions to their sons than to their daughters. The mothers' behavior alone, however, does not account for the effects. Infant sons of depressed mothers expressed less joy and were more agitated. These affective regulatory difficulties most likely reflect the interplay of the son's behavior, the mother's neutral and angry affect, and the ongoing interplay and self-reinforcing quality of the dyad's greater negativity. Thus, the negativity observed in the mother–son dyads is a mutually produced effect.

One can speculate on the long-term consequences of this early interaction pattern. For example, we would predict, although it has not been reported, that infant sons may be more likely to be insecurely attached to their depressed mothers than would be infant daughters. Furthermore, boys may be more likely to express negative affect, particularly anger, as they get older because of the frustrations experienced during social interactions. At the same time, depressed mothers would be more likely to express anger to their sons than to their daughters. The daughters' ability to self-regulate may induce more sadness in mothers, however, because daughters may seem disconnected from their mothers, leading to a mutual withdrawal on both their parts. These differentially mutually regulated pathways may increase the likelihood that as boys get older, they will express their disconnection in the form of angry interactions and behavioral disturbances such as conduct disorders, whereas girls will express their interactive problems in the form of withdrawal and depressive behavior.

Other developmental changes powerfully affect the emotional development of these infants. Toward the end of the first year of life, the infants develop a sense of *intersubjectivity*—or capacity to attribute a state of mind to the other and to oneself. Tronick and his colleagues (1998) have hypothesized that a serious outcome of the development of secondary intersubjectivity is that it may enable the infant to develop psychopathologic states. With the development of secondary intersubjectivity, the infant's reaction is no longer determined simply by what he or she directly experiences in interaction with the mother. The infant's reaction is increasingly based on an integration of immediate events with self-reflective representational processes. With these developmental changes, distortions of reality become possible. For example, when children become aware of their depressed mother's affective state (e.g., her anger and sadness, which is apparently directed at themselves and their own intolerable feelings of rage directed at her), children may develop a pathological form of coping—denial, detachment, repression, and/or projection—in an attempt to control their awareness of these overwhelming feelings.

Representations of these experiences take time to develop. Early in development these experiences are instantiated in patterns of action and emotion, what Tronick referred to as *procedural knowledge,* before they become representations incorporating elements of the self, cognition, and history (Tronick, 1998). Critically, these representations are not simply stored information in a preformed or predetermined universal brain (e.g., the filing of information in some area of the brain dedicated to the storage of information) that can be accessed for present use. Rather, these representations are one of the processes that shapes the brain itself. Thus, the brain, like emotional experience, is jointly created. To invert the idea, the human brain is inherently dyadic and is created through interactive interchanges.

Tronick further hypothesized that there is a critical and emergent property of this collaboration—the creation of single dyadic states of consciousness (see Tronick et al., 1998 for details). This dyadic state organization is bound and has more components than the infant's (or mother's) own state of consciousness. Thus, this dyadic system contains more information and is more complex and coherent than either the infant's (or the mother's) endogenous state of consciousness alone. When infant and mother mutually create this dyadic state, they fulfill the system principle of gaining greater complexity and coherence. For example, the infant who is held and supported by the mother—the mother-held infant—is able to perform an action such as gesturing that he or she would not be able to perform by himself or herself without the maternal scaffolding. Most important, the mother-held infant, as contrasted to the alone infant, experiences a state of consciousness associated with gesturing that emerges from his or her participation in a dyadic system.

Creation of this dyadic system necessitates that the infant and mother apprehend elements of the other's state of consciousness. If they did not, it would not be possible to create a dyadic state. For example, if the mother's apprehension of the infant's state of consciousness is that the infant intends to reach for a ball when in fact the infant intended to stroke her face, a dyadic state will not be created. In this case, the two systems—infant and mother—will remain separate and uncoordinated. Thus, a principle governing the human dyadic system is that successful mutual regulation of social interactions requires a mutual mapping of (some of) the elements of the partner's state of consciousness into the partner's brain. This mutual mapping process may be a way of defining intersubjectivity. In the young infant, the process is one of emotional apprehension of the other's state, referred to as *primary intersubjectivity* (Campos, Barrett, Lamb, Goldsmith, & Stenberg, 1983; Tronick, Als, & Brazelton, 1980). In the older infant, the process is one of *secondary intersubjectivity* because the infant becomes aware of his or her apprehension of the other's state. In older children and adults, the process may be what is called *empathy*—a state that contains an awareness of the other's state and a paradoxical awareness of the differentiation between one's state and the state of the other.

The *Dyadic Consciousness hypothesis* suggests that each individual is a self-organizing system that creates its own states of consciousness—states of brain organization—that can be expanded into more coherent and complex states in collaboration with another self-organizing system. When the collaboration of two brains is successful, each fulfills the system principle of increasing its coherence and complexity. The states of consciousness of the infant and the mother are more inclusive and coherent the moment they form a dyadic state that incorporates the state of the other.

An important consequence of the Dyadic Consciousness hypothesis relates to the toxic effects on the infant of maternal depression. Maternal depression disrupts the establishment of a dyadic infant–mother system. The infant is deprived of experiencing dyadically expanded states of consciousness (see Tronick, 1998, for details). This deprivation forces the infant into a self-regulatory pattern of coping that further constricts his or her experience. Yet, there is an even more insidious possibility suggested by the Dyadic Consciousness hypothesis. Given that the infant's system functions to expand its complexity and coherence, the infant of the depressed mother may be able to accomplish this expansion by taking on elements of the mother's state of consciousness. These elements, however, are likely to be negative (e.g., sad and hostile affect, withdrawal, and disengagement). Intersubjectivity is established and with it, the infant's state is expanded. Thus, in the service of becoming more complex and coherent, the infant incorporates a state of consciousness that mimics the depressive elements of the mother. That this intersubjective state contains painful elements does not override the need for expansion. From the perspective of dyadic states of consciousness, neither boys nor girls are more vulnerable to the effects of maternal depression because for both sons and daughters, their interactive and subjective states are constricted and restricted. Both experience a failure to achieve dyadic states and, for both, the consequence is a limitation of the affective development of their mind.

ACKNOWLEDGMENTS

This research was funded by grants from NIMH (RO1 MH45547, RO1 MH43398 and RO3 MH 5226500) and NSF (BNS 85-06987) awarded to E. Z. Tronick and M. K. Weinberg. We would like to thank all the mothers and infants who participated in these studies, and Henrietta Kernan, Joan Riley, Jennifer Scott-Sutherland, Yana Markov and April Prewitt for their tireless effort on this research.

REFERENCES

Beebe, B., & Lachmann, F. M. (1994). Representation and internalization in infancy: Three principles of salience. *Psycoanalytic Psychology, 11*, 127–165.

Bowlby, J. (1951). Maternal care and mental health. *World Health Organization, Monograph Series* (No. 2, 2nd ed.),

Bowlby, J. (1980). *Attachment and loss, vol. 1: Attachment.* New York: Basic Books.

Campos, J. J., Barrett, K. C., Lamb, M. E., Goldsmith, H. H., & Stenberg, C. (1983). Socioemotional development. In P. H. Mussen (Ed.), *Handbook of child psychology, Vol 2.* (pp. 783–915). New York: Wiley.

Cohn, J. F., & Tronick, E. Z. (1987). Mother–infant face-to-face interaction: The sequence of dyadic states at 3, 6, and 9 months. *Developmental Psychology, 23*, 68–77.

Cohn, J. F., & Tronick, E. Z. (1989). Specificity of infants' response to mothers' affective behavior. *Journal of the American Academy of Child and Adolescent Psychiatry, 28*, 242–248.

Downey, G., & Coyne, J. C. (1990). Children of Depressed Parents: An Integrative Review, *Psychological Bulletin, 108(1)*, 50–76.

Emde, R. N., Kligman, D. H., Reich, J. H., & Wade, T. D. (1978). Emotional expression in infancy: I. Initial studies of social signaling and an emergent model. In M. Lewis & L. A. Rosenblum (Eds.), *The development of affect* (pp. 125–148). New York: Plenum.

Field, T. (1995). Infants of depressed mothers. *Infant Behavior and Development, 18*, 1–13.

Gianino, A., & Tronick, E. Z. (1988). The mutual regulation model: The infant's self and interactive regulation, coping, and defense. In T. Field, P. McCabe, & N. Schneiderman (Eds.). *Stress and coping* (pp. 47–68). Hillsdale, NJ: Lawrence Erlbaum Associates.

Hofer, M. A. (1981). Relationships as regulators: A psychobiologic perspective on bereavement. *Pyschosomatic Medicine, 46*, 183–197.

Hofer, M. A. (1984). Relationships as regulators: A psychobiologic perspective on bereavement. *Psychosomatic Medicine, 46*, 183–197.

Isabella, R., & Belsky, J. (1991). Interactional synchrony and the origins of mother–infant attachment: A replication study. *Child Development, 62*, 373–384.

Lyons-Ruth, K., Connell, D. B., & Grunebaum, H. U. (1990). Infants at social risk: maternal depression and family support services as mediators of infant development and security of attachment. *Child Development, 61*, 85–98.

Melson, G. F., & Fogel, A. (1982). Young children's interests in unfamiliar infants. *Child Development, 53*, 693–700.

Murray, L., & Cooper, P. (1997). *Postpartum depression and child development.* London, England: Guilford.

Spitz, R. (1965). *The first year of life.* New York: International Universities Press.

Tronick, E. Z. (1980). On the primacy of social skills. In D. B. Sawin, L. O. Walker, & J. H. Penticuff (Eds.), *The exceptional infant* (pp. 144–157). New York: Brunner/Mazel.

Tronick, E. Z. (1989). Emotions and emotional communication in infants. *American Psychologist, 44*, 112–119.

Tronick, E. Z. (Ed.). (1998, Fall). Interactions that effect change in psychotherapy: A model used on infant research. *Infant Mental Health Journal, 19*(3).

Tronick, E. Z., Als, H., Adamson, L., Wise, S., & Brazelton, T. B. (1978). The infant's response to entrapment between contradictory messages in face-to-face interaction. *Journal of American Academy of Child Psychiatry, 17*, 1–13.

Tronick, E. Z., Als, H., & Brazelton, T. B. (1980). The infant's communicative competencies and the achievement of intersubjectivity. In M. R. Key (Ed.), *The relationship of verbal and nonverbal communication* (pp. 261–274). The Hague, the Netherlands: Mouton.

Tronick, E. Z., Brushweller-Stern, N., Harrison, A. M., Lyons-Ruth, K., Morgan, A. C., Nahum, J. P., Sander, L., & Stern, D. N. (1998, Fall). Dyadically expanded states of consciousness and the process of therapeutic change. In E. Z. Tronick (Ed.), Interactions that effect change in psychotherapy: A model used on infant research. *Infant Mental Health Journal, 19*(3), 290–299.

Tronick, E. Z., & Cohn, J. F. (1989). Infant–mother face-to-face interaction: Age and gender differences in coordination and the occurrence of miscoordination. *Child Development, 60,* 85–92.

Tronick, E. Z., Cohn, J., & Shea, E. (1986). The transfer of affect between mother and infants. In T. B. Brazelton & M. W. Yogman (Eds.), *Affective development in infancy* (pp. 11–25). Norwood, NJ: Ablex.

Tronick, E. Z., & Gianino, A. (1980). An accounting of the transmission of maternal disturbance to the infant. *New Directions for Child Development,* , 5–11.

Tronick, E. Z., & Weinberg, M. K. (1997). Depressed mothers and infants: Failure to form dyadic states of consciousness. In L. Murray & P. Cooper (Eds.), *Postpartum depression and child development* (pp. 54–81). New York: Guilford.

Weinberg, M. K., & Tronick, E. (1994). Beyond the face: An empirical study of infant affective configurations of facial, vocal, gestural, and regulatory behaviors. *Child Development, 65,* 1495–1507.

Weinberg, M. K., & Tronick, E. (1996). Infant affective reactions to the resumption of maternal interaction after the still-face. *Child Development, 67,* 905–914.

Weinberg, M. K., & Tronick, E. (1997). Maternal depression and infant maladjustment: A failure of mutual regulation. In J. Noshpitz (Ed.), *The handbook of child and adolescent psychiatry* (pp. 177–191). New York: Wiley.

Weinberg, M. K., & Tronick, E. Z. (1998). The impact of maternal psychiatric illness on infant development. *Journal of Clinical Psychiatry, 59*(2), 53–61.

Weinberg, M. K., Tronick, E. Z., Cohn, J. F., & Olson, K. L. (1999). Gender differences in emotional expressivity and self-regulation during early infancy. *Developmental Psychology, 35*(1), 175–188.

Chapter 3

Emotion Regulation, Depression, and Hemispheric Asymmetry

Peter J. Marshall
Nathan A. Fox
University of Maryland

In this chapter, we review some of the research on the psychophysiological correlates of personality and social behavior that has been carried out in our laboratory and others, with specific emphasis on depression. Much of the research described is based on a model that stresses the importance of individual differences in the likelihood of expressing and modulating different emotions. There are individuals whose modal response to mild stress or novelty is one of approach and positive emotions, whereas other individuals display withdrawal responses and negative emotions. There are also individual differences within these groups in the intensity of emotion expression and in the ability to modulate expression. In this model, differences in the tendency to express either approach (positive) or withdrawal (negative) patterns in response to stress or novelty are fundamental to the motivational core of individuals. These differences are seen as being subsumed by different brain systems, with the tendency to express negative emotions and withdrawal organized within the right hemisphere and the tendency to express positive emotions and approach-related behaviors organized within the left hemisphere. Individual differences in the patterning of hemispheric activation may thus reflect individual differences in emotion regulation strategies, which may, in turn, determine vulnerability to affective disorders such as depression.

HEMISPHERIC ASYMMETRIES IN EMOTION EXPRESSION

Evidence suggests that the left frontal region of the cortex is associated with the expression and experience of positive affect, whereas the right frontal region is associated with the expression and experience of negative affect (Silberman & Weingartner, 1986). One source of such evidence comes from studies of intracarotid injection of sodium amytal, a procedure that is commonly used in presurgical evaluation of patients who have intractable epilepsy. Although in this context it is mainly used to determine the lateralization of language and memory functions, the procedure also provides a means to study putative hemispheric asymmetries in the organization of emotional behavior (see Snyder & Harris, 1997). Injection of sodium amytal into one of the carotid arteries essentially results in a loss of hemispheric functions on the side of injection, leaving the other hemisphere to dominate emotional expression. Unilateral injection of sodium amytal results in the production of severe emotional reactions, with striking differences in the nature of these reactions depending on the side of injection (e.g., Lee, Loring, Meader, & Brooks, 1990; Perria, Rosadini, & Rossi, 1961). Following injection into the left carotid artery, descriptions of patients' behaviors included crying, pessimistic statements, feelings of nothingness, indignity or despair, and inability to hold back fears or negative thoughts. Unilateral injection into the right carotid artery elicited an opposite response, characterized by a euphoric reaction, including smiling, optimism, and overall well-being. Related findings were reported in a retrospective study by Sackeim and colleagues, who found that pathological overexpression of positive affect (i.e., laughing) was associated with predominantly right-sided brain damage, whereas pathological overexpression of negative affect (i.e., crying) was mainly associated with left-sided damage (Sackeim et al., 1982). Thus, these studies lend some support to the hypothesis that the left hemisphere is specialized for the expression of positive emotions, whereas the right hemisphere is specialized for the expression of negative emotions.

Other work on hemispheric lateralization of emotion has focused on the frontal (i.e., anterior) region of the cortex. This area of the brain is unique in its integrative function, as it receives input from all other regions of the cortex as well as from those subcortical areas thought to be directly involved in the expression of emotion (LeDoux, 1993). A variety of data has implicated the anterior regions of the left and right cerebral hemispheres in the expression and/or experience of different emotions (Fox, 1994). Our focus in this chapter is on the evidence from electroencephalographic (EEG) studies, which are outlined in the following sections.

One method of assessing hemispheric asymmetry in brain activity is to record electrical activity from various sites on the left and right sides of the scalp to obtain an EEG signal. The component of the EEG signal that is usually of interest in this respect is alpha-wave activity, which occurs in the frequency range of 8 to 13 Hz in adults and at lower frequencies in children. EEG alpha-wave activity has been shown to be inversely related to brain glucose metabolism as measured by positron emission tomography (PET; Larson et al., 1998). Thus, a difference in EEG alpha power between the left and right frontal EEG electrodes is contended to reflect relative differences in neuronal activity between the right and left regions of the frontal cortex. Bearing in mind that the relation is inverse, decreased alpha power in the EEG from the left frontal electrode relative to alpha power from the right frontal electrode can be taken as indicating increased neuronal activity in the left frontal region of the cortex compared to the right frontal region. Such a pattern may be referred to as *left frontal asymmetry* as it reflects greater activation of the left frontal region compared to the right. *Right frontal asymmetry* refers to a pattern in which activation in the right frontal region is greater than activation in the left frontal region, with lower alpha power from the right frontal electrode relative to the left frontal electrode.

A number of studies have shown a relation between frontal EEG asymmetry and patterns of emotion expression. Wheeler and colleagues presented adult women with nine film clips designed to elicit different discrete emotions (Wheeler, Davidson, & Tomarken, 1993). Of the nine clips, two were designed to elicit positive emotion (i.e., happiness), and seven were designed to elicit negative emotions (i.e., fear or disgust). After viewing each clip, each participant rated the level of emotion that she experienced during the clip. These self-report scores were compared to resting EEG asymmetry scores as measured at two separate sessions separated by 3 weeks. The main findings concerned participants whose asymmetry pattern was stable over this period: A stable pattern of greater EEG activation on the left side of the frontal region relative to the right side (i.e., left frontal asymmetry) was associated with reports of more intense positive affect following the two positively valenced film clips. Conversely, greater relative activation on the right side (i.e., right frontal asymmetry) was associated with reports of more intense negative affect following the seven negatively valenced film clips. A related study of male participants showed that greater relative left frontal EEG activation during baseline was associated with increased positive affect and decreased negative affect on a self-report affect scale (Jacobs & Snyder, 1996).

Studies of frontal asymmetry and emotion have also been completed with infants and young children. Davidson and Fox (1982) found that 10-month-old infants viewing a video of an actress portraying either positive affect (i.e., smiling and laughter) or negative affect (i.e., sad expression and crying) exhibited asymmetric frontal activation depending on the valence of the video. While viewing the positive segment, infants exhibited greater left frontal EEG activation relative to right frontal activation. A further study found this asymmetry in frontal EEG activity to be present in infants' response to sweet and sour tastes (Fox & Davidson, 1986). Fox and Davidson (1988) also isolated instances of disgust and joy expressions in infants and found that frontal asymmetry differed as a function of the coincident type of expression. During the expression of positive affect, infants exhibited left frontal EEG asymmetry, whereas during the expression of negative affect, infants displayed right frontal EEG asymmetry.

Fox (1991, 1994) and Davidson (1992) have argued that the functional significance of frontal EEG asymmetry with regard to emotion may be conceptualized in terms of motivational systems of approach and withdrawal. In this perspective, the left frontal region promotes positive, approach-directed emotional responses, whereas the right frontal region promotes negative, withdrawal-directed responses. Individual differences in frontal asymmetry may, therefore, be expected to be associated with different patterns of emotion expression and regulation. Based on this, it also may be expected that particular patterns of frontal asymmetry represent an imbalance between approach and withdrawal behaviors that may be manifested in dysfunctional patterns of emotion regulation. This point is further explored in the following sections, with particular emphasis on the relation between frontal asymmetry and depression.

Hemispheric Asymmetry and Depression

The model of frontal asymmetry and emotion expression that has been described may be integrated with various data concerning affective disorder and frontal brain activity. One source of such data is studies by Robinson and his colleagues of lesion location and depressive symptoms in stroke patients. Early studies by this group implicated the frontal lobes in depression, as the severity of poststroke depressive symptoms was correlated with the proximity of the lesion to the frontal pole (Robinson & Szetela, 1981). More specifically, recent work from the Stroke Data Bank study has shown an association between depression and left hemisphere lesions, particularly when such lesions occur in the left prefrontal region. For patients with comparable small-sized lesions, depression was more frequent in patients with left hemisphere lesions than in patients with right hemisphere lesions (Morris, Robinson, de Carvalho, et al., 1996). Furthermore, within the left hemisphere, there was a higher frequency of depression in patients with lesions involving the left prefrontal or basal ganglia regions compared to other left hemisphere lesions (Morris, Robinson, Raphael, & Hopwood, 1996).

There is also evidence from EEG studies that the left frontal region plays a role in depression, with an association between depression and decreased left frontal EEG activation apparent in both nonclinical and clinical samples. Schaffer, Davidson, and Saron (1983) compared individuals with high and low scores on the Beck Depression Inventory on resting EEG asymmetry. They found that dysphoric participants showed less activation of the left frontal region relative to the right frontal region compared with nondysphoric participants. Henriques and Davidson (1991) recorded resting EEG activity from 15 clinically depressed participants and 13 control participants. Depressed participants displayed less left-sided activation than did control participants, which was interpreted as indicating a deficit in approach mechanisms in depressed participants. In another study, the same researchers also compared six individuals with remitted depression with eight control participants who had no history of depression (Henriques & Davidson, 1990). Previously depressed participants displayed less left-sided frontal activation than did never-depressed participants, which is similar to the pattern found in acutely depressed participants and raises the possibility that left frontal hypoactivation may be a state-independent marker for depression. A recent study has provided further support for this idea. Currently depressed and remitted depressed individuals displayed significantly lower left frontal activation compared to a never-depressed control group. Furthermore, currently depressed and remitted depressed participants did not differ with respect to frontal EEG asymmetry (Gotlib, Ranganath, & Rosenfeld, 1998).

A related point is that a tendency to express approach behaviors or positive affect may also be seen in the context of obtaining a reward or incentive, and a tendency to express withdrawal behaviors or negative affect may be seen in the context of avoiding punishment.

Although this discussion focused mainly on the association of decreased left frontal EEG activation with decreased expression of positive affect and increased vulnerability to depression, it is notable that increased relative left frontal activation has been associated with heightened motivational sensitivity toward incentive and decreased vulnerability to affective disorder. Harmon-Jones and Allen (1997) found that higher relative left frontal activation was associated with higher scores on a self-report scale assessing motivational sensitivity to signals of reward.

Increased relative left frontal EEG activation also has been associated with the self-enhancing cognitive style of individuals classified as repressors (Tomarken & Davidson, 1994). *Repressors* obtain low scores on self-reported anxiety, but high scores on self-reported defensiveness, which distinguishes them from other low anxious participants (Weinberger, Schwartz, & Davidson, 1979). Defensiveness is often measured using the *Marlowe–Crowne Social Desirability Scale* (Crowne & Marlowe, 1960), which assesses the tendency to see oneself in an overly positive light. High defensiveness on this scale has been associated with a decreased lifetime incidence of affective disorders (Lane, Merikangas, Schwartz, Huang, & Prusoff, 1990). There is a variety of further evidence indicating that a self-enhancing cognitive style, such as repression, may confer lowered risk for psychopathology (for review, see Taylor & Brown, 1988). Individuals demonstrating such a style often make self-serving attributions, overestimate their control over situations, and demonstrate unrealistic optimism. Several findings support the notion that depression can be characterized by the breakdown of these kinds of self-deceptive mechanisms (Alloy & Abramson, 1988). Further studies are needed to explore the links between right frontal asymmetry, repressive defensiveness, and motivational sensitivity to reward.

FUNCTIONAL NEUROIMAGING STUDIES OF DEPRESSION

Other evidence that is concordant with a model of depression that involves underactivation of the frontal lobes, and in particular the left frontal region, comes from studies of functional brain imaging. Over the last 20 years, PET has been used increasingly to study the functional neurophysiology of affective disorders. PET employs a computerized reconstruction technique to produce tomographic images that represent the spatial distribution of radionuclides in the brain. The two main PET approaches involve the assessment of regional cerebral blood flow (rCBF) using ^{15}O-labeled water, or cerebral metabolic rate of glucose (CMR_{glu}) using 2-fluoro-2-deoxyglucose (FDG) labeled with ^{18}F. Both methods are used to identify patterns of differential neuronal activity across the various regions of the brain.

A number of investigators using PET studies with FDG have reported frontal abnormalities in patients with unipolar depression, with the most consistent finding being reductions in the metabolic rate in the frontal region of the brain among depressed individuals compared to nondepressed individuals (for reviews, see Dougherty & Rauch, 1997; Kennedy, Javanmard, & Vaccarino, 1997). Hurwitz et al. (1990) reported significant reductions in metabolic rate in the frontal region for unipolar depressed patients compared to normal controls. Similarly, Biver et al. (1994) found that metabolic rates were decreased in the frontal dorsolateral area in unipolar depressed patients compared to normal controls. Ho et al. (1996) found that frontal hypometabolism was present during non-REM sleep in unipolar depressed patients relative to controls, with this effect being particularly strong in the medio-orbital prefrontal cortex. Drevets et al. (1997) reported decreased metabolic activity in the subgenual prefrontal cortex in individuals with family histories of unipolar and bipolar depression compared to controls. In the same study, magnetic resonance imaging (MRI) was used to provide structural information alongside the functional information provided by the PET scans. The MRI scans showed a significant reduction in gray matter volume in the left subgenual prefrontal cortex for depressed individuals compared with control participants, which would partly explain the decreased metabolic activity in that region displayed on PET scans of depressed individuals.

Whereas many of the clinical studies referred to thus far involve primary depression, another line of research has explored the functional correlates of depression occurring secondary to neurological disorders such as Parkinson's Disease (PD) and Huntington's Disease (HD). Among patients with such disorders, Mayberg (1994) compared PET scans of depressed and nondepressed patients. Depression secondary to PD and HD was associated with hypometabolism in the orbitofrontal and inferior prefrontal regions. A recent study also has found decreased frontal-lobe activity associated with depression secondary to Alzheimer's disease (Hirono et al., 1998).

Drevets et al. (1992) found that individuals with a family history of depression showed hypermetabolism in the prefrontal cortex, amygdala, and medial thalamus. Although findings appear at odds with the previously mentioned findings of hypometabolism in prefrontal regions, some researchers have recently suggested that frontal hypermetabolism accompanying depression may occur in the postero-medial frontal (i.e., paralimbic) cortex, whereas hypometabolism may occur in the anterior and dorsolateral prefrontal cortex (Dougherty & Rauch, 1997).

Whereas most of the previously mentioned studies refer only to decreased frontal activity in depression, other studies have found this effect to be lateralized, with decreased activity specific to the left frontal region. Baxter et al. (1985) observed that a subgroup of their unipolar depressed sample (i.e., 3 out of 11) demonstrated a strikingly lower metabolic rate in the left frontal region of the cortex compared to the right frontal region. A subsequent study of unipolar depressed, bipolar depressed, and obsessive–compulsive disordered (OCD) patients also provided evidence that depression is associated with abnormal metabolic function in the left prefrontal cortex (Baxter et al., 1989). Although there was no difference between unipolar depressed individuals and controls in relative levels of left frontal metabolism, OCD patients with depression displayed significantly lower left frontal metabolism than OCD patients without depression, and depressed bipolar patients showed left frontal hypometabolism compared with manic bipolar patients. Clearer evidence for left frontal dysfunction in depression comes from a rCBF study by Bench and colleagues. Regional blood flow was decreased in the left dorsolateral prefrontal cortex and left anterior cingulate in unipolar depressed patients versus nondepressed controls (Bench et al., 1992).

Using an extended sample, Bench et al. (1993) conducted further analyses of rCBF patterning in relation to depressive symptoms. Factor analysis of patients' symptoms suggested three factors: anxiety, cognitive performance, and depressed mood. Whereas the anxiety factor was unrelated to frontal rCBF, the other two factors were associated with differing patterns of frontal blood flow. The cognitive performance factor was positively correlated with rCBF in the left medial prefrontal cortex, and the depressed mood factor was negatively correlated with rCBF in the left dorsolateral prefrontal cortex. A related finding comes from a study of self-generated sad mood in a nondepressed male sample (Gemar, Kapur, Segal, Brown, & Houle, 1996). Sad mood was associated with a decrease in rCBF in the left dorsolateral prefrontal, left medial prefrontal, and left temporal cortex when compared with recall of affectively neutral events or a resting baseline.

Thus, there are a number of PET findings that mirror EEG findings of an association between depression and left frontal hypoactivation. Given that EEG alpha-wave activity is inversely proportional to brain activity as measured by PET (Larson et al., 1998), there may be links between the findings from the two methodological approaches. Due to the paucity of studies relating EEG and PET, the nature of these links is not entirely clear yet, but the evidence from both approaches suggests an association between left frontal hypoactivation and depression.

HEMISPHERIC ASYMMETRY, COGNITIONS, AND DEPRESSION

Further questions concern the nature of the associations between frontal EEG asymmetry, depression, and emotional processing. As previously discussed, Davidson (1992) and Fox (1994) have suggested that frontal EEG asymmetry reflects individual differences in patterns of emotion expression and regulation. In particular, it has been suggested that left frontal hypoactivation may be associated with an inability to generate positive affect (e.g, Henriques & Davidson, 1991). In contrast, some current models of depression emphasize other aspects of affect regulation. For instance, Beck (1967) suggested that negative schemata play a causal role in depression, by biasing the individual to attend to negative information in the environment and to evaluate stimuli more negatively. Empirical investigations of this model have often found that self-report measures, such as the dysfunctional attitudes scale, are elevated in depressed participants. Related work by Nolen-Hoeksema has shown that among initially nondepressed participants, a cognitive-response style of rumination predicts the onset of longer and more severe depressive episodes (Nolen-Hoeksema, Morrow, & Fredrickson, 1993).

Another research approach has utilized information-processing tasks to study cognitive processes in depression (cf. Gotlib & Neubauer, chap. 7, this volume; Scott, Winters, & Beevers, chap. 8, this volume). Using a modified version of the *Stroop Color-Naming task,* in which participants are asked to name the ink colors of negative-content, positive-content, and neutral-content words, depressed participants take longer to name the colors of negative-content words, whereas nondepressed participants do not differ in time to name colors across the three word types (Gotlib & McCann, 1984).

If left frontal EEG hypoactivation represents a vulnerability to depression, participants with such a pattern of frontal asymmetry may be expected to show the kind of negative information-processing biases that are manifested by depressed individuals. At present, there is no evidence to support such a connection. A recent study found that participants with left frontal hypoactivation did not exhibit attentional biases toward negative stimuli on the modified Stroop Color-Naming task, and furthermore, they did not obtain higher scores on a self-report measure of dysfunctional attitudes compared to participants with increased left frontal activation (Gotlib et al., 1998). In the model of depression as lack of positive affect, however, these null results make sense. As Gotlib et al. discussed, anxiety rather than depression may bias attention toward threat-relevant stimuli. In support of this, Clark and Watson (1991) argued that depression is associated with low positive affect, whereas anxiety is associated with high negative affect. In fact, it has been suggested that the Stroop test findings among depressed individuals may be due to high comorbid anxiety (Williams, Watts, MacLeod, & Mathews, 1988). A recent study of EEG, depression, and anxiety illustrated the importance of considering anxiety comorbid with depression. Bruder et al. (1997) found that an anxious–depressed group showed decreased relative left frontal EEG activation, but a nonanxious depressed group did not. Further studies need to be conducted on the interaction of anxiety and depression as relates to emotion expression and EEG asymmetry.

EEG ASYMMETRY AND EMOTION EXPRESSION: DEVELOPMENTAL FINDINGS

Developmental data suggest that the links between frontal asymmetry, emotion regulation, and depression may be traced back to infancy. Infants of depressed mothers show relative right frontal asymmetry in baseline conditions and in mother–infant play (Dawson, Klinger, Panagiotides, Hill, & Spieker, 1992; Field, chap. 1, this volume; Field, Fox, Pickens, & Nawrocki, 1995; Jones, Field, Fox, Lundy, & Davalos, 1997). Consistent with the findings among depressed adults, 1-month-old infants of depressed mothers exhibited right frontal EEG asymmetry that was due to reduced left frontal activation (Jones, Field, Fox, et al., 1997). This frontal asymmetry at 1 month was significantly related to 3-month EEG asymmetry. Right frontal EEG asymmetry was also related to more frequent negative facial expressions (i.e., sad and precry faces) during the Brazelton exam. Dawson et al. (1992) further demonstrated that EEG asymmetry was a more sensitive indicator of a young child's response to maternal depression than behavioral measures of facial expression and vocal indicators of distress. Across a variety of emotion conditions, facial expression was unrelated to maternal depression and vocal distress displayed only one association with maternal depression, whereas EEG patterns were associated with maternal depression consistently across conditions.

Further research is needed to determine whether the frontal asymmetry found in infants of depressed mothers is a proximal response to a depressed parent or whether it continues when the parent is absent or no longer depressed. Behavioral effects of interacting with a depressed mother carry over for a short time (Field et al., 1988), and the effects of maternal depression are most striking when depression is chronic or recurrent (Campbell, Cohn, & Meyers, 1995). It is possible that continued interaction with a depressed parent may bring about a stable pattern of frontal asymmetry that influences the subsequent course of emotion regulation. Evidence for such a developmental pathway emerges from a study by Jones, Field, Davalos, and Pickens (1997), who examined the stability of EEG asymmetry in infants of depressed and nondepressed mothers from 3 months to 3 years. Seven of the eight children who had exhibited right frontal EEG asymmetry as infants still showed right frontal asymmetry at 3 years. Furthermore, 3-year-olds showing right frontal asymmetry were more withdrawn during an exploratory play task, and children of depressed versus nondepressed mothers were less empathic during simulated maternal distress.

The EEG work described in this chapter has mostly focused on right frontal asymmetry due to hypoactivation of the left frontal region. Nonetheless, it is important to note that right frontal asymmetry can also arise through activation of the right frontal region with no left frontal hypoactivation. This pattern of asymmetry has also been associated with individual differences in emotion expression. As discussed throughout this chapter, Fox (1994) has argued that the pattern of resting or tonic frontal EEG activation may be thought of as reflecting a predisposition toward the expression and/or experience of affects associated with approach or withdrawal. From a theoretical point of view, this model would predict that right frontal asymmetry that was a function of right frontal activation would be associated with the overexpression of negative affect. There are a number of findings to support this prediction. Davidson and Fox (1989) found that infants with right frontal EEG asymmetry were more likely to cry at maternal separation compared to those displaying left frontal EEG activation. Fox, Bell, and Jones (1992) replicated this finding and reported that the locus of effect was in the right hemisphere, with infants who were most likely to cry displaying higher activation in the right frontal region.

Other work in this laboratory has expanded understanding of the relations between EEG asymmetry and emotion expression. One particular focus of this work has been on behaviorally inhibited children who show reticence, wariness, and anxiety toward unfamiliar people and novel situations. Data from this laboratory and from others have shown that infants who display more irritability and negative affect during the early months of life are more likely to exhibit inhibited social behavior as toddlers. Calkins and Fox (1992) found that infants displaying more negative reactivity at 5 months were more likely to display separation distress at 14 months and also were more likely to be behaviorally inhibited at 24 months of age. Kagan and Snidman (1991) reported that 4-month-old infants selected for characteristics such as high motor activity and high frequency of crying were more likely than other infants to exhibit behavioral inhibition as toddlers.

We investigated whether the active irritable infants, who displayed behavioral inhibition as toddlers, would display a unique EEG activation pattern. We screened over 300 infants at 4 months of age and selected three distinct groups: infants who exhibited high motor behavior and frequent crying and negative affect; infants who exhibited high motor activity and frequent smiling and positive vocalizations; and infants who exhibited low motor behavior and infrequent positive or negative affect. These infants were seen in the laboratory twice—first at 9 months of age, at which time EEG was recorded while the infants attended to an attractive visual stimulus, and again at 14 months, at which time they were presented with a series of novel stimuli designed to elicit approach or withdrawal behaviors. The findings from this study confirmed our hypotheses regarding the relations between approach–withdrawal behaviors, infant temperament, and the pattern of frontal EEG activity (Calkins, Fox, & Marshall, 1996). Infants who displayed high motor behavior and frequent crying at 4 months exhibited right frontal EEG asymmetry at 9 months, whereas infants who showed high motor behavior and high positive affect exhibited left frontal asymmetry. In addition, the high-motor–high-cry infants who exhibited right frontal EEG asymmetry were more likely to show inhibited behaviors at 14 months. By categorizing infants at 4 months of age, we were able to predict which infants would display inhibited behavior 10 months later.

In another study, we again found relations between frontal EEG asymmetry and the disposition to display negative or positive affect in a social situation. Fox et al. (1995) observed a sample of 4-year-olds in laboratory play sessions involving four children of the same sex. The children came into the laboratory as a group and were videotaped in two free-play sessions that were separated by a clean-up session, a cooperation task, and a self-presentation task in which each child described their recent fourth-year birthday party. Measures of inhibition and social competence were coded from the videotapes. Each child returned to the laboratory 2 weeks later, at which time EEG was recorded during a visual attention task. Children who showed inhibited behavior in the quartet were more likely to present with right frontal asymmetry at the second lab visit that was a function of greater left frontal alpha power, that is, left frontal hypoactivation. Children who exhibited high sociability in the group session exhibited left frontal asymmetry that was a function of less left frontal power, that is, left frontal hyperactivation.

It is interesting to note that the differences in frontal asymmetry between inhibited and uninhibited children were a function of power in the left and not the right frontal region, which is similar to the pattern described earlier for depressed adults. This is not to argue that the 4-year-olds were depressed or at risk for depression, but rather that similar patterns of emotion regulation (i.e., an absence of positive affect and approach behavior in the inhibited children) may characterize both types of social interactions. Likewise, the depressed adult also appears unable to generate appropriate positive affect.

One related finding that fits the current model concerns a pattern of EEG asymmetry that has not yet been discussed. Shahinfar, Schmidt, and Fox (1996) found that toddlers selected for externalizing behaviors exhibited left frontal EEG asymmetry that was a function of lower right frontal activation. They speculate that this pattern may reflect the inability to experience negative affect among aggressive children.

CONCLUSION

In this chapter, we have attempted to bring together some current findings relating brain asymmetry to individual differences in the tendency to express and experience positive or negative emotions, with a particular focus on depression. It is clear that the frontal lobes are implicated in depression by various sources of data and this involvement has been integrated into current neurobiological models of depression (e.g., Mayberg, 1997). Nonetheless, it is reasonable to imagine the frontal region as a multimodal component in a series of networks rather than subserving a predictable local function (Goodwin, 1997). Thus, the frontal region is likely to be involved in many aspects of emotion expression, and models of diverse affective processes may in fact share some commonalities. Dougherty and Rauch (1997) suggested that primary major depression may involve hyperactivity or hypersensitivity of the amygdala. In their model, the amygdala may direct a reallocation of frontal resources by eventuating emotional and motivational processing in paralimbic areas and deactivating areas of the prefrontal cortex. This limbic shift represents a transient and adaptive response to an aversive stimulus, with depression being a maladaptive prolongation of this amygdala-mediated shift. Although prefrontal deactivation in this model is presumed to underlie cognitive deficits in depression, there are similarities with a current model of behavioral inhibition in childhood that emphasizes hypersensitivity of the amygdala (Kagan, 1994). This illustrates a point that was touched on during the description of the findings concerning EEG asymmetry. Fox (1994) suggested that frontal EEG activity should be viewed as reflecting a dynamic process of emotion regulation. Individuals will use multiple strategies, including the expression of different discrete emotions, use of verbal strategies, and manipulation of attention in order to modulate their positive and negative affective states. The frontal lobes are intimately involved in the expression of these different regulatory strategies. As such, during periods of affective challenge, the pattern of frontal activity will reflect the individual's attempt to regulate emotional arousal. This means that patterns of brain activity may not be specific to any particular behavior or affective disorder, but rather that these patterns reflect regulatory processes that may be manifested behaviorally in multiple ways.

REFERENCES

Alloy, L. B., & Abramson, L. Y. (1988). Depressive realism: Four theoretical perspectives. In L. B. Alloy (Ed.), *Cognitive processes in depression* (pp. 223–265). New York: Guilford.

Baxter, L. R., Jr., Phelps, M. E., Mazziotta, J. C., Schwartz, J. M., Gerner, R. H., Selin, C. E., & Sumida, R. M. (1985). Cerebral metabolic rates for glucose in mood disorders. Studies with positron emission tomography and fluorodeoxyglucose F 18. *Archives of General Psychiatry, 42,* 441–447.

Baxter, L. R., Jr., Schwartz, J. M., Phelps, M. E., Mazziotta, J. C., Guze, B. H., Selin, C. E., Gerner, R. H., & Sumida, R. M. (1989). Reduction of prefrontal cortex glucose metabolism common to three types of depression. *Archives of General Psychiatry, 46,* 243–250.

Beck, A. T. (1967). *Depression: Clinical, experimental, and theoretical aspects.* New York: Hoeber.

Bench, C. J., Friston, K. J., Brown, R. G., Frackowiak, R. S., & Dolan, R. J. (1993). Regional cerebral blood flow in depression measured by positron emission tomography: The relationship with clinical dimensions. *Psychological Medicine, 23,* 579–590.

Bench, C. J., Friston, K. J., Brown, R. G., Scott, L. C., Frackowiak, R. S., & Dolan, R. J. (1992). The anatomy of melancholia: Focal abnormalities of cerebral blood flow in major depression. *Psychological Medicine, 22,* 607–615.

Biver, F., Goldman, S., Delvenne, V., Luxen, A., De Maertelaer, V., Hubain, P., Mendlewicz, J., & Lotstra, F. (1994). Frontal and parietal metabolic disturbances in unipolar depression. *Biological Psychiatry, 36,* 381–388.

Bruder, G. E., Fong, R., Tenke, C. E., Leite, P., Towey, J. P., Stewart, J. E., McGrath, P. J., & Quitkin, F. M. (1997). Regional brain asymmetries in major depression with or without an anxiety disorder: A quantitative electroencephalographic study. *Biological Psychiatry, 41,* 939–948.

Calkins, S. D., & Fox, N. A. (1992). The relations among infant temperament, security of attachment, and behavioral inhibition at twenty-four months. *Child Development, 63,* 1456–1472.

Calkins, S. D., Fox, N. A., & Marshall, T. R. (1996). Behavioral and physiological antecedents of inhibited and uninhibited behavior. *Child Development, 67,* 523–540.

Campbell, S. B., Cohn, J. F., & Meyers, T. (1995). Depression in first-time mothers: Mother–infant interaction and depression chronicity. *Developmental Psychology, 31,* 349–357.

Clark, L. A., & Watson, D. (1991). Tripartite model of anxiety and depression: Psychometric evidence and taxonomic implications. *Journal of Abnormal Psychology, 100,* 316–336.

Crowne, D. P., & Marlowe, D. (1960). A new scale of social desirability independent of psychopathology. *Jounal of Consulting Psychology, 24,* 349–354.

Davidson, R. J. (1992). Anterior cerebral asymmetry and the nature of emotion. *Brain and Cognition, 20,* 125–151.

Davidson, R. J., & Fox, N. A. (1982). Asymmetrical brain activity discriminates between positive and negative affective stimuli in human infants. *Science, 218,* 1235–1237.

Davidson, R. J., & Fox, N. A. (1989). Frontal brain asymmetry predicts infants' response to maternal separation. *Journal of Abnormal Psychology, 98,* 127–131.

Dawson, G., Klinger, L. G., Panagiotides, H., Hill, D., & Spieker, S. (1992). Frontal lobe activity and affective behavior of infants of mothers with depressive symptoms. *Child Development, 63,* 725–737.

Dougherty, D., & Rauch, S. L. (1997). Neuroimaging and neurobiological models of depression. *Harvard Review of Psychiatry, 5,* 138–159.

Drevets, W. C., Price, J. L., Simpson, J. R., Jr., Todd, R. D., Reich, T., Vannier, M., & Raichle, M. E. (1997). Subgenual prefrontal cortex abnormalities in mood disorders. *Nature, 386,* 824–827.

Drevets, W. C., Videen, T. O., Price, J. L., Preskorn, S. H., Carmichael, S. T., & Raichle, M. E. (1992). A functional anatomical study of unipolar depression. *Journal of Neuroscience, 12,* 3628–3641.

Field, T., Fox, N. A., Pickens, J., & Nawrocki, T. (1995). Relative right frontal EEG activation in 3- to 6-month-old infants of depressed mothers. *Developmental Psychology, 31,* 358–363.

Field, T., Healy, B., Goldstein, S., Perry, S., Bendell, D., Schanberg, S., Zimmerman, E. A., & Kuhn, C. (1988). Infants of depressed mothers show "depressed" behavior even with nondepressed adults. *Child Development, 59,* 1569–1579.

Fox, N. A. (1991). If it's not left, it's right. Electroencephalograph asymmetry and the development of emotion. *American Psychologist, 46,* 863–872.

Fox, N. A. (1994). Dynamic cerebral processes underlying emotion regulation. In N. A. Fox (Ed.), The development of emotion regulation: Biological and behavioral considerations (pp. 152–166). *Monographs of the Society for Research in Child Development, 59*(2–3, Serial No. 240).

Fox, N. A., Bell, M. A., & Jones, N. A. (1992). Individual differences in response to stress and cerebral asymmetry. *Developmental Neuropsychology, 8,* 161–184.

Fox, N. A., & Davidson, R. J. (1986). Taste-elicited changes in facial signs of emotion and the asymmetry of brain electrical activity in human newborns. *Neuropsychologia, 24,* 417–422.

Fox, N. A., & Davidson, R. J. (1988). Patterns of brain electrical activity during facial signs of emotion in ten month old infants. *Developmental Psychology, 24,* 230–236.

Fox, N. A., Rubin, K. H., Calkins, S. D., Marshall, T. R., Coplan, R. J., Porges, S. W., Long, J. M., & Stewart, S. (1995). Frontal activation asymmetry and social competence at four years of age. *Child Development, 66,* 1770–1784.

Gemar, M. C., Kapur, S., Segal, Z. V., Brown, G. M., & Houle, S. (1996). Effects of self-generated sad mood on regional cerebral activity: A PET study in normal subjects. *Depression, 4,* 81–88.

Goodwin, G. M. (1997). Neuropsychological and neuroimaging evidence for the involvement of the frontal lobes in depression. *Journal of Psychopharmacology, 11*, 115–122.

Gotlib, I. H., & McCann, C. D. (1984). Construct accessibility and depression: An examination of cognitive and affective factors. *Journal of Personality and Social Psychology, 47*, 427–439.

Gotlib, I. H., Ranganath, C., & Rosenfeld, J. P. (1998). Frontal EEG alpha asymmetry, depression, and cognitive functioning. *Cognition and Emotion, 12*, 449–478.

Harmon-Jones, E., & Allen, J. J. (1997). Behavioral activation sensitivity and resting frontal EEG asymmetry: Covariation of putative indicators related to risk for mood disorders. *Journal of Abnormal Psychology, 106*, 159–163.

Henriques, J. B., & Davidson, R. J. (1990). Regional brain electrical asymmetries discriminate between previously depressed and healthy control subjects. *Journal of Abnormal Psychology, 99*, 22–31.

Henriques, J. B., & Davidson, R. J. (1991). Left frontal hypoactivation in depression. *Journal of Abnormal Psychology, 100*, 535–545.

Hirono, N., Mori, E., Ishii, K., Ikejiri, Y., Imamura, T., Shimomura, T., Hashimoto, M., Yamashita, H., & Sasaki, M. (1998). Frontal lobe hypometabolism and depression in Alzheimer's disease. *Neurology, 50*, 380–383.

Ho, A. P., Gillin, J. C., Buchsbaum, M. S., Wu, J. C., Abel, L., & Bunney, W. E., Jr. (1996). Brain glucose metabolism during non-rapid eye movement sleep in major depression. A positron emission tomography study. *Archives of General Psychiatry, 53*, 645–652.

Hurwitz, T. A., Clark, C., Murphy, E., Klonoff, H., Martin, W. R., & Pate, B. D. (1990). Regional cerebral glucose metabolism in major depressive disorder. *Canadian Journal of Psychiatry, 35*, 684–688.

Jacobs, G. D., & Snyder, D. (1996). Frontal brain asymmetry predicts affective style in men. *Behavioral Neuroscience, 110*, 3–6.

Jones, N. A., Field, T., Davalos, M., & Pickens, J. (1997). EEG stability in infants/children of depressed mothers. *Child Psychiatry and Human Development, 28*, 59–70.

Jones, N. A., Field, T., Fox, N. A., Lundy, B., & Davalos, M. (1997). EEG activation in 1-month-old infants of depressed mothers. *Development and Psychopathology, 9*, 491–505.

Kagan, J. (1994). *Galen's Prophecy*. New York: Basic Books.

Kagan, J., & Snidman, N. (1991). Temperamental factors in human development. *American Psychologist, 46*, 856–862.

Kennedy, S. H., Javanmard, M., & Vaccarino, F. J. (1997). A review of functional neuroimaging in mood disorders: Positron emission tomography and depression. *Canadian Journal of Psychiatry, 42*, 467–475.

Lane, R. D., Merikangas, K. R., Schwartz, G. E., Huang, S. S., & Prusoff, B. A. (1990). Inverse relationship between defensiveness and lifetime prevalence of psychiatric disorder. *American Journal of Psychiatry, 147*, 573–578.

Larson, C. L., Davidson, R. J., Abercrombie, H. C., Ward, R. T., Schaefer, S. M., Jackson, D. C., Holden, J. E., & Perlman, S. B. (1998). Relations between PET-derived measures of thalamic glucose metabolism and EEG alpha power. *Psychophysiology, 35*, 162–169.

LeDoux, J. E. (1993). Emotional memory systems in the brain. *Behavioral Brain Research, 58*, 69–79.

Lee, G. P., Loring, D. W., Meader, K. J., & Brooks, B. B. (1990). Hemispheric specialization for emotional expression: A reexamination of results from intracarotid administration of sodium amobarbital. *Brain and Cognition, 12*, 267–280.

Mayberg, H. S. (1994). Frontal lobe dysfunction in secondary depression. *Journal of Neuropsychiatry and Clinical Neurosciences, 6*, 428–442.

Mayberg, H. S. (1997). Limbic-cortical dysregulation: a proposed model of depression. *Journal of Neuropsychiatry and Clinical Neurosciences, 9*, 471–481.

Morris, P. L., Robinson, R. G., de Carvalho, M. L., Albert, P., Wells, J. C., Samuels, J. F., Eden-Fetzer, D., & Price, T. R. (1996). Lesion characteristics and depressed mood in the Stroke Data Bank study. *Journal of Neuropsychiatry and Clinical Neurosciences, 8*, 153–159.

Morris, P. L., Robinson, R. G., Raphael, B., & Hopwood, M. J. (1996). Lesion location and poststroke depression. *Journal of Neuropsychiatry and Clinical Neurosciences, 8*, 399–403.

Nolen-Hoeksema, S., Morrow, J., & Fredrickson, B. L. (1993). Response styles and the duration of episodes of depressed mood. *Journal of Abnormal Psychology, 102*, 20–28.

Perria, L., Rosadini, G., & Rossi, G. F. (1961). Determination of side of cerebral dominance with amobarbital. *Archives of Neurology, 4*, 173–181.

Robinson, R. G., & Szetela, B. (1981). Mood change following left hemispheric brain injury. *Annals of Neurology, 9*, 447–453.

Sackeim, H. A., Greenberg, M. A., Weiman, A. L., Gur, R. C., Hungerbuhler, J. P., & Geschwind, N. (1982). Hemispheric asymmetry in the expression of positive and negative emotions. *Archives of Neurology, 39*, 210–218.

Schaffer, C. E., Davidson, R. J., & Saron, C. (1983). Frontal and parietal electroencephalogram asymmetry in depressed and nondepressed subjects. *Biological Psychiatry, 18*, 753–762.

Shahinfar, A., Schmidt, L. A., & Fox, N. A. (1996, October). *Right frontal EEG hypoactivation in aggressive toddlers.* Paper presented at the 36th Annual Meeting of the Society for Psychophysiological Research, Vancouver, British Columbia, Canada.

Silberman, E. K., & Weingartner, H. (1986). Hemispheric lateralization of functions related to emotion. *Brain and Cognition, 5*, 322–353.

Snyder, P. J., & Harris, L. J. (1997). The intracarotid amobarbital procedure: An historical perspective. *Brain and Cognition, 33*, 18–32.

Taylor, S. E., & Brown, J. D. (1988). Illusion and well-being: A social psychological perspective on mental health. *Psychological Bulletin, 103*, 193–210.

Tomarken, A. J., & Davidson, R. J. (1994). Frontal brain activation in repressors and nonrepressors. *Journal of Abnormal Psychology, 103*, 339–349.

Weinberger, D. A., Schwartz, G. E., & Davidson, R. J. (1979). Low-anxious, high-anxious, and repressive coping styles: Psychometric patterns and behavioral and physiological responses to stress. *Journal of Abnormal Psychology, 88*, 369–380.

Wheeler, R. E., Davidson, R. J., & Tomarken, A. J. (1993). Frontal brain asymmetry and emotional reactivity: A biological substrate of affective style. *Psychophysiology, 30*, 82–89.

Williams, J. M. G., Watts, F. N., MacLeod, C., & Mathews, A. (1988). *Cognitive psychology and emotional disorders.* Chichester, England: Wiley.

Chapter 4

Moderators of Child Outcome in Families With Depressed Mothers and Fathers

Sheri L. Johnson
University of Miami

Theodore Jacob
Palo Alto Veterans Affairs Health Care System, Palo Alto, California

We begin this chapter by reviewing the impact of maternal and paternal depression on child outcome. Although parental depression is a major risk factor for child outcome, it is also clear that offspring of both depressed fathers and depressed mothers are highly varied in outcome and that many children demonstrate no social or behavioral difficulties at all. One of the issues highlighted by our review is that despite this heterogeneity of offspring adjustment, little is known about which of these children will display difficulties.

With this literature review as background, we then describe a study aimed at examining variables that may increase or decrease risk of behavioral problems for children with a depressed parent. In examining moderators, we use hierarchical linear modeling, which allowed us to simultaneously consider each child within the family. We believe that this provides an important advantage for understanding family systems and outcome. The results of this study suggest that marital longevity is a significant buffer for children with a depressed father, but is not protective for children of a depressed mother or children of normal controls. In the final section of this chapter, we attempt to place these findings in a broader context.

BACKGROUND

To date, most research on parental depression has focused on children with a depressed mother rather than those with a depressed father. Overall, children of depressed mothers (CODMs) experience a range of difficulties compared to children with a nondisturbed or medically ill mother, including more emotional symptoms, behavioral impairment, social problems, and school problems (Beardslee, Keller, & Klerman, 1985; Billings & Moos, 1983; Downey & Coyne, 1990). Given this constellation of behavioral and social difficulties, it is not surprising that children with depressed mothers, like children whose mothers exhibit other psychiatric disorders, demonstrate increased risk for psychiatric disorder (Goodman, Adamson, Riniti, & Cole, 1994; Hammen, Burge, Burney, & Adrian, 1990). CODMs are particularly prone to major depression, with rates of major depression ranging from 7% to 13% per year among these children. By adolescence, these children exhibit a lifetime risk for depression as high as 45% (Hammen, chap. 5, this volume). Furthermore, some studies indicate that the rate for affective disorders is three times higher in CODMs than in normal control families. Even a full year after the remission of maternal depression, these children display significant impairment (Billings & Moos, 1985; Lee & Gotlib, 1989). In short, CODMs demonstrate a host of difficulties, most importantly, elevated rates of depression.

In contrast with the considerable research interest in CODMs, less is known about the role of paternal depression in predicting child outcome. Several studies have reported that children of depressed fathers (CODFs) are at greater risk for behavioral problems compared to children of nondisturbed fathers (Compas, Howell, Phares, Williams, & Giunta, 1989; Forehand, Long, Brody, & Fauber, 1986). Studies contrasting the impact of a depressed father versus a depressed mother, however, have been less clearcut. For example, congruent with patterns of more intensive childrearing involvement among women than among men, Hops (1992) found that maternal depression exerted a stronger impact on child adjustment than paternal depression. In contrast, our own studies, as well as those of other investigators, have found comparable levels of disturbance associated with maternal and paternal depression (Billings & Moos, 1983; Ge, Conger, Lorenz, Shanahan, & Elder, 1995; Jacob & Johnson, 1997; Weissman et al., 1987). In short, although CODFs appear to be at increased risk for depression and other child behavior problems, research remains inconclusive regarding whether maternal versus paternal depression exert a comparable effect on offsprings' psychosocial and psychiatric functioning.

Whereas many children of depressed parents exhibit difficulties, it is also true that some of these children appear quite resilient and do not display significant behavior problems. Understanding the variability in outcome among children from these families is a fundamental need of current research. In this chapter, we examine factors that might increase or decrease the risk associated with parental depression, with particular interest in whether the same moderators operate in families with a depressed mother versus a depressed father.

In considering potential moderators among children of depressed parents, the variable of child gender has received the most attention in the relevant research literature. For example, in longitudinal research, maternal depression has been more associated with daughters' depression, whereas paternal depression appears more closely associated with sons' depression (Hops, 1992; Thomas & Forehand, 1991). Other research, however, with younger samples, has been inconsistent in documenting parental depression effects for the crossgender offspring (Ge et al., 1995). It is likely that gender effects will need to be considered within the context of child age, given that boys manifest problem behavior during early or middle childhood, whereas rates of depression for girls increase during adolescence (Hops, 1995; Lewinsohn, Hops, Roberts, Seeley, & Andrews, 1993).

Beyond examining child gender and age, we were interested in examining a few key, relatively uncorrelated, variables that appeared likely to be moderators on the basis of previous literature. Previous literature suggested that marital satisfaction (Downey & Coyne, 1990; Emery, Weintraub, & Neale, 1982), marital longevity (cf. Fendrich, Warner, & Weissman, 1990) and parental psychopathology influence outcomes among children with depressed parents (Compas et al., 1989). In summary, we were interested in evaluating the following variables as potential moderators of the impact of parental depression on child outcome: child age, child gender, marital satisfaction, marital longevity, and parental psychopathology.

Of these potential moderators, some are family-level characteristics that will be constant for all children in the family (e.g., parental psychopathology, marital satisfaction, and marital longevity), whereas others vary across children within the family (e.g., age and gender). Although all children in a family are exposed to the same levels of parental and marital functioning, the unique characteristics of each child within the family may impact vulnerability to a particular family environment. The conjoint examination of family-level and child-level predictors of risk should enhance understanding of family influences on outcome. By examining both family and child characteristics at the same time, one opens the door for addressing questions of why some children within a family do poorly, whereas other children from the same family do relatively well.

To fully model any child's level of risk, then, would require an approach that could simultaneously examine characteristics of both the family environment and each child within that family. This goal has been unobtainable within traditional analysis of variance (ANOVA) or regression-based approaches, in which one of the assumptions is that all observations are independent. This assumption is violated if more than one child from the same family is included in analyses. To avoid this statistical violation, researchers have traditionally focused on one randomly selected child from each family, without considering the other children in the family. Alternatively, they have utilized an average of all the children in the family as the dependent variable. Neither of these approaches can simultaneously consider the family environment while capturing each child's unique risk factors and outcome.

To be able to predict outcomes for each of the children within a family, we turned to a data analytic approach that received comparably little attention within the family literature—hierarchical linear modeling (HLM). In conducting analyses that utilize outcomes from multiple children within the same family, one of the statistical issues is how to account for the correlation or dependency of observations among siblings within the same family. HLM computes the intraclass correlation within families, estimating the extent of dependency in observations within each family. All analyses include a correction parameter for this dependency. This allows us to examine family-level indices (i.e., parental depression, marital satisfaction, marital longevity, and parental psychopathology) as well as child-level variables (i.e., child gender and child age) conjointly.

METHOD

Participants

Participants were recruited as part of a larger study, one part of which examined the relation between parental depression and family interaction (Jacob, Seilhamer, & Rushe, 1989). All participants, including depressed and control families, were recruited from the Pittsburgh area via newspaper advertisements. For the depressed families, the advertisements indicated that the study was to involve families in which either the male or female head of the household was experiencing depression. Families, recruited between 1979 and 1986, completed a wide range of assessment procedures over a 1-month period and were paid from $300 to $500 for participation.

Participating couples had been married and living together for at least 5 years and had at least one child between 10 and 18 years of age. Additionally, families contained a father who satisfied Research Diagnostic Criteria (RDC; Endicott & Spitzer, 1978) for depressive disorder (50 families with a depressed husband), a mother who satisfied RDC for depressive disorder (41 families with a depressed wife), or no current psychopathology in either parent (50 control couples). RDC were assessed by the Schedule for Affective Disorders and Schizophrenia Lifetime Version (SADS; Spitzer, Endicott & Robins, 1978). Families were excluded if the index spouse satisfied any RDC for current or previous major disorder other than depression or if the nondepressed spouse satisfied any RDC for current major disorder. No family member was actively involved in therapy at the time of the family's participation in the study.

Although sample selection was originally based on RDC criteria, SADS interviews, as well as original phone screens, were reviewed to determine whether index participants met criteria for DSM–IV major depression. Only one individual failed to meet these criteria and the data from this family was excluded from all subsequent analyses.

Measures

Family members were asked to complete a series of questionnaires, laboratory and home-based observations, and interviews as part of a larger data collection effort. Only results from the questionnaires are presented in this report. (For detailed descriptions, see Jacob et al., 1989.)

To assess marital adjustment, both spouses completed the Dyadic Adjustment Scale (DAS; Spanier, 1976; Spanier & Thompson, 1982). The DAS is a widely used, 32-item self-report scale that has high internal consistency and successfully differentiates married and divorced couples, distressed and nondistressed couples, and clinical and nonclinical samples. Within this sample, husband and wife DAS scores were highly correlated ($r = .67$, $N = 131$).

Depression was further assessed using the Beck Depression Inventory (BDI; Beck, Ward, Mendelson, Mock, & Erbaugh, 1961) and the Minnesota Multiphasic Personality Inventory Scale 2 (MMPI; Hathaway & McKinley, 1983). The BDI is a 21-item self-report scale that assesses mood, cognitive, and somatic aspects of depression. It is the most frequently used self-report instrument for assessing depression severity and has been shown to exhibit good psychometric properties. Estimates of internal consistency and test–retest reliability are high; the measure appears sensitive to severity across a broad range of community and clinical populations; and gender bias across items is low (Norman, Miller, & Klee, 1983; Rush et al., 1986; Santor, Ramsay, & Zuroff, 1994). The MMPI Scale 2 differentiates depressed and nondepressed samples (Greene, 1980). One-month retest reliability for this scale has been found to vary between .80 and .90 (Dahlstrom, Welsh, & Dahlstrom, 1975). The 60-item scale incorporates symptoms of depression such as poor morale, hopelessness, dissatisfaction, apathy, sleep disturbance, and social withdrawal.

As an index of parental psychopathology symptom levels, we included the MMPI Goldberg Index (Goldberg, 1965, 1969). This summation of *k*-corrected scales has been shown to be a robust predictor of clinician and other indices of psychosis and clinical severity (Greene, 1980).

Child Behavior Checklist

The CBCL is the most widely used parental report measure of child functioning. It is well standardized with extensive normative data, and previous research strongly demonstrated the ability of the CBCL to differentiate clinic-referred children from nonreferred children (Achenbach, 1978, 1991a, 1991b). The CBCL provides a general index of behavior problems—*Total Behavior Problems,* two factor-analytically derived broad indices, *Internalization* and *Externalization,* and of particular interest for this study, *Depression.* Internal consistency and test–retest coefficients for each scale are well established. These parent-report indices have also been shown to correlate highly with child self-report ($r = .71$ to .86) (Achenbach, 1991b).

We relied exclusively on *t* scores that are age- and gender-normed. That is, we were not interested in possible main effects for age nor for gender; rather, we were interested in potential interactions between parental depression status and these variables.

Within the current study, maternal and paternal scores on the CBCL were moderately correlated ($r_{\text{Depression}} = .33$, $N = 136$, $p = .000$; $r_{\text{Total Behavior Problems}} = .56$, $N = 136$, $p = .000$; $r_{\text{Internalizing}} = .49$, $N = 136$, $p = .000$; $r_{\text{Externalizing}} = .59$, $N = 136$, $p = .000$). The limited strength of these correlations raised concerns that mothers and fathers could be evaluating their children differently, with depressed parents potentially exhibiting a systematic negative bias. Although a recent comprehensive review provides substantial evidence that this is not a major concern (Richters, 1992), paired *t* tests were computed separately within each group to examine whether parents with depression were being overly negative in evaluating their children. As expected, for the normal controls, no significant differences emerged between mother and father report of Depression, Total Behavior Problems, Internalizing, or Externalizing. Similarly, no significant differences between maternal and paternal report emerged within either the paternal depression group or the maternal depression group.

Despite these reassuring findings, we adopted a particularly conservative approach to avoid any risk that these indices would be biased by parental depression. That is, we used a dependent variable that included the average of maternal and paternal ratings for the control group, the maternal ratings for the paternal depression group, and the paternal ratings for the maternal depression group.

Sample Description

Across a number of demographic variables (see Table 4.1), ANOVAs were conducted to examine group differences. These ANOVAs revealed that groups differed on marital longevity (number of years married), husband

TABLE 4.1
Sample Means (+ SDs) for Demographic Variables

	Normal Control (*n* = 50)		*Depressed Husband* (*n* = 49)		*Depressed Wife* (*n* = 41)		
	M	*SD*	*M*	*SD*	*M*	*SD*	*F*
Marital Longevity	19.34 ±	5.43	17.18 ±	5.63	15.46 ±	5..71	5.52***
Husband Age	43.44 ±	6.61	42.37 ±	6.78	39.80 ±	5.79	3.71*
Wife Age	40.74 ±	6.47	39.24 ±	6.33	38.12 ±	5.00	2.17
Husband Education	12.66 ±	1.27	14.24 ±	2.31	14.53 ±	2.03	13.24****
Wife Education	12.54 ±	1.40	12.69 ±	2.60	13.15 ±	1.68	1.12
Mean DAS	111.23 ±	12.16	95.00 ±	14.13	96.05 ±	19.56	17.61****
Index BDI	--		23.00 ±	7.52	19.08 ±	7.22	4.02*
Index Episodes	--		3.42 +	5.72	2.80 +	2.29	.66
Index MMPI Scale 2	--		86.98 ±	12.18	73.00 ±	13.20	20.12****
Index DAS	--		93.91 ±	16.05	94.00 ±	21.48	1.06

Note. Mean DAS = average of wife and husband DAS; index = index spouse; BDI = Beck Depression Inventory; Episodes = number of lifetime episoes of depression; DAS scores were missing for 6 of the depressed husband couples; M = Mean; SD = standard deviation; $^{*}p \leq .05$; $^{**}p \leq .01$; $^{***}p \leq .005$; $^{****}p \leq .001$.

age, and husband education (see Table 4.1). Univariate *t* tests were conducted to compare the control group versus the depressed groups and couples with a depressed husband versus couples with a depressed wife. Contrasts revealed that the depressed groups had been married fewer years and were more highly educated than the controls. In addition, husbands in the depressed groups were younger than control husbands. Couples with a depressed wife versus a depressed husband, however, did not differ on marital longevity, husband age, or husband education. Furthermore, there were no significant group differences for husband occupation, wife age, or wife education. Finally, the three samples were comparable on husband and wife employment status, child gender, child age, and family religion.

As expected, groups differed on marital satisfaction (average of the mother and father scores; see Table 4.1). Depressed groups were significantly lower on marital satisfaction than the control group was [t (132) = 5.72, $p < .001$], whereas couples with a depressed husband did not differ from couples with a depressed wife [t (82) = –.31, $p = .76$]. Results were entirely comparable when wives' DAS and husbands' DAS were examined separately. Using the standard cut-off score for marital distress of less than or equal to 100, 18% of the control couples, 64% of the depressed husband couples, and 50% of the depressed wife couples reported marital distress [X^2 (2) = 21.21, $p \leq .0001$]. Finally, for depressed husbands and depressed wives, depression and marital satisfaction for the depressed individuals were examined. Depressed husbands reported higher levels of depression than the depressed wives on the BDI [t (84) = 2.45, $p = .02$] and MMPI Scale 2 [t (86) = 5.16, $p < .001$), whereas depressed husbands and depressed wives reported comparable levels of marital distress.

On average, couples had been married for 17 years and had three children. Their offspring ranged in age from 4 to 19 years. Approximately 17% of the couples had been previously married. Of the children, 92.6% were living with both biological parents. Children of depressed fathers or depressed mothers were less likely to be living with both biological parents (99.4% of children of nondepressed parents, 91.8% of the children of depressed fathers, and 85.5% of the children of depressed mothers were living with both biological parents; $X^2 = 21.18$, $df = 2$, $N = 471$, $p = .000$). Preliminary analyses suggested that living with a stepparent was not associated with child behavior problem scores. Of the husbands, 77.9% worked full-time, 1.4% worked part-time, 19.3% were unemployed, .7% were retired, and .7% were disabled. Among the wives, 30% worked full-time, 25.7% worked part-time, 6.4% were unemployed, 37.6% were housewives, and .7% were students.

RESULTS

Our primary analyses utilized HLM to achieve two goals. First, our previous research had been limited to examining child behavior problems associated with maternal versus paternal depression for only one randomly selected child per family. To examine the impact of maternal and paternal depression when including all children in the family, we conducted analyses of the impact of maternal and paternal depression on child outcome. After describing these results, we present HLM analyses conducted to examine moderators of maternal and paternal depression.

Impact of Paternal and Maternal Depression on Child Outcome

Within these analyses, we used parental depression and maternal versus paternal depression as independent variables. Four parallel analyses were conducted to examine the dependent variables of Total Behavior Problems, Depression, Internalization, and Externalization.

HLM provides an intraclass correlation coefficient, indicating the degree of correlation among children within the same family, which is used to

TABLE 4.2
HLM Analyses: Effects of Parental Depression on Scores

Criterion Variable	*Predictor Variable*	*Estimate*	*SE*	*P*
Total Behavior	Parental Depression	8.48	2.01	.0000
	Maternal versus Paternal Depression	.34	.17	.86
Depression	Paternal Depression	2.83	.89	.001
	Maternal versus Paternal Depression	-.07	.88	.93
Internalization	Parental Depression	7.72	1.88	.0000
	Maternal versus Paternal Depression	.30	1.87	.87
Externalization	Parental Depression	5.99	1.75	.0006
	Maternal versus Paternal Depression	.58	1.75	.74

Note. SE = Standard error.

correct for the dependency of observations within each cluster (or correlations among siblings). The intraclass correlation coefficient was equal to .48 for Total Behavior Problems and .52 for Internalization, suggesting that for each of these two variables, approximately 25% of the variance was accounted for by shared family variance. The intraclass correlation coefficient was equal to .30 for Depression and .36 for Externalization, suggesting that only 9% to 13% of the variance was accounted for by shared family variance.

For each of the four scales, results were comparable in revealing a significant effect for parental depression, but not for maternal versus paternal depression (see Table 4.2). That is, children with either a depressed mother or father obtained higher Total Behavior Problem, Depression, Internalization, and Externalization scores than children without a depressed parent.

To provide a more concrete estimate of risk, we also calculated the proportion of children in each group who were above the 90th percentile (a t score of 63) on the Total Behavior Problems and Depression scales. In examining Total Behavior Problems, 1.9% of the control children (n = 105) were at or above the 90th percentile compared to 18.8% of the paternal depression children (n = 96) and 20.6% of the maternal depression children (n = 97). For depression, 4.8% of the control children obtained a score at or above the 90th percentile compared to 19.8% of the paternal depression children (n = 96) and 17.1% of the maternal depression children (n = 97).

Moderators of Paternal and Maternal Depression

To assess moderators of risk, we extended the Baron and Kenny (1986) suggestions concerning regression models to HLM. First, analyses were conducted to examine which variables predicted outcome among the children with a depressed parent. Second, we conducted analyses of whether children with a depressed parent were more vulnerable to these risk factors than were children of a nondepressed parent by examining interactions between group (e.g., depressed–nondepressed and maternal versus paternal depression) and potential moderator variables. In conducting analyses of moderators, the dependent variable was Total Behavior Problems, the CBCL index capturing the broadest range of behaviors, with the most robust psychometric support.

First, to determine which variables were associated with increased risk among children of depressed parents, we conducted analyses with paternal and maternal BDI, paternal and maternal MMPI Goldberg Index, DAS, marital longevity, child gender, and child age as the independent variables. We utilized the Total Behavior Problems *t* score as the dependent variable. Within this analysis, only marital longevity was significant (see Table 4.3). Among children with a depressed parent, children of parents who had been married longer had fewer behavior problems. Marital longevity appeared to be a protective factor among children with a depressed parent.

To address whether marital longevity was a moderator (associated with greater risk among children of depressed parents than children of normal controls), we conducted a second HLM analysis. In this analysis, we included control, paternal depression, and maternal depression families. Independent variables included whether or not a parent was depressed, whether the mother or father was depressed, marital longevity, the interaction of Parental depression × Marital longevity and the interaction of Maternal or paternal depression × Marital longevity. Within this analysis, marital longevity was not significant, nor was the interaction of Parental depression × Marital longevity (see Table 4.4). Significant results were

TABLE 4.3
HLM Analyses: Predictors of CBCL Total Behavior Problems in Children With a Depressed Parent

Predictor Variable	*Estimate*	*SE*	*p*
Paternal BDI	.20	.13	.12
Maternal BDI	.10	.12	.40
Paternal MMPI	.02	.06	.80
Maternal MMPI	.05	.06	.36
Maternal Satisfaction	-.07	.07	.32
Marital Longevity	-.58	.20	.004
Maternal versus Paternal Depression	1.78	1.61	.27
Child Gender	-2.80	2.77	.31
Child Age	.31	.23	.17

Note. SE = Standard error.

TABLE 4.4
HLM Analyses: Moderators of the Impact of Parental Depression on Total Behavaior Problems

Predictor Variable	*Estimate*	*SE*	*p*
Parental Depression	17.86	7.07	.01
Maternal or Paternal Depression	-15.85	6.24	.01
Years Married	-.63	.58	.28
Depression x Years Married	-.57	.37	.12
Maternal or Paternal Depression x Marital Longevity	.96	.36	.008

Note. SE = Standard error.

obtained for depression, maternal versus paternal depression, and the interaction of Maternal versus paternal depression × Marital longevity.

These results suggest that children with a depressed father or a depressed mother were experiencing more behavioral difficulties than those with nondepressed parents. Although children of depressed mothers were experiencing more behavior problems than were children of depressed fathers, this effect only emerged after we accounted for group differences in marital longevity. For families with a depressed father, children have fewer behavior problems as the couple has been married longer, whereas behavior problems were not associated with marital longevity among families with a depressed mother.

The significant finding for maternal versus paternal depression was somewhat surprising, as this effect did not emerge in our initial analyses. The contrasting findings from these two sets of analyses suggest that marital longevity was operating as a suppressor variable.

Given the array of factors associated with marital longevity, we conducted analyses to examine whether correlates of marital longevity might explain outcome among the children of depressed fathers.[1] In particular, we conducted another HLM analysis to examine whether behavior problems among children with a depressed father could be explained by paternal age, stepfamily status, or number of lifetime depression episodes. None of these variables were significant predictors of child behavior outcome among children with a depressed father.

[1]These variables were not included in primary analyses for several reasons. First, we attempted to select variables that would be less correlated with each other. Second, although we were interested in the number of episodes of depression, this information was not available for the families with no depressed parent, so that it was not an appropriate variable for moderator analyses.

DISCUSSION

Within this study, paternal and maternal depression both influence child functioning and symptoms. Compared to children of control parents, children with a depressed parent display more behavior problems, internalization, externalization, and depression. As many as 19% of the children with a depressed parent demonstrated clinical levels of behavior problems, highlighting the need to increase understanding about the ways in which parental depression operates as a risk factor for offspring behavior problems. The magnitude of problems suggests a strong need for further attention to paternal depression.

Moderator analyses suggested one important variable—marital longevity—that appeared to operate differently for depressed mothers versus depressed fathers. For families with depressed fathers, marital longevity was associated with less child impairment, whereas for families with depressed mothers and for families with no parental depression, marital longevity was not significantly associated with child impairment. Assuming that this result is replicable, this suggests that paternal depression effects need to be interpreted within a longitudinal context that incorporates the time a couple has been married. This finding is difficult to interpret in that there are a myriad of factors associated with marital longevity (cf. Levenson, Carstensen, & Gottman, 1994; Thomas, Fletcher, & Lange, 1997). We examined several variables that correlate with marital longevity, but found that child age, paternal age, stepchild status, marital satisfaction, and depression recurrence all failed to explain child outcome. Although a vast array of family characteristics are likely to shift and evolve across years of being married, our own reflection on current findings led us to hypothesize that they might hint at the development of family coping and communication strategies that buffer children during paternal episodes of depression. More specifically, we believe that mothers and fathers differ in their responses to repeated episodes of depression.

Across years of marriage and repeated episodes of depression, mothers may become more adept at explaining the father's depression to the child. Alternatively, mothers may learn to take on a larger share of the parenting role to maintain continuity in the child's life, such as helping with homework, talking with a child about school and friendship problems, or bolstering the child's self-esteem as the depressed parent is less positive. It is also possible that with more time together, mothers and fathers learn to buffer the impact of the depression on family interaction, so that parenting remains preserved in the context of depression. For example, fathers' behavioral and communicative expressions of depression may shift over time, with consequent protection for the child. The combination of increased personal maturity and experience within the marriage may allow the couple to develop more skillful strategies. In contrast to the families with depressed husbands, families with depressed wives do not seem protected by marital longevity; coping strategies do not seem to evolve across years of marriage.

More research is necessary to understand how the family learns to protect the child from the impact of father's depression over time; variables that may be particularly important to study include family interaction patterns and parenting. Overall, there has been an increasing recognition within family studies of the need to understand the process through which marital difficulties and problems for individual parents become translated into child risk (Davies & Cummings, 1994; Gottman, Katz, & Hooven, 1997). Understanding naturalistic shifts in depression-related variables across time may have important implications for the development of prevention interventions; if families with depressed fathers are independently finding ways to protect children's outcomes, understanding these shifts may suggest natural windows to intervention. From the current results, however, it is apparent that the functional context and meaning of paternal depression may shift with marital longevity. Longitudinal research will be necessary to understand more about this process.

Although current findings may be understood as a developmental shift in coping or communication strategies associated with paternal depression, other possibilities exist. For example, families with more severe depression are more likely to experience marital dissolution; within this sample, depressed parents were more likely to be remarried and to have stepchildren. Other research has indicated that depression among women may increase the likelihood of marriage, whereas depression among men may decrease the likelihood of marriage (Forthofer, Kessler, Story, & Gotlib, 1996). Gender differences in the impact of depression on initiation and longevity of marital status may have important implications for these findings.

Beyond marital longevity, the current study revealed no other protective or risk factors for children with a depressed parent—mirroring our previous findings that children of nondepressed parents are as affected by negative communication as children of depressed parents (Jacob & Johnson, 1997). Current findings also mirror previous literature on marital distress. Although some research has found that marital distress is a moderator of parental depression on child behavior, other research suggests that marital distress is as detrimental in nondepressed families as in families with a depressed parent (Fendrich et al., 1990). Taken together, these results suggest that it is hard to identify variables that are specifically detrimental for children of depressed parents.

Strongest effects have emerged for child gender as a moderator of paternal versus maternal depression. In understanding the role of gender, it will be important to be sensitive to developmental milestones, such as puberty. Approaches such as life table analyses incorporating the timing of onset may be helpful. Investigations of moderators may be most successful when embedded within a developmental context with attention to ages when risk for depression becomes elevated for girls compared to boys.

In summary, questions still remain about the ways in which some children of depressed parents escape from disturbance, whereas other children appear vulnerable to parental depression. In considering such variability in outcome, it must be emphasized that depression is an extremely heterogeneous disorder and families with a depressed member are likely to have substantially differing experiences. In terms of the depressive symptoms, some individuals experience symptoms that are predominantly physiological and endogenomorphic, but others experience symptom patterns such as negative self-esteem, hopelessness, and suicidality. Differences in functional impairment are also likely to be vast, as are differences in course, including relapse rates and chronicity. Each of these dimensions is likely to be of importance in understanding how depression influences the family. Moreover, there is great variability in psychosocial concomitants and repercussions of depression, such as social skill, coping, problem solving, and negative communication. The degree to which a parent exhibits difficulties coping with negative stressors should influence the development of difficulties coping among the children (Nolen-Hoeksema, Mumme, Wolfson, & Guskin, 1995). Similarly, a parent who voices his or her negative cognitions of the child and the family is likely to have a much different impact on the child's self-concept than a parent who maintains highly positive views of the child (Goodman et al., 1994; Hammen, 1988). In short, the course and expression of depression are important considerations for understanding child outcome.

Although this investigation focused on family functioning, research has documented that factors outside of the family, such as stress, are important moderators (Hammen, 1992). Additionally, recent research has highlighted that the intergenerational transmission of depression may be best understood by conjoint consideration of physiological and maternal interaction variables (Field, chap. 1, this volume; Tronick & Weinberg, chap. 2, this volume). In summary, children with depressed parents are at elevated risk for behavior problems and depression. More precise models of risk are needed before an understanding of this phenomenon can be advanced. From our view, such models must ultimately involve the careful integration of family environment, physiological, and extrafamilial variables. HLM may be a helpful statistical tool for building these integrated models of social, familial, and child variables influencing outcome.

ACKNOWLEDGMENTS

Support for this project has been provided by Grant R01-AA03037 from the National Institute on Alcohol Abuse and Alcoholism and by a Research Career Scientist Award from the Palo Alto Veterans Affairs Health Care System awarded to the second author.

We thank Michael Windle for his helpful comments regarding the analytic strategy.

REFERENCES

Achenbach, T. M. (1978). The Child Behavior Profile: I. Boys aged 6-11. *Journal of Consulting and Clinical Psychology, 46,* 478–488.

Achenbach, T. M. (1991a). *Integrative guide for the 1991 CBCL/4-18, YSR, and TRF profiles.* Burlington, VT: University of Vermont, Department of Psychiatry.

Achenbach, T. M. (1991b). *Manual for the Child Behavior Checklist and 1991 profile.* Burlington, VT: University of Vermont, Department of Psychiatry.

Baron, R. M., & Kenny, D. A. (1986). The moderator-mediator variable distinction in social psychological research: Conceptual, strategic, and statistical considerations. *Journal of Personality and Social Psychology, 51,* 1173–1182.

Beardslee, W. R., Keller, M. B., & Klerman, G. L. (1985). Children of parents with affective disorder. *International Journal of Family Psychiatry, 6,* 283–299.

Beck, A. T., Ward, C., Mendelson, M., Mock, J., & Erbaugh, J. (1961). An inventory for measuring depression. *Archives of General Psychiatry, 4,* 53–63.

Billings, A. G., & Moos, R. H. (1983). Comparisons of children of depressed and nondepressed parents: A social-environmental perspective. *Journal of Abnormal Child Psychology, 11*(4), 463–486.

Billings, A. G., & Moos, R. H. (1985). Children of parents with unipolar depression: A controlled 1-year follow-up. *Journal of Abnormal Child Psychology, 14*(1), 149–166.

Compas, B. E., Howell, D. C., Phares, V., Williams, R. A., & Giunta, C. T. (1989). Risk factors for emotional/behavioral problems in young adolescents: A prospective analysis of adolescent and parental stress and symptoms. *Journal of Consulting and Clinical Psychology, 57*(6), 732–740.

Dahlstrom, W. G., Welsh, G. S., & Dahlstrom, L. E. (1975). *An MMPI Handbook, Vol II. Research Applications* (Rev. Edition). Minneapolis: University of Minnesota Press.

Davies, P., & Cummings, E. M. (1994). Marital conflict and child adjustment: An emotional security hypothesis. *Psychological Bulletin, 116,* 387–411.

Downey, G., &. Coyne, J. C. (1990). Children of depressed parents: An integrative review. *Psychological Bulletin, 108*(1), 50–76.

Emery, R., Weintraub, S., & Neale, J. M. (1982). Effects of marital discord on the school behavior of children of schizophrenic, affectively disordered, and normal parents. *Journal of Abnormal Child Psychology, 10*(2), 215–228.

Endicott, J., & Spitzer, R. L. (1978). A diagnostic interview: The schedule for affective disorders and schizophrenia. *Archives of General Psychiatry, 35,* 837–844.

Fendrich, M., Warner, V., &. Weissman, M. M. (1990). Family risk factors, parental depression, and psychopathology in offspring. *Developmental Psychology, 26*(1), 40–50.

Forehand, R., Long, N., Brody, G. H., & Fauber, R. (1986). Home predictors of young adolescents' school behavior and academic performance. *Child Development, 57*(6), 1528–1533.

Forthofer, M. S., Kessler, R. C., Story, A. L., & Gotlib, I. H. (1996). The effects of psychiatric disorders on the probability of timing of first marriage. *Journal of Health and Social Behavior, 37*, 121–132.

Ge, X., Conger, R. D., Lorenz, R. O., Shanahan, M., & Elder, G. H., Jr. (1995). Mutual influences in parent and adolescent psychological distress. *Developmental Psychology, 31*(3), 406–419.

Goldberg, L. R. (1965). Diagnosticians versus diagnostic signs: The diagnosis of psychosis versus neurosis from the MMPI. *Psychological Monographs, 79*(9, Whole no. 602),

Goldberg, L. R. (1969). The search for configural relationships in personality assessment: The diagnosis of psychosis versus neurosis from the MMPI. *Multivariate Behavioral Research, 4*, 523–536.

Goodman, S. H., Adamson, L. B., Riniti, J., & Cole, S. (1994). Mothers' expressed attitudes: Associations with maternal depression and children's self-esteem and psychopathology. *Journal of the American Academy of Child and Adolescent Psychiatry, 33*, 1265–1274.

Gottman, J. M., Katz, L. F., & Hooven, C. (1997). *Meta-emotion: The emotional life of families.* Mahwah, NJ: Lawrence Erlbaum Associates.

Greene, R. L. (1980). *An MMPI Interpretive Manual.* Orlando, FL: Grune & Stratton.

Hammen, C. (1988). Self-cognitions, stressful events, and the prediction of depression in children of depressed mothers. *Journal of Abnormal Child Psychology, 16*(3), 347–360.

Hammen, C. (1992). Life events and depression: The plot thickens. *American Journal of Community Psychology, 20*(2), 179–193.

Hammen, C., Burge, D., Burney, E., & Adrian, C. (1990). Longitudinal study of diagnoses in children of women with unipolar and bipolar affective disorder. *Archives of General Psychiatry, 47*(12), 1112–1117.

Hathaway, S. R., & McKinley, J. C. (1983). *Minnesota Multiphasic Personality Inventory: Manual for Administration and Scoring.* Minneapolis: University of Minnesota Press.

Hops, H. (1992). Parental depression and child behavior problems: Implications for behavioral family intervention. *Behaviour Change, 9*(3), 126–138.

Hops, H. (1995). Age- and gender-specific effects of parental depression: A commentary. *Developmental Psychology, 31*, 428–431.

Jacob, T., & Johnson, S. (1997). Parent–child interactions of depressed men and women. *Journal of Family Psychology, 11*(4), 1–19.

Jacob, T., Seilhamer, R. A., & Rushe, R. (1989). Alcoholism and family interaction: An experimental paradigm. *American Journal of Drug and Alcohol Abuse, 15*(1), 73–91.

Lee, C. M., & Gotlib, I. H. (1989). Maternal depression and child adjustment: A longitudinal analysis. *Journal of Abnormal Psychology, 98*(1), 78–85.

Levenson, R. W., Carstensen, L. L., & Gottman, J. M. (1994). The influence of age and gender on affect, physiology, and their interrelations: A study of long-term marriages. *Journal of Personality and Social Psychology, 67*(1), 56–68.

Lewinsohn, P. M., Hops, H., Roberts, R. E., Seeley, J. R., & Andrews, J. A. (1993). Adolescent psychopathology: I. Prevalence and incidence of depression and other DSM–III–R disorders in high school students. *Journal of Abnormal Psychology, 102*(1), 133–144.

Nolen-Hoeksema, S., Mumme, D., Wolfson, A., & Guskin, K. (1995). Helplessness in children of depressed and nondepressed mothers. *Developmental Psychology, 31(3)*, 377–387.

Norman, W. H., Miller, I. W., & Klee, S. H. (1983). Assessment of cognitive distortion in a clinically depressed population. *Cognitive Therapy and Research, 7*(2), 133–140.

Richters, J. E. (1992). Depressed mothers as informants about their children: A critical review of the evidence for distortion. *Psychological Bulletin, 112*(3), 485–499.

Rush, A. J., Giles, D. E., Schlesser, M. A., Fulton, C. L., Weissenburger, J., & Burns, C. (1986). The Inventory for Depressive Symptomatology (IDS): Preliminary findings. *Psychiatry Research, 18,* 65–87.

Santor, D. A., Ramsay, J. O., & Zuroff, D. C. (1994). Nonparametric item analyses of the Beck Depression Inventory: Evaluating gender item bias and response option weights. *Psychological Assessment, 6*(3), 255–270.

Spanier, G. (1976). Measuring dyadic adjustment: New scales for assessing the quality of marriage and similar dyads. *Journal of Marriage and the Family, 38,* 15–30.

Spanier, G., & Thompson, L. (1982). A confirmatory analysis of the Dyadic Adjustment Scale. *Journal of Marriage and the Family, 44,* 731–738.

Spitzer, R. L., Endicott, J., & Robins, T. (1978). Research diagnostic criteria: Rationale and reliability. *Archives of General Psychiatry, 35,* 773–782.

Thomas, A. M., & Forehand, R. (1991). The relationship between paternal depressive mood and early adolescent functioning. *Journal of Family Psychology, 4*(3), 260–271.

Thomas, G., Fletcher, G. J. O., & Lange, C. (1997). On-line empathic accuracy in marital interaction. *Journal of Personality and Social Psychology, 72*(4), 839–850.

Weissman, M. H., Davis, M., Gammon, J. K., Merikangas, K. R., Warner, V., Prusoff, B. A., & Sholomskas, D. (1987). Children of depressed parents. *Archives of General Psychiatry, 44,* 847–853.

Part II

BASIC ADULT PSYCHOPATHOLOGY

Chapter 5

Interpersonal Factors in an Emerging Developmental Model of Depression

Constance Hammen
University of California, Los Angeles

Over 20 years have passed since psychologists turned significant attention toward depression. The topic had heretofore attracted relatively little research interest—or for that matter, scant clinical interest. There were many reasons for the relative neglect, but by the early 1970s, a new era of interest in depression was underway, one that continues today. The interest was spurred by improved diagnostic rules and methods, ground-breaking new models of etiology and treatment, applications of existing theoretical models to embrace the complexities of depression, and certainly, by the growing recognition of the frequency and debilitating effects of depressive disorders.

Reflecting some of the highways and byways of the depression research agenda over this period, my research has attended to cognitions, stressful life events, and the family context of depression. In exploring these topics, my goal has always been to understand the individual in context—not only what the person is feeling and thinking, but also what is happening to the person and what forces impinge on his or her life. Over time, it has become apparent that many seemingly disparate themes share a common thread: the importance of interpersonal relationships in the origin and course of depression.

Key themes of this chapter and their interrelations are illustrated in Fig. 5.1. The discussion begins with brief consideration of topics in depression that were early focuses of our work—cognitions and life stress. In retrospect, we found that some of these topics kindled an interest in

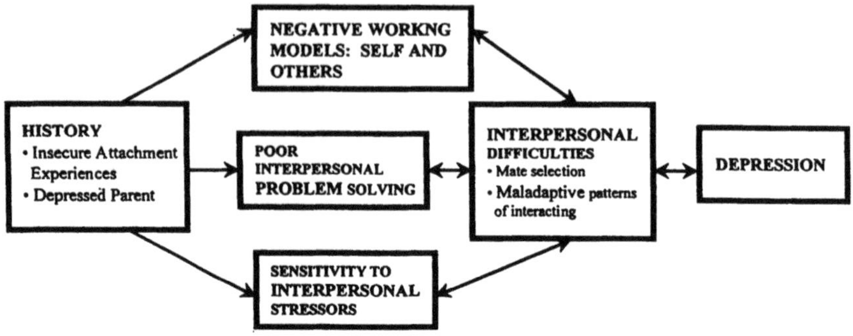

FIG. 5.1. Overview of the association of depression risk factors with interpersonal themes in the prediction of depression. Additional bidirectional influences not shown here are possible. As one example, depression influences cognitions and behaviors, thereby contributing to a potentially self-perpetuating process.

interpersonal themes, leading to a more explicit focus on interpersonal aspects of depression in recent years. As our research has more directly studied interpersonal processes, the final section reviews some of our most recent work on this topic and our increasing emphasis on depression as an interpersonal disorder. A related goal of this chapter is to illustrate a transactional perspective on depression, viewing it as a disorder that not only affects the vulnerable individual, but in which such individuals affect their environments. Indeed, we focus in part on how creation of a vulnerable environment contributes to the onset, as well as recurrence, of depression.

OVERVIEW OF RECENT RESEARCH PROJECTS

Most of the data presented in this chapter are drawn from three longitudinal studies of characteristics and predictors of depression in samples of different ages and contexts.

Children of Depressed Women

A sample of 68 families (with 96 children) of women with recurrent unipolar disorder, bipolar disorder, chronic medical illness, or nonill comparison women were studied intensively and followed for up to 3 years. The children were between the ages of 8 and 16 years. Children's psychiatric and psychosocial functioning were studied, along with children's stress, cognitions, and observed mother–child interaction quality. Data about the mothers included not only their own psychiatric histories and family histories of disorder in first-degree relatives, but also ongoing chronic and episodic stress as well as information about the biological fathers of the children.

Depressed Children and Adolescents in Treatment

A sample of 88 families (43 in which the child's primary diagnosis included major depression or dysthymia) was recruited from an ongoing study of treatment delivery in community clinics. The youngsters were between the ages of 8 and 16 years and participated for up to 2 years in a study of psychiatric and psychosocial functioning. Information was obtained concerning the children's psychiatric status and history and also that of their mothers and fathers. Information about chronic and episodic stress in the youngsters and their mothers was also obtained at periodic intervals.

Adolescent Women in the Transition to Adulthood

A sample of 155 representative high-school senior women was studied for up to 5 years. The goals of the study were to understand risk for depressive disorders during the transition to adulthood, a period known to be associated with elevated risk for depression in women. The risk factors studied included symptoms, family functioning and psychiatric history, cognitions, and interpersonal adjustment and stressors. The women were interviewed annually, covering symptoms, chronic and episodic stress, and role functioning in work, school, family, and relationship domains. Information about the participants was also obtained from best-friend informants and boyfriends.

DYSFUNCTIONAL COGNITIONS AND COGNITIVE VULNERABILITY

Beck's seminal cognitive theory of depression stimulated a generation of research on maladaptive cognitions about the self, world, and the future as vulnerability factors for depression (Beck, 1967). This model has proven to be extremely useful and productive for two primary reasons. First, it emphasizes the central role of individuals' interpretations of themselves and circumstances, rather than just the occurrence of painful realities as critical to understanding why some individuals become depressed and others do not. Beck contributed the observation that individuals sometimes distort the meaning of events, and that self-deprecating, helpless, and hopeless interpretations led to depressive reactions. Second, the cognitive model gave rise to an extremely fruitful and empirically validated treatment for depression, one that appears to fare as well as, and according to some of the treatment outcome studies, sometimes better than psychotropic medications (Beck, Rush, Shaw, & Emery, 1979; see also DeRubeis, Tang, Gelfand, & Feeley, chap. 10, this volume; Hollon, Shelton, & Davis, 1993 for a review).

Despite these positive features, however, the cognitive approaches were limited in several ways. Because many dysfunctional cognitions were found to be associated with the depressed state and not observable when the person was no longer depressed, more elaborated models and methods of measurement that do not depend on self-report have needed to be developed (e.g., reviewed in Segal & Ingram, 1994; see also Gotlib & Neubauer, chap. 7, this volume). Also, despite the emphasis on various forms of cognitive distortions about the self, world, and the future, it appeared that cognitions about the *self*—one's worth and competence—were the key to depressive reactions. Another problem was the initial neglect of the stress portion of the implied diathesis–stress models in which the cognitions caused depression if triggered by stressful circumstances. Over time, Beck and others (e.g., Arieti & Bemporad, 1980; Beck, 1983) acknowledged that individuals might be susceptible to depression following the occurrence not just of any stressful event, but more particularly, if an event occurred within the domain of experiences to which the individual attached particular significance with respect to self-worth and competence.

Specific Vulnerability for Interpersonal Life Events

Several of our earlier studies demonstrated that a match between event content and either interpersonal or achievement domains of personal importance resulted in depression to a greater extent than stressors occurring in the nonrelevant content domain. Various methods were used in different studies to characterize the relative salience and personal significance to achievement and relationships with others; then, participants were followed longitudinally to observe stressors and depression. A particularly interesting feature of these findings was the relative importance of the interpersonal domain to most individuals. Several studies that used different populations, such as college students (Hammen, Marks, Mayol, & deMayo, 1985), adult outpatients with unipolar or bipolar mood disorder (Hammen, Ellicott, & Gitlin, 1992; Hammen, Ellicott, Gitlin & Jamison, 1989), and children of depressed women (Hammen & Goodman-Brown, 1990), demonstrated that the match between interpersonal negative life events and attaching great importance to personal relationships with others was especially predictive of depressive reactions. Although matches between achievement- or autonomy-oriented individuals and failures or disappointments in the achievement domain also produced depressive reactions, such matches were neither as frequent nor as reliable a predictor of depression as were matches in the interpersonal domain.

Attachment Cognitions and Early Acquisition of Vulnerability

Additional limitations of the earlier cognitive models of depression were the relatively narrow definition of cognitive vulnerability and the comparative neglect of studies of how such vulnerability is acquired. Dysfunctional cognitions had typically been defined as bias or distortions of interpretation, negative attribution style, harsh self-regulatory standards, and the like (e.g., review by Haaga, Ernst, & Dyck, 1991). In an attempt both to broaden the scope of potentially dysfunctional depressive cognitions, as well as to integrate a developmental psychopathology approach to the origin of such maladaptive beliefs, our group included attachment cognitions in a test of the cognitive diathesis–stress model of depression. Bowlby's attachment model of children's development posits the acquisition of secure or insecure working models of the self and others as internal cognitive representations derived from the nature of the caretaker–infant bond (Bowlby, 1969, 1980). Insecure attachment experiences with their resulting negative working models confer on the individual a tendency to see the self as unlovable and others as rejecting, unreliable, or unresponsive. Such cognitions may constitute a vulnerability for depressive experiences later in life, especially in the face of interpersonal losses. Measures of adult attachment regarding romantic relationships derived from self-report questionnaires are thought to capture central concerns of the attachment system that are continuous through life regarding the availability and responsiveness of close others. Attachment representations may indicate dysfunctional working models relevant to attachment organization, although it cannot be said that they reflect infant attachment without actually demonstrating the link between infant development of attachment status and later adult attachment cognitions.

In two studies, our group tested the association between such internal (i.e., cognitive) representations and depression. Burge, Hammen, et al. (1997) showed that two measures of adult attachment cognitions, the Revised Adult Attachment Scale (RAAS; Collins & Read, 1990) and the Inventory of Parent and Peer Attachment (IPPA; Armsden & Greenberg, 1987) predicted depressive and other symptoms 1 year later. The scales were administered to high-school senior women at graduation, and showed that even when initial symptom levels were controlled, those with more insecure cognitions were more likely to experience depression and other symptoms such as anxiety and personality pathology. Parallel analyses conducted to predict academic, work, and relationship adjustment also demonstrated that these areas of functioning were significantly impaired in women with insecure attachment cognitions compared to those with secure beliefs, over a prospective 2-year period (Burge et al., 1997).

A second study explored the role of attachment representations as vulnerability factors for depression, specifically their role in a diathesis–stress model. Examining both stressors and symptoms over a 1-year period in the same sample of women in the transition from high school to adulthood, we predicted that interpersonal stressful events would be especially likely to predict changes in depression among young women with insecure attachment cognitions (Hammen, Burge, et al., 1995). Using the Collins and Read (1990) RAAS, we found that the subscale representing anxiety about abandonment and fears of loss of the other was particularly likely to predict depressive reactions following interpersonal stress, while controlling for initial symptoms. Additionally, the effects were generally not specific to depression symptoms alone, and the interaction of insecure cognitions and interpersonal stressors also predicted increments in general psychopathology as well.

These analyses suggest that cognitions representing individuals' beliefs about the availability of others and their dependability—beliefs that we hypothesize to arise from early relationships with caretakers—may be important in understanding cognitive vulnerability to depression and other disorders. These cognitive representations of interpersonal processes expand the territory of depressive cognitive vulnerability and represent a topic to which we return later.

STRESSFUL LIFE EVENTS AND DEPRESSION

One of the most robust predictors of depression is the domain of stressful life events. The majority of individuals who experience a major depressive episode, both in community and clinical samples, report the prior occurrence of a severely stressful life event (Brown & Harris, 1989). Typically, the events that trigger depressive reactions are those that match a person's area of vulnerability as defined by the importance of such experiences to self-worth and sense of competence as previously described (see also Brown, Bifulco, & Harris, 1987). At the same time, the majority of individuals who experience a stressful life event do not experience clinically severe depressive experiences. They either have transitory or relatively minor depression after a loss, disappointment, or major readjustment—or they have little emotional distress at all. Thus, some underlying predisposition is hypothesized, and a depressive diathesis of a psychological or biological nature is typically understood to moderate the association between stress and depression.

The Stress Context as a Trigger of Depressive Reactions

Despite the importance of stress in depression, however, until fairly recently, relatively little psychological research on depression explored the topic. Understanding the stressful experiences to which an individual is exposed is an essential step in understanding the context of depression. Beck's cognitive model of depression provided, perhaps, an undue emphasis on misappraisal of circumstances as a precipitant of depression. In contrast, the work of sociologist George Brown indicated that much depression is a response to actual severe negative events (Brown & Harris, 1978). Brown also contributed important methodology to the measurement of stressors—assessment without contamination by the depressed person's cognitive appraisal of the meaning of an event. Interview assessment of the context in which each event occurred permits ratings of the objective impact of a stressor, without knowledge of the person's actual reaction to the event. Our group adapted Brown's contextual threat approach to the interview assessment of life events and evaluation of their impact and independence (e.g., fatefulness).

In the course of studying the exposure of various research populations to both chronic and episodic stressors, we made several observations that reinforced our emphasis on understanding the life context, and especially interpersonal life, of individuals. One observation, as previously noted, suggested that the combination of information about stress and the cognitive vulnerability in a particular content area is a better predictor of depressive reactions than either variable alone.

Second, our longitudinal studies revealed the importance of stress as a precipitant of depressive reactions in various populations: children at risk for depression (Hammen, 1988) and patients with bipolar illness (Ellicott, Hammen, Gitlin, Brown, & Jamison, 1990)—in addition to numerous studies of adults in the community and in clinical populations. Although some cases of depression doubtlessly arise in the absence of significant stressors, it seems likely that majority of cases occur in response to the stressor and its meaning to the individual.

The Generation of Stress

Another observation in the course of our various longitudinal studies of mood disorder and stressful life events concerned patterns of stress that we came to label *the generation of stress.* It seemed that some individuals experience more stressful life events than do others, and such stressors are frequently, at least partly, of their own making. During the course of our study of children of depressed women, for instance, we observed that certain women—due to their circumstances, behaviors, and characteristics—appeared to frequently experience stressful life events, and in turn, such stressors often precipitated further depression. Hammen (1991b) tested this observation and found that women with recurrent unipolar depression were more likely than were women with bipolar disorder, chronic medical illness, or nonill women to experience such patterns of elevated stress over a 1-year period. Although the groups did not differ in levels of independent or fateful events, the unipolar depressed group was especially likely to have higher total rates of stress, particularly events to which they had at least partly contributed (i.e., dependent events). Among the dependent events, the highest frequencies of stressors occurred in the interpersonal content domain, with particularly significantly elevated rates of interpersonal conflict events, compared to the other groups of women.

This intriguing pattern that we termed *stress generation* has important implications. It may help to understand the commonly observed pattern of recurrent depression among some individuals, and it may therefore serve as a target for therapeutic change in order to reduce depressive episodes. Moreover, it suggests that simple unidimensional models of stress and depression are too static to accurately capture the dynamic transaction between the person and the environment in understanding psychopathology, maybe especially depression. Moreover, the elevated levels of interpersonal stress suggest that interpersonal experiences are of particular importance in understanding depressive vulnerability.

Before drawing firm conclusions, however, we planned a series of analyses in new studies to help determine whether this stress generation pattern would be observed in other depressed samples, and what factors might help us to understand its nature and mechanisms. Several analyses showed that the effect may be seen in children of depressed women, compared with children of bipolar, medically ill, and nonill women (Adrian & Hammen, 1993)—and that such children were especially likely to display elevated rates of interpersonal conflict events, such as problematic relationships and losses with peers and romantic partners. In the community sample of women in the transition to adulthood, Daley et al. (1997) showed that women who were depressed during Year 1 of the longitudinal study had significantly more dependent stressors during Year 2 than either women with no diagnoses or women with other nondepressive diagnoses. The groups did not differ in independent, or fateful, events.

What factors characterize those with higher levels of stress to which they had at least in part contributed? In the previously mentioned study, Daley et al. (1997) showed that those with the most elevated levels of stress were those with comorbid depression, that is, women who had depression along with other psychopathology such as anxiety disorders or substance abuse. These women had the highest levels of dependent events—and notably, interpersonal conflict events—than any other group including those with pure depression. Daley et al. (1997) also found that chronic stressful conditions in interpersonal domains exerted an independent predictive effect on subsequent level of episodic dependent stress. Also, the personality style of *autonomy* (preference of independence, achievement, and self-reliance) also predicted the generation of stressful dependent and interpersonal conflict events. Thus, this study suggests that women with more comorbid psychopathology including depression, who have preexisting levels of ongoing difficulties in their social and family relationships and who prefer autonomy to the possible disregard of others' needs, are especially at risk for creating stressful environments.

The impact of the generation of stress as a factor in recurrent depression was further tested in analyses reported by Davila, Hammen, Burge, Paley, and Daley (1995). Davila et al. (1995) found that increased interpersonal stress led to elevated depression above initial levels. Moreover, Davila found that women with relatively lower levels of interpersonal problem-solving capability (based on adaptations of the Interpersonal Negotiation Strategies interview of Schultz, Yeates, & Selman, 1989) were especially likely to have elevated levels of interpersonal stressors. In turn, Davila, Hammen, Burge, Daley, and Paley (1996) found that interpersonal problem solving was associated with attachment cognitions and self-worth such that those with insecure attachment beliefs had lower interpersonal problem-solving skills, likely mediated in part by reduced self-concept. Consistent with a developmental psychopathology model of depression, these results suggest that insecure attachment leads to negative views of the self, which, in turn, may lead to poor interpersonal problem solving and hence, to stressful life events in the interpersonal domain that serve as triggers for depressive reactions.

The stress generation phenomenon serves to remind us that individuals help to create environments for themselves. Depression vulnerability may consist, in part, in the construction of environments that are stressful and unsupportive, potentially overwhelming a susceptible individual's coping and problem-solving capabilities. The interpersonal environment appears to be particularly salient in this process, and this is the topic to which we turn now.

Stress Sensitivity Due to Early Adversity

The typical diathesis–stress model of depression examines variability in the amount of the diathesis required in interaction with stress to produce depression. Under conditions of high stress and high vulnerability, people display depression. A further refinement of this model, however, is that there may be variability in the amount of stress needed to trigger depression even in a vulnerable individual. In a recent study, we hypothesized that exposure to adverse family conditions may actually create a vulnerability whereby the threshold for the triggering of depression is lowered (Hammen, Henry, Daley, & Burge, 1999). Noting that Kessler and Magee (1993) found that various family adversities, such as violence, parental death, and divorce, were statistically associated with major depression in the large national comorbidity epidemiological sample, we predicted that such adversities might sensitize the individual—potentially through biological as well as psychological mechanisms. In our study of high-school women in the transition to adulthood, we tested the sensitization hypothesis by examining the amount of stress occurring prior to the onset of a significant increase in depression, comparing those who had one or more major childhood family difficulties and those who had none. As predicted, depressed women with early adversity exposure were less likely to experience a severe stressor prior to depression onset and had a lower total level of stress when compared to depressed women who did not have one of these adversities.

One of the implications of this finding is its compatibility with a truly developmental model of depression, emphasizing the early acquisition of vulnerability in the family context. We now turn to this topic for a fuller discussion of the interpersonal context of depression.

INTERPERSONAL CONTEXT OF DEPRESSION

Up to this point, we discussed the importance to depression of dysfunctional interpersonal cognitions and interpersonal stressors. A further area of relevance to understanding depression concerns the nature and quality of family and relationship experiences. These relationships might cause interpersonal stressors, and therefore, much of our recent work has explored relationship formation and quality and how these factors might lead to stressful interpersonal life events.

Our close observation of depressed adults and their families and relationships over the course of several longitudinal studies suggests two hypotheses about the link between depression and interpersonal functioning. One is that certain family attributes create a risk for depressive disorders and the other is that depression-prone adults create interpersonal environments that may trigger or at least increase the likelihood of depressive reactions.

Depression Runs in Families

Considerable research has documented that parental depression—studied chiefly as maternal depression—increases the risk of depression in offspring. Studies of school-age children based on direct interview methods have been consistent in displaying high rates of disorder in general and depressive disorders in particular. For instance, current or lifetime major depression rates ranged between 45% in the 8- to 16-year-old offspring in Hammen, Burge, Burney, and Adrian (1990; see also Hammen, 1991a), to 38% among 6- to 23-year-olds in Weissman et al. (1987) to 24% in Keller et al. (1986), and 20% in Goodman, Adamson, Riniti, and Cole (1994), with rates depending in part on children's ages. In contrast, children of normal comparison families reported significantly lower rates of depressive disorders. Rates of other disorders were also higher than those in comparison groups, with children of depressed parents displaying elevated rates of anxiety disorders, disruptive disorders, and substance-use disorders—as well as high proportions of comorbid disorders. For instance, rates of any diagnosis ranged between 65% in Keller, 73% Weissman, 80% Goodman, and 82% in Hammen.

In addition to clinical studies, numerous investigations of women with elevated symptom levels, who are often studied with their infants and toddlers, indicate emotional and behavioral disruptions among the children. In general, face-to-face interactions have shown that infants respond with withdrawal, anger, and reduced activity to dysphoric mothers' displays of flat affect, withdrawn behavior, or intrusiveness (e.g., Cohn & Tronick, 1989; Field, Healy, Goldstein, & Gutherz, 1990). Also, several studies of women with nonclinical dysphoric states indicated that their infants displayed higher rates of insecure attachment than did infants of nondysphoric women (e.g., Cohn, Matias, Tronick, Connell, & Lyons-Ruth, 1986; Lyons-Ruth, Zoll, Connell, & Grunebaum, 1986). This volume of research indicates that negative effects for children are especially pronounced for women whose dysphoria persists over time. Other chapters in this volume review infant research in detail (see Field, chap. 1, this volume; Marshall & Fox, chap. 3, this volume; Tronick & Weinberg, chap. 2, this volume).

The pattern of depression transmission (or in infants, of distress and negative behaviors that might portend depressive reactions at a later developmental stage) has been demonstrated mainly for clinical samples or for nonclinical dysphoric adults and their children. Yet, another demonstration of risk for offspring depression comes from clinically depressed community samples. Our recent longitudinal study of young women in the transition from adolescence to adulthood obtained not only Structured Clinical Interview for DSM (SCID) diagnoses on the young women, but also obtained Family History Research Diagnostic Criteria (FHRDC) data on their mothers from the participants' reports. There was a marked intergenerational pattern of depression. Only 21% of daughters of nondepressed women had diagnosable depression (including minor depression), whereas 44% of the daughters of depressed mothers had diagnoses of depression in the first year of observation. Furthermore, in the study of depressed children and adolescents referred for treatment, fully 70% of their mothers had a lifetime history of major depression or dysthymic disorder, and 30% were currently depressed. Thus, whether among children of clinical samples of depressed adults, offspring of depressed adults in the community, or parents of clinical samples of depressed children, the data suggest that parental depression is one of the strongest predictors of depression in offspring.

Assortative Mating

Initially viewed as something of a nuisance factor in the methodology of behavioral genetics studies, the tendency of individuals with depressive disorders to marry others with disorders should attract the attention of developmental psychopathologists interested in the creation of dysfunctional contexts. Offspring studies by Rutter and Quinton (1984) and Merikangas, Weissman, Prusoff, and John (1988) initially observed the elevated rates of disorder in husbands of depressed women. Due to the potentially disruptive consequences for the families of such pairings, we explored the generality of the patterns in three samples. Table 5.1 presents rates of paternal disorder when the mother is known to have a diagnosis. These data are based on direct diagnostic interviews of the mothers and indirect family history interviews of the mothers about the fathers (except in the high-school study where all data about parents were obtained from the family history interviews of the participant–daughter).

The patterns of nonrandom mating raise intriguing questions not only about the potentially negative impact on the marital and family life affecting the children, but also about the nature and origins of such mate choices.

Relationships and the Creation of Stressful Environments

As noted at the outset, the emphasis of our work on interpersonal functioning in the origin of depression has gradually emerged from concerns with cognitive, life-stress, and family factors. Slowly, we have begun to formulate a developmental model of depression, in which maladaptive

TABLE 5.1
Psychiatric Diagnosis in Husbands of Depressed Women

	Father Psychiatric Status	
Study and Sample	*Probable/Definite Diagnosis*	*No Diagnosis*
Children of Depressed Mothers Unipolar depressed women	64%	36%
Child and Adolescent Treatment Presence of depression history in mothers of depressed youngsters	74%	26%
High School Senior Study Presence of depression history in mothers	58%	42%

parenting contributes to negative cognitions about the self and others and to the acquisition of dysfunctional interpersonal problem-solving capabilities. When faced with a stressor—especially loss or failure—individuals with these characteristics may experience further erosion of self-esteem or may interpret the event as further evidence of unworthiness and of the unreliability or unsupportiveness of significant others, thereby precipitating depression. We add to this formulation the important step that individuals with such vulnerabilities may create interpersonal environments that increase the chances of stressful life events. One of the areas most likely to be central in such dysfunctional personal environments is close relationships. It would appear that women with depressive histories are highly likely to form intimate relationships, and often have children with men whose own psychopathology might increase the likelihood of marital instability and stressful family lives. Eventually, such women may be depressed mothers of depressed children.

Our high-school transition study was aimed in part at further exploration of the formation of intimate relationships among young women as part of the goal of studying risk factors for depression. In this concluding section, therefore, we present preliminary data on the prediction of relationship characteristics (Burge, Davila, Hammen, & Daley, 1997).

In view of the apparent utility of including attachment cognitions in models of vulnerability to depression as a means of linking childhood experiences to later adjustment, we focused on the romantic relationship experiences of women who scored as insecure or secure at one point in time over a subsequent 3-year period. The hypothesis guiding the analyses was that women with relatively negative attachment cognitions about others would display most dysfunctional relationship patterns. These analyses make use of the Hazan and Shaver (1987) classification of adult attachment, which attempts to classify participants by self-report into categories commonly used in infant attachment: *secure, avoidant,* and *anxious–ambivalent.* A fourth category was also used for this study: *unclassifiable,* comprised of women who rated themselves equally high on two or more descriptions.

Of the 133 women retained in the study at the 3-year follow-up, 12 were engaged to be married and 10 had married; 21 had not had a romantic relationship of at least 1-month duration. The mean number of relationships for the group was 1.69 ($SD = 1.08$) over a 3-year period. The groups formed from attachment representations did not differ by ethnic composition or socioeconomic status (SES).

Survival analyses were used to characterize the interval until the event of interest occurred, with comparison of survival curves for the four attachment groups. There were differences in age at first intercourse, with avoidant attachment women reporting this event significantly later than those with the anxious–ambivalent style, with secure and unclassifiable women falling midway between these two extremes. Approximately 50% of the anxious–ambivalent women had sex by age 16½, whereas only about 10% of the avoidant women did so. Length of longest relationship reported during the 3 years did not indicate significant differences between the groups, as relatively frequent changes of partners are generally common during this transition period. Nonetheless, the most recent relationship did show patterns consistent with attachment style: avoidant women were significantly more likely to report breakups over time than were anxious–ambivalent women and marginally more likely than were secure women.

Length of the interval between relationships may provide a clue about the experienced urgency of having a relationship. Avoidant women resisted being in relationships for the longest time, becoming involved again significantly later than secure women. The other groups did not differ markedly, but unclassifiable women showed the least tolerance for extended periods of being out of a relationship.

Other characteristics of relationship patterns are noteworthy. Involvement in abusive relationships would certainly be one measure of a dysfunctional environment due in part to the woman's choice of mates. When women's reports of no abuse, verbal abuse, and physical abuse were evaluated by attachment style, the overall patterns were statistically significant. Twenty-eight percent of the anxious–ambivalent women had experienced verbal abuse, compared to 10% of the secure women, 3% of the avoidant women, and 7% of the unclassifiable women. With respect to physical abuse, 20% of the unclassifiable women reported such experiences, compared with 6% to 7% of each of the other three groups.

Finally, unwanted pregnancy with termination serves as an indicator of an interpersonal event with highly stressful implications. The secure women had the lowest rate of terminations of unwanted pregnancies (8.9%) and the unclassifiable women had the highest rate (35.3%) when compared to 9.4% of avoidant and 13% of anxious–ambivalent women—a statistically significant chi-square distribution.

Overall, avoidant women may be somewhat reluctant to engage in intimate relationships and their reluctance may create conflict in the relationships they have—or alternatively, prevent the acquisition of relationship skills that may contribute to stable marriages. We might speculate that relatively anxious–ambivalent women seek out relationships out of fear of being alone but creating the risk of making precipitous choices. Also, they may be conflict-aversive, hoping to hold onto the relationships they have but at some cost in failing to resolve tensions and difficulties. The unclassifiable women may be likened to the emerging definition of *disorganized attachment* in infants (e.g., Lyons-Ruth, Alpern, & Repacholi, 1993; see also Tronick & Weinberg, chap. 2, this volume)—a type of insecurity marked by lack of coherence in underlying mental representations portending maladjustment and interpersonal dysfunction. Indeed, this group provided some of the clearest evidence of interpersonal dysfunction: They entered new relationships very quickly after break ups and they were most likely to have abortions and to experience physical abuse.

This research continues at the present time, with an attempt to study the relationships more directly, including observations of interaction patterns and assessment of boyfriends' or husbands' psychological characteristics. Over time, we hope to shed more light on the nature and processes of mate selection by women at risk for depression.

SUMMARY AND CONCLUSIONS

This brief summary of research over the past 10 years illustrates the emergence of a developmental framework for understanding depression vulnerability, with a particular focus on interpersonal relationships. We showed that adverse family events, such as parental depression, other parental mental disorders, and violence, may contribute to increased likelihood of depression in the offspring. We speculated that such experiences create maladaptive cognitive schemata about the self, including dysfunctional attachment beliefs about the self in relation to others and the availability and reliability of others—and also that adverse family experiences impair the acquisition of effective interpersonal problem-solving strategies. The outcome of these processes appears to be an increased risk for depression when an interpersonal negative event occurs, presumably causing the person to interpret the event as further depletion of the self. There is preliminary evidence that early adversities may also alter the threshold of stress needed to trigger a depressive reaction. A further outcome of adverse family experiences is the experience of stressful events that are caused at least in part by the person. The generation of such stressors—especially interpersonal events—may arise from dysfunctional ways of solving emerging difficulties and from conflict arising from maladaptive expectations about others. Such vulnerabilities may also contribute to the selection of romantic partners and mates who are themselves maladjusted and who contribute to a context of instability and unfulfilled expectations. In such ways, depression may come to be a recurrent theme in the lives of such individuals.

Many gaps remain to be filled in this developmental perspective, and our work continues to address such issues. We also look forward to the work of other investigators who are clarifying our understanding of the interpersonal world of depression, and the processes by which this debilitating disorder occurs.

REFERENCES

Adrian, C., & Hammen, C. (1993). Stress exposure and stress generation in children of depressed mothers. *Journal of Consulting and Clinical Psychology, 61,* 354–359.

Arieti, S., & Bemporad, J. (1980). The psychological organization of depression. *American Journal of Psychiatry, 137,* 1360–1365.

Armsden, G., & Greenberg, M. (1987). The Inventory of Parent and Peer Attachment: Individual differences and their relationship to psychological well-being in adolescence. *Journal of Youth and Adolescence, 16,* 427–454.

Beck, A. T. (1967). *Depression: Clinical, experimental, and theoretical aspects.* New York: Harper & Row.

Beck, A. T. (1983). Cognitive therapy of depression: New perspectives. In P. J. Clayton & J. E. Barrett (Eds.), *Treatment of depression: Old controversies and new approaches.* New York: Raven.

Beck, A. T., Rush, A. J., Shaw, B., & Emery, G. (1979). *Cognitive therapy of depression.* New York: Guilford.

Bowlby, J. (1969). *Attachment and loss: Vol. I. Attachment.* New York: Basic Books.

Bowlby, J. (1980). *Loss: Sadness and depression.* New York: Basic Books.

Brown, G. W., Bifulco, A., & Harris, T. O. (1987). Life events, vulnerability and onset of depression: Some refinements. *British Journal of Psychiatry, 150,* 30–42.

Brown, G. W., & Harris, T. (1978). *Social origins of depression.* London: The Free Press.

Brown, G. W., & Harris, T. O. (1989). Depression. In G. W. Harris & T. O. Harris (Eds.), *Life events and illness* (pp. 49–93). New York: Guilford.

Burge, D., Davila, J., Hammen, C., & Daley, S. (1997). *Attachment styles and the prediction of young women's romantic relationship course and sexual behavior over a 3-year period.* Manuscript under review.

Burge, D., Hammen, C., Davila, J., Daley, S., Paley, B., Herzberg, D., & Lindberg, N. (1997). Attachment cognitions and college and work functioning two years later in late adolescent women. *Journal of Youth and Adolescence, 26,* 285–301.

Burge, D., Hammen, C., Davila, J., Daley, S., Paley, B., Lindberg, N., Herzberg, D., & Rudolph, K. (1997). The relationship between attachment cognitions and psychological adjustment in late adolescent women. *Development and Psychopathology, 9,* 151–168.

Cohn, J. F., Matias, R., Tronick, E., Connell, D., & Lyons-Ruth, K. (1986). Face-to-face interactions of depressed mothers and their infants. In E. Tronick & T. Field (Eds.), *Maternal depression and infant disturbance.* (New Directions for Child Development, No. 34, pp. 31–46). San Francisco: Jossey-Bass.

Cohn, J. F., & Tronick, E. (1989). Specificity of infants' response to mothers' affective behavior. *Journal of the American Academy of Child and Adolescent Psychiatry, 28,* 242–248.

Collins, N., & Read, S. (1990). Adult attachment, working models, and relationship quality in dating couples. *Journal of Personality and Social Psychology, 58,* 644–663.

Daley, S., Hammen, C., Burge, D., Davila, J., Paley, B., Lindberg, N., & Herzberg, D. (1997). Predictors of the generation of episodic stress: A longitudinal study of late adolescent women. *Journal of Abnormal Psychology, 106,* 251–259.

Davila, J., Hammen, C., Burge, D., Daley, S., & Paley, B. (1996). Cognitive/interpersonal correlates of adult interpersonal problem-solving strategies. *Cognitive Therapy and Research, 20,* 465–480.

Davila, J., Hammen, C., Burge, D., Paley, B., & Daley, S. (1995). Poor interpersonal problem-solving as a mechanism of stress generation in depression among adolescent women. *Journal of Abnormal Psychology, 104,* 592–600.

Ellicott, A., Hammen, C., Gitlin, M., Brown, G., & Jamison, K. (1990). Life events and the course of bipolar disorder. *American Journal of Psychiatry, 147,* 1194–1198.

Field, T., Healy, B., Goldstein, S., & Guthertz, M. (1990). Behavior-state matching and synchrony in mother–infant interactions of nondepressed versus depressed dyads. *Developmental Psychology, 26,* 7–14.

Goodman, S. H., Adamson, L. B., Riniti, J., & Cole, S. (1994). Mothers' expressed attitudes: Associations with maternal depression and children's self-esteem and psychopathology. *Journal of the American Academy of Child and Adolescent Psychiatry, 33,* 1265–1274.

Haaga, D. A., Ernst, D., & Dyck, M. J. (1991). Empirical status of cognitive theory of depression. *Psychological Bulletin, 110,* 215–236.

Hammen, C. (1988). Self cognitions, stressful events, and the prediction of depression in children of depressed mothers. *Journal of Abnormal Child Psychology, 16,* 347–360.

Hammen, C., Ellicott, A., & Gitlin, M. (1992). Stressors and sociotropy/autonomy: A longitudinal study of their relationship to the course of bipolar disorder. *Cognitive Therapy and Research, 16,* 409–418.

Hammen, C., & Goodman-Brown, T. (1990). Self-schemas and vulnerability to specific life stress in children at risk for depression. *Cognitive Therapy and Research, 14,* 215–227.

Hammen, C., Henry, R., Daley, S., & Burge, D. (1999). *Sensitization to stressful life events as a function of early adversity.* Manuscript under review.

Hammen, C. L. (1991a). *Depression runs in families: The social context of risk and resilience in children of depressed mothers.* New York: Springer-Verlag.

Hammen, C. L. (1991b). The generation of stress in the course of unipolar depression. *Journal of Abnormal Psychology, 100,* 555–561.

Hammen, C. L., Burge, D., Burney, E., & Adrian, C. (1990). Longitudinal study of diagnoses in children of women with unipolar and bipolar affective disorder. *Archives of General Psychiatry, 47,* 1112–1117.

Hammen, C. L., Burge, D., Daley, S. E., Davila, J., Paley, B., & Rudolph, K. D. (1995). Interpersonal attachment cognitions and prediction of symptomatic responses to interpersonal stress. *Journal of Abnormal Psychology, 104,* 436–443.

Hammen, C. L., Ellicott, A., Gitlin, M., & Jamison, K. R. (1989). Sociotropy/autonomy and vulnerability to specific life events in unipolar and bipolar patients. *Journal of Abnormal Psychology, 98,* 154–160.

Hammen, C. L., Marks, T., Mayol, A., & deMayo, R. (1985). Depressive self-schemas, life stress, and vulnerability to depression. *Journal of Abnormal Psychology, 94,* 308–319.

Hazan, C., & Shaver, P. (1987). Romantic love conceptualized as an attachment process. *Journal of Social and Personality Psychology, 52,* 511–524.

Hollon, S. D., Shelton, R. C., & Davis, D. D. (1993). Cognitive therapy for depression: Conceptual issues and clinical efficacy. *Journal of Consulting and Clinical Psychology, 61,* 270–275.

Keller, M. B., Beardslee, W. R., Dorer, D. J., Lavori, P. W., Samuelson, H., & Klerman, G. R. (1986). Impact of severity and chronicity of parental affective illness on adaptive functioning and psychopathology in children. *Archives of General Psychiatry, 43,* 930–937.

Kessler, R., & Magee, W. (1993). Childhood adversities and adult depression: basic patterns of association in a U.S. national survey. *Psychological Medicine, 23,* 679–690.

Lyons-Ruth, K., Alpern, L., & Repacholi, B. (1993). Disorganized infant attachment classification and maternal psychosocial problems as predictors of hostile-aggressive behavior in the preschool classroom. *Child Development, 64,* 572–585.

Lyons-Ruth, K., Zoll, D., Connell, D., & Grunebaum, H. U. (1986). The depressed mother and her one-year-old infant: Environment, interaction, attachment, and infant development. In E. Tronick & T. Field (Eds.), *Maternal depression and infant disturbance* (New Directions for Child Development, 34; pp. 31–46). San Francisco: Jossey-Bass.

Merikangas, K., Weissman, M., Prusoff, B., & John, K. (1988). Assortative mating and affective disorders: Psychopathology in offspring. *Psychiatry, 51,* 48–57.

Rutter, M., & Quinton, P. (1984). Parental psychiatric disorder: Effects on children. *Psychological Medicine, 14,* 853–880.

Schultz, L., Yeates, K., & Selman, R. (1989). *The Interpersonal Negotitation Strategies (INS) interview: A scoring manual.* Cambridge, MA: Harvard Graduate School of Education, The Group for the Study of Interpersonal Development.

Segal, Z. V., & Ingram, R. E. (1994). Mood priming and construct activation in tests of cognitive vulnerability to unipolar depression. *Clinical Psychology Review, 14,* 663–695.

Weissman, M. M., Gammon, G. D., John, D., Merikangas, K. R., Warner, V., Prusoff, B. A., & Sholomskas, D. (1987). Children of depressed parents: Increased psychopathology and early onset of major depression. *Archives of General Psychiatry, 44,* 847–853.

Chapter 6

Stress and Depression: A Personality–Situation Interaction Approach

Paul H. Blaney
University of Miami

That there is a relation between exposure to negative events and depression is well established. It is also well established, however, that the simple stressor–depression relation is a modest one, leaving considerable variance unaccounted for, even when all variables are carefully assessed. The quest for a more powerful predictive model has mostly involved consideration of personal or contextual variables that might increase the individual's vulnerability to any and all stressors. For instance, it has been suggested that lacking a hardy personality and/or social support renders one relatively vulnerable to stressors (cf. Blaney & Ganellen, 1990). Such models are sometimes described as interactional, denoting only that there is a statistical interaction between the purported vulnerability factor and stressor level.

The research verdict on the usefulness of such models is decidedly mixed, leading one to consider other kinds of interactional models. The corpus of events normatively viewed as stressful is remarkably heterogeneous, even controlling for severity. This raises the possibility that particular kinds of events are particularly difficult for particular kinds of people. That is, personal characteristics may interact with event characteristics in accounting for response outcome, yielding a personality–situation interaction model.[1] In this chapter, I review existing studies relevant to such a model

[1]A distinction can be made between *statistical* (i.e., mechanistic) and *classical* (i.e., dynamic, reciprocal) personality–situation interaction (e.g., Emmons, Diener, & Larsen, 1986; Endler, 1983). This chapter addresses the former. The latter acknowledges the role persons play in

of depression onset, summarize encouraging findings from our laboratory, and outline the range of questions that await further attention in this area.

THE PREVAILING MODEL

Anyone wishing to flesh out such an interaction model in the last 25 years would be confronted with an interesting phenomenon. Starting in the mid-1970s, a number of authors (Arieti & Bemporad, 1980; Beck, 1983; Blatt, 1974), having varied theoretical pedigrees and using somewhat varied terminologies, converged in suggesting that two groups of persons have a particular vulnerability to depression: interpersonally dependent persons and those with a strong personal achievement orientation.[2] This distinction has, as well, emerged repeatedly in diverse literatures beyond those having a primary focus on depression, often designated by such terms as *communion* and *agency*; see Wiggins (1991) for a historical review. Moreover, two research groups came forth with pairs of self-report scales purporting to measure such variables in a fashion pertinent to depression vulnerability: Blatt, D'Afflitti, and Quinlan's (1976) Depressive Experiences Questionnaire (DEQ), measuring self-criticism and dependency; and Beck, Epstein, Harrison, and Emery's (1983) Sociotropy-Autonomy Scale (SAS).[3] The attractiveness of this personality taxonomy is enhanced by the ease with which many stressful events can be placed in categories that have strong apparent parallels with it: interpersonal loss[4] or rejection and achievement failure.

---

selecting their situations. Classical personality–situation interactions are probably of limited importance in stress research, at least when the situations are so negative that virtually no one ever selects them. Nonetheless, there is evidence of situation selection as a function of variables relevant to this chapter (cf. Zuroff & de Lorimier, 1989), perhaps in ways that pertain to the generation of stress (Daley et al., 1997).

[2]These conceptualizations are by no means identical, however. See Blatt and Maroudas (1992) and Robins (1995) regarding differences.

[3]In recent years, agency and communion have often been assessed via masculinity and femininity scales. Interestingly, whereas it is bad to be both self-critical and dependent (e.g., Blatt, Quinlan, Chevron, McDonald, & Zuroff, 1982), it is good to be both masculine and feminine (e.g., Shaver et al., 1996). Although the literature on *unmitigated* agency and communion (cf. Helgeson, 1993; Shaver et al., 1996, Study 3; Spence, Helmreich, & Holahan, 1979) considers the negative side of these characteristics, the items found in unmitigated scales have more to do with arrogance and subservience (respectively) than with self-criticism and dependency.

[4]It may appear that all losses are, by definition, interpersonal. Some writers (e.g., Finlay-Jones, 1989), however, have used *losses* to describe a broad category that encompasses all negative events (including achievement failures) with a quality of finality.

In this context (and using the dependency and self-criticism idioms), the personality–situation interaction model predicts the following specific vulnerabilities:

- Dependent people are especially prone to react to rejection or loss with depression—more so than dependent people react to failure and more so than self-critical people react to rejection.
- Self-critical people are especially prone to react to failure with depression—more so than self-critical people react to rejection and more so than dependent people react to failure.

There are, in fact, two kinds of outcome questions that can be entertained: whether there is an intense (but perhaps time-limited) depressive reaction to a stressor, and whether whatever reaction is aroused does not dissipate but persists and becomes entrenched, perhaps even clinical. Laboratory studies address the former and are relevant to the latter only insofar as an affective response cannot become entrenched unless it first occurs and a severe affective response is more likely to become entrenched than a weak one. Only longitudinal observational studies can address issues surrounding clinical depression directly.

The relevant observational (i.e., nonexperimental) literature has been substantial, including a number of longitudinal studies involving clinical depression, in addition to some that are crosssectional and/or involve nonclinical samples. The findings of this literature have been well reviewed elsewhere (Blatt & Zuroff, 1992; Coyne & Whiffen, 1995; Nietzel & Harris, 1990; Robins, 1995). Briefly, though no conclusion has received uniform support or nonsupport, the predominant thrust of the nonexperimental literature has been much more supportive of the dependency–rejection tie than of the self-criticism–failure tie. I turn now to experimental research.

AN ELEGANT STUDY

My students (primarily Gary Kutcher and Eva Helleotes) and I approached these questions inspired largely by Zuroff and Mongrain's (1987) experimental study of a personality–situation specificity model of depression. The Zuroff and Mongrain study is uncommonly elegant in that it used measures of two personality variables from the same instrument (Dependency and Self-criticism from the DEQ), and two very similar stressors as situation variables—an interpersonal rejection mood induction and an achievement failure mood induction. Both were conveyed via an audiotape describing a negative event that the participant was asked to imagine himself or herself experiencing. Although the notion of laboratory mood inductions has a long and complex history (usually seen as originating with Velten, 1968), mood induction studies have rarely employed more than one negative induction, and doing so allows comparisons between them. Although Robins (1988) suggested a similar strategy at about the same time, Zuroff and Mongrain were the first to actually implement a two-induction approach in this domain. Whereas Zuroff and Mongrain's scenarios involved a sense of finality (i.e., certainty of negative outcome), other researchers (e.g., Lassner, Matthews, & Stoney, 1994; Radecki-Bush, Farrell, & Bush, 1993) employed achievement and interpersonal stressors that do not; it is presumably this finality aspect of Zuroff and Mongrain's stressors that rendered them relevant to depression.

Zuroff and Mongrain employed not only two personality and two situation variables, but also several response variables, most notably two scales assessing affective states—anaclitic and introjective—posited as congruent with one or the other of the personality–situation pairs. This opened the door for consideration of three interaction models beyond personality–situation as previously described: personality–response, situation–response, and personality–situation–response specificity. The following are dependency-relevant hypotheses pertinent to these models; self-criticism predictions mirror them:

- Personality–Response Specificity: Dependent people are especially prone to reacting to stressors with *anaclitic feelings* (e.g., feelings of abandonment)—more so than self-critical people react to stressors with anaclitic feelings and more so than dependent people respond to stressors with *introjective feelings* (e.g., feelings of being a failure).
- Situation–Response Specificity: Rejection is especially likely to engender an anaclitic state—more so than failure engenders anaclitic affect and more so than rejection engenders introjective feelings.
- Personality–Situation–Response Specificity: Dependent persons react to rejection with anaclitic affect—more so (a) than dependent persons react to rejection with introjective affect, (b) than dependent persons react to failure with anaclitic affect, and (c) than self-critical persons react to any stressor with anaclitic affect.

Although all are specificity (or congruence) models involving the same kinds of variable pairs, they are dramatically different from one another. Among personality–situation, personality–response, and situation–response, support for one has no bearing on whether either of the other two is also supported. I mention these models mainly to note that the tendency, found occasionally in the literature, to refer to *the* interaction (or the specificity or the congruence) model (as if there were just one of them, or as if support for one constituted support for all) is unwarranted and misleading. The majority of so-called specificity studies have addressed personality–situation, with personality–response a distant second.[5] Zuroff and Mongrain's analyses addressed some of these hypotheses more thoroughly than others.

Although Zuroff and Mongrain included a neutral response measure (i.e., nonspecific depressive state), they only included self-criticism and dependency as personality variables and failure and rejection as situation variables. In the absence of a nonfailure, nonrejection negative mood induction, personality–response specificity could be assessed only by analyses in which the two situation groups were combined, or by demonstrating that parallel effects were manifest in each group. In their design, self-criticism and dependency were treated categorically, such that these two groups could be compared with each other and with controls (i.e., persons whose scores were elevated on neither DEQ scale).

In any case, Zuroff and Mongrain's (1987) most straightforward test of personality–situation specificity involved examination of six postinduction nonspecific depressive affect means: self-critical, dependent, and control participants (personality) following rejection and failure inductions (situation). Following rejection, dependent participants were more upset than were self-critical and control participants. Contrary to prediction, following failure self-critical participants were not more upset than dependent participants were. Although these results could be taken to indicate that DEQ Dependency is a marker for nonspecific vulnerability, my students and I focused on the fact that Zuroff and Mongrain's failure induction seemed to incorporate an element of interpersonal rejection. We wondered if more complete support for personality–situation specificity might be obtainable with a cleaner failure induction.

Despite its theoretical import, its elegant design, and its ambiguous findings, there was apparently no published replication, partial or otherwise, of Zuroff and Mongrain's (1987) study until a paper recently appeared by Allen, Horne, and Trinder (1996). Allen et al.'s study paralleled Zuroff and Mongrain's, with the following major changes: The scales employed for the personality variable were Sociotropy and Autonomy from the Personal Style Inventory (PSI; Robins et al., 1994); the inductions were adapted from Robins (1988); and response (anaclitic vs. introjective) was not a variable in the study, although psychophysiological as well as self-report,

[5]In developing a statistical model to deal with data such as these, it is easier to show some effects are significant whereas others are not, or to eyeball means, than it is to back up all of the "more so than" statements inherent in the various specificity hypotheses with significance tests.

nonspecific, affect data were obtained. The Allen et al. results were remarkably similar to Zuroff and Mongrain's, with sociotropy predicting affect following rejection (and, to a lesser extent, following failure), and with autonomy failing to predict affect following both.

Gruen, Silva, Ehrlich, Schweitzer, and Friedhoff (1997) reported what may be construed as a partial replication of Zuroff and Mongrain (1987). Gruen et al.'s study differed in a number of respects, including the following: (a) an abbreviated version of the DEQ was employed to assess self-criticism and dependency; (b) there was no rejection manipulation; (c) the failure induction was a cognitive problem-solving task; and, (d) the outcome variables, although including only nonspecific, self-reported affect, also involved preinduction and postinduction assays of plasma *homovanillic acid* (HVA), an indicator of central dopamine activity. Results showed that self-criticism predicted change in HVA and in self-reported affect following failure. Dependency, in contrast, did not predict HVA change. The relation between dependency and affect change was not reported, thus one cannot know if self-criticism was more effective in predicting depressed affect following failure than was dependency. In addition, the absence of a rejection (or other nonfailure) stressor makes it impossible to know if the vulnerability measured by self-criticism was specific to failure. Still, given that these positive results are on the self-criticism–failure side of the court, they provide an interesting complement to the results reported by Zuroff and Mongrain and by Allen et al.

In addition several experimental or quasi-experimental studies may be viewed as corroborating the link between dependency and vulnerability to interpersonal disruption (without addressing the link between self-criticism and failure). These have been reported in the following papers: Fichman, Koestner, and Zuroff (1997), Keinan and Hobfoll (1989), Masling, O'Neill, and Katkin (1982), and Simpson, Rholes, and Phillips (1995).

OUR REPLICATIONS

Although no attempt to replicate Zuroff and Mongrain (1987) was published until Allen et al. (1996), we conducted three large-scale quasireplications, only one of which is likely to be published. The first two (Kutcher, 1990, 1992) were not because design problems inherent in those (and also in Zuroff & Mongrain's and Allen et al.'s) studies became apparent to us in the process of analysis. As previously noted, our initial suspicion had been that the crucial reason for Zuroff and Mongrain's incomplete support for the personality–situation hypothesis was simply that their failure induction contained too much rejection. (In that tape, the subject's father expressed disappointment over what had happened—a feature that our version avoided.) Our eventual success at showing complete support for this hypothesis may rest partly on induction improvements we initiated at the outset, although we are not certain (we never compared Zuroff and Mongrain's failure induction with our own adaptation of it). There were a number of lessons to be learned in the process of the Kutcher 1990 and 1992 studies, which we took to heart in designing the third study:

- It is unwise to incorporate failure versus rejection as a within-participants variable (at least if the inductions are presented within a single session). Whereas Zuroff and Mongrain (1987) reported that order effects were nonsignificant, in Kutcher's (1990) larger sample study, such effects were often significant. Given that it is risky to base inferences on responses to the second of two inductions, situation should be a between-participants variable.
- When one or more personality variables show reliable relations with the response variables, it is unwise to rely solely on postinduction responses in the assessment of the effects of those inductions. Analyses of postinduction responses must control for preinduction level. Otherwise, inferences regarding what effects are induction-based, as opposed to preexisting, are too tenuous.
- Unfortunately, DEQ Self-criticism is so closely related to depression that statistical control of preinduction depression is not a fully satisfactory solution—a disconcerting turn of events, given that one of the appealing aspects of the Zuroff and Mongrain study was its reliance on two seemingly comparable scales from the same instrument. That is, as DEQ Self-criticism is much more closely related to depression than DEQ Dependency is, the comparability is more apparent than real. DEQ Self-criticism appears to measure a central aspect of depression, and it is hard for something to be a suitable vulnerability marker for the development of a condition of which it is a central aspect (cf. Blaney & Kutcher, 1991; Coyne & Whiffen, 1995).

The results of Kutcher's (1990, 1992) studies were encouraging with respect to personality–situation specificity (and for that matter, the other specificity models), else we would have dropped the quest. We viewed reliance on the DEQ Self-criticism scale as the sole serious problem remaining with the Kutcher (1992) study,[6] giving rise to our third study (Helleotes, Kutcher & Blaney, 1998; see also Helleotes, 1995). In approaching that study, the key question was: What measure should be used in

---

[6]Gruen et al.'s (1997) recent findings raise the possibility that the self-criticism scale from Welkowitz, Lish, and Bond's (1985) revision of the DEQ may not be as problematic as that from the original DEQ.

place of DEQ Self-criticism as a predictor of specific vulnerability to depressed affect following failure?

It may appear that a measure of autonomy (from the SAS or PSI) would have been an obvious choice, especially given that Allen et al.'s (1996) negative findings regarding PSI Autonomy had not yet appeared and autonomy scales do not correlate as highly with depression as DEQ Self-criticism does (cf. Blaney & Kutcher, 1991; Moore & Blackburn, 1996; Robins et al., 1994). We steered clear of autonomy measures for two reasons. First, in the nonexperimental literature, autonomy scales had been no more consistent in predicting specific failure vulnerability than DEQ Self-criticism. Second, autonomy scales—tracking a distinctive aspect of Beck's (1983) thinking on the matter—tend to include many items focusing on issues such as self-determination, and we were unsure what this had to do with failure–vulnerability. (This betrays our bias in favor of face-valid scales—a bias that we would readily abandon if provided with a nonface-valid predictor of specific vulnerability.)

In casting about for a scale having the right kinds of items and external validity, we came upon the revised Attitudes Toward Self scale (ATS-R; Carver, LaVoie, Kuhl, & Ganellen, 1988). We were particularly impressed with the weak association between self-reported depression and the ATS-R Self-criticism subscale, so we focused on that subscale. We retained DEQ Dependency as the rejection-relevant measure, as it appears no better nor worse than the obvious alternatives (SAS or PSI Sociotropy). Indeed, these various scales tend to correlate well with one another (e.g., Blaney & Kutcher, 1991; Robins et al., 1994) and they have all shown interpersonal loss or rejection vulnerability in one or more studies. We also included the three depressed affect scales employed by Zuroff and Mongrain, with minor modification. It should be emphasized that, despite the tortuous pathway traversed in reaching it, the Helleotes et al. (1998) study was still a relatively close methodological replication of the original Zuroff and Mongrain (1987) report that inspired it.

The support in Helleotes et al. (1998) for personality–situation specificity, as set forth previously, was quite strong across the board, and even clearer for self-criticism–failure than for dependency–rejection. Although the key analyses involved multiple regression, here the specificity findings are summarized in terms of comparisons between groups at the extremes on the two personality variables with respect to preinduction to postinduction change scores. In regard to personality–situation specificity:

- DEQ Dependency (i.e., high vs. low) made a greater difference for those in the rejection induction than for those who experienced failure.
- ATS-R Self-criticism made a greater difference for those in the failure condition than for those who experienced rejection.

- Among those exposed to rejection, dependency made more difference than did self-criticism.
- Among failure-induction participants, self-criticism mattered more than dependency.

As an aside, support for the other two-element specificity models (personality–response and situation–response) was mixed but largely positive; at the personality–situation–response level, there seemed to be a strong self-criticism—failure—introjective-affect link.

In turning to the ATS-R Self-criticism scale, we (Helleotes et al., 1998) had, in fact, come to the sad suspicion that a substantial literature—consisting not only of the Zuroff and Mongrain (1987) and Allen et al. (1996) experimental studies, but also of the substantial number of nonexperimental studies of naturally occurring stressful experiences—had proceeded with insufficient attention to basic measurement issues. The fact that ATS-R Self-criticism worked so well lends credence to the inference that experimental and nonexperimental literatures on failure vulnerability would be less inconsistent if better measures had been used all along. The broader lesson is that major efforts at model testing can be largely wasted unless they are preceded by thorough efforts at obtaining conceptual clarity and measurement sophistication.

DEPENDENCY REVISITED

One could even say that the field has been lucky not to have had the same kinds of problems with dependency–rejection that it had with self-criticism–failure. In various studies, personality–situation specificity effects have been demonstrated with various dependency or sociotropy scales. The items found in such scales are quite diverse, and it remains unclear which items contribute to these effects. Birtchnell (1991) suggested that the "insecurity and lack of trust" aspect of dependency is crucial, but neither this nor any other narrow hypothesis appears to have been tested (p. 291). Only quite recently have researchers taken a particularly close look at the item subsets within DEQ Dependency, SAS Sociotropy, and related scales (e.g., Blatt, Zohar, Quinlan, Zuroff, & Mongrain, 1995; Gilbert, Allan, & Trent, 1995; Pincus & Gurtman, 1995; Rude & Burnham, 1995). That work should arguably have preceded all personality–situation research involving dependency.

Major relevant efforts had been reported earlier, regarding variables such as attachment styles (e.g., Bartholomew & Horowitz, 1991; West, Sheldon, & Reiffer, 1987) and affiliation motives (e.g., Hill, 1987). There has been research linking attachment styles to dependency (Heiss, Berman, &

Sperling, 1996; Livesley, Schroeder, & Jackson, 1990; Murphy & Bates, 1997; Zuroff & Fitzpatrick, 1995), to depression (Burge et al., 1997; Cole-Detke & Kobak, 1996; Fonagy et al., 1996; Hammen et al., 1995; Radecki-Bush et al., 1993; Roberts, Gotlib, & Kassel, 1996) and to response to noninterpersonal (Armsden & Greenberg, 1987; Mikulincer, Florian, & Weller, 1993; Simpson, Rholes, & Nelligan, 1992) and interpersonal (Hammen et al., 1995) stressors. Still, the literature on the measurement of attachment, like that on dependency, is very much in flux (Heiss et al., 1996; Carver, 1997), and there are concerns that attachment measures (like DEQ Self-criticism), in part, assess pathological distress itself.

Regarding affiliation motives, Mehrabian and Ksionsky (1974) argued that dependency is best viewed as the confluence of two variables: affiliative tendency and sensitivity to rejection. More recently, Hill (1987) proposed four distinguishable variants of affiliation motivation (i.e., emotional support, attention, positive stimulation, and social comparison) and presented data indicating that each of these four relates rather congruently with (self-reported) responses in various kinds of situations (see also Hill, 1991). In addition, Emmons (1991) reported data indicating that having many affiliative strivings is associated with higher positive affect as a function of experiencing good interpersonal events and with higher negative affect as a function of bad interpersonal events. The literature on the measurement of affiliation motivation, however, is unsettled too (e.g., King, 1995); arguably, need for affiliation is ripe for replacement with the similar (but more communally-oriented) construct need for intimacy, which in turn has implicit and self-attributed variants (cf. Craig, Koestner, & Zuroff, 1994).

INDUCTIONS AS BEHAVIORAL ASSESSMENTS

Several broader issues become apparent as one considers research of this sort. One concerns the relation between experimental inductions and vulnerability assessment. Studies such as Allen et al. (1996), Helleotes et al. (1998), and Zuroff and Mongrain (1987) can be framed as addressing whether personality predicts depressive outcome in a situation-specific fashion. Alternatively, a given induction can be viewed as an element in an elaborate personality assessment tool. One does not have to be a card-carrying behaviorist to acknowledge that among the best assessment procedures are those that present participants with a real (or realistic) stimulus, then ascertain how they respond. Although participants can be asked how, say, rejection experiences influence their moods, we trust our findings more if we expose our participants to some kind of rejection experience and monitor their preinduction and postinduction mood states. Both can be seen as tests, and in fact, both usually rely on self-report, although when inductions are used pre-to-post psychobiological monitoring is also possible (cf. Allen et al. 1996, Gruen et al., 1997). Even when reliance is on affective self-report, preinduction to postinduction assessments are probably not vulnerable to the biases inherent in participants' retrospective and generalized reports about their behavior.

In this light, the Helleotes et al. (1998) study can be seen as addressing the construct validation of four measures of vulnerability via a multitrait–multimethod matrix. The measures are:

1. Prerejection to postrejection induction change.
2. Prefailure to postfailure induction change.
3. DEQ Dependency.
4. ATS-R Self-criticism.

The first and third address the same trait (rejection vulnerability), as do the second and fourth (failure vulnerability). The first and second share a method (scenario-based behavioral assessment), as do the third and fourth (self-report questionnaire). In such a design, the hope is that the correlations between two measures of the same trait will be higher than the others in the matrix. Although this is not the way Helleotes et al. (1998) actually reported their data, when one views their data in this light, one sees evidence for convergent and discriminant validity.

One could, however, take this line of reasoning a step further: One could view a given preinduction to postinduction change score not merely as a measure but as *the* criterion measure of the variable in question. Batson, Shaw, and Oleson (1992) advocated something similar, suggesting that the way to discern an individual's true goals and values (i.e., aspects of personality) is to attend closely to his or her emotional reactions in different situations. This can be viewed as a radical personality–situation model, one in which the presence of personality–situation interactions is a given rather than a testable hypothesis, because personality dimensions are viewed as demonstrable only insofar as individuals differ with respect to the situations to which they respond. Seen in that light, the present study can be viewed as addressing the criterion validity of DEQ-Dependency and ATS-R Self-criticism.

The wisdom of this step should not be taken for granted. Frijda (1994), in effect, cautioned against it on logical grounds, as follows: "The statement that emotions serve satisfaction or protection of one's concerns is meaningful only to the extent that concerns (or . . . motives or goals) can be defined or ascertained *independently* from emotions" (p. 118; emphasis added). Even if one were to put aside such misgivings and accept Batson et al.'s (1992) premise, one faces difficult questions about the adequacy of the inductions one has chosen to employ. Presumably, no single induction, no matter how realistic or carefully designed, could bear the burden of being the key component in the assessment of a broad construct such as dependency. This is also the case with respect to naturally occurring stressors (as in nonexperimental longitudinal research). Two persons can be equally upset at the same event for very different reasons, and clarification of what it was about an event that evoked a given response might require exposing the individual to a variety of additional events. Moreover, the premise that each of the two situation classes considered in this chapter (rejection–loss and failure) is, in fact, functionally homogeneous warrants further examination. For instance, it is a good working assumption that the state that ensues on the death of a parent is similar to that which ensues on being dumped by a fiancé (and that an individual who is particularly vulnerable to the one will be to the other as well), but that is all it is: a good working assumption.

In addition, one had best be cautious in drawing inferences about what a scale measures solely on the basis of its ability to predict a given response to a particular kind of situation. For instance, Fenigstein (1979, Study 1) showed that a self-report measure of public self-consciousness was able to predict affective responses following rejection. Can one infer from such a finding that the self-consciousness measure is really just a measure of dependency? Probably not, especially given that the study did not include a nonrejection stressor. Variables other than dependency (perhaps, as Fenigstein suggested, public self-consciousness per se) may presumably influence intensity of negative reaction to rejection.

Furthermore, it is not clear that one would want to specify any one outcome as the sole criterion in a challenge-based assessment. For example, with respect to the dependency-relevant notion of intensity of attachment, Berman and Sperling (1994) listed a number of criterion outcomes, including: (a) frequency of intrusive thoughts about the attachment figure, (b) efforts to seek or make contact with or rejoin the attachment figure, and (c) the intensity of jealousy or insecurity. In line with Helleotes et al. (1998), one might suggest the addition of depressed affect to this list, and, based on related research by Bornstein (1995), one might add outcomes involving physical symptoms. Moreover, the research by Hammen (chap. 5, this volume) suggests other variables that may be relevant. Finally, Frijda, Ortony, Sonnemans, and Clore (1992) pointed out that, even within the ostensibly narrow response variable of affect intensity, the specific indexes on which one could reasonably rely are legion. The point is, of course, that—even taking a relatively operational approach to personality construct definition—there can be a variety of responses, as well as situations, that would deserve consideration.

LABORATORY SITUATIONS

Returning to the manipulations employed by Helleotes et al. (1998), the fact that the hypotheses were so well supported does not exempt us from questioning the use of simulated or role-played rejection and failure scenarios. Having heard the tapes employed in these studies, I can testify that they provide powerful portrayals. Moreover, persons who had just actually undergone the experiences set forth in these tapes (and who really did care about the relationship or occupational goal as set forth) would probably show far less variability than our participants showed; virtually all such persons would, I suspect, be devastated by the respective rejection or failure. Participants who were relatively unaffected by our laboratory inductions may have achieved this imperviousness by avoiding full engagement in the simulation experience. If so, one wonders what this ability to distance oneself from such inductions says about how individuals handle the real-life situations that the inductions parallel.

In contrast, deception-borne inductions may help ensure that all participants are fully engaged in the experimental situation. As far as the participant knows, the event in such inductions is actual. For example, deception-based rejection inductions have placed participants in staged interactions in which they were ignored or treated coolly and given negative interpersonal feedback (e.g., Fenigstein, 1979, Study 1; Masling et al., 1982; Wallace & Alden, 1997), whereas deception-based failure inductions have involved feedback of poor performance at a cognitive task (e.g., Gruen et al., 1997). Although deception approaches do not provide the participant with an obvious option to be uninvolved, they do entail rejection or failure that is pallid and nonspecific, compared with what can be set forth in a scenario. For instance, being briefly ignored by a stranger (e.g., Fenigstein, 1979) is hardly in the same league with being dumped permanently by one's fiancé (e.g., Helleotes et al., 1998). It would be impractical and unethical, however, to lead participants to believe they were really being dumped by their fiancé. Given the limitations both of scenario-based and of deception-based approaches, a case can be made for quasireplications of all findings, using both approaches.

PERSONALITY, SELF-REPORT, AND FACE VALIDITY

As previously noted, there may be reasons not to define constructs such as dependency and self-criticism too operationally. For instance, to treat intensity of response to a particular rejection induction as the criterion measure of dependency places great weight on the characteristics of the induction in question. When relying on a self-report approach, one may employ an inventory of face-valid items that ask the individual if she or he would be upset by the occurrence of various instances of the class of situations and/or events in the class (described as a class). To use dependency as an example, one can ask: "How upset would you be if your best friend ignored you? . . . if your fiancé dumped you? . . . if your mother died?" and/or "How upset do feel when you experience interpersonal loss or rejection?" Either of these approaches increases the chances that one will be able to infer something about how an individual will respond in a generalized range of situations. That, plus the ease of self-report assessment, presumably accounts for the heavy reliance on inventories in research domains such as this one.

Still, it is not clear that our field should rely exclusively on personality variables as captured in face-valid, self-report items. That is, it is not clear that we have made headway in understanding personality processes when we simply show that persons who report that a particular stressor situation distresses them do, in fact, become distressed when confronted with that situation. Isn't there more to the notion of personality dimensions than situation-specific stressor vulnerability? Aren't indirect research findings more intriguing than direct ones? The DEQ Dependency, ATS-R Self-criticism scales, and others used in this tradition of research include items that are relatively direct and face-valid. Furthermore, to my knowledge, no study has shown that a scale consisting only of subtle items could predict specific vulnerability. Ascertaining whether this is possible will surely be one of the challenges of personality–situation research in coming years. Indeed, it is central to the question of what we mean by *personality.*

In the quest for promising indirect items, one would presumably look first to face-valid items that express an aversion for the respective stressor less directly (e.g., "It is normal to dislike being rejected") or that express affinity for something that seems antithetical to the stressor. The latter could be either an activity preference (e.g., "Being able to share experiences with other people makes them much more enjoyable for me"—an actual item from SAS Sociotropy), a positive motive or goal (e.g., "I strive to have close relationships with other people"), or some combination thereof (e.g., "People who need people are the luckiest people in the world").

GOALS AND VULNERABILITIES

The foregoing has implications beyond personality-scale development, involving questions of key relevance to our understanding of personality: How closely tied are vulnerabilities to positive goals and rewards? Is what makes one sad the loss or absence of what makes one happy? In the case of dependency, are wanting to be loved and being depressed by rejection simply two sides of the same coin?[7]

Although it may appear obvious that an individual will not be upset by the loss of something that she or he does not value, there are theoretical perspectives (e.g., Coats, Janoff-Bulman, & Alpert, 1996; Higgins, 1996) that specify a major distinction between striving toward a good outcome and striving to avoid a bad outcome, and reliance must in any case be placed on empirical answers to these questions. The vintage literature on affiliative motivation (cf. Carrera, 1964; Mehrabian & Ksionzky, 1974) suggests that affiliative tendency and sensitivity to rejection are distinct, although some findings may reflect the heavy loading of submissiveness in the measurement of the latter (cf. Mehrabian, 1997). Among recent studies, the following seem most relevant:

- Emmons and Diener (1986) reported that affiliation needs correlated both positively with friendly feelings in social situations that one was in by choice and negatively with such feelings in solitary situations that one was in by imposition; similarly, achievement needs correlated positively with feeling productive in chosen work situations and negatively with feeling productive in imposed recreation situations (see also Emmons, 1991).
- Mongrain and Zuroff (1995) reported substantial correlations between DEQ Dependency and Self-criticism scales and measures of personal strivings; the pattern of associations is consistent with the view that vulnerabilities and goals are inversely related, although some DEQ strivings associations are virtually assured by the presence of motive-relevant items in the DEQ.
- Solomon and Haaga (1994) sorted SAS items into positive and negative subscales; their data—focusing on the external correlates of these two subscales—indicate that, within SAS Sociotropy and Autonomy, positively valenced subscales do not mirror the pattern of correlations shown by respective negatively valenced subscales.

[7]It is also of interest to compare the item "I get depressed when I am rejected" with the item "I often worry about being rejected," and to compare the item "I get depressed when I fail" with "I worry a lot about failing." Because factor analyses seem not to segregate "worry about" from "depressed when" items, scales such as those mentioned in this chapter tend to mix them together. However, if pressed, many people could probably list events that would be personally devastating, but about which they ordinarily spend little time brooding. Factor analysis of self-report items is probably not a trustworthy way to address whether uncued worry about a given event is a predictor of specific vulnerability to that event, because people probably do not ordinarily focus on such phrasing distinctions when they respond to self-report items.

- Carver (1997) reported that, within the interpersonal attachment domain, a positively oriented scale called *Security* (e.g., "It feels relaxing and good to be close to someone") was unrelated to an *Ambivalence–Worry scale* (e.g., "I often worry that my partner doesn't really love me").
- Karoly and Ruehlman (1995) reported that, across several goal domains, scores on positive (e.g., "This goal is a source of pleasure for me") and negative (e.g., "The thought of not achieving this goal frightens me") scales were essentially uncorrelated, although both were related (in opposite directions) to depression.
- Elliot and Church (1997) considered approach and avoidance achievement motivation scales (e.g., "It is important to me to do better than the other students," and "I often think to myself, 'What if I do badly in this class?' " respectively) and found them to be modestly correlated and to have differing external correlates.

The results of these self-report studies provide no straightforward answer to the question: Is what makes one distressed simply the loss (or absence, or endangerment) of what makes one happy? The Emmons–Diener and Mongrain–Zuroff findings suggest that the answer is yes, the Mehrabian–Ksionzky, Solomon–Haaga, Karoly–Ruehlman, and Carver data suggest that it is no, and the Elliot–Church findings suggest that it is somewhat.

Note that this question could be addressed in a fashion that avoids reliance on personality self-report. A study modeled after Zuroff and Mongrain's (1987), but that employed not only rejection and failure inductions but also acceptance and success inductions (and included an affective state measure able to show increases in both elation and depression), would achieve this end (though having truly symmetrical inductions within a given domain may not be easy; see Fenigstein, 1979). The key questions in such research would be: Is there a uniquely strong association between amount of depressive shift following failure and of euphoric shift following success? Similarly, is there one between depressive shift after rejection and euphoric shift following acceptance?

LEVEL OF ANALYSIS

Especially if one favors the view that self-report personality assessment is most useful when direct, face-valid items are employed (i.e., the individual reports what she or he finds upsetting), one may expect that, if people can report accurately what upsets them in general, they are probably even more accurate in reporting what upsets them in particular. For instance, it would be unsurprising if, in predicting depression vulnerability to being dumped by one's fiancé, one were to find the strongest predictive power with a scale containing items having a very narrow motivational (cf. Raynor & Nochajski, 1986) or situational focus (e.g., "I would be very upset if my fiancé dumped me"). If this level is where personality–situation specificity is strongest, is this the level at which we should focus?

Probably not, at least if one has goals that go beyond mere prediction of behavior via self report. The reason is that any kind of narrow definition invites misapprehension regarding the root source of a vulnerability. Though being dumped by a fiancé may be particularly prototypical of dependency-relevant events, it is still possible that, among persons upset by this event, in some cases an ensuing depression has more to do with, say, lust for wealth than with dependency. For this reason, assessments that utilize multiple instances of a category are better suited than single-event assessments to mapping out the range of stressors to which an individual is vulnerable. This parallels the reasoning just provided, that if one were to employ induction assessments as one's criterion measures, one should employ more than one induction per variable.

On the other hand, if needs and vulnerabilities are hierarchically organized, a blanket choice among levels of generality is not necessary; various levels may each have utility. It is, however, an open question whether situation classes and hierarchies that emerge from examination of self-report items will parallel those that emerge from induction-based and/or naturalistic observations. For instance, if it were to be ascertained that the items "I would be extremely upset if my fiancé dumped me" and "I would be extremely upset if one of my parents died" correlated particularly highly with one another and with the item "Rejection and interpersonal loss experiences upset me a great deal," this would support the notion that there is a general rejection–loss class, of which being dumped by fiancé and parental death are instances. Such data would not, however, obviate direct information regarding whether individuals who are particularly affected by being dumped by a fiancé are also, in fact, particularly affected by the death of a spouse. If the situation hierarchies differ between self-report and observational findings, the latter should presumably be taken more seriously.

STRESSOR PERCEPTION

Demonstrating personality–situation specificity is not the same thing as understanding what processes underlie it. It was previously noted, for instance, that in a study using a role-playing, scenario-based induction, response variation may arise from variation in task engagement. Alternatively, individuals may attend to different aspects of a standard experience. That is, two individuals may perceive the same event quite differently, and they may be upset by different aspects of the event.

In several of our studies (including Helleotes et al., 1998), we attempted to address this issue systematically—by asking participants if they viewed the failure or rejection induction they had experienced as entailing failure or rejection. We suspected that dependent persons would report seeing even the rejection induction as entailing failure. Results have been complex, difficult to make sense of and to summarize, and useful largely in showing how difficult it may be to address these issues. One source of difficulty is probably related to the idioms that we happily, but perhaps unwisely, adopted. Although we had in mind that *failure* is noninterpersonal, whereas *rejection* is interpersonal, both failure and rejection have meanings in both interpersonal and achievement contexts. One can fail (or succeed) not only at work or school, but also in relationships and interpersonal interactions (cf. Wallace & Alden, 1997); both one's marriage proposal and one's job application can be rejected (or accepted). We surmise that the terms we used muddied the waters.[8]

In short, the matter of differential perceptions of events continues to await clarification. More generally, the question of the processes underlying personality–situation effects—and specific vulnerabilities—is ripe for further attention.

TRAITS VERSUS STATES

Another complexity pertains to the possibility that variables such as dependency and self-criticism function as states in addition to traits.[9] This shows up in colloquial usage: We talk of people being particularly needy (i.e., in a

[8]The term *self-criticism* also has fuzzy referents. One can be self-critical in interpersonal as well as in achievement realms and being self-critical may render one dependent on others for encouragement. Indeed, Birtchnell's (1991) list of defining characteristics of *dependency* includes "Self-judging: inclined to dislike, blame, and punish oneself" (p. 284). Blatt (1995) has shown a recent preference for the term *perfectionism* rather than *self-criticism.* Notwithstanding that one can presumably be perfectionistic in interpersonal relationships, this is a step in the direction of greater clarity. Nonetheless, perfectionism and self-criticism may not be interchangeable notions. Standard measures of perfectionism typically show only modest correlations with depression (Frost, Heimberg, Holt, Mattia, & Neubauer, 1993). *Self-oriented Perfectionism,* the facet that interacts specifically with achievement stressors in predicting depression (Hewitt, Flett, & Ediger, 1996), is closely related to conscientiousness, especially to the achievement-striving facet thereof (Hill, McIntire, & Bacharach, 1997), whereas DEQ Self-criticism is closely related to neuroticism and minimally with conscientiousness (Mongrain, 1993; Zuroff, 1994).

[9]Of peripheral relevance is the issue of whether scores on scales such as the DEQ and SAS fluctuate as a function of degree of depression. The data on this question are mixed (cf. Bagby et al., 1994; Moore & Blackburn, 1996).

high-dependency state), and we say of someone who has fallen on hard times that she or he could really use a success experience just now.

If, say, experiencing an interpersonal loss specifically increases one's state dependency (and one's score on a dependency scale), this places crosssectional nonexperimental personality–situation specificity studies (of which several have been published) under a particularly dark cloud. If the loss event to which the dependency purportedly makes the individual vulnerable occurred before dependency was assessed, one cannot know if an apparently congruent reaction reflects specific-event vulnerability as a function of dependency or the specific impact of the event on dependency. There is a parallel concern with respect to self-criticism.

As previously noted, Zuroff and Mongrain (1987) assessed specific, momentary affective state response (e.g., introjective and anaclitic), and it might at first glance appear that such state measures provide the means to address the question of fluctuations in vulnerability. Such scales, however, are intended to be response measures, not vulnerability measures. For instance, it may be that a person who is, at the moment, experiencing a deep introjective distress response (thus, scoring high an introjective affect-state scale), would also be particularly vulnerable to a failure experience should it occur at that moment. To my knowledge, however, no one has taken a careful look at vulnerability states—distress driven or otherwise.[10]

SOCIAL SUPPORT AND COPING

I mentioned several kinds of specificity hypotheses: personality–situation, situation–response, etc. There may also be specificity effects with respect to still other classes of variables that have pervaded stress research in recent decades—social support and coping—and it may be that major progress with respect to those variables awaits attention to specificity effects. For instance, a specificity model can be proposed regarding what kind of social support is especially ameliorative following particular kinds of stressors (cf. Cutrona & Russell, 1990; Hill, 1991; Kaniasty & Norris, 1992). The claim that individuals tend to engage in social-support-seeking coping following rejection is, in effect, a situation–coping specificity model (assuming that

[10]Overholser (1992) suggested that exposure to loss events may temporarily increase dependency levels and he presented data that may be viewed as providing modest support. Kutcher's (1990) finding of order effects among participants exposed to both failure and rejection inductions (in a within-participants design) is also probably relevant, as is the long (Shipley & Veroff, 1952) and continuing (Elliot & Harackiewicz, 1996) tradition in which relevant motivational states are purportedly influenced by means of experimental induction. The notion of emotional transfer (cf. Zillmann, 1996) implies that sequential elicitors need not be thematically similar for a prior elicitor to potentiate the effect of a subsequent one.

this tendency exceeds the tendency to engage in support-seeking following failure or to engage in other coping behaviors following rejection). One can also conceive of other coping-related specificity models, that is, *personality–coping* (e.g., that dependent individuals tend to seek social support when exposed to any stressor), *response–coping* (e.g., that individuals in an introjective state tend to seek social support), *personality–support* (e.g., that self-reliant persons benefit less from support when stressed than dependent individuals do; cf. Funch & Marshall, 1984), and models involving more complex combinations (cf. O'Brien & DeLongis, 1996).

Although these possibilities would appear worthy of consideration, pursuit of them could easily run afoul of the fuzzy boundaries between variable-types (e.g., between personality and coping). Factor-analytic work on coping styles has yielded a variable called *self-criticism* (cf. Tobin, Holroyd, Reynolds, & Wigal, 1989), and the items one finds on dependency and sociotropy scales are sometimes difficult to distinguish from support-seeking coping assessments. In testing the hypothesis that dependent individuals engage in support-seeking coping, for instance, one would run the risk of tautology.

OTHER VARIABLES

Finally, the question can be asked whether the variables relevant to a personality–situation approach to the stress-depression relation are limited to dependency–self-criticism and rejection–failure.[11] There are findings that can be viewed as indicating that having a particular kind of self-image—perhaps as a future military officer (Kasl, Evans, & Niederman, 1979) or as an athletic person (Brewer, 1993)—renders one specifically vulnerable to events that challenge that image. One might argue that there are as many kinds of vulnerability as there are aspects of self-image.

Yet, the more interesting question is whether there are other broader personality types—and event groupings—that merit consideration. Although one can look for personality–situation interactions using personality and situation taxonomies that have no apparent prior relation to one another (e.g., Van Heck, Perugini, Caprara, & Fröger, 1994), a conceptually driven approach would appear more promising. This would involve one or both of the following: Start with an existing situation taxonomy, then ask whether variables in it are likely to be linked with particular kinds of personal characteristics; or start with an existing personality taxonomy, then ask whether variables in it are likely to be linked specifically with

[11]It is clear that the anaclitic–introjective distinction (cf. Zuroff & Mongrain, 1987), in merely addressing nuances of depressive state, provides a very limited response taxonomy.

particular kinds of (stressful) events. I pursued both approaches quite a bit and summarize the rather disappointing quest.

For the present purposes, useful situation taxonomies are most likely to be linked with stressor or life-event checklists and to consist of groupings of the entries on such lists. Beyond rejection–loss, failure, and their variants, groupings that have been proposed in the literature consist of odd assortments of events that do not seem to belong together (e.g., Cutrona & Russell's, 1990, loss-of-assets category, which includes everything from having a medical illness to being a crime victim). Although stressor and event lists may be the best place to find situation classes, there are two reasons not to assume that they are ideal for this purpose:

1. Such lists are comprised of normatively stressful events, and events that are stressful only to a minority of the population tend to be excluded. However, it is in attending to such events that a personality–situation approach may be most useful. Even if, say, 99% of the population were totally unfazed by instances of a given event class, if the other 1% shared some personality characteristic in common, that class would warrant consideration within a personality–situation framework. In this vein, note that in personnel and workplace psychology there has long been a person–environment tradition that posits that individuals can be at risk—even if their work environments are not inherently stressful—if there is a misfit between the person and the environment (e.g., Caplan, 1983).[12]
2. Because such lists tend to include only events that have some reasonable likelihood of being checked off, low-frequency events are excluded even if they are normatively stressful. For example, being at fault in a fatal car accident, although normatively stressful, is missing from usual stressor lists simply because it occurs so rarely. It probably is an instance of an event class that may be characterized as "having acted in abject contradiction of one's values." Although the frequency of any given high-intensity event in this class is presumably minimized by the choices people make, it is a large and phenotypically diverse class, and instances of it, taken together, probably occur with considerably frequency. Still, study of most stressor lists would provide no clue that such a class exists. There is, inci-

[12]The person–environment fit research tradition (which encompasses person–organization, person–vocation, person–group, and person–job fit; cf. Kristof, 1996) has conceptual commonality with the personality–situation specificity tradition. Despite commonalities, (a) person–environment addresses permanent aspects of the situation, whereas personality–situation addresses events; (b) person–environment often addresses both competencies and personality variables, whereas personality–situation focuses on personality variables; and, (c) the personality variables in person–environment are needs and values (and fit is good), whereas those in personality–situation are vulnerabilities (and specificity is toxic). Hence, it is person–environment *misfit* that is most similar to personality–situation specificity.

dentally, a research literature on the effects of such events (cf. Klass, 1978; McGraw, 1987), although it is rarely cited in the stress research literature. Furthermore, in both cases (events that are stressful to a minority and low frequency events), even if there are instances of a respective class on a given checklist, there may not be enough such instances for an examination of the checklist to render it apparent that there is, indeed, an underlying class.

Turning from situation to personality in the search for additional variables, consideration of existing lists (see, e.g., Table 1 of Clark, Livesley, Schroeder, & Irish, 1996, for lists of personality-disorder related variables) reveals mainly those that reflect generalized perceptual or response tendencies (plus, of course, those relevant to affiliation and achievement). Somewhat more promising are taxonomies of motives and personal strivings (e.g., Emmons, 1991; Murray, 1938), the relevance of which is tied to the assumption that people are more upset by the frustration of goals they care about than by the frustration of unimportant ones. As previously noted, however, the question of the relation between positive strivings and depression vulnerability has received remarkably little direct attention.

COMMENT

One interesting aspect of personality–situation interaction research—whether naturalistic or longitudinal—is that there is never a shortage of ways to explain negative results. Ambiguous data can always be blamed on the manipulation (or event definition) or the personality measure one has used, allowing one to maintain the illusion that, with a little tinkering, the model will surely be supported next time around. This can, of course, be a prescription for self-delusion. Fortunately, once (on the basis of an examination of research "failures") we did the study in the "right" way (Helleotes et al., 1998), we, in fact, obtained virtually unambiguous findings. Coupled with prior partial support, these results would seem to vindicate our (and others') continuing faith in the personality–situation specificity approach.

It seems likely that the kind of personality–situation approach supported by these findings has potential usefulness beyond the taxonomies employed here, that is, self-critical–dependent (personality) and rejection–failure (situation). Still, it is unclear what additions and modifications are most likely to be productive. The challenge is to develop a good taxonomy of vulnerability-relevant traits that links with a good taxonomy of stressful (and perhaps positive) events. Doing so is difficult because the goodness of each must be judged against its match with a good version of the other. Still, the successes thus far would seem to mandate the effort—even if only with respect to what it has to offer for our understanding of brief emotional states.

REFERENCES

Allen, N. B., Horne, D. J., & Trinder, J. (1996). Sociotropy, autonomy, and dysphoric emotional responses to specific classes of stress: A psychophysiological evaluation. *Journal of Abnormal Psychology, 105*, 25–33.

Arieti, S., & Bemporad, J. R. (1980). The psychological organization of depression. *American Journal of Psychiatry, 137*, 1360–1365.

Armsden, G. C., & Greenberg, M. T. (1987). The Inventory of Parent and Peer Attachment: Individual differences and their relationship to psychological well-being in adolescence. *Journal of Youth and Adolescence, 16*, 427–454.

Bagby, R. M., Schuller, D. R., Parker, J. D. A., Levitt, A., Joffe, R. T., & Shafir, M. S. (1994). Major depression and the self-criticism and dependency personality dimensions. *American Journal of Psychiatry, 151*, 597–599.

Bartholomew, K., & Horowitz, L. M. (1991). Attachment styles among young adults: A test of a four-category model. *Journal of Personality and Social Psychology, 61*, 226–244.

Batson, C. D., Shaw, L. L., & Oleson, K. C. (1992). Differentiating affect, mood, and emotion: Toward functionally based conceptual distinctions. In M. S. Clark (Ed.), *Emotion* (pp. 294–326). Newbury Park, CA: Sage.

Beck, A. T. (1983). Cognitive therapy of depression: New perspectives. In P. Clayton & J. Barrett (Eds.), *Treatment of depression: Old controversies and new approaches* (pp. 265–290). New York: Raven.

Beck, A. T., Epstein, N., Harrison, R. P., & Emery, G. (1983). *Development of the Sociotropy-Autonomy Scale: A measure of personality factors in psychopathology.* Unpublished manuscript. Philadelphia: University of Pennsylvania.

Berman, W. H., & Sperling, M. B. (1994). The structure and function of adult attachment. In M. B. Sperling & W. H. Berman (Eds.), *Attachment in adults: Clinical and developmental perspectives* (pp. 1–28). New York: Guilford.

Birtchnell, J. (1991). The measurement of dependence by questionnaire. *Journal of Personality Disorders, 5*, 281–295.

Blaney, P. H., & Ganellen, R. J. (1990). Hardiness and social support. In B. R. Sarason, I. G. Sarason, & G. R. Pierce (Eds.), *Social support: An interactional view* (pp. 297–318). New York: Wiley-Interscience.

Blaney, P. H., & Kutcher, G. S. (1991). Measures of depressive dimensions: Are they interchangeable? *Journal of Personality Assessment, 53*, 502–513.

Blatt, S. J. (1974). Levels of object representation in anaclitic and introjective depression. *Psychoanalytic Study of the Child, 29*, 107–157.

Blatt, S. J. (1995). The destructiveness of perfectionism: Implications for the treatment of depression. *American Psychologist, 50*, 1003–1020.

Blatt, S. J., D'Afflitti, J. P., & Quinlan, D. M. (1976). Experiences of depression in normal young adults. *Journal of Abnormal Psychology, 85*, 383–389.

Blatt, S. J., & Maroudas, C. (1992). Convergences among psychoanalytic and cognitive-behavioral theories of depression. *Psychoanalytic Psychology, 9*, 157–190.

Blatt, S. J., Quinlan, D. M., Chevron, E. S., McDonald, C., & Zuroff, D. (1982). Dependency and self criticism: Psychological dimensions of depression. *Journal of Consulting and Clinical Psychology, 50*, 113–114.

Blatt, S. J., Zohar, A. H., Quinlan, D. M., Zuroff, D. C., & Mongrain, M. (1995). Subscales within the dependency factor of the Depressive Experiences Questionnaire. *Journal of Personality Assessment, 64*, 319–339.

Blatt, S. J., & Zuroff, D. C. (1992). Interpersonal relatedness and self-definition: Two prototypes for depression. *Clinical Psychology Review, 12*, 527–562.

Bornstein, R. F. (1995). Interpersonal dependency and physical illness: The mediating roles of stress and social support. *Journal of Social and Clinical Psychology, 14*, 225–243.
Brewer, B. W. (1993). Self-identity and specific vulnerability to depressed mood. *Journal of Personality, 61*, 343–364.
Burge, D., Hammen, C., Davila, J., Daley, S. E., Paley, B., Lindberg, N., Herzberg, D., & Rudolph, K. D. (1997). The relationship between attachment cognitions and psychological adjustment in late adolescent women. *Development and Psychopathology, 9*, 151–167.
Caplan, R. D. (1983). Person–environment fit: Past, present, and future. In C. L. Cooper (Ed.), *Stress research: New directions for the 1980s* (pp. 35–78). New York: Wiley.
Carrera, R. N. (1964). Need for affiliation: Approach and avoidant aspects. *Journal of Clinical Psychology, 20*, 429–432.
Carver, C. S. (1997). Adult attachment and personality: Converging evidence and a new measure. *Personality and Social Psychology Bulletin, 23*, 865–883.
Carver, C. S., LaVoie, L., Kuhl, J., & Ganellen, R. J. (1988). Cognitive concomitants of depression: A further examination of the roles of generalization, high standards, and self-criticism. *Journal of Social and Clinical Psychology, 7*, 350–365.
Clark, L. A., Livesley, W. J., Schroeder, M. L., & Irish, S. L. (1996). Convergence of two systems for assessing specific traits of personality disorder. *Psychological Assessment, 8*, 294–303.
Coats, E. J., Janoff-Bulman, R., & Alpert, N. (1996). Approach versus avoidance goals: Differences in self evaluation and well-being. *Personality and Social Psychology Bulletin, 22*, 1057–1067.
Cole-Detke, H., & Kobak, R. (1996). Attachment processes in eating disorder and depression. *Journal of Consulting and Clinical Psychology, 64*, 282–290.
Coyne, J. C., & Whiffen, V. E. (1995). Issues in personality as diathesis for depression: The case of sociotropy—dependency and autonomy—self-criticism. *Psychological Bulletin, 118*, 358–378.
Craig, J. A., Koestner, R., & Zuroff, D. C. (1994). Implicit and self-attributed intimacy motivation. *Journal of Social and Personal Relationships, 11*, 491–507.
Cutrona, C. E., & Russell, D. W. (1990). Type of social support and specific stress: Toward a theory of optimal matching. In B. R. Sarason, I. G. Sarason, & G. R. Pierce (Eds.), *Social support: An interactional view* (pp. 319–366). New York: Wiley.
Daley, S. E., Hammen, C., Burge, D., Davila, J., Paley, B., Lindberg, N., & Herzberg, D. S. (1997). Predictors of the generation of episodic stress: A longitudinal study of late adolescent women. *Journal of Abnormal Psychology, 106*, 251–259.
Elliot, A. J., & Church, M. A. (1997). A hierarchical model of approach and avoidance achievement motivation. *Journal of Personality and Social Psychology, 72*, 218–232.
Elliot, A. J., & Harackiewicz, J. M. (1996). Approach and avoidance achievement goals and intrinsic motivation: A mediational analysis. *Journal of Personality and Social Psychology, 70*, 461–475.
Emmons, R. A. (1991). Personal strivings, daily life events, and psychological and physical well-being. *Journal of Personality, 59*, 453–472.
Emmons, R. A., & Diener, E. (1986). An interactional approach to the study of personality and emotion. *Journal of Personality, 54*, 371–384.
Emmons, R. A., Diener, E., & Larsen, R. J. (1986). Choice and avoidance of everyday situations and affect congruence: Two models of reciprocal interactionism. *Journal of Personality and Social Psychology, 51*, 815–826.
Endler, N. S. (1983). Interactionism: A personality model, but not yet a theory. In M. M. Page (Ed.), *Personality—Current theory and research* (pp. 155–200). Lincoln, NE: University of Nebraska Press.
Fenigstein, A. (1979). Self-consciousness, self-attention, and social interaction. *Journal of Personality and Social Psychology, 37*, 75–86.

Fichman, L., Koestner, R., & Zuroff, D. C. (1997). Dependency and distress at summer camp. *Journal of Youth and Adolescence, 26*, 217–232.

Finlay-Jones, R. (1989). Anxiety. In G. W. Brown & T. O. Harris (Eds.), *Life events and illness* (pp. 96–112). New York: Guilford.

Fonagy, P., Leigh, T., Steele, M., Steele, H., Kennedy, R., Mattoon, G., Target, M., & Gerber, A. (1996). The relation of attachment status, psychiatric classification, and response to psychotherapy. *Journal of Consulting and Clinical Psychology, 64*, 22–31.

Frijda, N. H. (1994). Emotions are functional, most of the time. In P. Ekman & R. J. Davidson (Eds.), *The nature of emotion: Fundamental questions* (pp. 112–122). New York: Oxford University Press.

Frijda, N. H., Ortony, A., Sonnemans, J., & Clore, G. (1992). The complexity of intensity. In M. Clark (Ed.), *Emotion: Review of personality and social psychology* (Vol. 13, pp. 60–89). Beverly Hills, CA: Sage.

Frost, R. O., Heimberg, R. G., Holt, C. S., Mattia, J. I., & Neubauer, A. L. (1993). A comparison of two measures of perfectionism. *Personality and Individual Differences, 14*, 119–126.

Funch, D. P., & Marshall, J. R. (1984). Self-reliance as a modifier of the effects of life stress and social support. *Journal of Psychosomatic Research, 28*, 9–15.

Gilbert, P., Allan, S., & Trent, D. R. (1995). Involuntary subordination or dependency as key dimensions of depressive vulnerability? *Journal of Clinical Psychology, 51*, 740–752.

Gruen, R. J., Silva, R., Ehrlich, J., Schweitzer, J. W., & Friedhoff, A. J. (1997). Vulnerability to stress: Self-criticism and stress-induced changes in biochemistry. *Journal of Personality, 65*, 33–47.

Hammen, C. L., Burge, D., Daley, S. E., Davila, J., Paley, B., & Rudolph, K. D. (1995). Interpersonal attachment cognitions and prediction of symptomatic responses to interpersonal stress. *Journal of Abnormal Psychology, 104*, 436–443.

Heiss, G. E., Berman, W. H., & Sperling, M. B. (1996). Five scales in search of a construct: Exploring continued attachment to parents in college students. *Journal of Personality Assessment, 67*, 102–115.

Helgeson, V. S. (1993). Implications of agency and communion for patient and spouse adjustment to a first coronary event. *Journal of Personality and Social Psychology, 64*, 807–816.

Helleotes, E. (1995). *Self-criticism, dependency and vulnerability to failure and rejection.* Doctoral dissertation, University of Miami, Coral Gables, Florida.

Helleotes, E., Kutcher, G. S., & Blaney, P. H. (1998). *Self-criticism, dependency, and vulnerability to failure and rejection.* Unpublished manuscript, University of Miami, Coral Gables, Florida.

Hewitt, P. L., Flett, G. L., & Ediger, E. (1996). Perfectionism and depression: Longitudinal assessment of a specific vulnerability hypothesis. *Journal of Abnormal Psychology, 102*, 276–280.

Higgins, E. T. (1996). Emotional experiences: The pains and pleasures of distinct regulatory systems. In R. D. Kavanaugh, B. Zimmerberg, & S. Fein (Eds.), *Emotion: Interdisciplinary perspectives* (pp. 203–241). Mahwah, NJ: Lawrence Erlbaum Associates.

Hill, C. A. (1987). Affiliation motivation: People who need people . . . but in different ways. *Journal of Personality and Social Psychology, 52*, 1008–1018.

Hill, C. A. (1991). Seeking emotional support: The influence of affiliative need and partner warmth. *Journal of Personality and Social Psychology, 60*, 112–121.

Hill, R. W., McIntire, K., & Bacharach, V. R. (1997). Perfectionism and the big five factors. *Journal of Social Behavior and Personality, 12*, 257–270.

Kaniasty, K., & Norris, F. H. (1992). Social support and victims of crime: Matching event, support, and outcome. *American Journal of Community Psychology, 20*, 211–421.

Karoly, P., & Ruehlman, L. S. (1995). Goal cognition and its clinical implications: Development and preliminary validation of four motivational assessment instruments. *Assessment, 2*, 113–129.

Kasl, S. V., Evans, A. S., & Niederman, J. C. (1979). Psychosocial risk factors in the development of infectious mononucleosis. *Psychosomatic Medicine, 41*, 445–466.

Keinan, G., & Hobfall, S. E. (1989). Stress, dependency, and social support: Who benefits from husband's presence in delivery? *Journal of Social and Clinical Psychology, 8*, 32–44.

King, L. A. (1995). Wishes, motives, goals, and personal memories: Relations of measures of human motivation. *Journal of Personality, 63*, 985–1007.

Klass, E. T. (1978). Psychological effects of immoral actions: The experimental evidence. *Psychological Bulletin, 85*, 756–771.

Kristof, A. M. (1996). Person-organization fit: An integrative review of its conceptualizations, measurement, and implication. *Personnel Psychology, 49*, 1–49.

Kutcher, G. S. (1990). *Styles of depressive vulnerability: A test of specificity.* Unpublished manuscript, University of Miami, Coral Gables, Florida.

Kutcher, G. S. (1992). *Dependency and self-criticism as predictors of depressive mood states: A test of specificity.* Ph.D. dissertation, University of Miami, Coral Gables, Florida.

Lassner, J. B., Matthews, K. A., & Stoney, C. M. (1994). Are cardiovascular reactors to asocial stress also reactors to social stress? *Journal of Personality and Social Psychology, 66*, 69–77.

Livesley, W. J., Schroeder, M. L., & Jackson, D. N. (1990). Dependent personality disorder and attachment problems. *Journal of Personality Disorders, 4*, 131–140.

Masling, J., O'Neill, R., & Katkin, E. S. (1982). Autonomic arousal, interpersonal climate, and orality. *Journal of Personality and Social Psychology, 42*, 529–534.

McGraw, K. M. (1987). Guilt following transgression: An attribution of responsibility approach. *Journal of Personality and Social Psychology, 53*, 247–256.

Mehrabian, A. (1997). Analysis of affiliation-related traits in terms of the PAD temperament model. *Journal of Psychology, 13*, 101–117.

Mehrabian, A., & Ksionzky, S. (1974). *A theory of affiliation.* Lexington, MA: D.C. Heath.

Mikulincer, M., Florian, V., & Weller, A. (1993). Attachment styles, coping strategies, and posttraumatic psychological distress: The impact of the Gulf War in Israel. *Journal of Personality and Social Psychology, 64*, 817–826.

Mongrain, M. (1993). Dependency and self-criticism located within the five-factor model of personality. *Personality and Individual Differences, 15*, 445–462.

Mongrain, M., & Zuroff, D. C. (1995). Motivational and affective correlates of dependency and self-criticism. *Personality and Individual Differences, 18*, 347–354.

Moore, R. G., & Blackburn, I. M. (1996). The stability of sociotropy and autonomy in depressed patients undergoing treatment. *Cognitive Therapy and Research, 20*, 69–80.

Murphy, B., & Bates, G. W. (1997). Adult attachment style and vulnerability to depression. *Personality and Individual Differences, 22*, 835–844.

Murray, E. M. (1938). *Explorations in personality.* New York: Oxford University Press.

Nietzel, M. T., & Harris, M. J. (1990). Relationship of dependency and achievement/autonomy to depression. *Clinical Psychology Review, 10*, 279–297.

O'Brien, T. B., & DeLongis, A. (1996). The interactional context of problem-, emotion- and relationship-focused coping: The role of the big five factors. *Journal of Personality, 64*, 775–813.

Overholser, J. C. (1992). Interpersonal dependency and social loss. *Personality and Individual Differences, 13*, 17–23.

Pincus, A. L., & Gurtman, M. B. (1995). The three faces of interpersonal dependency: Structural analyses of self-report dependency measures. *Journal of Personality and Social Psychology, 69*, 744–758.

Radecki-Bush, C., Farrell, A. D., & Bush, J. P. (1993). Predicting jealous responses: The influence of adult attachment and depression on threat appraisal. *Journal of Social and Personal Relationships, 10*, 569–588.

Raynor, J. O., & Nochajski, T. H. (1986). Development of the Motivation for Particular Activity Scale. In D. R. Brown & J. Veroff (Eds.), *Frontiers of motivational psychology* (pp. 1–25). Berlin: Springer-Verlag.

Roberts, J. E., Gotlib, I. H., & Kassel, J. D. (1996). Adult attachment security and symptoms of depression: The mediating roles of dysfunctional attitudes and low self-esteem. *Journal of Personality and Social Psychology, 70*, 310–320.

Robins, C. J. (1988). Development of experimental mood induction procedures for testing personality-event interaction models of depression. *Journal of Clinical Psychology, 44*, 958–963.

Robins, C. J. (1995). Personality-event interaction models of depression. *European Journal of Personality, 9*, 367–378.

Robins, C. J., Ladd, J., Welkowitz, J., Blaney, P. H., Diaz, R., & Kutcher, G. (1994). The Personal Style Inventory: Preliminary validation studies of new measures of sociotropy and autonomy. *Journal of Psychopathology and Behavioral Assessment, 16*, 277–299.

Rude, S. S., & Burnham, B. L. (1995). Connectedness and neediness: Factors of the DEQ and SAS dependency scales. *Cognitive Therapy and Research, 19*, 323–340.

Shaver, P. R., Papalia, D., Clark, C. L., Koski, L. R., Tidwell, M. C., & Nalbone, D. (1996). Androgyny and attachment security: Two related models of optimal personality. *Personality and Social Psychology, 22*, 582–597.

Shipley, T. E., & Veroff, J. (1952). A projective measure of need for affiliation. *Journal of Experimental Psychology, 43*, 349–356.

Simpson, J. A., Rholes, W. S., & Nelligan, J. S. (1992). Support seeking and support giving within couples in an anxiety-provoking situation: The role of attachment styles. *Journal of Personality and Social Psychology, 62*, 434–446.

Simpson, J. A., Rholes, W. S., & Phillips, D. (1996). Conflict in close relationships: An attachment perspective. *Journal of Personality and Social Psychology, 71*, 899–914.

Solomon, A., & Haaga, D. A. F. (1994). Positive and negative aspects of sociotropy and autonomy. *Journal of Psychopathology and Behavioral Assessment, 16*, 243–252.

Spence, J. T., Helmreich, R. L., & Holahan, C. K. (1979). Negative and positive components of psychological masculinity and femininity and their relationship to self-reports of neurotic and acting out behavior. *Journal of Personality and Social Psychology, 37*, 1673–1682.

Tobin, D. L., Holroyd, K. A., Reynolds, R. V., & Wigal, J. K. (1989). The hierarchical factor structure of the Coping Strategies Inventory. *Cognitive Therapy and Research, 13*, 343–361.

Van Heck, G. L., Perugini, M., Caprara, G. V., & Fröger, J. (1994). The big five as tendencies in situations. *Personality and Individual Differences, 16*, 715–731.

Velten, E. (1968). A laboratory task for induction of mood states. *Behaviour Research and Therapy, 6*, 473–482.

Wallace, S. T., & Alden, L. E. (1997). Social phobia and positive social events: The price of success. *Journal of Abnormal Psychology, 106*, 416–424.

Welkowitz, J., Lish, J. D., & Bond, R. N. (1985). The Depressive Experiences Questionnaire: Revision and validation. *Journal of Personality Assessment, 49*, 89–94.

West, M., Sheldon, A., & Reiffer, L. (1987). An approach to the delineation of adult attachment: Scale development and reliability. *Journal of Nervous and Mental Disease, 175*, 738–741.

Wiggins, J. S. (1991). Agency and communion as conceptual coordinates for the understanding and measurement of interpersonal behavior. In W. M. Grove & D. Cicchetti (Eds.), *Thinking clearly about psychology, Volume 2: Personality and psychopathology* (pp. 89–113). Minneapolis: University of Minnesota Press.

Zillmann, D. (1996). Sequential dependencies in emotional experience and behavior. In R. D. Kavanaugh, B. Zimmerberg, & S. Fein, (Eds.), *Emotion: Interdisciplinary perspectives* (pp. 243–272). Mahwah, NJ: Lawrence Erlbaum Associates.

Zuroff, D. C. (1994). Depressive personality styles and the five-factor model of personality. *Journal of Personality Assessment, 63*, 453–472.

Zuroff, D. C., & de Lorimier, S. (1989). Ideal and actual romantic partners of women varying in dependency and self-criticism. *Journal of Personality, 57*, 825–846.

Zuroff, D. C., & Fitzpatrick, D. K. (1995). Depressive personality styles: Implications for adult attachment. *Personality and Individual Differences, 18*, 253–265.

Zuroff, D. C., & Mongrain, M. (1987). Dependency and self-criticism: Vulnerability factors for depressive affective states. *Journal of Abnormal Psychology, 96*, 14–22.

Chapter 7

Information-Processing Approaches to the Study of Cognitive Biases in Depression

Ian H. Gotlib
Dana L. Neubauer
Stanford University

DEPRESSION: SYMPTOMS AND PREVALENCE

Depression is among the most common of all psychiatric disorders. It is estimated that between 8% and 18% of the general population will experience at least one clinically significant episode of depression during their lifetime (Kessler, McGonagle, Swartz, & Blazer, 1993), and that approximately twice as many women as men will be affected by this disorder (Blehar & Oren, 1995). Depression is also a recurrent disorder: Over 80% of depressed patients have more than one depressive episode (Belsher & Costello, 1988). In fact, over 50% of depressed patients have been found to relapse within 2 years of recovery (e.g., Keller & Shapiro, 1981); individuals with three or more previous episodes of depression may have a relapse rate as high as 40% within only 12 to 15 weeks after recovery (Keller et al., 1992; Mueller et al., 1996).

The high rate of recurrence of depression almost certainly reflects the presence of some stable vulnerability factor, or factors, that place certain individuals at increased risk for experiencing depressive disorders repeatedly over the course of their lives. Over the last 20 years, considerable research has been conducted in an effort to identify potential vulnerability factors for depression. Much of this research has been guided by cognitive theories of depression, which emphasize the importance of the role played by cognitive constructs in placing individuals at elevated risk for experiencing episodes of depression. Whereas early empirical studies in this area assessed the self reports of depressed persons concerning their beliefs and attitudes, more recent investigations have utilized information-processing approaches to the study of cognitive functioning derived from research in experimental cognitive psychology. We have three main goals in writing this chapter. First, we describe the various tasks that have been used to assess the processing of valenced stimuli in depressed persons. Second, we examine findings of studies that have used these information-processing tasks and paradigms to assess depression-associated biases in attention and memory. In this context, we attempt to integrate these findings to present a coherent picture of the current status of our knowledge of the cognitive functioning of depressed individuals and of the role that biases in attention and memory may play in the etiology of depression, in recovery from this disorder, and in relapse of depression. Finally, we discuss what we believe are important directions for future research in this area. Because it will be helpful in placing in a broader context the various information-processing tasks that investigators have used to examine cognitive functioning in depression, we begin the following section with a brief overview of the major cognitive theories of depression.

Cognitive Theories of Depression

As noted earlier, cognitive theories of depression provide a theoretical foundation for research examining potential vulnerability factors for this disorder. Perhaps most prominently, Beck (1967, 1976) formulated a theory of depression that ascribes the onset of this disorder in large part to cognitive biases, contending that dysfunctional cognitive processes represent a significant vulnerability factor for depression. According to this model, individuals who experience loss or adversity in childhood develop negative schemata concerning loss, failure, or abandonment. These schemata become reactivated when the individual later experiences a life event that is reminiscent of the original trauma. The reactivated schemata take the form of excessively rigid and inappropriate beliefs or attitudes about the self and the world, as well as unrealistic, perfectionistic standards by which the self is judged.

The schemata act as filters through which stimuli and events in the environment are perceived, evaluated, attended to, and remembered. Thus, individuals interpret the information from the environment so that it is consistent with the schemata, selectively attending to particular stimuli or distorting the information to achieve congruence; positive stimuli may be selectively filtered out, and negative or neutral information may be perceived as being more negative than is actually the case. This negative information-processing bias is postulated to lead to depressive affect, which, in turn, further innervates the negative schemata and reinforces their activity. Thus, in Beck's model, schemata are postulated to play a critical etiological role in predisposing an individual to experience clinically significant episodes of depression, particularly in the face of specific stressful life events that activate schematic information-processing biases.

In a conceptually similar model, Bower (1981, 1987) postulated that depressed individuals are characterized by cognitions that are more negative in content than those experienced and reported by nondepressed persons. Whereas Beck (1967, 1976) utilized a schema model to account for the negative thoughts or cognitions of depressed individuals, Bower formulated a network model of emotion, based on his earlier model of human associative memory (HAM; Anderson & Bower, 1973). In the HAM model, Bower conceptualized human memory as containing a vast collection of nodes. Within this system, each node is composed of distinct representations. Accessing a representation activates its associated node to a threshold level. When nodes are repeatedly activated simultaneously, associative connections develop and strengthen between the activated nodes. Activation of one node will partially activate, or *prime,* other nodes with which it has associative connections. Because little additional activation is necessary for partially activated nodes to reach the threshold level necessary for access to occur, the representations of nodes that have been primed are easier to access than are the representations of nonprimed nodes.

In his network model of emotion, Bower (1981, 1987) introduced the concept of emotion nodes into the HAM formulation. In this model, each emotion node corresponds to a distinct emotional state; the node is activated whenever its corresponding emotional state is experienced. Associative connections between nodes develop and strengthen when the nodes are frequenly activated together. Nodes that are activated with an emotion node will contain representations that are affectively congruent with this node. Thus, for example, associative connections tend to develop between a depression emotion node and nodes containing information relevant to failure and loss. The strong associations among these nodes result in more efficient processing of information that is congruent with an individual's mood, leading, in particular, to mood-congruent biases in memory.

Finally, Teasdale (1988) proposed an extension of Beck's and Bower's theories, essentially postulating an interaction between mood state and vulnerability to depression. Specifically, Teasdale hypothesized that depression-prone and nonvulnerable individuals respond differently to sad moods. Offering a positive feedback formulation, Teasdale hypothesized that vulnerable individuals respond to a negative mood state with patterns of thinking that exacerbate this mood (e.g., increased attention to, and memory for, negative information); thus, depressed mood and cognitive processing are mutually reinforcing, with negative cognitions functioning to increase the severity and duration of depressive affect. In contrast, nonvulnerable individuals do not exhibit this dysfunctional cognitive response to negative mood and, therefore, recover relatively easily from a dysphoric mood state.

Over the past 20 years there has been a surge of research examining predictions derived from these cognitive theories of depression. Early studies examining postulates and hypotheses derived from these theories relied in large part on the responses of depressed individuals to self-report questionnaire measures of cognitive functioning. In this context, there is a large literature documenting the association of depression with dysfunctional attitudes and a negative attributional style (for detailed reviews of this literature, see Gotlib & Hammen, 1992, and Gotlib & Abramson, 1999). It is important to note here that these investigations were much more consistent in demonstrating a relation between cognitive dysfunction and concurrent depression than they were in supporting causal aspects of these models, that cognitive dysfunction precedes the onset of depression, and that it plays a role in the course of depression. This differential pattern of results suggested that biases in cognitive functioning may be viewed more parsimoniously as a symptom of depression than as a casual factor in this disorder.

Although these investigations were important in drawing empirical attention to the cognitive styles of depressed persons, this conclusion regarding the role of cognitive biases in depression must be tempered by the use in these studies of self-report measures of cognitive biases. This methodology has a number of limitations (see Gotlib & MacLeod, 1997, and Gotlib & McCabe, 1992, for extended discussions of this issue), two of which are particularly relevant here. First, the cognitive theories that are being tested with these measures are, in large part, theories of cognitive processes as well as cognitive content. That is, Beck, Bower, and Teasdale formulated hypotheses concerning not only the content of depressive biases, which include themes of failure and loss, but also, more important, how stimuli and information involving these themes and this content are attended to, interpreted, and remembered, as well as how these cognitive processes are related to the course of depression. Unfortunately, questionnaire studies are not well suited to an examination of issues regarding cognitive processes. Second, and perhaps more important, it is unlikely that self-report questionnaire measures, which typically require participants to make conscious, deliberate, and thoughtful responses, are able to assess the existence and functioning of schemata or associative networks, which are hypothesized to be activated automatically and to operate outside of individuals' awareness. Indeed, these problems with the use of self-report measures to assess cognitive functioning may lie at the heart of the inconsistencies in the results of studies in this area.

To address these limitations, investigators have now begun to develop and adapt methodologies, many derived from research in experimental cognitive psychology, to examine the functional role of cognitive biases in depression. In contrast to self-report questionnaire measures, these methodologies permit the assessment of automatic cognitive processes and schematic functioning in depressed persons. In this context, investigators have begun to use tasks, such as the Stroop color-naming task, self-referent encoding tasks, dichotic listening tasks, deployment of attention tasks, and negative priming tasks, to study cognition in depression. The use of these tasks both extends the scope of previous investigations of cognitive functioning in depression to include cognitive processes as well as cognitive content, and also allows the assessment of more automatic, as opposed to strategic or controlled, functioning. Importantly, the results of investigations using these methods appear to be more promising in testing the hypothesis that biased cognitive functioning represents a vulnerability factor for depression and, more generally, in elucidating the nature of cognitive functioning in this disorder.

Despite the promise of information-processing paradigms and tasks to assess cognitive functioning in depressed individuals, the rapid increase over the past 10 years in the use of these measures has led to seemingly discrepant findings across studies using ostensibly similar tasks. In the next two sections of this chapter, we briefly describe the information-processing tasks that are used most commonly to examine attentional and memory functioning of depressed persons, and we examine the patterns of empirical findings that have been obtained across studies with each of these procedures. In presenting this discussion, we attempt to highlight both consistencies and discrepancies across investigations and paradigms. We begin with a description of tasks that assess attentional processing and then turn to procedures designed to examine depression-associated biases in memory.

TASKS USED TO ASSESS ATTENTIONAL BIASES

In assessing selective attention in depression, investigators have traditionally examined whether individuals who are (or who have been) depressed exhibit particular patterns of selective attention. More specifically, studies in this area have examined whether depressed or depression-vulnerable individuals, compared with nondepressed controls, demonstrate greater interference for negative than for positive stimuli, and whether their attention is drawn selectively to negative information. In examining the interference question, investigators have utilized the emotion Stroop task and a dichotic listening task; in examining the selective attention question, researchers have utilized dot-probe and color-perception tasks.

Emotion Stroop Task

The Stroop task has been used for over 50 years to study response interference. Essentially, participants are presented with words printed in different colors and are required to name the ink colors of each word, not the word itself, as quickly as possible. Participants invariably take longer to name the ink colors of words that are color names (e.g., red or green) printed in competing colors than they do the ink colors of other words (e.g., door or church). The common explanation for this finding is that the content of the color-name words interferes with the competing response of naming the (different) ink color of the words.

This task has recently been adapted for use in the study of attentional processes in depression. In the Stroop task, depressed and nondepressed participants are presented with emotionally valenced stimuli printed in different colors. Typically, the stimuli are depressed-content, positive-content, and neutral words. As in the original Stroop task, participants are instructed to ignore the meaning of the stimuli and name the color in which each word is presented. If the cognitive structures, or schemata, of depressed individuals facilitate their attention to negative stimuli, they should attend more to the content of the depressed-content than the nondepressed-content words and, consequently, exhibit longer latencies (greater interference) to naming the ink colors of these words.

Dichotic Listening Task

The dichotic listening task is conceptually similar to the Stroop task. In this task, different information or stimuli is presented simultaneously through headphones to each ear. Participants are instructed to attend to and repeat (shadow) neutral, target stimuli that are presented to either the left or right ear and to ignore distractor stimuli that are presented simultaneously to the other ear. Given these instructions, participants attempt to direct their attention to the ear in which the target stimuli are presented, and ignore stimuli presented in the unattended ear. As is the case in the Stroop task, the negative schemata of depressed persons are hypothesized to make it more difficult for them to ignore stimuli presented to the unattended ear when the stimuli are negatively valenced than when the stimuli are neutral or positively valenced. This diversion of attention to negative stimuli presented in the unattended ear means that fewer attentional processing resources are available for tracking information presented in the attended ear. Consequently, depressed participants are hypothesized to exhibit a greater number of shadowing errors of the neutral target stimuli on those trials in which the distractor stimuli are negatively valenced.

Dot-Probe Task

In the original version of the dot-probe task, pairs of words are presented simultaneously on a computer screen for a brief time (generally 500 to 750 msecs). Both words then disappear from the screen and, on approximately one third of the trials, a small dot appears in the spatial location of one of the words. Participants are asked to press one of two buttons to indicate, as quickly as they can, when they see the dot. The rationale underlying the use of this task is that participants are quicker to detect the dot probe when it appears in the spatial location of the word to which they had directed their attention than when it appears in the location of the word to which they were not attending. When the dot probe appears in the location of the word to which participants were attending, detection of the probe does not involve a shift in spatial attention and, consequently, participants are quicker to detect the probe. Thus, because depressed individuals are hypothesized to direct their attention toward negatively valenced information, they should be faster to detect probes that appear in the location of negatively valenced words, to which they had been attending, than probes that appear in the location of the other word in the pair. In a subsequent revision of this paradigm, a dot probe appeared on every trial, rather than on just one third of the trials, and participants had to indicate whether the probe appeared in the left or right side of the display.

Deployment of Attention Task

A task conceptually similar to the dot-probe task is the deployment of attention task. This task is based on Titchener's (1908) *Law of Prior Entry*, which states that a stimulus that is presented in a visual field to which a person is already attending will appear to occur before a stimulus that is presented simultaneously, but outside the person's field of attention. We have used this law in developing a paradigm that assesses where depressed individuals focus their attention. In this task, pairs of words are presented for a short duration (generally between 500 and 1,000 msecs), one above the other. The words are paired in mixed combinations of negatively valenced, positively valenced, and neutral content. Following this presentation, bars of different colors simultaneously replace each of the words. Participants are instructed to report which color bar they perceived as appearing first. Because perception of the color bar that replaces the word to which participants were attending does not involve a shift in attention, the color bar that participants identify as appearing first indicates the word to which they were attending. If the schematic functioning of depressed individuals leads them to direct their attention toward negatively valenced information, then they should perceive the color bars that replace negatively valenced words as occurring first in each trial.

TASKS USED TO ASSESS MEMORY BIASES

Researchers interested in assessing biases in memory in depressed individuals have examined either recall of autobiographical memory or recall of experimentally presented stimuli. Investigators in this area have made a further distinction between explicit memory and implicit memory. We discuss these two type of tasks and two forms of memory in greater detail.

Autobiographical Memory

In autobiographical memory paradigms, investigators typically present participants with several negative and positive words or phrases (e.g., lonely and happy) one at a time, and the participants' task is to recall, for each word, the first memory that comes to mind. The speed of participants' responses in generating memories to the negative and positive cue words serves as the dependent variable. Depressed persons have been found to be faster to recall memories to negative than to positive cues. A number of researchers argued that this difference could be due to the possibility that depressed persons have experienced more recent negative than positive events in their lives (e.g., MacLeod & Mathews, 1991; Mathews & MacLeod, 1994). Consequently, investigators have moved away from this methodology and have begun to present the same standardized emotional stimuli to depressed and nondepressed participants in the laboratory and examine their memory for these stimuli.

Memory for Experimental Stimuli

Laboratory studies examining memory biases in depression have typically utilized one of two types of encoding tasks in ensuring that participants process the stimuli presented to them: a self-rating task and an imagination task. In both of these tasks, participants receive words that differ in emotional valence and are asked to encode these words in reference to themselves. In the self-rating task, participants are asked to rate emotionally valenced adjectives with respect to how well the words describe them. In contrast, in the imagination task, participants are presented with emotionally valenced words one at a time and are asked, for each word, to imagine a scene that involves both themselves and the word.

As noted earlier, investigators have assessed explicit and implicit memory for the stimuli that participants were required to encode. In studies examining explicit memory biases in depression, after the encoding task, participants are asked either to write down as many stimuli as they can remember from the encoding task (i.e., free recall procedure), or to complete word stems with words from the encoding task (i.e., cued-recall procedure). In studies examining implicit memory biases in depression, participants are asked, following the encoding task, either to make perceptual judgments as quickly as possible of words that were or were not presented in the encoding task (i.e., lexical decision task), or to complete word stems of old and new words with the first word that comes to mind (i.e., word completion task).

Measures of explicit and implicit memory differ with respect to whether stimuli that were encoded are intentionally recalled. Measures of explicit memory require participants to recall directly material presented in the encoding task and involve conscious control. In contrast, measures of implicit memory assess nonintentional recall of items from memory and do not explicitly refer to stimuli presented in the encoding task. Typically, in implicit memory measures, learning of the material presented earlier is inferred when performance on the presented stimuli is better than task performance involving new stimuli (Roediger & McDermott, 1992; see Richardson-Klavehn & Bjork, 1988, for a review of tests of implicit and explicit memory).

ATTENTIONAL BIASES IN DEPRESSION

According to the cognitive models of depression described earlier, depressed individuals should encode negative stimuli more quickly and efficiently than they do positive stimuli. Thus, depressed (and depression-vulnerable) individuals should: (a) experience interference when trying to ignore the semantic content of negative words on the Stroop task; (b) make a greater number of shadowing errors or exhibit longer latencies on a secondary reaction-time task on a dichotic listening task when they are attempting to ignore negative words that are presented to the unattended ear; (c) be faster to detect dot-probes that appear in the spatial location of negative than of positive words; and (d) perceive color bars that replace negative words as appearing first on an attention deployment task. However, empirical support for these predictions is equivocal.

Findings From Studies Using the Stroop Task

Several researchers have reported results indicating that depressed individuals exhibit longer latencies to name the ink color of depressotypic stimuli than of other, nondepressed, words. In the first study to use a Stroop task with depressed individuals, Gotlib and McCann (1984) found that subclinically depressed college students took longer to name the color of depressed-content than of manic-content words. This pattern of results was not observed in the nondepressed control participants; indeed, the nondepressed participants did not respond differentially to either word type. These results were subsequently replicated by both Klieger and Cordner (1990) and Williams and Nulty (1986), and by Gotlib and Cane (1987) in a sample of clinically depressed psychiatric patients. It is important to note, however, that other researchers failed to find evidence in depressed individuals of an attentional bias for depressotypic information on the Stroop task. For example, Hill and Knowles (1991) examined the response latencies of depressed individuals to name the colors of self-esteem threatening nouns, as well as nouns with unpleasant or pleasant connotations. Depressed individuals in this study exhibited elevated response latencies to all three types of emotional stimuli, calling into question the specificity to negative stimuli of an attentional bias in depressed persons. Other researchers, too, have failed to find evidence of increased interference for negative words in depressed participants (e.g., Mogg, Bradley, Williams, & Mathews, 1993; Williams & Broadbent, 1986).

Findings From Studies Using the Dichotic Listening Task

McCabe and Gotlib (1993) used a dichotic listening task to examine attentional bias in depressed participants. In this version of the task, participants were required to shadow neutral words in the attended ear while positive-content, negative-content, and neutral-content distractor words were presented in the unattended ear. In addition, in a secondary reaction-time task, participants were required to press a button whenever a light in front of them was illuminated. McCabe and Gotlib found that depressed participants took longer to respond on the secondary reaction-time task when the light appeared during the presentation of negative-content distractor words than when positive-content or neutral-content distractor words were presented; nondepressed participants did not exhibit this pattern of attentional functioning. This finding indicates that depressed participants had fewer attentional resources to devote to the secondary reaction-time task when negative-content words (that they were attempting to ignore) were playing in the unattended channel, suggesting that depressed individuals are less able than nondepressed controls to ignore negative stimuli.

In a similar study, Ingram, Bernet, and McLaughlin (1994) examined performance on a dichotic listening task of nondepressed and formerly depressed (but currently nondepressed) participants. Ingram et al. also included a negative mood induction procedure in this study in an attempt to prime attentional biases in the formerly depressed participants. (We discuss the importance of this priming procedure in a later section of this chapter.) In the neutral (unprimed) condition, there was no difference in the shadowing performance of nondepressed and formerly depressed participants. In contrast, however, when exposed to a negative mood-induction procedure, formerly depressed individuals exhibited elevated attention to emotional stimuli; this pattern was not observed in nondepressed participants exposed to a negative mood-induction procedure. Thus, consistent with Teasdale's (1988) formulation, individuals who are vulnerable to depression appear to respond to a negative mood state differently than do nonvulnerable individuals.

Findings From Studies Using the Dot-Probe Task

Initial investigations using the dot-probe task failed to find an attentional bias for negative words in depressed individuals (e.g., Hill & Dutton, 1989; MacLeod, Mathews, & Tata, 1986). More recently, researchers discussed the possibility of a confound in this task. Because dot probes appeared on only one third of the trials, participants may have become aware of the association between the presentation of a negatively valenced stimuli and the subsequent presentation of a dot probe. Importantly, when investigators modified the dot-probe task by presenting a dot probe on each trial, rather than on only one third of the trials, they obtained a different pattern of results. The results of these more recent investigations indicated that depressed participants exhibit an attentional bias for negative words (Mathews, Ridgeway, & Williamson, 1996; Mogg, Bradley, Millar, & White, 1995). Similarly, Westra and Kuiper (1997) used this dot-probe task with carefully selected stimuli, and they also found that depressed individuals differentially allocate their attention to negative stimuli.

Findings From Studies Using the Deployment of Attention Task

The results of studies that used the deployment of attention task also report differences between depressed and nondepressed participants; the pattern of these differences, however, is not the same as that typically obtained in investigations of attentional biases in depression. In these studies, it is nondepressed participants who demonstrate an attentional bias away from negative stimuli, whereas depressed participants are even-handed in their attention to positive and negative stimuli. This pattern of findings has now been reported in samples of mildly depressed university students (Gotlib, McLachlan, & Katz, 1988; Mogg et al., 1993) and clinically depressed participants (McCabe & Gotlib, 1995). The even handedness of depressed individuals, combined with the avoidance of negative stimuli exhibited by nondepressed person, is consistent with a view of depressed persons as having lost the positive bias that characterizes nondepressed persons (see Alloy & Abramson, 1979, for a similar perspective).

MEMORY BIASES IN DEPRESSION

Findings From Studies Examining Explicit Memory

Given the confound in studies just described, using autobiographical memory to investigate memory biases in depression, it is not surprising that the pattern of results obtained in those studies differs somewhat from that obtained in studies in which the number and type of material encoded and recalled is controlled by presenting participants with preselected stimuli. Whereas autobiographical memory studies typically find that depressed persons exhibit poor recall for positive material, laboratory studies using structured stimuli and an incidental recall paradigm consistently report that depressed individuals recall more negative-content than positive-content words (cf. Blaney, 1986). For instance, Denny and Hunt (1992) used a self-rating explicit memory task with clinically depressed and nondepressed participants and found that the depressed participants recalled significantly more of the negatively than the positively valenced items from the rating task; nondepressed participants exhibited exactly the opposite pattern of bias. Virtually identical results for both depressed and nondepressed participants were also reported by Watkins, Mathews, Williamson, and Fuller (1992). In fact, Matt, Vazquez, & Campbell (1992) recently conducted a meta-analysis of 30 studies that examined the explicit recall of emotionally valenced material in nondepressed, mood-induced nondepressed, subclinically depressed, and clinically depressed individuals. Matt et al. concluded that biases in explicit memory for negative material are a reliable function of the severity of depression.

Findings From Studies Examining Implicit Memory

In contrast to the results of studies examining depression-associated biases in explicit memory, early investigations generally failed to find biases in implicit memory in depressed participants (see Roediger & McDermott,

1992, for a review of this literature). Researchers disagree in their interpretations of the absence of an implicit memory bias in depressed individuals. Some investigators cite Graf and Mandler's (1984) work, which proposes that explicit memory tasks measure the degree of elaboration of the test material. These researchers argued that the pattern of findings in depression of biases in explicit, but not implicit, memory indicates that these memory biases are occurring at a later, elaborative, stage of information processing, rather than at an early, perceptual stage (e.g., Williams, Watts, MacLeod, & Mathews, 1988).

Results from two lines of research are consistent with this position. First, several studies demonstrated that having participants increase their elaboration during encoding improves their performance on tests of explicit memory, but not on tests of implicit memory (see Richardson-Klavehn & Bjork, 1988, for a review this literature). Second, a number of investigators found that memory biases in depression occur only when the material is self-referentially encoded, which presumably means that the material is encoded with greater elaboration (e.g., MacLeod & Mathews, 1991). Other researchers contend, however, that studies of depression-associated biases in implicit memory are difficult to interpret because implicit memory tasks typically involve two different types of processing in the encoding of stimuli and memory for the material; whereas the encoding tasks in these studies involve *conceptual processing* (i.e., focusing on the meaning of the stimuli), the retrieval tasks involve *perceptual processing* (i.e., matching word stems or number of letters; cf. Roediger & McDermott, 1992). Consequently, these researchers argued that the results of these studies may not adequately examine whether depression is characterized by biases in implicit memory. More recent studies examined performance on tasks using only conceptual (and not perceptual) processing. In these investigations participants are asked to engage in conceptual processing at encoding (e.g., by imagining a scene involving themselves and the stimulus item) as well as at retrieval (e.g., produce as many one-word associations for various cue words, rather than completing independent fill-in-the-blanks or word-stem items). Interestingly, these studies obtained evidence for depression-associated negative biases in implicit memory (e.g., Bradley, Mogg, & Williams, 1994; Watkins, Vache, Verney, & Mathews, 1996).

EVALUATION, CONCLUSIONS, AND FUTURE DIRECTIONS

The use of information-processing paradigms to examine biases in attention and memory in depression represents a significant improvement over earlier self-report methodologies. Nevertheless, the results of these studies raise a number of important questions and issues. In general terms, the most consistent findings come from research examining biases in explicit memory: Depressed persons almost invariably demonstrate better memory for negative than for positive stimuli, and this pattern is not exhibited by nondepressed participants. The findings concerning depression-associated biases in attentional functioning are less consistent: Depressed individuals are often found to demonstrate selective attention to negative stimuli, but this is not always the case. In the final section of this chapter, we discuss a number of possible explanations for these inconsistencies, as well as several of the issues raised by this research. We then conclude with a discussion of what we believe are important future directions for research in this area.

Discrepancies Across Studies

When the findings of these studies are considered collectively, there seem to be four factors that may help to explain the inconsistencies in this body of research. First, attentional biases in depression are likely influenced by a high level of comorbid anxiety (Gotlib & Cane, 1989; Gotlib & MacLeod, 1997; Williams et al., 1988; see also Bradley, Mogg, Millar, & White, 1995). Indeed, Williams et al. formulated a model of cognitive biases in emotional disorders in which they hypothesize that anxiety, rather than depression, is responsible for biases in attention. Moreover, the results of recent research suggests that, as stimulus presentation durations become shorter, approaching subliminal levels, anxious, but not depressed, participants continue to exhibit attentional biases (e.g., Bradley et al., 1995; Mathews et al., 1996). Thus, it is possible some of the inconsistencies may be due to the effects on attentional functioning of different levels of (unreported) anxiety across studies.

Second, attentional biases in depression are almost certainly a function of the relevance of the stimuli to the concerns of depressed individuals. The more strongly that stimuli reflect depressed individuals' concerns, the more probable it is that investigators will find attentional biases in depression. It is likely, therefore, that some of the inconsistencies in this area of research are due to varying quality of matches across those studies between the stimuli used and the concerns of the depressed participants. For example, Hill and Dutton (1989) used pleasant and unpleasant stimuli that do not appear to be particularly relevant to depression, and they did not find depression-associated biases in attention; as noted earlier, other studies that have used stimuli more relevant to depression found attentional biases in depressed individuals (e.g., Gotlib & Cane, 1987; Gotlib & McCann, 1984; Westra & Kuiper, 1997).

Third, it is beginning to appear that attentional biases in depressed individuals are influenced by whether the task or paradigm involves the presentation of more than one stimulus for the participant to process and, therefore, allows distinct processing options. For example, whereas studies using the original dot-probe task failed to find an attentional bias for depressed individuals (e.g., Hill & Dutton, 1989; MacLeod et al., 1986), the two most recent studies using a modification that creates a forced choice reaction-time task on each trial both found clear attentional biases in depressed individuals (Mathews et al., 1996; Mogg et al., 1995). Investigators have not explicitly examined the impact of processing options on the production of attentional biases in depressed participants, and this appears to be a promising direction for future research.

The fourth factor that may contribute to the inconsistencies across studies examining attentional biases in depression is whether the processing task implicitly encourages the use of a guessing strategy. For example, the deployment of attention task, in which participants are required to indicate which of two simultaneously presented color bars they perceived as occurring first, yields findings indicating an evenhandedness in the attentional functioning of depressed participants. Interestingly, some researchers using this task report that a substantial number of participants complain that the task is impossible because both color bars seem to appear simultaneously, and they express a reluctance to guess (e.g., Mogg, Matthews, May, & Grove, 1991). Therefore, it is likely that various strategies are employed by participants in making judgments on this task. Thus, the lack of an attentional bias in depressed participants and the positive attentional bias in nondepressed individuals may be reflecting different approaches to making judgments in an ambiguous situation rather than different patterns of attentional processing of emotional information. At the present time, we cannot distinguish between these two possibilities, but this is clearly an important question for future research.

Content Specificity

The cognitive theories described earlier posit that attentional and memory biases associated with depression (and with anxiety) are due to specific associations of the words with features of the disorder, rather than to the more general negative tone of the words. In one of the first examinations of content specificity of attentional biases in depression, Williams and Broadbent (1986) compared the Stroop performance of patients who had recently attempted suicide by overdose, hospital control patients, and nonhospital participants. Their results indicated that the patients who attempted suicide by overdose showed greater attentional bias for words that were specifically related to aspects of a suicidal overdose (e.g., *drug*) than for words associated more generally with depression (e.g., *lonely*), suggesting that Stroop findings reflect specificity of the stimuli. More recently,

Westra and Kuiper (1997) examined the content specificity of attentional allocation using a dot-probe task across four domains of maladjustment (i.e., depression, anxiety, bulimia, and Type A personality). Westra and Kuiper found the most consistent support for content-specificity effects in depression: Depressed participants allocated their attention differentially toward stimuli related to themes of hopelessness and loss.

Similar findings have been obtained by investigators examining stimulus specificity in memory biases in depression. For example, Watkins et al. (1992) found that depressed participants demonstrated enhanced recall for negative material that was depression-relevant, but not for negative material that was relevant to physical threat (see also Bellew & Hill, 1990). Interestingly, the memory bias in depression appears not only to be specific to depressotypic concerns, but further, to depend on whether the stimulus material is encoded with respect to the self. As noted earlier, research suggests that depressed individuals exhibit negative biases in explicit memory more consistently when they are required to encode the presented stimuli as self-referent (e.g., Clark & Teasdale, 1985; Denny & Hunt, 1992; Kuiper, Olinger, MacDonald, & Shaw, 1985; see also Matt et al., 1992).

Causality and Stability

The three major cognitive theories of depression described earlier differ somewhat in their hypotheses concerning whether depression-associated biases in attention and memory represent a vulnerability factor for depression, or alternatively, reflect a cognitive response to a negative mood state. Most explicitly, perhaps, Beck (1967) postulated that negative cognitive biases represent a stable vulnerability factor for depression that play a causal role in the onset of clinical depression. Bower's (1981) associative network theory suggests that memory biases observed in depression are due primarily to the depressed individual's current negative mood state, with specific memories being activated by negative mood. Finally, taking a middle position, Teasdale (1988) suggested that cognitive biases in depression are a function of both an enduring vulnerability to depression and a more transient negative mood state.

Clearly, studies comparing cognitive biases in currently depressed participants and nondepressed controls cannot address the issue of causality, given the likely confounding in depressed participants of high levels of both state and trait emotion. Consequently, researchers utilized several different strategies in attempts to separate the relative contributions of state and trait emotion. For example, Gotlib and Cane (1987) used the Stroop task to assess attentional biases in depressed patients both during episode and following discharge from hospital, and they found that although depressed patients demonstrated increased interference to negative words when they were in episode, they no longer showed differential response latencies to negative-content, neutral-content, or positive-content words following discharge. A similar pattern of results was obtained in a subsequent longitudinal study using a dichotic listening task (McCabe & Gotlib, 1993), as well as in crosssectional comparisons of formerly and never depressed individuals using a Stroop task (Gilboa & Gotlib, 1997; Hedlund & Rude, 1995).

Although these findings may suggest that attentional bias is due simply to transient negative mood in depression, the results of other studies suggest that this is not the case. Gotlib and McCann (1984), for example, found no differences in patterns of Stroop interference among participants in whom transient depressed, elated, or neutral mood had been induced. Moreover, Williams and Nulty (1986) found that Stroop interference to negative words was better predicted by levels of depression 12 months prior to testing than by current levels of depression. In an intriguing study, MacLeod and Hagan (1992) presented evidence that an attentional bias for threatening events predicted subsequent emotional reactions to a stressful life event. In this study, women awaiting an appointment for a colposcopy test for cervical pathology participated in a Stoop task with threat and neutral words. The degree of attentional interference to threat words was found to be the single best predictor of the emotional response 8 weeks later for the 15 women who received a diagnosis of cervical pathology. Finally, in a study described earlier, Ingram et al. (1994) examined the performance of previously depressed and never depressed individuals on a dichotic listening task, and presented data suggesting that attentional biases may be reinstated in previously depressed individuals through a negative mood-induction procedure. Importantly, a negative mood induction had no effect on the attentional processing of individuals who were not previously depressed (i.e., nonvulnerable subjects). These findings replicate Gotlib and McCann's (1984) earlier demonstration of the inability of negative mood to lead to cognitive biases among never-depressed participants. This pattern of findings indicates that depression-vulnerable individuals respond to a negative mood state differently than do nonvulnerable persons (cf. Teasdale, 1988) and suggests that negative attentional biases, when primed, or activated by negative mood, may play a role in placing particular individuals at risk for experiencing more severe depression.

Studies examining the causal status and stability of memory biases in depression have yielded inconsistent results. For example, both Slife, Miura, Thompson, Shapiro, and Gallagher (1984) and Dobson and Shaw (1987) found that memory biases disappear following recovery from a depressive episode. In other studies, however, depression-associated memory biases have been found to persist following recovery from depression, particularly if the depressive schemata or associative networks are reactivated or primed through some form of negative mood induction (cf. Gilboa & Gotlib, 1997; Hedlund & Rude, 1995; Teasdale & Dent, 1987). This pattern of findings suggests that the negative memory bias exhibited by depressed individuals may be a function both of mood and of more stable cognitive structures (see also Clark & Teasdale, 1982).

Interestingly, there is also now evidence that memory biases may predict the onset or course of depressive symptoms. Bellew and Hill (1991) found that pregnant women who demonstrated a recall bias for self-esteem-threatening words and who later experienced stressful life events had higher levels of depression at 3 months postpartum than did women who experienced comparable levels of stress, but who had not exhibited a negative recall bias during pregnancy. Similarly, Dent and Teasdale (1988) found that the number of negative trait words that depressed women endorsed as self-descriptive and recalled on an incidental recall task predicted how severely depressed they were 5 months later. Finally, Brittlebank, Scott, Williams, and Ferrier (1993) followed a sample of depressed patients for 7 months and found that overgeneral recall on an autobiographical memory test at the initial assessment predicted the course of depression and, importantly, was also highly correlated with failure to recover from depression. Thus, there is evidence to suggest that, under the particular experimental conditions, biases in attention and memory functioning can be reactivated in some formerly depressed patients, suggesting that these biases remain active between depressive episodes among a subgroup of depression-prone individuals. Furthermore, data from a small number of studies indicate that these biases may play a role in affecting the duration and the severity of depression. It remains for future research to delineate these particular experimental conditions and depressed individuals more systematically and explicitly.

Future Directions

In this final section of the chapter, we discuss what we believe are three important directions for future research to undertake: the examination of inhibitory processes that may underlie attentional biases in depression, the elucidation of precisely what symptoms of depression are most strongly associated with specific biases in attention and memory, and the consideration of developmental aspects of cognitive biases in depression.

Inhibitory Processes. The cognitive theories of depression described in this chapter essentially predict that depressed individuals encode and/or recall negative stimuli more quickly and efficiently than they do positive stimuli. In developing the theories that lead to this prediction, Beck, Bower, and Teasdale all focused on the activation, or excitation, of cognitive processes. Recently, however, cognitive theorists conceptualized attention and memory as involving not only an excitatory process, but an inhibitory process as well. Thus, in addition to this excitatory process, an inhibitory mechanism is hypothesized to enhance the excitatory process by preventing or inhibiting distracting information from being processed further (e.g., Houghton & Tipper, 1994; Neumann & Deschepper, 1992). According to this view of selective attention, all stimuli are first identified and processed to semantic levels of analysis. Then, an excitatory and an inhibitory process occur simultaneously. Whereas the excitatory process acts on stimuli that are selected for further processing, the inhibitory process actively suppresses further processing of irrelevant stimuli. Therefore, efficient selection is achieved not only by enhancing the availability of selected information, but also by suppressing, or inhibiting, irrelevant or to-be-ignored information. As would be expected, this dual process serves to facilitate responses to selected information and to slow responses to irrelevant information (e.g., Milliken, Tipper, & Weaver, 1994; Tipper, Weaver, Kirkpatrick, & Lewis, 1991).

Considering this dual-process view of attentional functioning against the background of Beck's, Bower's, and Teasdale's theories, it is likely that depressed individuals are characterized by an inhibitory bias for negative stimuli. The logic of this hypothesis is relatively simple: When negative stimuli are presented to depressed individuals as distractors, these stimuli are relatively more activated and, thus, more easily accessed. This greater activation would require greater inhibition on the part of depressed persons to ignore the negative distractors. Indeed, research manipulating the level of activation of the distractor stimulus in a negative priming (i.e., inhibition) task supports this positive relation between the level of activation of the to-be-ignored stimulus and the magnitude of inhibition (Malley & Strayer, 1995). We have conducted an initial study in our laboratory examining inhibitory biases for negative stimuli in depressed and formerly depressed participants (Neubauer & Gotlib, 1998). We developed a negative priming information-processing task that allowed us to examine specific activation and inhibition processes that are implicated in attentional functioning in depression.

In this task, a trial consists of two consecutive displays. Each display contains a target stimulus and a distractor stimulus, presented one above the other, with one stimulus presented in green ink and the other in red ink. For each display, participants are required to name the target (e.g., the word in red) and ignore the distractor (e.g., the word in green). On *interference* trials within this task, an emotionally valenced stimulus is presented as a distractor in the first display, with unrelated neutral stimuli appearing in the target position of the first display, as well as in the target and distractor positions of the second display. Thus, on the first display of interference trials, participants are required to name a neutral word while ignoring an emotional word. These trials provide information concerning how difficult depressed individuals find it to ignore negative stimuli and select a neutral stimulus for further processing. Like the predictions of the Stroop and dichotic listening tasks, depressed individuals are expected to show increased interference and, thus, show increased response latency for negative stimuli on this task. In contrast, on *inhibition*, or *negative priming*, trials within this task, an emotionally valenced distractor stimulus in the first display also appears as the target stimulus in the second display. Unrelated neutral stimuli are presented in the remaining positions of these two displays. Consequently, on the second display of these negative priming trials, participants are required to name a target stimulus that they had just attempted to ignore. Individuals who inhibit the distractors on the first display should take more time to respond to these stimuli when they are presented as targets on the subsequent display because it takes longer to access and activate an inhibited representation. If depressed individuals are able to successfully inhibit the negative stimulus, then they should show an increase in inhibition that is proportional to the initial activation of the representation.

Neubauer, Thomas, and Gotlib (1997) found that both currently and previously depressed individuals demonstrated significantly more interference and inhibition for negative-content than for positive-content words. In contrast, never-depressed individuals showed equivalent levels of interference and inhibition for both types of stimuli. These findings provide important information concerning selective attention processes in depression. As noted earlier, cognitive theories of depression hypothesize that depression is associated with increased activation of negative cognitive structures and, consequently, with facilitated processing of negatively valenced information. This negative priming study extends the findings from the Stroop and dichotic listening tasks by demonstrating not only that depression is associated with facilitated processing of negative stimuli, but furthermore, that this processing is followed immediately by increased inhibition of that stimulus. Certainly, this finding must be replicated in future studies, but it appears that depression is characterized by both increased interference for, and subsequent inhibition of, negative-content stimuli.

Association of Specific Symptoms With Specific Biases. There is little question from results of studies reviewed in this chapter that individuals who are experiencing elevated levels of depressive symptoms (and, for that matter, symptoms of anxiety) are characterized by negative biases in attention and/or memory. Moreover, it appears that persons who are vulnerable to becoming depressed can also exhibit these biases when they are experiencing negative affect. A second important direction for future research is to examine whether there are specific symptoms of depression and/or anxiety that are more strongly related to biases in attention and memory than are other symptoms. It seems clear that both subclinical and clinically significant levels of depression are associated at least to some extent with cognitive biases. What is less clear is whether there is a specific constellation of depressive symptoms that is most strongly associated with biases in attention and/or memory.

Alloy, Abramson, Hogan, Murray, and Whitehouse (1997) recently reported promising results indicating that participants who were identified as cognitively vulnerable by virtue of obtaining high scores on self-report measures of depressotypic cognitions in the absence of significant depressive symptoms were characterized by negative biases on self-referent information-processing tasks. Although not fully developed by Alloy et al., it may be that when cognitively vulnerable individuals become depressed, they exhibit a specific constellation of symptoms of depression that is different from that manifested by depressed persons who are not characterized by cognitive biases. Moreover, given the similarity across a number of studies in the nature of cognitive biases that are associated with both depression and anxiety, it is possible that this symptom constellation will include a number of symptoms that are common to depression and anxiety, such as dysphoric mood and rumination or worry (cf. Gotlib & Cane, 1989). In the same vein, however, it is important to recognize that investigators also reported differences in information processing between depressed and anxious participants (e.g., MacLeod et al., 1986; Neubauer et al., 1997). For example, Watkins et al. (1992) found depression, but not anxiety, to be associated with a bias in explicit memory. It may be the case more specifically, therefore, that different patterns of cognitive biases are associated with different symptom patterns. It remains for future research to examine this possibility more explicitly.

Developmental Considerations. The results of epidemiological studies of the incidence and prevalence of depression in children and adolescents highlight the need to gain a better understanding of this disorder in these age groups. Recent figures indicate a point prevalence of depression in adolescents of 8% (Kashani, Carlson, Beck, & Hoeper, 1987) and a lifetime prevalence of 20% (Lewinsohn, Hops, Roberts, Seeley, & Andrews, 1993). In addition to these high rates of diagnosable depression in adolescence, there is an extraordinary level of self-reported depression and unhappiness in the teenage years. In his Isle of Wight study, for example, Rutter (1966) found that depressed feelings were reported by 12% of boys when they were 10 to 11 years old, but jumped to 40% among the same youngsters when they were 14 to 15 years of age. Adding to the gravity of these figures, several investigators now documented the adverse effects of depression during adolescence on psychosocial functioning in adulthood. For example, individuals whose first episode of depression occurred at an early age have been found to experience a more negative, severe, and long-lasting course of depression than have individuals whose first depressive episode occurred later in their lives (e.g., Bland, Newman, & Orn, 1986; Hammen, Davila, Brown, & Ellicott, 1992). Moreover, Gotlib, Lewinsohn, and Seeley (1998) documented the adverse effects of depression during adolescence on subsequent marital satisfaction.

Clearly, it is important for researchers to understand the nature of depression in children and adolescents. Unfortunately, most of the research examining depression-associated cognitive biases in younger populations focused on the content rather than the function of negative cognitions in these age groups, and has also, for the most part, utilized self-report measures (cf. Garber & Robinson, 1997). A few studies, however, examined memory biases for negative and positive material in depressed and nondepressed children. The results of these investigations indicate that depressed children do not exhibit the positive memory bias demonstrated by nondepressed children (e.g., Prieto, Cole, & Tageson, 1992; Whitman & Leitenberg, 1990).

Although studies such as these have yielded promising results, there remain a number of important issues concerning the role of cognitive biases in depression in children and adolescents. First, further research with depressed children and adolescents is required to elucidate the role of cognitive biases in the development of depression. We noted earlier that this is an important question in adult samples; we believe that examining this issue in children will yield significant information concerning the function of cognitive biases in affecting the course of depression. Second, future studies in this area could profitably examine the origins of cognitive biases in depressed children; that is, are the cognitive biases that have been found to be associated with depression learned from significant persons in the child's immediate environment, or alternatively, do they represent an emotional response that is an integral part of the disorder (Gotlib & MacLeod, 1997)?

Finally, studies are required to examine whether (and how) cognitive biases that are associated with depression develop and change over the life span. Vasey (1993) argued that associative memory networks change with age. He suggested that the associative network of a young child contains few specific events, but becomes more intricate, richly developed, and detailed with age. Consequently, cognitive models might predict that the nature and quantity of thoughts produced by depressed mood should also differ with age. Indeed, Vasey predicted that younger children should respond to a negative mood state with a relatively narrow attentional bias, and that attentional biases in children should begin to resemble those observed in adults as children age and their associative networks become more fully developed. In our laboratory, we are currently examining the nature and concordance of cognitive biases exhibited by depressed children and their parents. The results of this research could have important implications for our understanding of the development of cognitive biases over the life course.

In this chapter, we provided an overview of the diverse range of information-processing tasks currently used by researchers examining the nature of cognitive biases, both in depressed individuals and in persons who are at elevated risk for depression. We also presented broad findings that were obtained with these tasks, and we discussed implications of these findings for our understanding of the cognitive functioning of depressed persons. Finally, we outlined three important directions for future research in this area. In closing, we emphasize that a comprehensive theory of depression will undoubtedly go beyond an exclusive focus on information processing to also include a consideration of social and biological factors (cf. Gotlib, Kurtzman, & Blehar, 1997). Only by integrating the knowledge obtained through the use of the kinds of information-processing tasks described in this chapter with the results of studies examining biological and social functioning in depression can we begin to develop effective programs for the prevention and treatment of this disorder.

REFERENCES

Alloy, L. B., & Abramson, L. Y. (1979). Judgement of contingency in depressed and nondepressed students: Sadder but wiser? *Journal of Experimental Psychology: General, 108,* 441–485.

Alloy, L. B., Abramson, L. Y., Hogan, M. E., Murray, L. A., & Whitehouse, W. G. (1997). Self-referent information-processing in individuals at high and low cognitive risk for depression. *Cognition and Emotion, 11,* 539–568.

Anderson, J. R., & Bower, G. H. (1973). *Human associative memory.* New York: Halsted.

Beck, A. T. (1967). *Depression: Clinical, experimental, and theoretical aspects.* New York: Harper & Row.

Beck, A. T. (1976). *Cognitive therapy and the emotional disorders.* New York: International Universities Press.

Bellew, M., & Hill, A. B. (1990). Negative recall bias as a predictor of susceptibility to induced depressive mood. *Personality & Individual Differences, 11,* 471–480.

Bellew, M., & Hill, A. B. (1991). Schematic processing and the prediction of depression following childbirth. *Personality & Individual Differences, 12,* 943–949.

Belsher, G., & Costello, C. G. (1988). Relapse after recovery from unipolar depression: A critical review. *Psychological Bulletin, 104,* 84–96.

Bland, R. C., Newman, S. C., & Orn, H. (1986). Recurrent and nonrecurrent depression: A family study. *Archives of General Psychiatry, 43,* 1085–1089.

Blaney, P. H. (1986). Affect and memory: A review. *Psychological Bulletin, 99,* 229–246.

Blehar, M. C., & Oren, D. A. (1995). Women's increased vulnerability to mood disorders: Integrating psychobiology and epidemiology. *Depression, 3,* 3–12.

Bower, G. H. (1981). Mood and memory. *American Psychologist, 36,* 129–148.

Bower, G. H. (1987). Commentary on mood and memory. *Behaviour Research & Therapy, 25,* 443–455.

Bradley, B. P., Mogg, K., Millar, N., & White, J. (1995). Selective processing of negative information: Effects of clinical anxiety, concurrent depression, and awareness. *Journal of Abnormal Psychology, 104,* 532–536.

Bradley, B. P., Mogg, K., & Williams, R. (1994). Implicit and explicit memory for emotional information in non-clinical subjects. *Behaviour Research & Therapy, 32,* 65–78.

Brittlebank, A. D., Scott, J., Williams, J. M., & Ferrier, I. N. (1993). Autobiographical memory in depression: State or trait marker? *British Journal of Psychiatry, 162,* 118–121.

Clark, D. M., & Teasdale, J. D. (1982). Diurnal variation in clinical depression and accessibility of memories of positive and negative experiences. *Journal of Abnormal Psychology, 91,* 87–95.

Clark, D. M., & Teasdale, J. D. (1985). Constraints on the effects of mood and memory. *Journal of Personality and Social Psychology, 48,* 1595–1608.

Denny, E. B., & Hunt, R. R. (1992). Affective valence and memory in depression: Dissociation of recall and fragment completion. *Journal of Abnormal Psychology, 101,* 575–580.

Dent, J., & Teasdale, J. D. (1988). Negative cognition and the persistence of depression. *Journal of Abnormal Psychology, 97*(1), 29–34.

Dobson, K. S., & Shaw, B. F. (1987). Specificity and stability of self-referent encoding in clinical depression. *Journal of Abnormal Psychology, 96*(1), 34–40.

Garber, J., & Robinson, N. S. (1997). Cognitive vulnerability in children at risk for depression. *Cognition and Emotion, 11,* 619–635.

Gilboa, E., & Gotlib, I. H. (1997). Cognitive biases and affect persistence in previously dysphoric and never-dysphoric individuals. *Cognition and Emotion, 11,* 517–538.

Gotlib, I. H., & Abramson, L. Y. (1999). Attributional theories of emotion. In T. Dalgleish & M. Power (Eds.), *The handbook of cognition and emotion* (pp. 613–636). Chichester, England: Wiley.

Gotlib, I. H., & Cane, D. B. (1987). Construct accessibility and clinical depression: A longitudinal investigation. *Journal of Abnormal Psychology, 96,* 199–204.

Gotlib, I. H., & Cane, D. B. (1989). Self-report assessment of depression and anxiety. In P. C. Kendall & D. Watson (Eds.), *Anxiety and depression: Distinctive and overlapping features* (pp. 131–169). Orlando, FL: Academic Press.

Gotlib, I. H., & Hammen, C. L. (1992). *Psychological aspects of depression: Toward a cognitive-interpersonal integration.* Chichester, England: Wiley.

Gotlib, I. H., Kurtzman, H. S., & Blehar, M. C. (1997). Cognition and depression: Issues and future directions. *Cognition and Emotion, 11,* 663–673.

Gotlib, I. H., Lewinsohn, P. M., & Seeley, J. R. (1998). Consequences of depression during adolescence: Marital status and marital functioning in early adulthood. *Journal of Abnormal Psychology, 107,* 686–690.

Gotlib, I. H., & MacLeod, C. (1997). Information processing in anxiety and depression: A cognitive developmental perspective. In J. Burack & J. Enns (Eds.), *Attention, development, and psychopathology* (pp. 350–378). New York: Guilford.

Gotlib, I. H., & McCabe, S. B. (1992). An information-processing approach to the study of cognitive functioning in depression. In E. F. Walker, B. A. Cornblatt, & R. H. Dworkin (Eds.), *Progress in experimental personality and psychopathological research* (Vol. 15, pp. 131–161). New York: Springer.

Gotlib, I. H., & McCann, C. D. (1984). Construct accessibility and depression: An examination of cognitive and affective factors. *Journal of Personality and Social Psychology, 47,* 427–439.

Gotlib, I. H., McLachlan, A. L., & Katz, A. N. (1988). Biases in visual attention in depressed and nondepressed individuals. Special Issue: Information processing and the emotional disorders. *Cognition & Emotion, 2,* 185–200.

Graf, P., & Mandler, G. (1984). Activation makes words more accessible, but not necessarily more retrievable. *Journal of Verbal Learning and Verbal Behaviour, 23,* 553–568.

Hammen, C., Davila, J., Brown, G., & Ellicott, A. (1992). Psychiatric history and stress: Predictors of severity of unipolar depression. *Journal of Abnormal Psychology, 101,* 45–52.

Hedlund, S., & Rude, S. S. (1995). Evidence of latent depressive schemas in formerly depressed individuals. *Journal of Abnormal Psychology, 104,* 517–525.

Hill, A. B., & Dutton, F. (1989). Depression and selective attention to self-esteem threatening words. *Personality & Individual Differences, 10,* 915–917.

Hill, A. B., & Knowles, T. H. (1991). Depression and the "emotional" Stroop effect. *Personality & Individual Differences, 12,* 481–485.

Houghton, G., & Tipper, S. P. (1994). A model of inhibitory mechanisms in selective attention. In D. Dagenbach & T. Carr (Eds.), *Inhibitory mechanisms in selective attention, memory, and language* (pp. 53–112). San Diego, CA: Academic Press.

Ingram, R. E., Bernet, C. Z., & McLaughlin, S. C. (1994). Attentional allocation processes in individuals at risk for depression. *Cognitive Therapy & Research, 18,* 317–332.

Kashani, J. H., Carlson, G. A., Beck, N. C., & Hoeper, E. W. (1987). Depression, depressive symptoms, and depressed mood among a community sample of adolescents. *American Journal of Psychiatry, 144,* 931–934.

Keller, M. B., Lavori, P. W., Mueller, T. I., Endicott, J., Coryell, W., Hirschfeld, R. M. A., & Shea, T. (1992). Time to recovery, chronicity, and levels of psychopathology in major depression: A 5-year prospective follow-up of 431 subjects. *Archives of General Psychiatry, 49,* 809–816.

Keller, M. B., & Shapiro, R. W. (1981). Major depressive disorder. Initial results from a one-year prospective naturalistic follow-up study. *Journal of Nervous and Mental Disorders, 169,* 761–768.

Kessler, R. C., McGonagle, K. A., Swartz, M., & Blazer, D. G. (1993). Sex and depression in the National Comorbidity Survey: I. Lifetime prevalence, chronicity and recurrence. Special Issue: Toward a new psychobiology of depression in women. *Journal of Affective Disorders, 29,* 85–96.

Klieger, D. M., & Cordner, M. D. (1990). The Stroop task as measure of construct accessibility in depression. *Personality & Individual Differences, 11,* 19–27.

Kuiper, N. A., Olinger, L. J., MacDonald, M. R., & Shaw, B. F. (1985). Self-schema processing of depressed and nondepressed content: The effects of vulnerability to depression. *Cognitive Therapy and Research, 8,* 443–478.

Lewinsohn, P. M., Hops, H., Roberts, R. E., Seeley, J. R., & Andrews, J. A. (1993). Adolescent psychopathology: I. Prevalence and incidence of depression and other DSM–III–R disorders in high school students. *Journal of Abnormal Psychology, 102,* 133–144.

MacLeod, C., & Hagan, R. (1992). Individual differences in the selective processing of threatening information, and emotional responses to a stressful life event. *Behaviour Research & Therapy, 30*(2), 151–161.

MacLeod, C., & Mathews, A. (1991). Biased cognitive operations in anxiety: Accessibility of information or assignment of processing priorities. *Behaviour Research & Therapy, 29,* 599–610.

MacLeod, C., Mathews, A., & Tata, P. (1986). Attentional bias in emotional disorders. *Journal of Abnormal Psychology, 95,* 15–20.

Malley, G. B., & Strayer, D. L. (1995). Effect of stimulus repetition on positive and negative identity priming. *Perception & Psychophysics, 57*(5), 657–667.

Mathews, A., & MacLeod, C. (1994). Cognitive approaches to emotion. *Annual Review of Psychology, 45,* 25–50.

Mathews, A., Ridgeway, V., & Williamson, D. A. (1996). Evidence for attention to threatening stimuli in depression. *Behaviour Research & Therapy, 34,* 695–705.

Matt, G. E., Vazquez, C., & Campbell, W. K. (1992). Mood-congruent recall of affectively toned stimuli: A meta-analytic review. *Clinical Psychology Review, 12,* 227–255.

McCabe, S. B., & Gotlib, I. H. (1993). Attentional processing in clinically depressed subjects: A longitudinal investigation. *Cognitive Therapy & Research, 17,* 359–377.

McCabe, S. B., & Gotlib, I. H. (1995). Selective attention and clinical depression: Performance on a deployment-of-attention task. *Journal of Abnormal Psychology, 104,* 241–245.

Milliken, B., Tipper, S. P., & Weaver, B. (1994). Negative priming in a spatial localization task: Feature mismatching and distractor inhibition. *Journal of Experimental Psychology: Human Perception & Performance, 20*(3), 624–646.

Mogg, K., Bradley, B. P., Millar, N., & White, J. (1995). A follow-up study of cognitive bias in generalized anxiety disorder. *Behaviour Research & Therapy, 33,* 927–935.

Mogg, K., Bradley, B. P., Williams, R., & Mathews, A. (1993). Subliminal processing of emotional information in anxiety and depression. *Journal of Abnormal Psychology, 102*(2), 304–311.

Mogg, K., Mathews, A., May, J., & Grove, M. (1991). Assessment of cognitive bias in anxiety and depression using a colour perception task. *Cognition & Emotion, 5*(3), 221–238.

Mueller, T. I., Keller, M. B., Leon, A. C., Solomon, D. A., Shea, M. T., Coryell, W., & Endicott, J. (1996). Recovery after 5 years of unremitting major depressive disorder. *Archives of General Psychiatry, 53,* 794–799.

Neubauer, D. L., & Gotlib, I. H. (1998). *Selective attention in currently and formerly depressed individuals: The role of interference and inhibition.* Unpublished manuscript, Stanford University, Stanford, CA.

Neubauer, D. L., Thomas, R. C., & Gotlib, I. H. (1997). *The role of elaboration and inhibition in memory biases associated with depression and anxiety.* Unpublished manuscript, Stanford University, Stanford, CA.

Neumann, E., & Deschepper, B. G. (1992). An inhibition-based fan effect: Evidence for an active suppression mechanism in selective attention. *Canadian Journal of Psychology, 46,* 1–40.

Prieto, S. L., Cole, D. A., & Tageson, C. W. (1992). Depressive self-schemas in clinic and nonclinic children. *Cognitive Therapy & Research, 16,* 521–534.

Richardson-Klavehn, A., & Bjork, R. A. (1988). Measures of memory. *Annual Review of Psychology, 39,* 475–543.

Roediger, H. L., & McDermott, K. B. (1992). Depression and implicit memory: A commentary. *Journal of Abnormal Psychology, 101,* 587–591.

Rutter, M. (1966). *Children of sick parents: An environmental and psychiatric study.* Oxford, England: Oxford University Press.

Slife, B. D., Miura, S., Thompson, L. W., Shapiro, J. L., & Gallagher, D. (1984). Differential recall as a function of mood disorder in clinically depressed patients: Between- and within-subject differences. *Journal of Abnormal Psychology, 93,* 391–400.

Teasdale, J. D. (1988). Cognitive vulnerability to persistent depression. Special Issue: Information processing and the emotional disorders. *Cognition & Emotion, 2,* 247–274.

Teasdale, J. D., & Dent, J. (1987). Cognitive vulnerability to depression: An investigation of two hypotheses. *British Journal of Clinical Psychology, 26,* 113–126.

Tipper, S. P., Weaver, B., Kirkpatrick, J., & Lewis, S. (1991). Inhibitory mechanisms of attention: Locus, stability, and relationship with distractor interference effects. *British Journal of Psychology, 82*(4), 507–520.

Titchener, E. B. (1908). *Lectures on the elementary psychology of feeling and attention.* New York: MacMillan.

Vasey, M. W. (1993). Development and cognition in childhood anxiety: The example of worry. *Advances in Clinical Child Psychology, 15,* 1–39.

Watkins, P. C., Mathews, A., Williamson, D. A., & Fuller, R. D. (1992). Mood-congruent memory in depression: Emotional priming or elaboration? *Journal of Abnormal Psychology, 101,* 581–586.

Watkins, P. C., Vache, K., Verney, S. P., & Mathews, A. (1996). Unconscious mood-congruent memory bias in depression. *Journal of Abnormal Psychology, 105,* 34–41.

Westra, H. A., & Kuiper, N. A. (1997). Cognitive content specificity in selective attention across four domains of maladjustment. *Behaviour Research and Therapy, 35,* 349–365.

Whitman, P. B., & Leitenberg, H. (1990). Negatively biased recall in children with self-reported symptoms of depression. *Journal of Abnormal Child Psychology, 18,* 15–27.

Williams, J. M. G., & Broadbent, K. (1986). Distraction by emotional stimuli: Use of a Stroop task with suicide attempters. *British Journal of Clinical Psychology, 25,* 101–110.

Williams, J. M. G., & Nulty, D. D. (1986). Construct accessibility, depression, and the emotional Stroop task: Transient mood or stable structure? *Personality and Individual Differences, 7*(4), 485–491.

Williams, J. M. G., Watts, F. N., MacLeod, C., & Mathews, A. (1988). *Cognitive psychology and emotional disorders.* Chichester, England: Wiley.

Chapter 8

Affective Distress as a Central and Organizing Symptom in Depression: Psychological Mechanisms

Walter D. Scott
Ray W. Winters
Christopher G. Beevers
University of Miami

As discussed in the Introduction of this volume, clinical depression presents as a multifaceted but coherent pattern of symptoms.[1] This coherency is more than a construction in the minds of psychopathology researchers. Multivariate statistical procedures confirm that a general set of cognitive, affective, behavioral, and vegetative symptoms tend to cooccur as clusters in depressive episodes (Blashfield & Morey, 1979; Eaton, Dryman, Sorenson, & McCutcheon, 1989; Grove & Andreason, 1989). Experienced in isolation, each of these symptoms is capable of generating significant distress and dysfunction. However, when experienced in combination, their cumulative impact is felt as a maelstrom that soon spirals the depressed individual into feelings of futility and despair (Karp, 1996).

One of the most challenging tasks for depression researchers is to unravel this maelstrom. The fact that depressive symptoms cluster suggests the operation of underlying causal processes responsible for their common grouping. What are the nature of these causal processes that bind symptoms in depression? Why is it that feelings of sadness tend to accompany such diverse symptoms as anhedonia, poor concentration, psychomotor retar-

[1]Specifically, the DSM–IV criteria for a major depressive episode require that either depressed mood or anhedonia be evident nearly every day, most of the day, for a 2-week period and during that same period, at least four of the following symptoms must also be present: *psychomotor retardation, sleep disruption, difficulties in thinking and concentration, changes in appetite and weight, fatigue, negative self evaluations and feelings of worthlessness,* and *suicidal ideation or plans.*

dation, pessimism, brooding, and hopelessness? How can any presumed causal process or processes linking such symptoms explain symptom clustering even when there appear to be diverse causes that lead to depression?

To better understand the inner dynamics of the depressive episode, Costello (1992a, 1993a) has argued for the advantages of a symptom-focused approach. This is not the usual research strategy. Studies examining depression more typically proceed by comparing groups of depressed and nondepressed individuals, where group status is based on whether a sufficient subset of symptoms are present. Theoretical models of causal processes are then inferred based on group differences. Although analyzing group differences is a valid and useful research strategy, it does lead to several problems, including the issue of within-group heterogeneity in depressive symptoms. The heterogeneity in depression becomes obvious when one considers that most of the nine DSM–IV depressive symptoms possess multiple variants. For example, sleep disturbance can include insomnia or hypersomnia. When these symptom variants are taken into account, there are actually 16 specific depressive symptoms. If research is limited to comparing groups of depressed and nondepressed individuals, or even to examine variables prospectively that predict future depression group status, this kind of extensive within-group symptom heterogeneity will necessarily limit progress in explaining how specific symptoms causally relate to each other. As a result, we will be less able to specify tight explanatory theories of depressive episodes (Costello, 1993b). This problem was highlighted in the 1992 Consensus Development Conference on Cognitive Models of Depression, where the need to circumvent problems of symptom heterogeneity by studying specific symptoms and symptom interrelations was one of the conference's consensual recommendations (Segal & Dobson, 1992).

In this and the following chapter, we focus on the symptom of affective distress, exploring the relations that exist between it and several other prominent and associated symptoms in depression. We maintain that persistent affective distress is a central and organizing symptom in depression. Clearly there are multiple causes of depression that can include the environment (e.g., impoverished socioeconomic background and high incidence of negative life events), medical disorders (e.g., premenstrual depression, postpartum depression, hypothyroidism, and Cushing's syndrome), genetically based individual differences in temperament (e.g., sensitivity to signals of reward and punishment), behaviors (e.g., low engagement in pleasant activities, poor social or interpersonal skills, and poor sleep and diet habits), and thinking patterns, to name but a few. Each of these causes, however, has been associated with persistent affective distress, which, we argue, serves as a sufficient proximal cause that can account for the cooccurring cognitive, behavioral, and vegetative symptoms of depression.

We begin this chapter by providing our definition of affective distress. We then present several arguments and empirical findings consistent with the notion that affective distress functions as a central, organizing symptom in depression. In the remainder of this chapter, we describe several psychological mechanisms that are responsible for the persistence and influence of affective distress. We include an account of how affective distress causally relates to other depressive symptoms. The role of neurobiological mechanisms in affective distress and their relations to specific depressive symptoms is the topic of the following companion chapter (chap. 9, this volume).

DEFINING AFFECTIVE DISTRESS

Emotion researchers usually define *affect* as a biologically based process that consists of several prototypical components (Ekman & Davidson, 1994). These components include a *cognitive appraisal process,* in which an individual attaches meaning to events that may have harmful or beneficial consequences for well-being. These meanings can vary in the degree to which they involve automatic or controlled information processing (Lazarus, 1991). The cognitive appraisal process is viewed as triggering changes in both the *pattern of physiological arousal* and in the *state of action readiness* to respond in a particular manner (e.g., to withdraw, flee, or attack). Finally, the affective response may be communicated by *overt expressive features,* especially in facial movements, which are more or less susceptible to controlled psychological processes.

Emotion researchers also make qualitative distinctions between different affective states. In describing these differences, one of two complementary approaches is usually taken: discrete or dimensional.

The Discrete Emotion Approach

Researchers taking a discrete emotion approach have identified several distinct biologically based categories of emotion. Although there is some disagreement over the number and names of these emotion categories, a strong case can be made for the following list: sadness, fear, anger, disgust, and happiness (Ekman, 1992; Smith & Lazarus, 1990). For each of these emotion categories, discrete emotion researchers have found evidence of specificity for each of the prototypical components, including cognitive appraisals (Roseman, Spindel, & Jose, 1990; Smith & Lazarus, 1990), physiological arousal patterns (Ekman, Levenson, & Friesen, 1983; Levenson, Ekman, & Friesen, 1990; Schwartz, Weinberger, & Singer, 1981), action tendencies (Frijda, Kuiper, & ter Schure, 1989), and expressive behaviors (e.g., facial expressions; Ekman, 1989). In the affective distress associated with depression, people most often report high levels of sadness, but they can also report elevated levels of fear–anxiety and anger–irritability. The relative profiles of this depression triumvirate can vary both between individuals and within an individual from moment to moment.

The Dimensional Emotion Approach

An alternative approach to the study of affect focuses on broad mood factors rather than distinct categories of emotions (Watson & Tellegen, 1985). Two factors emerge from factor analytic studies examining self-reports of current mood state: positive affect and negative affect (Watson, Clark, & Tellegen, 1988). These factors are characterized as orthogonal, although they are slightly negatively correlated at extremely high levels of intensity. Individuals in a state of high positive affect report a broad range of positive mood states such as excitement, enthusiasm, cheerfulness, self-confidence, pleasure, and alertness. In contrast, low positive affect is associated with sluggishness, low energy, and lack of interest in the environment. People experiencing high negative affect report being irritable, distressed, upset, nervous, dissatisfied with life, and discouraged. Individuals with low negative affect characterize themselves as calm and relaxed. In depressive episodes, people report combinations of low positive affect and high negative affect, although states of low positive affect appear to be particularly distinctive (Watson, Clark, et al., 1995; Watson, Weber, et al., 1995).

THE CENTRALITY OF AFFECTIVE DISTRESS IN DEPRESSION

As a symptom of depression, the centrality of affective distress is acknowledged to some extent by both the DSM–IV and the International Statistical Classification of Diseases and Related Health Problems–Tenth Edition (ICD–10). In DSM–IV, persistent (for 2 weeks) affective distress is one of the two entry criterion symptoms (the other entry symptom being anhedonia), of which only one must be present. ICD–10 describes distressed mood as the fundamental disturbance in each of the mood disorders. Depressed mood is also the most frequent (Judd, Rapaport, Paulus, & Brown, 1994) and the most reliably diagnosed of all the depressive symptoms (Costello, 1993a). Yet, why do we argue for the centrality of the symptom of affective distress as opposed to some other frequently occurring symptom of depression, such as sleep impairment or anhedonia? We now present several arguments and review empirical evidence supporting the proposal that affective distress is a central symptom in depressive episodes.

Arguments Supporting the Centrality of Affective Distress

Affect Is an Integrative Construct That Uniquely Explains Diverse Depressive Symptoms. In selecting a symptom for investigation, Costello (1993a) has recommended that researchers "choose a focal symptom for investigation . . . on the basis of some theory about the nature of depression and the role played by the symptom in the natural history of depression" (p. 293). Given the broad psychological, biological, and behavioral spectrum of symptoms that emerge in a depressive episode, a symptom-focused approach, in which a single symptom was viewed as central and organizing, would need to integrate across multiple levels of analysis. In this regard, the symptom of affective distress is somewhat unique. By definition, *affect* is an organizing process that integrates perceptual, cognitive, physiological, motivational, and behavioral systems (Ekman & Davidson, 1994). The nature of these organizational processes and mechanisms constitutes a large portion of the research agenda pursued by affect scientists. Therefore, not only is affective distress ideally suited as a construct for explaining multiple levels of symptom disturbance, but it is also the focus of a large and growing empirical literature that is shedding some light on the specific nature of these organizational processes. This literature potentially can inform how affective distress relates to specific depressive symptoms.

The Components of Sadness Parallel Depressive Symptoms. Typically, the most elevated discrete emotion in depression is sadness. Interestingly, the prototypical components and organizational characteristics of sadness mirror many of the processes and symptoms experienced in depression. For instance, sadness is instigated by cognitive appraisals of irrevocable loss (Smith & Lazarus, 1990). In clinical depression, life events that signify loss, particularly loss to self-identify or self-worth, are those most often associated with depression onset (Finlay-Jones & Brown, 1981; Paykel & Cooper, 1982). Studies examining rumination in depression also find that themes of personal loss and failure are prominent (Clark, Beck, & Beck, 1994). In terms of physiology and action tendencies, sadness is associated with psychomotor retardation and behavioral withdrawal (Frijda, 1986; Shaver, Schwartz, Kirson, & O'Connor, 1987). Both psychomotor retardation and behavioral withdrawal are frequent symptoms observed in depression as well (DSM–IV). In terms of behavior, crying is one of the characteristic expressions of sadness (Frijda, 1986; Plutchik, 1980; Shaver et al., 1987).

Crying episodes also happen to be one of the more distinguishing symptoms of depressive episodes (Clark et al., 1994).

Evidence Supporting the Centrality of Affective Distress

Experimentally Inducing Affective Distress Leads to Depression-Like Symptoms. Some of the strongest evidence supporting affective distress as a central symptom in depression comes from studies in which affective distress is experimentally induced in nonclinical populations. After the induction of affective distress, these otherwise normal individuals exhibit a number of depressive-like symptoms. They have a memory bias for negative self-information, recalling more unpleasant personal memories (Teasdale & Fogarty, 1979; see Matt, Vazquez, & Campbell, 1992) and more unfavorable personal feedback (Esses, 1989; Ingram, 1984a). They attend more to unfavorable self-information (Forgas & Bower, 1987; Mischel, Ebbesen, & Zeiss, 1973). They exhibit a general negative evaluative judgmental bias (Mayer, Gaschke, Braverman, & Evans, 1992), rating themselves lower on positively valued personality traits, such as intelligence, and higher on negatively valued personality traits, such as unfriendliness (Brown & Mankowski, 1993). When shown videotapes of their own social performances, they evaluate their social behaviors as more unskilled, incompetent, withdrawn, and antisocial, whereas objective judges rate them more favorably (Forgas, Bower, & Krantz, 1984). They are more dissatisfied with their lives (Schwarz & Clore, 1983) and the world (Forgas & Moylan, 1987; Isen, Shalker, Clark, & Karp, 1978). They rate imagined activities as less pleasant (Carson & Adams, 1980; Cunningham, 1988; Snyder & White, 1982) and they are more pessimistic about the future (Forgas & Moylan, 1987; Wright & Mischel, 1982). They also perceive less social support from others (Cohen, Towbes, & Flocco, 1988; Vinokur, Schul, & Caplan, 1987). In short, they tend to experience a constellation of diverse cognitive, motivational, and behavioral symptoms that parallel depressive symptoms, albeit in less persistent forms (Sedikides, 1992).

Affective Distress Appears to Be Prerequisite for Negative Cognitive Symptoms in Depression. Depressed individuals think more negatively about themselves, the future, and the world than do nondepressed people. In fact, negative thinking is so characteristic of depression that some have argued it should be considered along with "high probability of recurrence, running in families, and the like as facts about depression than any adequate theory ought to explain" (Haaga, Dyck, & Ernst, 1991, p. 232). These same authors, however, noted the mood-state dependence of these negative cognitive features in depression. Many studies have found that dysfunctional beliefs, critical self views, and negatively valenced information processing appear only when the depressed person is experiencing affective distress (see Gotlib & Neubauer, chap. 7, this volume; Segal & Ingram, 1994).

The Symptom of Affective Distress Appears as One of the First Symptoms in the Developing Depressive Episode. Understanding the temporal sequence of symptom occurrence in a depressive episode potentially reveals clues about the causal mechanisms that presumably link the various symptoms (Costello, 1993a). If affective distress is a central and organizing symptom that can causally determine the appearance of subsequent depressive symptoms, then it should be one of the first symptoms to appear in a developing depressive episode. We are aware of only one study that investigated the temporal sequence of depressive symptoms while not confounding depressed mood and anhedonia.[2] In that study, Young and Grabler (1985) administered the SADS (Endicott & Spitzer, 1978) to 11 hospitalized patients with current depressive episodes. After completing the SADS, each patient was given a set of index cards with each card describing a single symptom that was present for that individual in his or her current depressive episode. The patients were then told to arrange these cards to represent the order of symptom onset. Symptoms that the patients said occurred simultaneously were put into the same stack. The findings indicated that depressed mood tended to be the first symptom to present in a developing depressive episode.

The Presence of Affective Distress Appears Critical in Minor Depressive Conditions in Conferring Clinical Levels of Dysfunction. The importance of affective distress as an organizing symptom in depression is also supported in studies that compared characteristics of minor depressive conditions in which the symptom of affective distress was either present or not. *Minor depression* refers to a condition in which a number of depressive symptoms are present, but there are not enough symptoms to meet criteria for major depressive disorder. These studies show that sad, blue, or depressed mood may be a critical symptom in determining the extent of dysfunction in people with more minor depressive conditions (see Flett, Vredenburg, & Krames, 1997). For example, Broadhead, Blazer, George, and Tse (1990) compared groups of individuals who either had minor depression with mood disturbance or minor depression without mood disturbance. *Minor depression with mood disturbance* was found to more closely resemble clinical depression on several measures of disability and social dysfunction, including presence of comorbid anxiety disorders, increased number of missed work days, and greater

---

[2]Studies that have emerged from the U.S. National Institute of Mental Health Epidemiologic Catchment Area program have examined which depressive symptoms were most predictive of a first full major depressive episode at a follow-up period (e.g., Dryman & Eaton, 1991). These studies, however, utilized the Diagnostic Interview Schedule (DIS), which confounds anhedonia with dysphoric mood and therefore does not permit conclusions about the unique role of affective distress.

incidence of future clinical depressive episodes. In regards to the latter, 10% of those participants who had minor depression with mood disturbance developed a full-blown major depression by a 1-year follow-up interview. In contrast, only 1.8% of those participants who had minor depression without mood disturbance developed a major depression by the 1-year follow-up. These findings have to be qualified, however, in that the mood disturbance criterion was confounded because it included affective distress or anhedonia.

Other studies have compared dysfunction in patients with adjustment disorder with depressed mood to patients with clinical depression (Bronisch & Hecht, 1989; Despland, Monod, & Ferrero, 1995; Fabrega, Mezzich, Mezzich, & Coffman, 1986; Snyder, Strain, & Wolf, 1990). In reviewing this literature, Flett, Vredenburg, and Krames (1997) concluded: "By and large, these studies suggest that adjustment disorders with depressed mood were quite comparable [with major depression] in terms of the degree of comorbidity with other diagnoses, gender ratio, and presence of comorbid medical conditions" (p. 400).

The importance of affective distress in more minor forms of depression is also implicated in studies investigating compromised immune functioning in depression. Weisse (1992) reviewed the literature examining immune functioning in clinical and nonclinical forms of depression (i.e., separation and bereavement). She found that impaired immune functioning, particularly as evidenced by decreased lymphocyte response to mitigens, was associated with both clinical and nonclinical depressions. Moreover, it was the intensity of the symptom of affective distress that appeared to account for these relations. Similar findings were reported by Herbert and Cohen (1993) in their meta-analytic review of depression and immune functioning. Specifically, these authors concluded that there appeared to be a linear association between the intensity of affective distress as a symptom and impairment in immune system functioning.

Early Improvement of Affective Distress With Antidepressants Predicts Improvement in Depression. Although antidepressants typically ameliorate each of the symptoms in a depressive episode (Casper et al., 1994; Healy, 1987; Worthington et al., 1995), there is some evidence that improvement in affective distress predicts improvement in other symptoms. Casper et al. (1994) examined the timing and pattern of symptom changes as depressed patients received antidepressant medications (either amitriptyline or imipramine). Although the first symptom to improve was difficulty falling asleep (i.e., initial insomnia), this occurred for both drug responders and nonresponders alike, and consequently did not predict improvement in other depressive symptoms. Moreover, the improvement in sleep was attributed to a sedative effect of the tricyclic antidepressants. It was only change in affective distress that was associated with improvement in depressive symptoms, including complete normalization of sleep and improvement in appetite, weight, and sexual interest.

AN OVERVIEW OF THE AFFECTIVE DISTRESS MODEL OF DEPRESSION: SAD, HOSTILE, AND ANXIOUS AFFECTIVE DIMENSIONS

We have argued that *persistent* affective distress is a central symptom in depression and can generate additional depressive symptoms. Yet, we all experience negative emotions such as sadness, anger, and fear. What are the characteristics that lead certain individuals to experience more persistent affective distress episodes? How does persistent affective distress lead to additional depressive symptoms? Finally, are different qualitative states of persistent affective distress associated with different depressive symptoms? These are the questions addressed in the remainder of this chapter.

We present an overview of affective distress processes in depression in Figure 8.1. In this model, neurobiological, environmental, and psychological processes are viewed as influencing the persistence of affective distress at both distal and proximal ends of the causal continuum. In terms of distal causal factors, we argue that temperament, early stressful life events, and development of cognitive schemata create vulnerabilities for discrete forms of persistent affective distress. By *temperament*, we refer to neurobiological circuits or neurotransmitter systems that have been identified in both animal and human research (see chap. 9, this volume). These circuits or transmitter systems are viewed as contextually activated systems that are associated with distinct behavioral tendencies and specific qualities of affective distress. By contextually activated, we mean that these temperament systems are not static, but respond to particular life circumstances and, in turn, are influenced by those circumstances (Rothbart & Ahadi, 1994). Although there are inherited individual differences in the baseline operation of these neurobiological systems, they may also develop in response to particular life events and/or cognitive styles. Furthermore, both environment and temperament influence, and are influenced by, cognitive schemata. *Cognitive schemata* refer to generalized beliefs about the self, others, or the world.

Due to the reciprocally influencing relations among temperament, events, and cognition (Bandura, 1986), we believe that each of these systems gradually converge over the course of development into distinctive affective dimensions. Each of these affective dimensions promote a specific type of bias in information processing, which results in a proneness toward appraising and generating life events that tap the dimension's specific vulnerabilities (see Hammen, chap. 5, this volume). As a result of generating particular events and making particular appraisals, the individual is

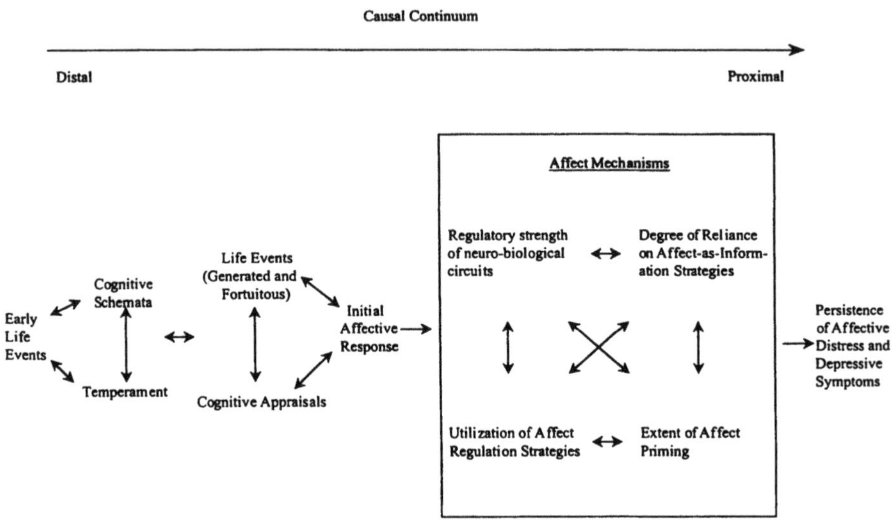

FIG. 8.1. Model of affective distress as a central and organizing symptom in depression.

prone to particular kinds of initial affective responses. The frequency and intensity of these affective responses is determined by temperamental, cognitive, behavioral, and environmental factors. Whether initial affective responses persist and subsequently influence the appearance of other depressive symptoms is viewed as depending on the operation of affective mechanisms—neurobiological and psychological—as well as moderators of those mechanisms. The key neurobiological mechanism is the regulatory strength of the specific circuit or transmitter system involved. These mechanisms are explained in depth in the following chapter (chap. 9, this volume). Although inherited individual differences play a role in establishing different set points for these regulatory systems, their strength is also impacted by such proximal moderators as the quality of sleep and diet (i.e., tryptophan), medical illness, additional negative life events, and antidepressants. Psychological mechanisms also determine whether affective distress persists and is the focus of a later section in this chapter.

In Table 8.1, we outline three affective dimensions that we believe are critical to understanding affective distress in depression. We argue that each of these affective dimensions is associated with specific depressive symptom profiles. Although not universally present, persistent sadness–dejection is certainly the prototypical affective dimension in depression. In terms of neurobiological factors, the sadness–dejection dimension is viewed as related to the sensitivity of dopamine neurons located in the ventral tegmental area of the brain. Low baseline levels of dopamine sensitivity in this circuit are associated with low positive affect and low behavioral ap-

TABLE 8.1
Symptom Profiles of Sadness, Hostile, and Anxious Depression

Affective Dimension	*DSM–IV Symptoms*		*Non-DSM–IV Associated Symptoms*
Persistent Sadness–Dejection	• Anhedonia • Psychomotor retardation • Fatigue and low energy • Poor thinking, slow decision making • Negative self-cognition • Hopelessness	• Hypersomnia • Weight loss • Feelings of worthlessness • Suicidal thinking	• Perseveration • Self-blame, Self-criticism
Persistent Hostility–Irritability	• Psychomotor agitation • Suicidal behaviors • Middle, terminal insomnia • weight gain		• High impulsivity • Early onset of REM • Increased pain sensitivity • Other-blame, Other-criticism • Emotional lability • Enhanced startle reflex • Inappropriate and decreased social behaviors • Altered circadian rhythms • Craving for high fat foots
Persistent Fear–Anxiety	• Initial insomnia • Feelings of guilt • Weight loss • Decreased concentration		• Worrying

proach. We argue that this neurobiological circuit tends to converge with the development of negative self schemata or beliefs about the self. This convergence may result from inherited low baseline levels of dopamine sensitivity, or these low baseline levels of dopamine may be a response to particular stressful life events, learning experiences, and/or cognitive styles. Regardless, the sadness–dejection affective dimension makes one prone toward generation and appraisal of irrevocable loss events; these events then maintain and intensify sadness–dejection affective states.

A second affective dimension, persistent anger–irritability, is related to low levels of the neurotransmitter serotonin. We believe that this neurobiological substrate converges with the development of negative other schemata, or negative beliefs about other people. Similar to the sadness–dejection dimension, this convergence may result from multiple causal pathways. The anger–irritability affective dimension makes one prone to blaming others and leads to generating life events in which such appraisals are likely. As a result, anger–irritability affective states are maintained and intensified.

Finally, a third affective dimension, persistent fear–anxiety, involves a neurobiological circuit that operates through the amygdala. Specifically, the functioning of this circuit reflects the ratio of norepinephrine to serotonin neurotransmitters, and the level of activity in an aversive motivational system. We believe these neurobiological features converge with the development of danger schemata or beliefs that the world is dangerous. Once again, as with the sadness–dejection and anger–irritability dimensions, this convergence can result from several different causal pathways. The fear–anxiety affective dimension is associated with being prone toward appraising and generating life events as threatening and dangerous, leading to the maintenance and intensification of fear–anxiety affective states.

Whether any particular acute episode of sadness, anger, or fear persists and causes the appearance of additional depressive symptoms depends on the operation of specific affect mechanisms and moderators of those affect mechanisms. With persistence of affective distress, however, we believe there is an increased likelihood of involvement and convergence across all neurobiological, cognitive, behavioral, and environmental systems.

A basic implication of our model is that each of these three affective dimensions (i.e., sadness–dejection, anger–irritability, and fear–anxiety) will be associated with specific depressive symptom profiles. In Table 8.1, we list the symptoms that we believe will be associated with sadness–dejection, anger–irritability, and fear–anxiety, respectively. Our list includes a number of symptoms, some of which are listed in DSM–IV's definition of depression, others of which have been associated with depression in clinical research, and a few of which we believe on a theoretical basis (given the neurobiological and psychological affective mechanisms involved) will be associated. The rationale for these predictions becomes clearer after we describe the psychological and neurobiological mechanisms (for a discussion of the latter, see chap. 9, this volume) that we propose lead to the emergence of these symptoms.

PSYCHOLOGICAL MECHANISMS OF PERSISTENT AFFECTIVE DISTRESS

Affect exerts its influence by means of multiple mechanisms (Forgas, 1995). In this chapter, we focus on two psychological mechanisms—affect priming and affect as information. Although not intended to be inclusive, we believe that these mechanisms are involved in the persistence of affective distress in depression-vulnerable individuals and can account for many of the observed relations between affective distress and specific depressive symptoms. Moreover, these mechanisms suggest several moderator variables that may function as risk factors. Following discussion of these psychological affective mechanisms and moderators, we describe how they relate to specific symptoms in depression.

The Affect Priming Mechanism

Affective distress has a priming effect on similarly valenced cognition. Just as the presentation of a category word (e.g., *tree*) cues the recall of previously learned category members (e.g., *elm, spruce*), affective distress facilitates recall of previously associated negatively valenced memories (Blaney, 1986; Matt et al., 1992; Singer & Salovey, 1988). In addition, affective distress primes self knowledge, online thinking, judgments, and associations with the same negative affective valence (Blaney, 1986; Matt et al., 1992; Mayer et al., 1992; Sedikedes, 1992; Singer & Salovey, 1988). In an attempt to explain these affect priming findings, Bower (1981, 1987, 1991) proposed that emotions be viewed as special nodes embedded within a general semantic memory network (see Gotlib & Neubauer, chap. 7, this volume, for a full discussion).

Moderators of Affect Priming

Bower's affect priming mechanism suggests specific moderators of whether affect priming leads to persistent affective distress and additional depressive symptoms.

Excessive Negative Self Knowledge. According to Bower's model, when affective distress occurs, it activates negative emotion nodes that then spread activation through interconnected cognitive networks to make negatively valenced information about the self more accessible. This is true for nondepressives and depressives alike. For individuals who possess more negative self-knowledge, however, affect priming has a greater effect, because there is more negative information to be primed. Therefore, for these cognitively vulnerable individuals, priming makes more negative self-information available for rumination, which further exacerbates and prolongs affective distress. A vicious cycle of increasing rumination and affective distress ensues (Ingram, 1984b). Consequently, the extent of self-knowledge content that is potentially primed moderates whether temporary affective distress subsides or persists, and whether or not it leads to other depressive symptoms.

Degree of Self Complexity. Some people employ too few categories in their self conceptions, and thus lack self complexity. An example would be the athlete who views himself only as an athlete. In contrast, an athlete with higher self complexity might think of himself as an athlete who is also a husband, father, friend, music lover, and a volunteer worker. Linville's work (1985, 1987) suggested that when cognitive representations of the self are too simplistic, a stressful event or significant loss leads to more extreme negative evaluations of the self and to greater affective distress. More complex self conceptions serve to buffer the impact of loss. Several empirical studies have found support for these predictions of the self-complexity model (Dixon & Baumeister, 1991; Linville, 1987; Niedenthal, Setterlund, & Wherry, 1992).

From an affect-priming perspective, a loss for someone with low self complexity threatens one's entire selfhood. In contrast, if one conceives of the self along a number of distinct and nonassociated dimensions, a loss experience in one domain primes only that relevant aspect of self knowledge, leaving a greater number of self aspects unprimed and unaffected. Thus, in states of affective distress, these more cognitively complex individuals can think positively about themselves in unaffected domains. Self complexity, then, may operate as yet another risk factor, or moderator of the consequences of induced affective distress, with those individuals having low self complexity being more susceptible to affect priming effects, and therefore to more persistent affective distress and depressive symptoms.

Organization of Self Knowledge. Sometimes vulnerability to affect priming is due not to the excessively negative content of self knowledge, but rather to the way self knowledge is organized. Showers (1992a, 1992b) proposed that one way in which self knowledge can be organized is in a compartmentalized fashion, in which self beliefs in various domains contain only positive or only negative features. In this type of self-knowledge organization, one's positive self view as a renaissance scholar might contain such exclusively positively valenced features as *curious, disciplined, motivated,* and *creative.* One's compartmentalized negative self belief as a testtaker would include only negatively valenced content, such as *worrying, tense, insecure,* and *competitive.* Self knowledge can also be represented in a more integrative fashion, in which any self belief contains both positive and negative features (e.g., self belief as a humanities student: *creative, insecure, motivated, distracted;* self belief as a science student: *disciplined, competitive, curious, tense*).

The way self knowledge is organized has implications for affect-priming mechanisms. In compartmentalized self schemata, positive emotions facilitate recall of only positive self information. Similarly, however, affective distress would facilitate recall of only negative self information. As long as life events are pleasant and positive, then a compartmentalized organization of self knowledge would be preferable. All individuals, however, experience affective distress from time to time. In these instances, a compartmentalized organization of self knowledge possesses a hidden vulnerability. Namely, because negative self beliefs with compartmentalized organizations contain only negative information, affect priming would activate only negative self information. For the person who possesses compartmentalized self beliefs as a testtaker, for example, affective distress primes only such negative self features as worrying, tense, insecure, and competitive. As a result, such exclusively negative rumination leads to greater intensity and persistence of affective distress. In contrast, individuals who possess integrated self beliefs are able to think of both negative and positive information when experiencing affective distress. As a result, these individuals experience states of affective distress that are both less intense and less persistent. These basic predictions of the self-knowledge organization model have received some empirical support (Showers & Kling, 1996). Therefore, in the face of negative life events, individuals whose self knowledge is organized in a compartmentalized fashion may be most vulnerable to affective distress, as for them, affect priming ought to lead to negative self information exclusively.

Awareness of Affect Priming. The effects of affect priming are not set in stone. Although affective distress tends to promote mood-congruent thinking, conscious awareness of priming influences can curtail and even reverse its effects (Forgas, 1995; Newman & Uleman, 1990). To the extent, then, that an individual is consciously aware of priming influences, he or she has more control over whether mood-congruent priming effects result, and thus, he or she is less susceptible to affective distress contaminating thinking and judgment.

Affect Regulatory Strategies. In response to affective distress and affect priming, individuals engage in a variety of regulatory strategies (Gross & Munoz, 1995). The regulatory strategies that individuals use moderate the extent to which affect priming occurs and influences subsequent thinking and affective distress.

The work of Nolen-Hoeksema (1991) has focused on two such strategies: rumination and distraction. Individuals with a *ruminative* focus tend to contemplate and dwell on various aspects of their affective distress. In contrast, other individuals utilize a variety of *distraction* strategies, such as engaging in pleasant activities. In order to be effective, such distraction strategies need to be engrossing and positively rewarding for the individual. Research has found that individuals who engage in distraction strategies tend to report shorter periods of affective distress compared to those who ruminate (Morrow, 1990). Thus, a mood regulatory strategy of distraction may moderate the influence of affect priming mechanisms.

Another regulatory strategy involves attempting to suppress or not think about either the state of affective distress or the cognitive material primed by affective distress. Research suggests that in either case, suppression can result in ironic consequences, particularly during conditions of cognitive load (Wegner, 1994; Wegner, Erber, & Zanakos, 1993). Beevers and Wenzlaff (1995), for example, asked subclinically depressed individuals to attempt to suppress negative thoughts while under a cognitive load. The content of thoughts was recorded in a stream-of-consciousness task. These investigators found that suppression under a cognitive load led to more negative thinking and to greater affective distress. In another study, individuals who were asked to suppress their emotional responses to a sad film had increased cardiovascular reactivity compared to individuals who were not asked to hide their emotions (Gross & Levenson, 1997). Avoiding unwanted thoughts or affective distress, particularly at times of stress, may exacerbate affect-priming influences, leading to prolonged negative thoughts and persistent affective distress.

Finally, *emotional disclosure*, or the expression of painful feelings and thoughts, appears to attenuate the persistence and deleterious consequences of affective distress (Pennebaker, 1995). The act of writing about affective distress and painful thoughts has been found to result in a strong sense of relief, both immediately and for extended periods (Pennebaker, 1997a, 1997b). Expressing affective distress also reduces emotional reactivity when the same situation reoccurs (Mendolia & Kleck, 1993). In addition to reducing affective distress, emotional disclosure may have practical benefits as well. Individuals who wrote about their feelings regarding their loss of employment were rehired more quickly (Spera, Buhrfeind, & Pennebaker, 1994). Other research has found emotional disclosure to be associated with improved immune functioning, fewer doctor visits, and better school and work performance (Pennebaker, 1995). These findings suggest that the impact of affect priming may be lessened by expressing both affective distress and the cognition that accompanies such distress.

Affect Priming and Specific Depressive Symptoms

The affect-priming mechanism is particularly suited for explaining how affective distress might lead to cognitive symptoms, such as increasing accessibility to negatively valenced memories, rumination, and self evaluations. These cognitive consequences of affect priming indirectly influence other symptoms in depression as well, such as anhedonia and sleep insomnia.

Cognitive Symptoms. Experimentally inducing affective distress has been shown to lead to negative cognitive symptoms for nondepressed individuals, particularly negative self-referent cognitive symptoms (Blaney, 1986; Mayer et al., 1992; Singer & Salovey, 1988). For those individuals who have excessive negative self information, lack self complexity, possess a compartmentalized self-knowledge organization, or for those who engage in ineffective mood regulatory strategies, affect priming is more likely to bias selective attention, processing, elaborating, and encoding of negative self-referent information (Bower, 1981, 1987; Ingram, 1984b). Consequently, for these vulnerable individuals, affective distress is predicted to launch a cascade of unrealistic negative self evaluations, guilty preoccupations, ruminations, and self criticism.

In addition, the sheer amount of excessive negative self information that becomes accessible for cognitively vulnerable individuals results in high levels of self absorption, an "excessive, sustained, and rigid attention to information emanating from internal sources" (Ingram, 1990, p. 169). Self absorption can lead to maladaptive behaviors in situations that demand externally focused attention, such as performance or social situations that require attention to task demands and social cues, respectively. Thus, the impact of affective distress on self-referent information processing and attention may have important behavioral and social implications as well.

Anhedonia. *Anhedonia*, or the diminished capacity to experience pleasure, is one of the hallmark symptoms of depression. Although behavioral theories emphasize that a reduction in the number of pleasant activities can induce depression, several experimental studies have shown that anhedonia can also be a consequence rather than a cause of affective distress. Carson and Adams (1980) tested the hypothesis that affective distress would cause changes in the perceived enjoyableness of pleasant events as measured by the Pleasant Event Schedule (PES; Lewinsohn & Graf, 1973; Lewinsohn & Libet, 1972). Groups of high- and low-dysphoric participants (measured by the BDI) were randomly assigned to negative, positive, and neutral mood manipulations. Following the mood manipulations, participants completed the PES. As predicted, experimentally inducing a negative mood state reduced the subjective enjoyableness of pleasant activities for both high- and low-dysphoric groups. In fact, for participants assigned to the negative mood condition, there was no significant difference between the dysphoric and nondysphoric groups in their ratings of the pleasantness of activities. These findings have been replicated in a group of nondistressed college students in which inducing negative mood led to significantly less interest in social, leisure, and physical activities (Cunningham, 1988).

In terms of psychological mechanisms, the influence of affective distress on anhedonia can be understood as a consequence of affect priming. Affective distress may prime negative interpretative sets (Bower, 1991) that then lead to negative evaluations of the potential enjoyableness of imagined activities. As a result of primed negative interpretive categories, the individual evaluates the activity as unenjoyable and therefore, lacks the necessary motivation to engage in the activity.

Sleep Disturbances. There is substantial evidence that rumination, which can result from affect priming, is an important determinant of insomnia. Several investigators have found that levels of cognitive activity before sleep predict late sleep onset (Nicassio, Mendlowitz, Russell, & Petras, 1985; Van Egeren, Haynes, Franzen, & Hamilton, 1983). More relevant, however, is research by Borkovec and colleagues (Borkovec, Lane, & Vanoot, 1981; Borkovec, Robinson, Pruzinsky, & DePree, 1983). Specifically, this research has found that insomniacs exhibit presleep cognitive activity that is significantly more negative and worried than that of normal sleepers. The contribution of worry to insomnia has been confirmed in more recent research as well (Watts, Coyle, & East, 1994). To the extent, then, that affect priming generates negative cognitive activity, or worry, prior to sleep, affective distress may indirectly contribute to sleep disturbances in depression, particularly to initial insomnia.

The Affect-as-Information Mechanism

In priming models, affective distress has an indirect influence on cognition: Affective distress primes self knowledge, which then leads to a bias in information processing. Although affect priming can explain many of the cognitive influences of affective distress, there is increasing evidence of another, more direct affective mechanism. Specifically, affective distress appears to directly influence people's evaluations by serving as a source of information (Schwarz & Clore, 1983; Schwarz, 1990). Rather than engage in an effortful, systematic analysis of positive and negative features when evaluating a target, individuals may adopt a "How do I feel about it?" heuristic, relying on the hedonic meaning of their affective states. Affective distress would then lead to negative evaluations. More importantly, preexisting affective distress can combine with any affective responses instigated by the target being judged, thereby exerting an unintended influence on unrelated evaluative judgments. For example, a feeling of dissatisfaction due to the fact that it is raining outside can influence evaluative judgments of overall life satisfaction (e.g., "I'm feeling lousy, I guess I'm dissatisfied with my life;" Schwarz & Clore, 1983; Exp. 2).

Moderators of the Affect-as-Information Mechanism

Affective distress does not necessarily inform unrelated evaluative judgments. The extent to which preexisting affective distress states contaminate subsequent judgments and evaluations depends on several moderator variables.

Affect Attributional Clarity. Individuals are aware of the causes of their moods to varying degrees. Some individuals monitor their moods very closely and are highly aware of the source of any affective distress. These individuals may be described as possessing high affect attributional clarity. Other individuals, in contrast, seem less aware of the antecedents of affective distress, and they can be described as possessing *low affect attributional clarity.* There is increasing evidence that affect attributional clarity moderates the extent to which affective distress contaminates subsequent judgments (Schwarz & Clore, 1983). Recall that they found that weather conditions influenced judgments of life satisfaction. Specifically, participants on rainy days evaluated their lives as less satisfactory. In a second high attributional clarity condition, however, Schwarz and Clore (1983) asked participants what the weather was like prior to asking the life satisfaction question, in effect drawing participant's attention to the rainy weather as a potential cause for their current affective distress. When the weather was highlighted as a possible attribution for mood, the effect of mood on life satisfaction ratings was eliminated. Presumably participants in the high affect attributional clarity condition attributed their affective distress to the rainy weather and thus, discounted the meaning of their distress as relevant to evaluating how satisfied they were with their lives. This discounting effect has been replicated in several other experiments when participants were provided clear attributions for their feeling states (Keltner, Locke, & Audrain, 1993; Schwarz & Clore, 1983, Exp. 1; Scott & Cervone, 1999; Tillema, Cervone, & Scott, in press).

The discounting effect under conditions of high affect attributional clarity suggests that affective distress can contaminate unrelated evaluative judgments, but only to the extent that people fail to make clear attributions for their feelings. The implication is that individuals who chronically fail to link their affective states to external or internal (i.e., some memory representation of a past event) stimuli are those who are most prone to affective distress contaminating subsequent unrelated judgments, which of course can lead to greater persistence of affective distress.

Controlled Information Processing. The affect-as-information mechanism functions as a heuristic, as an automatic process requiring minimal cognitive capacity. As such, Forgas (1995) has argued that affect informational mechanisms will be less apt to operate when individuals are engaged in more controlled, substantive modes of information processing. To the extent that people utilize controlled processing modes, their judgments should be less directly influenced by preexisting affective distress.

Affect-as-Information and Depressive Symptoms

Cognitive Symptoms. The affect-as-information mechanism has been used primarily to describe affective influences on evaluative judgments. When individuals characteristically fail to make clear attributions for their affective states and are prone to using heuristic judgment strategies, affective distress influences self evaluations and judgments of life satisfaction (Forgas, 1995; Schwarz, 1990). Clearly then, the affect-as-information mechanism can potentially explain many of the self-critical evaluations so characteristic of depression. A depressed person who experiences persistent affective distress may interpret these feeling states as meaning that he or she is dissatisfied with important features of the self, the world, and the future (e.g., Beck, 1967). Affect-as-information processes may also contribute to the lower perceived social support, self-esteem, and life satisfaction that is so frequently associated with depression. In addition to these cognitive symptoms, however, affect-as-information processes also may influence two noncognitive depressive symptoms: anhedonia and perfectionism.

Anhedonia. In a series of experiments, Martin, Ward, Achee, and Wyer (1993) provided some initial evidence suggesting that affect-as-informational processes may contribute to the influence of affective distress on anhedonia. Specifically, to induce positive or negative affective states, Martin et al. had nondepressed college students view a distressing film. Following the affective distress manipulation, participants completed a person impression-formation task in which they read a series of cards describing various behaviors of the target person. Within each mood condition, half of the participants were told to continue reading the cards until they "no longer enjoyed" the task and half were told to continue reading until they "had enough information." Interestingly, the influence of affective distress on the time spent reading the cards depended on the stop rule told to participants. When instructed to work on the task until they no longer enjoyed it, participants' affective distress led to less time spent reading the cards. In this condition, participants interpreted their affective distress to mean they were no longer enjoying the task and consequently they quit. In contrast, when instructed to read until they had enough information, participant's affective distress led to more time spent reading the cards, suggesting that in this condition, participants interpreted their affective distress to mean they were dissatisfied with how much information they had.

After replicating these findings using a different task (i.e., listing category exemplars), Martin et al. (1993) argued that the motivational implications of affective states depend on how they are interpreted. One of the implications of this research is that when the situational context involves judging how enjoyable a particular activity is (i.e., "Would you like to go the beach?"), people experiencing affective distress may interpret affective distress to mean that an activity would not be enjoyable, and thus, they would be less likely to elect to engage in the activity. These affect-informational processes, then, may contribute to anhedonia in depression.

Perfectionism. Affect-as-information mechanisms may also play a role in producing a maladaptive self-regulatory pattern sometimes observed in depression. Self-control models of depression propose that depressed individuals set stringent personal standards (Rehm, 1977). Although empirical findings have been somewhat equivocal, the evidence suggests that depression is associated with the adoption of personal standards that are relatively perfectionistic, in the sense of exceeding performance levels viewed as achieveable (Ahrens, 1987). This self-regulatory pattern has pernicious consequences, resulting in increased affective distress, decreased effort and persistence, poorer use of behavioral strategies essential to successful performance on complex tasks, and eventual goal abandonment (Bandura & Cervone, 1983; Cervone & Scott, 1995; Locke & Latham, 1990).

Cervone, Kopp, Schauman, and Scott (1994) found evidence that affective distress may contribute to this self-regulatory pattern. In a series of three experiments, experimentally inducing affective distress led people to adopt higher standards for both academic and social performances. The third experiment suggested that these findings were mediated by an affect-as-information mechanism. Specifically, affective distress led participants to evaluate moderate performance outcomes as dissatisfactory and adopt higher performance standards. The interpretation was that participants relied on their affectively distressed states to evaluate whether they would be satisfied with a moderate performance standard. Induced affective distress informed participants that they were dissatisfied with moderate performance standards, which resulted in the adoption of higher performance standards.

More conclusive evidence that affect-as-information processes were responsible for these findings was recently supplied by Scott and Cervone (1999). In two experiments, affect-as-information theory was tested as the mechanism for affective distress leading to high standards using a discounting manipulation. As predicted, induced affective distress generated higher minimal performance standards except under conditions when the induction procedure was made highly salient. This finding, then, directly supported the hypothesis that an affect-as-information mechanism accounted for the impact of affective distress on performance standards and provides experimental evidence supporting the importance of affect attributional clarity in moderating this relation.

SADNESS, HOSTILE, AND ANXIOUS AFFECTIVE DIMENSIONS IN DEPRESSION

Our focus on affective distress as a fulcrum symptom has implications for theories of depression and specifically argues for identifying sad, hostile, and anxious affective-depressive dimensions. Although our proposal is a theory-based approach, there is some support for these proposed affective dimensions in quantititative approaches, such as in cluster analytic research (Paykel, 1971, 1972). In a review of 11 cluster analytic studies of depression, for instance, Blashfield and Morey (1979) reported that all 11 studies found a retarded or melancholic depressive subtype that corresponds closely to the sadness dimension proposed in this chapter. In the factor analytic research, this melancholic subtype tended to contain more severe depressions, with characteristic symptoms including withdrawal, loss of appetite, psychomotor retardation, hopelessness, and more frequent delusions (only delusions is not included in our sadness dimension cluster). Cluster analytic studies also provide some support for the hostile and anxious depressive dimensions proposed in this chapter (Blashfield & Morey, 1979; Maes, Meltzer, Cosyns, & Schotte, 1994; Overall & Hollister, 1980). Blashfield and Morey (1979) found six studies that reported an anxious–depression cluster and four studies that discovered a hostile–depression cluster. Although there was some variation in the specific symptom constellations across these studies, the symptom profiles generally correspond to the anxious and hostile dimensions proposed in our model.

Convergent support for our sadness dimension can also be found in theoretical and empirical work investigating the hopelessness depression subtype proposed by Abramson, Metalsky, and Alloy (1989). The 12 symptoms proposed for the hopelessness depression subtype closely approximate the symptoms we propose for the sadness depression dimension. Specifically, these hopelessness symptoms include *sad affect, psychomotor retardation, lack of energy, apathy* (not anhedonia), *retarded initiation of voluntary responses, suicide, brooding, sleep disturbance, concentration difficulties, negative self cognitions, lowered self-esteem,* and *dependency.* There have been several empirical studies that have generally supported the proposed hopelessness depression symptom profile (see Abramson, Alloy, & Metalsky, 1995; also Alloy, 1997). Although the proposed symptom cluster of our sadness, depression dimension appears to be very similar to the hopelessness, depression symptom profile, there are a few important differences. In the hopelessness, depression subtype theory, anhedonia is not listed as a symptom. Our sadness dimension, however, includes anhedonia in its symptom profile. Second, hopelessness depression is viewed as having a single, proximal, sufficient, causal variable, namely *hopelessness*—the expectation that highly desired outcomes will not occur or that highly aversive outcomes will occur regardless of one's efforts. Our sadness dimension has multiple proximal causal determinants, only one of which is hopelessness. Finally, it is important to note that whereas in the hopelessness model sadness is a consequence and not a cause of hopelessness, the relation between sadness and hopelessness is bidirectional in our model, with persistent sadness often generating hopelessness.

Other than the few cluster analytic studies, there has been relatively less research examining the anxious and hostile subtypes. In a recent study, Scott, Ingram, and Shadel (1999) investigated whether hostile and sad moods in subclinical depression would be associated with specific cognitive symptoms, namely self-blaming or other-blaming attributions for a personal negative event. Participants were classified as Depressed–Sad if they met criteria for syndromal depression on a short questionnaire, scored above 16 on the BDI, and reported more sad than hostile mood on a measure of mood (i.e., Profile of Mood States; POMS). These same criteria were used to identify a Depressed–Hostile group, with the only difference being that they had to report more hostile than sad mood on the POMS. To ensure stability of depression syndrome and mood profile status (Kendall, Hollon, Beck, Hammen, & Ingram, 1987), participants were readministered these same questionnaires at the time of experimental testing 2 to 4 weeks after the initial screening. Only participants who retained both their original depression syndrome and original mood profile status were included in the study. Participants were classifed as nondepressed if they did not meet criteria for syndromal depression, scored below a 5 on the BDI, and reported the relative absence of sad and hostile mood states on the POMS at the initial screening and the experimental testing session.

The findings generally supported our predictions. Specifically, we (Scott, Ingram, & Shadel, 1999) found that the attributional patterns for negative personal events varied across the three groups. When the predominant mood was hostility, syndromally depressed people were more apt to blame others for negative life events and to view the cause as transient. In contrast, when predominantly sad, although syndromally depressed individuals did not make more internal attributions, they made more global attributions for negative life events. The cognitive features of syndromal depression, therefore, depended on which mood state—sadness or hostility—was the most elevated. In related research, melancholic depressed patients, whose symptoms corresponded closely to the sadness dimension cluster proposed here, were found to make more internal and stable attributions for negative events (Willner, Wilkes, & Orwin, 1990). Overall, these findings provide some preliminary evidence for the cognitive symptoms that we propose are uniquely associated with persistent hostile and sad moods in depression. More generally, these findings suggest that the levels of specific negative moods in depression may reflect specific cognitive profiles and that one cannot rely on a uniform conceptualization of cognition in depression.

FUTURE DIRECTIONS AND CONCLUSIONS

In this chapter we argued that persistent affective distress is a central and organizing symptom in depression that often serves as a sufficient proximal determinant of additional depressive symptoms. Our model also specifies the critical mechanisms and moderator variables that determine whether temporary states of affective distress persist and generate additional depressive symptoms. Future studies need to systematically assess the variables that are presumed to moderate the relations between affective distress and depressive symptoms. Incidentally, our model also implies that persistent affective distress, whether or not it occurs with officially diagnosed depression, will be related to other depressive symptoms given the presence of critical affective mechanisms and moderator variables. These relations are presumed to exist for both clinical and subclinical types of depression. Future studies might test these proposed relations by assessing daily levels of affective distress in subclinical and clinical depressed individuals as well as assessing their standings on the critical moderator variables. Then, one may examine whether the proposed relations to depressive symptoms are upheld. Our model also proposes distinct affective dimensions (e.g., sadness, hostile, and anxious) in depression. Future empirical work needs to investigate the symptom structures associated with each of these respective affective distress states.

Finally, as Costello (1993a) argued, there is a need for more basic data on symptoms in depressive episodes. For example, we are aware of only one study that has examined the temporal order of symptom appearance in depressive episodes without confounding affective distress and anhedonia (e.g., Young & Grabler, 1985). It would be important that future studies investigating the temporal pattern of depressive symptoms use unconfounded measures for each symptom. In addition, there is a need for more comprehensive symptom measures. This is particularly important when assessing affective distress, as we have argued that its relation to other symptoms depends on its specific quality (i.e., sadness, fear, or anger). Yet, this also applies to assessing such symptoms as sleep, weight, thinking and decision making, and suicidality where our model proposes that within each symptom type (i.e., sleep), more specific patterns (i.e., insomnia or hypersomnia) will be related to the predominant mood state. Our theory also suggests that a broader range of symptoms must be assessed beyond DSM–IV symptoms. This list ought to include symptoms that have been empirically associated (i.e., perfectionism) but might also include symptoms of theoretical importance for each affective dimensions (i.e., high impulsivity in depressed patients with high anger-irritability).

In summary, we have argued that there are several benefits to taking a symptom-focused approach to depression that emphasizes affective distress as a central, organizing depressive symptom and as a sufficient proximal determinant of depressive symptoms. First, we believe it offers a plausible explanation for the syndromal nature of depressive episodes that is consistent at both psychological and neurobiological levels of analysis. Our approach also reconciles with the evidence suggesting multiple distal causes of depressive episodes, all of which are associated with (states of persistent) affective distress. A focus on affective distress also highlights the role of specific affective mechanisms. In this chapter, our focus on psychological mechanisms suggests several moderator variables that confer risk to depression. Several of these moderator variables have been given scant attention thus far in depression research. We argue that these risk factors may be critical in determining whether affective distress in response to life events is a normative, temporary emotional response or an abnormally persistent mood state that culminates in a full-blown depressive episode. Finally, a focus on the symptom of affective distress also emphasizes the importance of the quality of affective distress, that is whether sadness, fear, or anger feeling states predominate. Specific affective profiles are argued to be associated with specific symptom profiles, a proposal that is consistent with existing cluster analytic and other empirical findings but which also proposes new symptom and affective distress relations that can be empirically tested.

As Costello (1992b) has argued, a research strategy of studying symptoms should not be an end in itself. Ultimately, the goal of such research will be to lead to diagnostic categories with better construct validity. It is our hope that future studies focusing on the symptom of persistent affective distress will contribute to this ultimate goal by identifying the causal relations that explain the coherence of depressive symptoms.

REFERENCES

Abramson, L. Y., Alloy, L. B., & Metalsky, G. I. (1995). Hopelessness depression. In G. M. Buchanen & M. E. P. Seligman (Eds.), *Explanatory Style* (pp. 113–134). Hillsdale, NJ: Lawrence Erlbaum Associates.

Abramson, L. Y., Metalsky, G. I., & Alloy, L. B. (1989). Hopelessness depression: A theory-based subtype of depression. *Psychological Review, 96*, 358–372.

Ahrens, A. H. (1987). Theories of depression: The role of goals and the self-evaluation process. *Cognitive Therapy and Research, 11*, 665–680.

Alloy, L. B. (Ed.). (1997). Carving depression at its joints: Cognitive/personality subtypes of depression [special issue]. *Cognitive Therapy and Research, 21*(3), 243–245.

Bandura, A. (1986). *Social foundations of thought and action: A social cognitive theory.* Englewood Cliffs, NJ: Prentice-Hall.

Bandura, A., & Cervone, D. (1983). Self-evaluative and self-efficacy mechanisms governing the motivational effects of goal systems. *Journal of Personality and Social Psychology, 45*, 1017–1028.

Beck, A. T. (1967). *Depression: Clinical, experimental, and theoretical aspects.* New York: Harper & Row.

Beevers, C. G., & Wenzlaff, R. M. (1995). *Depression and the paradoxical effects of thought suppression.* Paper presented at the 41st annual meeting of the Southwestern Psychological Association, San Antonio, TX.

Blaney, P. (1986). Affect and memory: A review. *Psychological Bulletin, 99,* 229–246.

Blashfield, R. K., & Morey, L. C. (1979). The classification of depression through cluster analysis. *Comprehensive Psychiatry, 20,* 516–527.

Borkovec, T. D., Lane, T. W., & Vanoot, P. A. (1981). Phenomenology of sleep among insomniacs and good sleepers: Wakefulness experience when cortically asleep. *Journal of Abnormal Psychology, 90,* 607–609.

Borkovec, T. D., Robinson, E., Pruzinsky, T., & DePree, J. A. (1983). Preliminary exploration of worry: Some characteristics and processes. *Behaviour Research and Therapy, 21,* 9–16.

Bower, G. H. (1981). Mood and memory. *American Psychologist, 36,* 129–148.

Bower, G. H. (1987). Commentary on mood and memory. *Behavioral Research and Therapy, 25,* 443–455.

Bower, G. H. (1991). Mood congruity of social judgments. In J. P. Forgas (Ed.), *Emotion and social judgments* (pp. 31–53). Oxford, England: Pergamon.

Broadhead, W. E., Blazer, D. G., George, L. K., & Tse, C. K. (1990). Depression, disability days, and days lost from work in a prospective epidemiological survey. *Journal of the American Medical Association, 264,* 2524–2528.

Bronisch, T., & Hecht, H. (1989). Validity of adjustment disorder, comparison with major depression. *Journal of Affective Disorders, 17,* 229–236.

Brown, J. D., & Mankowski, T. A. (1993). Self-esteem, mood, and self-evaluation: Changes in mood and the way you see you. *Journal of Personality and Social Psychology, 64,* 421–430.

Carson, T. P., & Adams, H. E. (1980). Activity valence as a function of mood change. *Journal of Abnormal Psychology, 89,* 368–377.

Casper, R. C., Katz, M. M., Bowden, C. L., Davis, J. M., Koslow, S. H., & Hanin, I. (1994). The pattern of physical symptom changes in major depressive disorder following treatment with amitrityline or imipramine. *Journal of Affective Disorders, 31,* 151–164.

Cervone, D., Kopp, D. A., Schaumann, L., & Scott, W.D. (1994). The influence of induced mood on personal standards, expectancies, and self-efficacy judgments. *Journal of Personality and Social Psychology, 67,* 1–14.

Cervone, D., & Scott, W. D. (1995). Self-efficacy theory of behavioral change: Foundations, conceptual issues, and therapeutic implications. In W. O'Donohue & L. Krasner (Eds.), *Theories of behavior therapy: Exploring behavior change* (pp. 349–383). Washington, DC: American Psychological Association.

Clark, D. A., Beck, A. T., & Beck, J. S. (1994). Symptom differences in major depression, dysthymia, panic disorder, and generalized anxiety disorder. *American Journal of Psychiatry, 151,* 205–209.

Cohen, L. H., Towbes, L. C., & Flocco, R. (1988). Effects of induced mood on self-reported life events and perceived and received social support. *Journal of Personality and Social Psychology, 55,* 669–674.

Costello, C. G. (1992a). Conceptual problems in current research on cognitive vulnerabilility to psychopathology. *Cognitive Therapy and Research, 16*(4), 379–390.

Costello, C. G. (1992b). Research on symptoms versus research on syndromes: Arguments in favor of allocating more research time to the study of symptoms. *British Journal of Psychiatry, 160,* 304–308.

Costello, C. G. (1993a). The advantages of the symptom approach to depression. In C. G. Costello (Ed.), *Symptoms of depression* (pp. 1–22). New York: Wiley.

Costello, C. G. (1993b). *Basic issues in psychopathology.* New York: Guilford.

Cunningham, M. R. (1988). What do you do when you're happy or blue? Mood, expectancies, and behavioral interest. *Motivation and Emotion, 12,* 309–331.

Despland, J. N., Monod, L., & Ferrero, F. (1995). Clinical relevance of adjustment disorder in DSM–III–R and DSM–IV. *Comprehensive Psychiatry, 36,* 454–460.

Dixon, T. M., & Baumeister, R. F. (1991). Escaping the self: Moderating effects of self-complexity. *Personality and Social Psychology Bulletin, 17,* 363–368.

Dryman, A., & Eaton, W. W. (1991). Affective symptoms associated with the onset of major depression in the community: Findings from the U.S. National Institute of Mental Health Epidemiologic Catchment Area Program. *Acta Psychiatrica Scandinavica, 84,* 1–5.

Eaton, W. W., Dryman, A., Sorenson, A., & McCutcheon, A. (1989). DSM–III major depressive disorder in the community: A latent class analysis of data from the NIMH Epidemiological Catchment Area programme. *British Journal of Psychiatry, 155,* 48–54.

Eich, E. (1995). Searching for mood-dependent memory. *Psychological Science, 6,* 67–75.

Ekman, P. (1989). The argument and evidence about universals in facial expressions of emotion. In H. Wagner & A. Manstead (Eds.), *Handbook of social psychophysiology* (pp. 143–164). Chichester, England: Wiley.

Ekman, P. (1992). An argument for basic emotions. *Cognition and Emotion, 6,* 169–200.

Ekman, P., & Davidson, R. J. (1994). *The nature of emotion: Fundamental questions.* New York: Oxford University Press.

Ekman, P., Levenson, R. W., & Friesen, W. V. (1983). Autonomic nervous system activity distinguishes emotions. *Science, 221,* 1208–1210.

Endicott, J., & Spitzer, R. L. (1978). A diagnostic interview: The Schedule for Affective Disorders and Schizophrenia. *Archives of General Psychiatry, 35,* 837–844.

Esses, V. M. (1989). Mood as a moderator of acceptance of interpersonal feedback. *Journal of Personality and Social Psychology, 57,* 769–781.

Fabrega, H., Mezzich, J. E., Mezzich, A. C., & Coffman, G. A. (1986). Descriptive validity of DSM–III depression. *Journal of Nervous and Mental Disease, 174,* 573–584.

Finlay-Jones, R., & Brown, G. W. (1981). Types of stressful life event and the onset of anxiety and depressive disorders. *Psychological Medicine, 11,* 803–815.

Flett, G. L., Vredenburg, K., & Krames, L. (1997). The continuity of depression in clinical and nonclinical samples. *Psychological Bulletin, 121*(3), 395–416.

Forgas, J. P. (1995). Mood and judgment: The affect infusion model (AIM). *Psychological Bulletin, 117,* 39–66.

Forgas, J. P., & Bower, G. H. (1987). Mood effects on person-perception judgments. *Journal of Personality and Social Psychology, 53,* 53–60.

Forgas, J. P., Bower, G. H., & Krantz, S. E. (1984). The influence of mood on perceptions of social interactions. *Journal of Experimental Social Psychology, 20,* 497–513.

Forgas, J. P., & Moylan, S. (1987). After the movies: Transient mood and social judgment. *Personality and Social Psychology Bulletin, 13,* 467–477.

Frijda, N. H. (1986). *The emotions.* New York: Cambridge University Press.

Frijda, N. H., Kuipers, P., & ter Schure, E. (1989). Relations among emotion, appraisal, and emotional action readiness. *Journal of Personality and Social Psychology, 57,* 212–228.

Gross, J. J., & Levenson, R. W. (1997). Hiding Feelings: The acute effects of inhibiting negative and positive emotion. *Journal of Abnormal Psychology, 106,* 95–103.

Gross, J. J., & Munoz, R. F. (1995). Emotion regulation and mental health. *Clinical Psychology: Science and Practice, 2,* 151–164.

Grove, W. M., & Andreason, N. C. (1989). Quantitative and qualitative distinctions between psychiatric disorders. In L. N. Robins & J. E. Barrett (Eds.), *The validity of psychiatric diagnoses* (pp. 127–138). New York: Raven.

Haaga, D. A. F., Dyck, M. J., & Ernst, D. (1991). Empirical status of cognitive theory of depression. *Psychological Bulletin, 110*(2), 215–236.

Healy, D. (1987). Rhythm and blues: Neurochemical, neuropharmacological and neuropsychological implications of a hypothesis of circadian rhythm dysfunction in the affective disorders. *Psychopharmacology, 93,* 271–285.

Herbert, T. B., & Cohen, S. (1993). Depression and immunity: A meta-analytic review. *Psychological Bulletin, 113*(3), 472–486.

Ingram, R. E. (1984a). Information processing and feedback: Effects of mood and information favorability on the cognitive processing of personally relevant information. *Cognitive Therapy and Research, 8,* 371–386.

Ingram, R. E. (1984b). Toward an information processing analysis of depression. *Cognitive Therapy and Research, 8*(5), 443–478.

Ingram, R. E. (1990). Self-focused attention in clinical disorders: Review and a conceptual model. *Psychological Bulletin, 107,* 156–176.

Isen, A. M., Shalker, T., Clark, M., & Karp, L. (1978). Affect, accessibility of material in memory and behavior: A cognitive loop? *Journal of Personality and Social Psychology, 36,* 1–12.

Judd, L. L., Rapaport, M. H., Paulus, M. P., & Brown, J. L. (1994). Subsyndromal symptomatic depression: A new mood disorder? *Journal of Clinical Psychiatry, 55*(4), 18–28.

Karp, D. A. (1996). *Speaking of sadness: Depression, disconnection, and the meanings of illness.* New York: Oxford University Press.

Keltner, D., Locke, K. D., & Audrain, P. C. (1993). The influence of attributions on the relevance of negative feelings to personal satisfaction. *Personality and Social Psychology Bulletin, 19,* 21–29.

Kendall, P. C., Hollon, S. D., Beck, A. T., Hammen, C. L., & Ingram, R. E. (1987). Issues and recommendations regarding the use of the Beck Depression Inventory. *Cognitive Therapy and Research, 11,* 289–299.

Lazarus, R. S. (1991). *Emotion and adaptation.* New York: Oxford University Press.

Levenson, R. W., Ekman, P., & Friesen, W. V. (1990). Voluntary facial expression generates emotion-specific nervous system activity. *Psychophysiology, 27,* 363–384.

Lewinsohn, P. M., & Graf, M. (1973). Pleasant activities and depression. *Journal of Consulting and Clinical Psychology, 41,* 261–268.

Lewinsohn, P. M., & Libet, J. (1972). Pleasant events, activity schedules, and depression. *Journal of Abnormal Psychology, 79,* 291–295.

Linville, P. W. (1985). Self-complexity and affective extremity: Don't put all your eggs in one cognitive basket. *Social Cognition, 3,* 94–120.

Linville, P. W. (1987). Self-complexity as a cognitive buffer against stress-related depression and illness. *Journal of Personality and Social Psychology, 52,* 663–676.

Locke, E. A., & Latham, G. P. (1990). *A theory of goal setting and task performance.* Englewood Cliffs, NJ: Prentice-Hall.

Maes, M., Meltzer, H. Y., Cosyns, P., & Schotte, C. (1994). Evidence for the existence of major depression with and without anxiety features. *Psychopathology, 27*(1–2), 1–13.

Martin, L. L., Ward, D. W., Achee, J. W., & Wyer, R. S., (1993). Mood as input: People have to interpret the motivational implications of their moods. *Journal of Personality and Social Psychology, 64*(3), 317–326.

Matt, G. E., Vazquez, C., & Campbell, W. K. (1992). Mood congruent recall of affectively toned stimuli: A meta-analytic review. *Clinical Psychology Review, 12,* 227–255.

Mayer, J. D., Gaschke, Y. N., Braverman, D. L., & Evans, T. W. (1992). Mood-congruent judgment is a general effect. *Journal of Personality and Social Psychology, 63,* 119–132.

Mendolia, M., & Kleck, R. E. (1993). Effects of talking about a stressful event on arousal: Does what we talk about make a difference? *Journal of Personality and Social Psychology, 64,* 283–292.

Mischel, W., Ebbesen, E. B., & Zeiss, A. R. (1973). Selective attention to the self: Situational and dispositional determinants. *Journal of Personality and Social Psychology, 27,* 129–142.

Morrow, J. (1990). *The effects of rumination, distraction, and negative mood on memories, evaluations, and problem solving.* Unpublished manuscript, Stanford University, Stanford, CA.

Newman, L. S., & Uleman, J. S. (1990). Spontaneous trait inference. In J. S. Uleman & J. A. Bargh (Eds.), *Unintended thought* (pp. 155–188). New York: Guilford.

Nicassio, P. M., Mendlowitz, D. R., Fussell, J. J., & Petras, L. (1985). The phenomenology of the pre-sleep state: The development of the Pre-Sleep Arousal Scale. *Behaviour Research and Therapy, 28,* 487–495.

Niedenthal, P., Setterlund, M., & Wherry, M. (1992). Possible self-complexity and affective reactions to goal-relevant evaluation. *Journal-of-Personality-and-Social-Psychology, 63*(1), 5–16.

Nolen-Hoeksema, S. (1991). Responses to depression and their effects on the duration of depressive episodes. *Journal of Abnormal Psychology, 100,* 569–682.

Overall, J. E., & Hollister, L. E. (1980). Phenomenological classification of depressive disorders. *Journal of Clinical Psychology, 36*(2), 372–377.

Paykel, E. S. (1971). Classification of depressed patients: Cluster analysis derived grouping. *British Journal of Psychiatry, 18,* 275–288.

Paykel, E. S. (1972). Depressive typologies and response to amitriptyline. *British Journal of Psychiatry, 120,* 147–156.

Paykel, E. S., & Cooper, Z. (1982). Life events and social stress. In E. S. Paykel (Ed.), *Handbook of affective disorders* (pp. 149–179). New York: Guilford Press.

Pennebaker, J. W. (1995). Emotion, disclosure, and health: An overview. In J. W. Pennebaker (Ed.), *Emotion, disclosure, and health* (pp. 3–10). Washington, DC: American Psychological Association.

Pennebaker, J. W. (1997a). *Opening up: The healing power of expressed emotions* (Rev. ed.). New York: Guilford.

Pennebaker, J. W. (1997b). Writing about emotional experience as a therapeutic process. *Psychological Science, 8,* 162–166.

Plutchik, R. (1980). *A psychoevolutionary synthesis.* New York: Harper & Row.

Rehm, L. P. (1977). A self-control model of depression. *Behavior Therapy, 8,* 787–804.

Roberts, J. E., & Kassel, J. D. (1996). Mood-state dependence in cognitive vulnerability to depression: The roles of positive and negative affect. *Cognitive Therapy and Research, 20,* 1–12.

Roseman, I. J., Spindel, M. S., & Jose, P. E. (1990). Appraisals of emotion-eliciting events: Testing a theory of discrete emotions. *Journal of Personality and Social Psychology, 59*(5), 899–915.

Rothbart, M. K., & Ahadi, S. A. (1994). Temperament and the development of personality. *Journal of Abnormal Psychology, 103*(1), 55–66.

Schwarz, N. (1990). Feelings as Information: Information and motivational functions of affective states. In E. T. Higgens & R. M. Sorrentino (Eds.), *Motivation and cognition: Foundations of social behavior* (Vol. 2, pp. 527–561). New York: Guilford.

Schwarz, N., & Clore, G. L. (1983). Mood, misattribution, and judgments of well-being: Informative and directive functions of affective states. *Journal of Personality and Social Psychology, 45,* 513–523.

Schwartz, G. E., Weinberger, D. A., & Singer, J. A. (1981). Cardiovascular differentiation of happiness, sadness, anger, and fear following imagery and exercise. *Psychosomatic Medicine, 43,* 343–364.

Scott, W. D., & Cervone, D. (1999). *The influence of negative mood on self-regulatory cognition.* Unpublished manuscript.

Scott, W. D., & Ingram, R. E. (1998). Affective influences in depression: Conceptual issues, multiple mechanisms, and cognitive consequences. In W. F. Flack & J. D. Laird (Eds.), *Emotions in psychopathology: Theory and research* (pp. 200–215). New York: Oxford University Press.

Scott, W. D., Ingram, R. E., & Shadel, W. G. (1999). *Hostile and sad mood profiles in dysphoria: Evidence for cognitive specificity.* Unpublished manuscript.

Sedikides, D. (1992). Changes in the valence of the self as a function of mood. In M. S. Clark (Ed.), *Emotion and social behavior: Review of personality and social psychology* (Vol. 14, pp. 271–311). Newbury Park, CA: Sage.

Segal, Z. V., & Dobson, K. S. (1992). Cognitive models of depression: Report from a consensus development conference. *Psychological Inquiry, 3*(3), 219–224.

Segal, Z. V., & Ingram, R. E. (1994). Mood priming and construct activation in tests of cognitive vulnerability to unipolar depression. *Clinical Psychology Review, 14,* 663–695.

Shaver, P., Schwartz, J., Kirson, D., & O'Connor, C. (1987). Emotion knowledge: Further exploration of a prototype approach. *Journal of Personality and Social Psychology, 52,* 1061–1086.

Showers, C. (1992a). Evaluatively integrative thinking about characteristics of the self. *Personality-and-Social-Psychology-Bulletin, 18* (6), 719–729.

Showers, C. J. (1992b). The motivational and emotional consequences of considering positive or negative possibilities for an upcoming event. *Journal-of-Personality-and-Social-Psychology, 63*(3), 474–484.

Showers, C. J., & Kling, K. C. (1996). Organization of self-knowledge: Implications for recovery from sad mood. *Journal of Personality and Social Psychology, 70*(3), 578–590.

Singer, J. A., & Salovey, P. (1988). Mood and memory: Evaluating the network theory of affect. *Clinical Psychology Review, 8,* 211–251.

Smith, C. A., & Lazarus, R. S. (1990). Emotion and adaptation. In L. A. Pervin (Ed.), *Handbook of personality: Theory and research* (pp. 609–637). New York: Guilford.

Snyder, M., & White, P. (1982). Moods and memories: Elation, depression, and the remembering of events of one's life. *Journal of Personality, 50,* 149–167.

Snyder, S., Strain, J. J., & Wolf, D. (1990). Differentiating major depression from adjustment disorder with depressed mood in the medical setting. *General Hospital Psychiatry, 12,* 159–165.

Spera, S. P., Buhrfield, E. D., & Pennebaker, J. W. (1994). Expressive writing and coping with job loss. *Academy of Management Journal, 37,* 722–733.

Teasdale, J. D., & Fogarty, S. J. (1979). Differential effects of induced mood on the recall of pleasant and unpleasant events from episodic memory. *Journal of Abnormal Psychology, 88,* 248–257.

Tillema, J. L., Cervone, D., & Scott, W. (in press). Negative mood, perceived self-efficacy, and personal standards in dysphoria: The effects of contextual cues on self-defeating patterns of cognition. *Cognition Therapy and Research.*

van Egeren, L., Haynes, S. N., Franzen, M., & Hamilton, J. (1983). Presleep cognitions and attributions in sleep-onset insomnia. *Journal of Behavioral Medicine, 6,* 217–232.

Vinokur, A., Schul, Y., & Caplan, R. D. (1987). Determinants of perceived social support: Interpersonal transactions, personal outlook, and transient affective states. *Journal of Personality and Social Psychology, 53,* 1137–1145.

Watson, D., Clark, L. A., & Tellegen, A. (1988). Development and validation of brief measures of positive and negative affect: The PANAS scales. *Journal of Personality and Social Psychology, 54*(6), 1063–1070.

Watson, D., Clark, L. A., Weber, K., Assenheimer, J. S., Strauss, M. E., & McCormick, R. A. (1995). Testing the tripartite model: II. Exploring the symptom structure of anxiety and depression in student, adult, and patient samples. *Journal of Abnormal Psychology, 104*(1), 15–25.

Watson, D., & Tellegen, A. (1985). Toward a consensual structure of mood. *Psychological Bulletin, 98,* 219–235.

Watson, D., Weber, K., Assenheimer, J. S., Clark, L. A., Strauss, M. E., & McCormick, R. A. (1995). Testing the tripartite model: I. Evaluating the convergent and discriminant validity of anxiety and depression symptom scales. *Journal of Abnormal Psychology, 104*(1), 3–14.

Watts, F. N., Coyle, K., & East, M. P. (1994). The contribution of worry to insomnia. *British Journal of Clinical Psychology, 33,* 211–220.

Wegner, D. M. (1994). Ironic processes of mental control. *Psychological Review, 101,* 34–42.

Wegner, D. M., Erber, R., & Zanakos, S. (1993). Ironic processes in the mental control of mood and mood-related thought. *Journal of Personality and Social Psychology, 65,* 1093–1104.

Weisse, C. S. (1992). Depression and immunocompetence: A review of the literature. *Psychological Bulletin, 111*(3), 475–489.

Willner, P., Wilkes, M., & Orwin, A. (1990). Attributional style and perceived stress in endogenous and reactive depression. *Journal of Affective Disorders, 18*(4), 281–287.

Worthington, J., Fava, M., Davidson, K., Alpert, J., Nierenberg, A. A., & Rosenbaum, J. F. (1995). Patterns of improvement in depressive symptoms with fluoxetine treatment. *Psychopharmacological Bulletin, 31*(2), 223–226.

Wright, J., & Mischel, W. (1982). Influence of affect on cognitive social learning person variables. *Journal of Personality and Social Psychology, 43,* 901–914.

Young, M. A., & Grabler, P. (1985). Rapidity of symptom onset in depression. *Psychiatry Research, 16,* 309–315.

Chapter 9

Affective Distress as a Central and Organizing Symptom in Depression: Neurobiological Mechanisms

Ray W. Winters
Walter D. Scott
Christopher G. Beevers
University of Miami

The findings presented in the preceding chapter (chap. 8, this volume) provide rather compelling evidence that altering the affective state of an individual leads to systematic biases in how information is processed. Changes in affective state reorder processing priorities involving working memory, attentional resources, and motivation; affective state also influences how information is represented and stored in memory, and what components of these representations are subsequently retrieved. The selective retrieval of stored information that results from affective distress, for example, can be used to account for mood-congruent biases in judgment (including self-evaluation), decision making and other cognitive processes. These effects of current emotional state on attention, motivation, cognition, and memory may be indirect, or alternatively, affect can be viewed as having informational properties, and this information is routinely integrated with other sources of information when making decisions and judgments. This affect-as-information view is based on observations that affective states can systematically bias judgment when the emotion is cognitively unconstrained.

This chapter seeks to elucidate the neural substrates of the affective distress linked to depression and in doing so, advance our understanding of how affective states can systematically bias the processing of emotionally significant information. Stressful life events lead to changes in the neural activity of central nervous system (CNS) structures involved in the processing of affective information. We present evidence that the symptoms of depression are directly linked to these changes in the brain's emotional systems or to homeostasis-promoting neural events that represent attempts by the CNS to regulate emotion in response to environmental stressors. The aim of the first part of this chapter is to characterize how affective information is processed by the CNS. The remainder of the chapter describes the neurobiological mechanisms that underlie specific symptoms of depression and the factors that render an individual vulnerable to a depressive episode. The processing of affective information and the symptoms of depression are viewed, throughout the chapter, from a biobehavioral control systems perspective in which the monoamines—dopamine, norepinephrine, and serotonin—play central roles in the regulation of affect. Dopamine-secreting neurons in the ventral tegmental area are thought to facilitate appetitive motivation and positive affect. Norepinephrine-secreting locus coeruleus neurons are seen as critical to the determination of the magnitude of significance conferred to incentive stimuli involved in reward-seeking behaviors (i.e., positive reinforcement) and threatening stimuli. Serotonin is viewed as a key component of a homeostasis-promoting negative feedback system designed to regulate positive and negative affect.

CENTRAL NERVOUS SYSTEM MECHANISMS UNDERLYING AFFECTIVE DISTRESS

Overview

Our understanding of neurobiological factors involved in affective distress and depression is based on research that has focused on how the CNS processes affective information. Neurobiological theories have focused on the role of one or more of the monoamines in the etiology and treatment of depression. In this section of the chapter, we describe the role of the monoamines in the regulation of information flow in the CNS during the processing of stimuli that have affective significance. The functions of the monoamines are discussed from a biobehavioral control systems perspective, which assumes that signal flow within various functional regions in the CNS is regulated and that changes in monoamine activity often help maintain neural homeostasis within these functional regions. The major sources of the monoamines are neurons whose cell bodies are housed in the brain stem and whose axons connect to forebrain structures involved in sensory processing, memory, emotion, cognition, and motivation. Specifically, the dorsal raphe and median raphe are the major sources of serotonin (5-hydroxytryptamine or 5-HT). Most of the norepinephrine (NE) in the CNS is secreted by the locus coeruleus (LC), and the ventral tegmental area (VTA) provides most of dopamine-secreting neurons involved in emotional behavior. A salient anatomical feature shared by the raphe, the LC, and the VTA is the widespread nature of their forebrain projections. It is this characteristic that has led to the view that monoamine systems modulate, rather than mediate, information flow in the CNS (Oades, 1985). The analogy provided by Oades (1985) is that neurons that modulate are comparable to a radio's volume control knob or tuning knob; these neurons regulate the flow of information between other neurons that are mediating the signal (the "melody" in his analogy). The important behavioral implication of this point of view is that a single monoamine can have an impact on several functional systems. As an example, by virtue of their widespread connections, dopamine-secreting VTA neurons have an effect on incentive motivation, subjective emotional experiences, emotional expression, and cognition.

Initial Processing of Sensory Information

The ability of a stimulus to evoke emotional behavior is dependent on the affective characteristics conferred to it when it is processed in the CNS. One or more of the monoamines are critically involved in the various stages of information processing of stimuli that have affective significance. Even when a stimulus is affectively neutral, in the earliest stages of sensory processing, the amplitude of the CNS signal that represents this stimulus appears dependent on serotonin (5-HT) activity. Although 5-HT-secreting raphe neurons make connections with all of the cortical lobes, there is substantial evidence that these neurons preferentially innervate sensory projection areas, especially primary visual, auditory, and somatic sensory regions (Azmitia & Gannon, 1986). Viewed from a biobehavioral control systems perspective (Depue & Zald, 1993; Dworkin, 1993; Collins & Depue, 1992; Spoont, 1992), 5-HT is thought to be a component of a homeostatic system designed to regulate the flow of information through a neural system; its role in regulation is to constrain signal flow. Specifically, 5-HT controls the sensitivity of the neural system (in this case, each sensory system involved in the initial processing of information) to perturbation by a new signal by setting the threshold for entry into the neural system; it also promotes neural homeostasis by serving as a negative feedback modulator of evoked activity. Thus, when a response in a neural system occurs, 5-HT has a constraining influence on both its magnitude and time course.

There are a number of findings that are consistent with the view that 5-HT has a constraining influence on neural activity at the initial stage of sensory processing. Increases in 5-HT transmission consistently attenuate the amplitude of the startle reflex and this reflex is potentiated by decreases in 5-HT activity (Davis, Astrachan, & Kass, 1980). Reductions in 5-HT increase pain sensitivity (Roberts, 1984) and increases in 5-HT decrease pain sensitivity (Andersen & Dafny, 1982). Similarly, reductions in 5-HT lower the threshold intensity for a tonal conditioned stimulus in Pavlovian conditioning of the nictitating membrane response (Gormezano & Harvey, 1980). In general, 5-HT has a constraining influence on stimulus reactivity, and investigators have consistently reported that low 5-HT activity leads to exaggerated reactivity to a wide variety of sensory stimuli. This exaggerated reactivity is experienced as aversive, so it may contribute to the irritability seen in many depressed patients (Depue & Zald, 1993). Low 5-HT activity may also be the basis for an increased sensitivity to pain found in many depressed patients (Meltzer & Lowy, 1987) and it may explain why many patients with chronic pain respond to antidepressant medications that enhance 5-HT activity (Gupta, 1986).

Appraisal

Appraisal is the process by which the CNS determines the emotional significance of an event or set of circumstances. During appraisal, environmental circumstances are assessed for significance to the physical and emotional well-being of the individual. The brain's appraisal mechanism, although automatic and often very rapid, draws on a number of hardwired structures and on stored memories. The *amygdala* is considered to be a nodal structure in the neural network that mediates appraisal (LeDoux, 1995). In order to determine the emotional significance of an event, this network must integrate contemporaneous sensory information with retrieved emotional memories and declarative memories, and with cognitive information. An *emotional memory* is a memory about the relation that discrete stimuli bear to reward and punishment. For example, a particular (conditioned) stimulus may signal an impending punishment, or a particular stimulus (conditioned incentive stimulus) may provide a signal for a behavior that leads to either reward or active avoidance of an aversive stimulus. The term *declarative memory*—conscious memory or explicit memory—is used in reference to the ability to consciously recall a past experience or previously learned information. The amygdala is a nodal structure in the storage and retrieval of emotional memories (LeDoux, 1993); it also modulates the activity in structures, such as the hippocampus, that are involved in the storage and retrieval of declarative memories (Cahill & McGaugh, 1998).

The appraisal process involves emotional memories to give meaning to discrete stimuli and declarative memories to place these stimuli in an appropriate context. For example, the sound of a gunshot would evoke emotional memories, but the appraised emotional significance and subsequent behaviors would be dependent on declarative memories that provide a context for the sound. The emotions and behaviors evoked by a gunshot heard when walking down a dark street, for example, would be quite different than those evoked from one that is perceived as coming from a television set.

The appraisal process is essential to: (a) the generation of incentive motivational states that are necessary for the activation of motor programs that evoke appetitive behaviors leading to reward (e.g., positive reinforcement); (b) the generation of incentive motivational states that lead to active coping (e.g., active avoidance) with a stressor where the reward is safety; and (c) aversive motivational states that lead to behavioral changes that serve to remove a source of threat to the well-being of the organism.

Tuned Appraisal

Selective attention is the process that allows CNS structures to focus on a selected portion of information that is being processed. This tuning process increases the saliency of affectively significant stimuli that will come to guide behavior. The stimuli may be *external* (changes in the environment) or *internal* (interoceptive stimuli, or representations of stimuli based on the retrieval of memories). NE is a monoamine that is essential to the process of selective attention. The major source of NE in the CNS is the LC, and one of the primary functions of this structure is to increase the relative saliency of stimuli that come to guide behavior.

The LC filters irrelevant stimuli by enhancing the signal-to-noise ratio in neurons that receive input from several stimuli (Aston-Jones, 1985). The activation of NE-secreting LC neurons enhances the reliability and efficiency of information processing by increasing the threshold for activation of a neuron so that only the most potent internal or external stimulus (the signal) can increase the discharge rate of that neuron. As this tuning mechanism augments the saliency of task-relevant stimuli, the effects of irrelevant stimuli (i.e., noise) are diminished. LC neurons are most responsive to phasic changes in the external or internal environment (e.g., a novel stimulus) and to tonic-threatening stimuli (Jacobs, 1986); they also are important in the processing of stimuli that lead to positive reinforcement (Aston-Jones, Rajkowski, & Kubiak, 1997).

The LC connections to the amygdala are thought to improve the ability of this structure to extract affective features of stimuli (Depue & Zald, 1993). Thus, NE-secreting LC neurons serve a modulatory role in a second stage of appraisal, referred to as *tuned appraisal* (see Fig. 9.1), in that increased LC activity increases the saliency of affectively significant stimuli. Stated differently, the process of tuned appraisal magnifies the importance of affective stimuli (relative to other stimuli) that guide behaviors that lead to reward and the active avoidance of aversive stimuli, and inhibit behavior

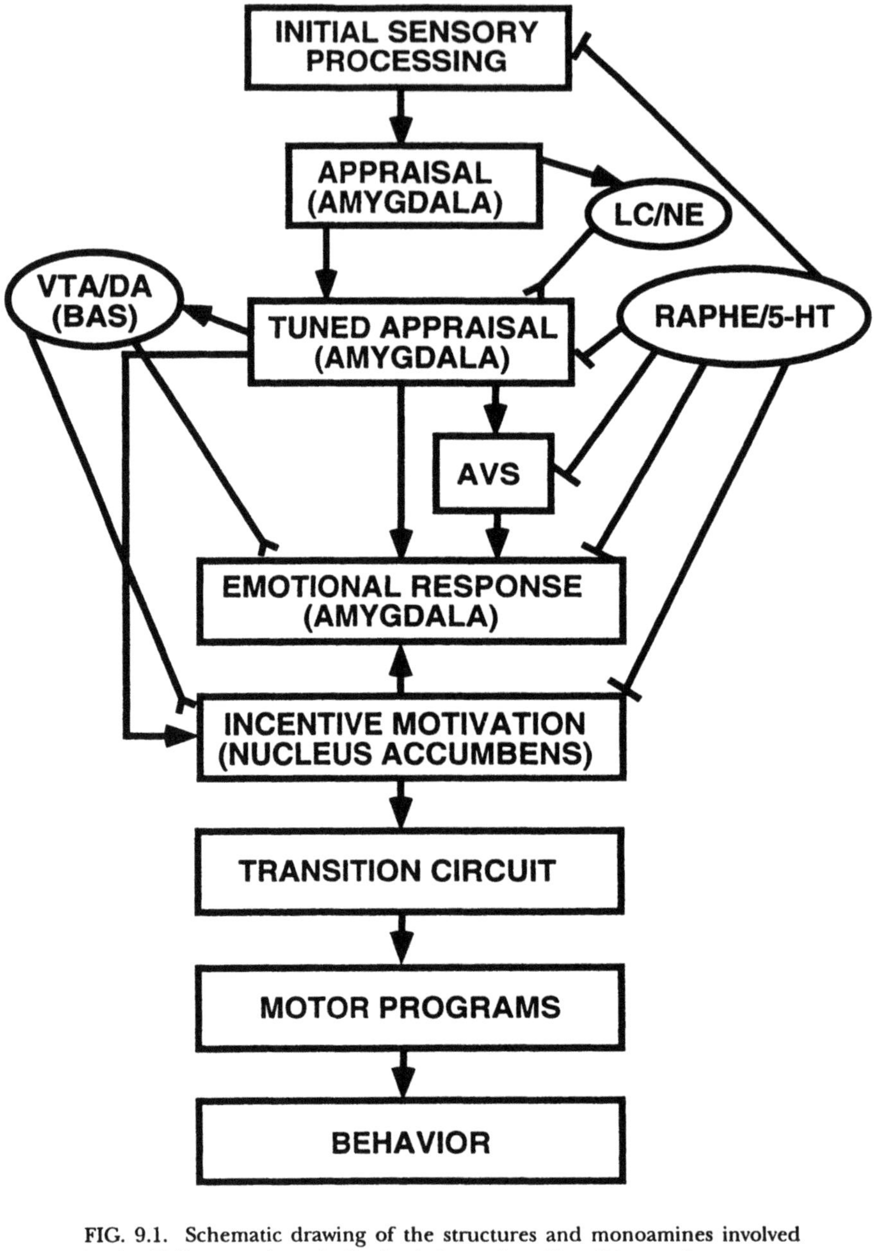

FIG. 9.1. Schematic drawing of the structures and monoamines involved in the CNS processing of affective information. *Note:* DA-secreting neurons from the VTA are referred to as VTA/DA in the figure (also referred to as the Behavioral Activation System or BAS). VTA/DA neurons, serotonin-secreting raphe neurons (Raphe/5-HT), and norepinephrine-secreting LC neurons (LC/NE) modulate signal flow at CNS structures involved in the processing of affective information. Arrows show direction of information flow; caret endings signify facilitation of signal flow; flat endings signify constraint of signal flow.

so as to avoid aversive stimuli (i.e., passive avoidance). Many of the stimuli that activate LC neurons have gone through considerable preprocessing by CNS structures involved in cognition and the retrieval of memories so as to confer meaning to these stimuli (i.e., the initial stage of appraisal). Furthermore, the response of LC neurons to conditioned stimuli is plastic in the sense that their conditioned responses are altered by changes in stimulus meaning (Aston-Jones et al., 1997) (e.g., a stimulus that was a "Go" signal may have become a "Stop" signal). LC neurons are also sensitive to the status of the internal milieu, such as blood gas levels, blood volume level, and the contractile state of smooth muscle of the gut. Abrupt changes in the internal environment, as occur when someone is withdrawing from a psychoactive drug, can lead to an alarm response that is mediated by the LC (Winters, Ironson, & Schneiderman, 1990). Information conveyed to the LC about current body state (e.g., activity in internal organs such as the heart and gut) become particularly important in situations involving threat. An aroused internal body state would enhance the saliency of threatening stimuli and thereby activate the Aversive Motivational System (AVS). As discussed later, the activation of the AVS leads to increases in vigilance, attention, and sensitivity to external stimuli. Thus, the neuronal structures involved in tuned appraisal are communicating to the AVS that the environment requires closer scrutiny. The activation of the AVS also provides a motivational imperative to generate behavioral and/or cognitive changes to cope with the threatening situation.

5-HT is also involved in the tuning of stimuli (see Fig. 9.1), and a number of studies provide evidence that this transmitter antagonizes the effects of NE (Haddjeri, de Montigny, & Blier, 1997; Kayama, Shimada, Hishikawa, & Ogawa, 1989; Marks, Speciale, Cobbey & Roffwarg, 1987; Ruiz-Ortega, Ugedo, Pineda, Garcia-Sevilla, 1995) and thus, the saliency of affective stimuli (Spoont, 1992)—perhaps by altering the signal to noise ratio at target sites (Spoont, 1992; Wilkinson & Jacobs, 1988). Indeed, one of the target sites at which 5-HT antagonizes NE is at the locus coeruleus (Aston-Jones, Akaoka, Charl'ety, & Chouvet 1991; Haddjeri et al., 1997; Ruiz-Ortega et al., 1995).

Why Is the Process of Tuned Appraisal Important to the Understanding of Affective Distress and Depression? One type of affective distress that is often linked to depression is anxiety. Anxiety disorders and depression are highly comorbid (Clark & Watson, 1991) and depressed patients often report anxiety coupled with low positive affect. One reason why tuned appraisal is important to the understanding of affective distress is that an exaggeration of the saliency of stimuli that signal punishment or loss of reward can lead to negative affect. If the saliency of threatening stimuli (i.e., the magnitude of emotional significance conferred to these stimuli) is exaggerated, the individual will show signs of anxiety, heightened nonspecific arousal, and hypervigilance.

The Aversive Motivational System

The fate of the CNS representation of a stimulus after the determination of its emotional significance is dependent on the meaning conferred to it in the appraisal process. If a stimulus is determined by the appraisal process to be associated with goal-directed behavior—either appetitive behaviors linked to reward or behaviors involved in active coping with stressors (active avoidance)—the amygdala activates neurons in brain structures involved in incentive motivation, particularly the nucleus accumbens (Fig. 9.1). The *nucleus accumbens* is a key component of the *Appetitive Motivational System (APMS*), which is activated during reward-seeking or active avoidance of aversive stimulation. If an environmental change signals threat or potential threat the AVS is activated (Fig. 9.1). The emotion that is most often linked to the AVS is anxiety. As an emotion, anxiety can be characterized as a state of the CNS associated with the anticipation of harm or vulnerability in response to perceived threat (Winters et al., 1990). The CNS structures that constitute the AVS are not shown in Fig. 9.1, although regions of the amygdala are considered to be essential components of this motivational system (see Rosen & Schulkin, 1998 for details of the circuitry).

As a subjective emotional experience, anxiety varies from one of tension and discomfort in situations in which effective coping responses are available, to a sense of helplessness, uncertainty, and distress, when no clear coping response is available (Winters et al., 1990). The uncontrollability associated with a sense of helplessness is often coupled with symptoms of depression. Anxiety also motivates behavioral changes to remove the threatening stimuli (or mitigate the impact of these stimuli; Miller, 1951; Mowrer, 1947; Rosen & Schulkin, 1998); activity in the neural circuitry that constitutes the AVS is considered to be the CNS substrate of this motivational state. There are a variety of coping responses that are motivated by threat, including phasic inhibition of behavior (i.e., passive avoidance), sustained withdrawal from the aversive situation, species-typical defensive behaviors (e.g., the fight–flight response), goal-directed behavior in which the reinforcer is safety (i.e., active avoidance that is mediated by the APMS), and cognitive coping (i.e., cognitively mediated changes in the emotional significance conferred to the threatening event).

When coping behaviors are available, the AVS is said to be involved in *predictive homeostasis* or regulation (Rosen & Schulkin, 1998). Predictive homeostasis is distinguished from *reactive homeostasis* by the time at which the regulatory response mechanism is engaged (Whybrow, 1997). Response mechanisms involved in reactive homeostasis are engaged after a regulatory challenge, such as an increase in blood pressure, a decrease in blood glucose, a pain-producing noxious stimulus, or a punitive psychosocial stimulus (e.g., failure or loss). The regulatory response usually remains engaged until the controlled variable is returned to some preset reference level (set point); examples of controlled variables would be blood pressure, blood glucose level, or mood state. In contrast to reactive homeostasis, a predictive homeostatic mechanism is engaged prior to the onset of the regulatory challenge. It is a preemptive physiological or behavioral response that mitigates or nullifies the impact of the forthcoming homeostasis-challenging stimulus. Thus, for example, a (conditioned) stimulus that signals impending physical punishment or punishment associated with psychosocial stimuli (e.g., failure, criticism, or loss) would activate the AVS, thereby creating a central motivational state. The central motivational state would lead to the engagement of behavioral changes that would nullify or mitigate the impact of the punitive stimulus in advance. For example, the organism may inhibit ongoing behavior (passive avoidance) or actively avoid the punishment by initiating a response pattern (e.g., working on a project to avoid failure).

Threatening stimuli usually fall into one of three categories (Gray, 1987): *a signal for an impending aversive stimulus* (e.g., criticism or other forms of negative feedback), *a signal for the withholding of a stimulus that had previously served as a positive reinforcer* (e.g., loss of a loved one), or a *novel stimulus.* Cognitive mechanisms are particularly important to the perceived threat associated with psychosocial stressors (Lazarus, 1991). The process of *cognitive appraisal* confers emotional meaning to a particular event or set of circumstances based on the goals, values, and beliefs of the individual doing the appraising (Lazarus, 1991). Often the terms *ego threat* or *threat to self-esteem* are used to refer to threat linked to psychosocial stressors.

As pointed out by Rosen and Schulkin (1998), the activation of the AVS (what they refer to as the *fear circuit*) not only motivates behavioral changes, but it also alters the organism's orientation toward the environment by increasing nonspecific arousal, vigilance, and by reallocating attentional resources. It seems likely that changes in selective attention are mediated, in part, by increased LC activity. These CNS changes enhance the processing of sensory stimuli that may be linked to danger and threat or that may guide coping responses. In situations in which the AVS is hyperexcitable, as with individuals with anxiety disorders (Rosen & Schulkin, 1998), the promotion of vigilant scanning of the environment by the AVS may interfere with appetitive motivation and goal-directed behaviors, and hence lead to several symptoms of depression. Indeed, depression and anxiety disorders are highly comorbid. It should be pointed out, however, that activation of the AVS would not be expected to interfere with appetitive motivation under normal circumstances. In fact, an element of threat is inherent in most goal-directed behaviors involving psychosocial stimuli, that is, the individual may fail to reach the goal. If perceived threat is not too high, the increased AVS activity may actually be beneficial in that it would increase the vigor of the goal-directed behaviors.

The Appetitive Motivational System

Although the amygdala is essential to the generation of representations of stimuli that may be linked to reward or active coping (active avoidance), the activity of this structure and others involved in appraisal do not form the neural substrate for the motivational state linked to goal-directed behavior. Representations of stimuli that have emotional significance are translated into an incentive–reward motivational state within an appetitive motivational system (APMS) (Kalivas, Churchill, & Klitenick, 1993). Kalivas et al. refer to the APMS as a motive circuit. A nodal structure in the APMS is the nucleus accumbens (Fig. 9.1). This structure serves as an interface between limbic structures that process motivational information and the extrapyramidal motor system that integrates the neural activity necessary for the generation of motor activity involved in goal-directed behavior. The nucleus accumbens is a focal point for the convergence of motivationally relevant information and may be involved in the encoding of the motivating power of an affective stimulus. It receives input from a variety of CNS structures involved in the processing of emotional information, including the amygdala, hippocampus, and dopamine-secreting neurons from the ventral tegmental area. This structure is thought to encode motivational intensity based on current environmental circumstances (such as availability of rewards or goal proximity), on the physiological state of the organism (e.g., food-deprived state), and cognitive activity. A separate network (i.e., transition circuit in Fig. 9.1) transforms the incentive motivational state encoded in the nucleus accumbens (and other structures within the APMS) to motor programs that generate goal-directed behavior. The nucleus accumbens also determines whether motor programs associated with goal-directed behavior will be activated and the vigor with which the responses will be performed. It is likely that nucleus accumbens activity contributes to subjective affective states by its connections to the amygdala (emotional response in Fig. 9.1).

Cognitive Modulation of the APMS. Cognition is defined as a complex form of information processing that often involves the utilization of ideas and thoughts to enhance the adaptability of emotional behavior in complex environments. Complex information processing is often required when reinforcement contingencies change and new behavioral strategies must be generated to reach a goal. A key region in cognitive modulation of goal-directed behavior is the prefrontal cortex (PFC). As is discussed later, many of the cognitive changes that occur during depression are thought to be the result of changes in functioning in the PFC. Lesions of the PFC lead to a severe reduction in cognitive flexibility. Humans with damage to the PFC are limited in their ability to change response set when reinforcement contingencies change, as reflected by the observation that they perseverate on previously learned behavior patterns. Damage to the PFC also leads to inappropriate social behaviors, reduced behavioral inhibition, and severe restrictions in response selection when reward contingencies change (e.g., Struss & Benson, 1986).

The PFC contains the circuitry for *working memory*, a temporary, erasable form of memory that is essential to cognitive modification of goal-directed behaviors. *Working memory* refers to the mnemonic process by which information can be kept in a state of moment-to-moment awareness and continuously updated (Goldman-Rakic, 1990). The information held online in working memory may be internal and external contemporaneous sensory information, retrieved long-term declarative or emotional memories, or information about current motivational and emotional states (Goldman-Rakic, 1995). The PFC uses this information to modify behavior in the face of changing reinforcement contingencies. When goal-directed behaviors lead to unexpected outcomes, the PFC, in collaboration with structures such as the amygdala, modifies the affective significance of stimuli and thereby alters expected outcomes and response strategies (Everitt & Robbins, 1992). The PFC is capable of holding a number of representations of affective stimuli online, in working memory, and updating expectancies associated with response strategies as events unfold. The effects of the PFC on goal-directed behaviors are mediated by connections to structures within the APMS (such as the nucleus accumbens), and to the neural network that conveys motivational information to structures involved in the control of movement, particularly the basal ganglia and thalamus (transition circuit in Fig. 9.1).

Monoamine Modulation of Signal Flow Through the APMS. Both the raphe (5-HT neurons) and dopamine (DA)-secreting neurons from the ventral tegmental area (VTA DA) are components of a homeostatic system that regulates signal flow through the APMS (i.e., its output to CNS systems that control motor programs involved in goal-directed behavior) by controlling its *gain* (Hestenes, 1992). *Gain* is defined as the ratio of the magnitude of the output of a system to the strength of an input signal. The gain of the APMS is typically a reflection of its sensitivity to incentive stimuli. An everyday example of a variable gain control mechanism is the volume control of a radio. Turning the volume control knob changes the gain setting so that perceived loudness (the reference level or set point) is the same for signals with differing strengths. Weak signals from distant sources require a higher gain setting than strong signals from sources that are closer to the radio's antenna. The gain setting for the APMS is dependent on the reference level (set point) for this motivational system at a particular time. APMS reference level (i.e., appetitive motivational strength) is influenced by environmental circumstances such as goal proximity and the availability of rewards, and the organism's internal physiological state (e.g., food deprived, satiated). The reference level may be lowered in order to conserve energy resources, as appears to occur in some forms of depression.

VTA DA neurons, also referred to as the Behavioral Activation System (BAS), that connect to the nucleus accumbens can alter the incentive value conferred to stimuli. VTA DA neurons are activated by stimuli that are determined by the amygdala to have affective significance (i.e., through the processes of appraisal and tuned appraisal) with respect to goal-directed behavior (projection from the amygdala to the VTA/DA in Fig. 9.1). Single cell recording studies reveal that VTA DA neurons respond to incentive stimuli, but rarely to stimuli that signal punishment (Mirenowicz & Schultz, 1996). Moreover, the effective incentive value of a stimulus is dependent on both its signal strength, as determined by the processes of appraisal and tuned appraisal, and the sensitivity of VTA DA neurons to conditioned incentive stimuli. The sensitivity of VTA neurons to conditioned incentive stimuli is dependent on their steady state level of neural activity, independent of evoked activity (Beninger, 1983; Blackburn, Phillips, Jakubovic, & Fibiger, 1989). Thus, if the level of activity in the nucleus accumbens and other structures in the APMS form the neural substrate of incentive motivation, the ability of environmental stimuli to motivate goal-directed behavior is dependent on the steady-state level of DA activity in VTA neurons. The results of animal studies provide support for this interpretation. The elevation of VTA DA steady-state synaptic activity by DA agonists enhances a number of APMS-mediated goal-directed behaviors, including affective aggression, social behaviors, sexual activity and goal-directed behaviors involving learning. A reduction in steady-state synaptic activity of VTA DA neurons produced by DA antagonists leads to impairment of the same behaviors (see reviews by Bozarth, 1987; Deutch, Bourdelais, & Zahm, 1993; Fibiger & Phillips, 1987; Le Moal & Simon, 1991; Oades, 1985).

It is important to make a conceptual distinction between the emotional system in the brain that is activated by reward and the emotional system that leads to reward, that is, the APMS. To illustrate this distinction let us examine the activity of VTA DA neurons during instrumental learning. VTA DA neurons are essential to the formation of mnesic traces of the stimulus–response associations formed during the learning of a goal-directed behavior. Suppose that a rat receives a food reward when it presses a lever. VTA DA neurons are activated when the reward occurs, and this activation is essential to the formation of the memory trace (i.e., the change in the strength of synaptic connections that take place during learning) of the relation between the sight of the bar and the instrumental response that leads to the reward. Interestingly, VTA DA neurons respond to the reward in the early phases of the learning process, but once the connection between the stimulus (sight of lever) and response (lever press) become established in memory, the VTA DA neurons cease to respond to the rewarding stimulus. Instead, these neurons respond to stimuli in the environment that predict reward, such as the lever (Houk, Adams, & Barto, 1995). The stimuli that initially were affectively neutral have become conditioned incentive stimuli. Once learning has taken place, stimuli such as the lever gain affective significance, but the sight of the lever would only lead to bar pressing if the appropriate incentive motivation state exists in the APMS. If so, the appropriate motor programs for bar pressing would be activated.

5-HT neurons that connect to neurons of the APMS constrain the facilitating effects of DA on incentive motivation. As examples, 5-HT injections into the nucleus accumbens can completely abolish DA-facilitated locomotor activity, whereas a reduction in 5-HT activity by electrolytic lesions, chemical lesions, or tryptophan-free diets potentiates DA-facilitated locomotor activity (Gerson & Baldessarini, 1980; Grabowska, 1974; Pycock, Horton, & Carter 1978). Similarly, 5-HT agonists suppress DA-facilitated aggressive behavior, whereas 5-HT antagonists enhance DA-facilitated affective aggression (Hahn, Hynes, & Fuller, 1982; McKenzie, 1981). In addition, VTA DA agonists enhance sexual behavior and increased 5-HT activity suppresses sexual behavior (Zemlan, 1978). Thus, 5-HT activity is particularly important to the control of the gain of the APMS.

There is compelling evidence that 5-HT antagonizes VTA DA activity at the nucleus accumbens by presynaptic inhibition. 5-HT inhibits DA release and synthesis at 5-HT heteroreceptors located on the axon terminals of VTA DA neurons that make synaptic connections with nucleus accumbens neurons (Hetey, Kudrin, Shemanow, Rayevsky, & Oelssner, 1985). Thus, increases in the gain of the APMS resulting from increases in VTA DA activity can be counteracted by increases in 5-HT activity upstream to the nucleus accumbens.

Why Is VTA DA and 5-HT Modulation of the Nucleus Accumbens Activity Important to the Understanding of Depression? The core feature of most depressive episodes is a reduction in sensitivity to conditioned incentive stimuli and the associated loss of appetitive motivation. In terms of current mood state, this is referred to as *low positive affect*. Positive affect is one of two superfactors that emerge from a factor analysis of self-reports of current mood state: positive affect and negative affect (Watson, Clark, & Tellegen, 1988). Individuals in a state of *high positive affect* report a broad range of positive mood states such as excitement, enthusiasm, cheerfulness, self-confidence, pleasure, and alertness. In contrast, *low levels of positive affect* are associated with sluggishness, low levels of energy, and a lack of interest in the environment. People experiencing high negative affect report being anxious, distressed, upset, nervous, dissatisfied with life, and discouraged. Individuals with low negative affect characterize themselves as calm and relaxed.

The terms *positive affectivity* and *negative affectivity* are used to refer to the traits that account for self-reports of current mood state and personality characteristics that are based on emotional traits (Clark, Watson, & Mineka, 1994). The term *trait* is used here to refer to a constitutionally based, stable individual difference that is influenced over time by heredity, maturation, and experience (Rothbart & Ahadi, 1994). In addition to showing a proclivity for positive mood states, people high on the dimension of the emotion-based personality trait of positive affectivity report a sense of personal efficacy and incentive motivation, particularly in regard to interpersonal relationships. They tend to be gregarious, assertive, and friendly and characterize themselves as enthusiastic and optimistic. People low in positive affectivity, in contrast, tend to be less responsive to incentives, less socially inclined, reserved, and aloof. Individuals high on the dimension of negative affectivity, in addition to being more likely to report negative mood states, are introspective, have more somatic complaints, have a less favorable self-concept, and in general, report higher levels of stress.

Tellegen (1985) proposed that positive affectivity and negative affectivity reflect differential sensitivities to incentive stimuli and threat, respectively. If the neuronal activity in the brain's emotional systems that underlie affective states exhibit homeostasis (Depue & Zald, 1993), differential sensitivities to incentive stimuli and threat will be reflected in emotion-based personality traits and in current mood states (i.e., positive affect and negative affect). As expected, these two measures—trait and state—are highly correlated (Tellegen & Walker, 1992). The sensitivity of VTA DA neurons to conditioned incentive stimuli is thought to provide the neurobiological foundation for the construct of positive affectivity (Depue, Luciana, Arbisi, Collins, & Leon, 1994). Accordingly, because reduced DA activity is the only consistent monoamine marker for depression (Davis et al., 1988), it seems reasonable to hypothesize that a reduction in the activity of VTA DA neurons is the neural substrate of the low positive affect and low incentive motivation that are the hallmarks of depression. As is discussed in greater detail in the second part of this chapter, a reduction in VTA DA activity may be due to a loss of a source of positive reinforcement, such as the death of a loved one, or it may result from presynaptic inhibition of VTA DA neurons by 5-HT-secreting raphe neurons. An enhancement of 5-HT activity (and inhibition of VTA DA neurons) occurs when prolonged stress leads to a high level of negative affect.

In terms of the information-processing model offered in this chapter, individual differences in sensitivity to threat may result from the mechanisms involved in tuned appraisal or from an AVS with heightened sensitivity to threat. One structure that appears to be a particularly good candidate for involvement in sensitivity to threat is the LC because of its role in increasing the saliency of affective stimuli processed at the amygdala; LC activation can lead to heightened AVS activity and LC reactivity is probably enhanced when the AVS becomes active. The results of animal studies are consistent with this hypothesis. High intensity electrical stimulation of the LC in monkeys produces fear-like behaviors that cannot be distinguished from those observed in learning and conditioning studies (Redmond & Huang, 1979), and these responses can be blocked by anxiolytic drugs. Moderate levels of activity of LC neurons in the awake monkey are associated with attentiveness and vigilance (Foote, Bloom, & Aston-Jones, 1983) and low levels of activity are coupled with signs of fearlessness and inattentiveness (Redmond, 1979). Stimuli that have been linked to fear through learning increase the level of activity in these neurons (Grant & Redmond, 1981) and, in general, drugs that reduce the activity of LC neurons, such as the benzodiazepines, have anxiolytic effects (Redmond, 1977). There is substantial evidence that disregulation of LC neuronal activity, due to diminished sensitivity of alpha-2 autoreceptors, underlies the symptoms of an uncued panic attack in panic disorder patients (Heninger & Charney, 1988).

Findings reviewed by Rosen and Schulkin (1998) provide evidence that a heightened sensitivity to threat may result from a hyperexcitable AVS (what they refer to as the *fear circuit*). By hyperexcitability, they mean a reduction in the threshold for activation of neurons in the AVS. This change in threshold is reflected by a selective perceptual bias in viewing stimuli as threatening and interpreting the environment as dangerous. This perceptual bias is accompanied by heightened arousal, attentiveness, vigilance, and readiness to respond. They contend that both genetic factors and stressful life experiences play roles in the development of hyperexcitability in the neural circuits that mediate functionally adaptive behavioral and perceptual responses to danger. Several types of life experiences are thought to contribute to a hyperexcitable AVS, including trauma (as would occur in individuals with postraumatic stress disorder), sustained maternal separation at an early age, traumatic socially aversive events during adolescence (as occurs in an individual with a social phobia), or a history of uncontrollable or unpredictable stressors.

To summarize, Tellegen (1985) proposed that the trait of negative affectivity was based on differential sensitivity to threat. According to the neural model of information processing presented here, heightened sensitivity to threat may result from the mechanisms involved in tuned appraisal (e.g., LC neurons that are particularly sensitive) or enhanced sensitivity of the AVS to (learned) cues for punishment. These mechanisms should not be considered to be equivalent however. Recall that the process of tuned appraisal occurs earlier in the processing of affective information than the activation of the AVS. Thus, an individual with a tuned appraisal mechanism that shows increased sensitivity to affective stimuli would show both an enhanced sensitivity to threat and to incentive stimuli that activate the APMS, whereas the individual with a highly reactive AVS system would show only enhanced sensitivity to threat. Similarly, high positive affectivity may result from tuned appraisal mechanisms or heightened sensitivity of the APMS to incentive stimuli (specifically the VTA DA neurons shown in Fig. 9.1). High positive affectivity would be linked to heightened sensitivity to threat and negative affectivity when tuned appraisal is involved but heightened sensitivity to incentive stimuli exclusively when VTA DA sensitivity to incentive stimuli is the neural substrate.

Generation of an Emotional Response

The term *emotional response* is used here to refer to both a subjective emotional experience and the changes in body state (e.g., cardiovascular responses, sweating, pupil dilation, hormonal responses, and changes in facial expression) that occur when an emotion is expressed. As shown in Fig. 9.1, the amygdala is considered to be the nodal structure in the neural circuitry responsible for the generation of an emotional response. An emotional response is dependent on appraisal mechanisms and the individual's current motivational state, as reflected by AVS and APMS activity (Fig. 9.1). It also seems likely that subjective emotional experiences are dependent on feedback signals generated by changes in body state (e.g., increases in heart rate and hormonal responses) and sent to the amygdala and other CNS structures (Damasio, 1994).

Dopamine-Secreting Neurons From the VTA Facilitate Emotional Responding. There are extensive projections from the VTA to the amygdala (Fig. 9.1) and these connections appear to lower the threshold for emotional responding, as exemplified by the facilitation of affective aggression when DA activity in the amygdala is increased (Depue & Spoont, 1986; Depue & Iacono, 1989). The VTA is apprised of the emotional significance of a stimulus by projections from the amygdala (Fig. 9.1), and if the stimulus has incentive value VTA DA neuronal connections to the nucleus accumbens augment the incentive motivational state and increase positive affect. The magnitude of this effect is dependent on stimulus intensity and the steady-state level of activity of VTA DA neurons.

One way that DA enhances emotional responding is by facilitating the flow of signals entering and exiting a neural circuit. This is accomplished by promoting "switching" among signal sources within the CNS (Oades, 1985). For example, a number of stimuli may elicit an emotional reaction and subsequent goal-directed behaviors if their CNS representations can gain access to the amygdala; DA promotes the *switching* between these signal sources. In addition to switching between CNS representations of affectively significant stimuli, DA also promotes switching among various memory traces.

Serotonin (5-HT) Activity Promotes Emotional Stability. The 5-HT-secreting raphe neurons are a part of a negative feedback system designed to regulate affect when it is modulated by changes in environmental circumstances (i.e., challenges). The phrase *5-HT functioning* is used to refer to the ability of the 5-HT system to return the level of positive affect or negative affect to its original level (i.e., set point) when challenged by these environmental changes. It accomplishes this by altering the gain of feed forward mechanisms such as the APMS and the AVS. As an example, in a 5-HT system showing high functioning (i.e., effective negative feedback control), the increase in negative affect elicited by threat or punishment should lead to an increase in 5-HT activity (increased constraint of signal flow). Similarly, the decrease in positive affect due to the loss of a major source of reinforcement, such as the death of a loved one, should lead to a decrease in 5-HT activity (decrease in constraint of signal flow through the APMS and increase in APMS gain) so as to bring positive affect back to its set point. Paradoxically, an increase in positive affect resulting from reward or other mood-elevating experiences should also lead to an increase in 5-HT activity thereby reducing the gain of the APMS. Indeed, there is evidence that the 5-HT system is a component of the negative feedback system (satiety mechanism) involved in the reward associated with food intake, and disregulation of the 5-HT system may contribute to the impairment of mood regulation and psychopathological behaviors associated with the eating disorders anorexia nervosa and bulimia nervosa (Kaye & Weltzin, 1991; Wolfe, Metzger, & Jamerson, 1997). More specifically, low 5-HT activity would be associated with binge eating in the patient with bulimia nervosa due to a reduction in the strength of the satiety mechanism. Low 5-HT activity is usually accompanied by mood changes and thus, may account for the dysphoric mood that precedes binge eating in these patients. Similarly, the weight loss in the anorexia nervosa patient could be accounted for by an overfunctioning 5-HT system that is associated with an enhancement in the strength of the satiety mechanism. An overfunctioning 5-HT system may also account for the limited social spontaneity and overly restrained emotional expression observed in anorexia nervosa patients.

A general principle regarding the effects of 5-HT on emotional behavior is that this transmitter antagonizes the facilitating effect of DA (Spoont, 1992). Thus, low 5-HT functioning is associated with emotional lability, and high 5-HT functioning is linked to emotional stability. Individuals with extremely high levels of 5-HT functioning (i.e., negative feedback control is too strong) show restrained emotional expression and a general paucity of emotions, whereas low 5-HT functioning is linked to a lower threshold for eliciting an emotional reaction, an increased magnitude of the emotional reaction once it occurs, and an increased propensity to experience a variety of emotions per unit of time (Depue & Zald, 1993); the valence of these emotional states may be either positive or negative. The lower threshold for emotional responding results from unconstrained DA facilitation at the regions in the amygdala associated with the generation of an emotional response. Similarly, emotional response magnitude would be greater due to reduced 5-HT-mediated negative feedback inhibitory modulation of signal flow in these same regions of the amygdala. Emotional lability would be observed because DA's switching of signal sources (i.e., various stimuli that might elicit an emotional reaction) would be unconstrained.

It is important to note that many of the characteristics of an individual showing low 5-HT functioning are also displayed by an individual with a sensitive VTA DA system (e.g., impulsivity, aggressive behaviors, increased suicidal tendencies, and emotional lability). DA facilitates signal flow at many of the CNS structures, such as the amygdala, at which signal flow is constrained by 5-HT, although the effects of the two transmitters do not add in any simple way. In fact, 5-HT constraining influences are often not observed unless a behavior has been facilitated by increased DA activity (Spoont, 1992).

Why Is the Promotion of Emotional Stability by 5-HT Important to the Understanding of Affective Distress and Depression? 5-HT functioning becomes particularly important when an individual is faced with psychosocial stressors. 5-HT constrains signal flow so low 5-HT functioning is associated with both a stronger initial emotional reaction to a stressor (5-HT affects the threshold for responding) and prolonged affective distress due to slow engagement of negative feedback attenuation of the emotional response evoked (increase in negative affect or decrease in positive affect).

Summary

An examination of the CNS mechanisms involved in the processing of stimuli that have emotional significance reveals several potential sources for the affective distress linked to depression. First, low activity in VTA DA neurons leads to reduced signal flow through the nucleus accumbens, a key component of the APMS. This would lead to two core features of most forms of depression, a reduction in incentive motivation, and a low level of positive affect. Affective distress can also result from neural mechanisms involved in the tuning of affective stimuli in situations involving threat. If the sensitivity of NE-secreting LC neurons is high, the saliency of tuned stimuli that signal punishment or loss of reward would be enhanced, thereby leading to heightened negative affect (i.e., anxiety); hyperexcitable AVS neurons would also lead to high anxiety. Anxiety and depression are highly comorbid. Finally, affective distress is also linked to a low functioning 5-HT system because of its important homeostatic role in the processing of affective information. 5-HT has a constraining influence on neural activity at each stage in the processing of affective information and thus, would play a key role in attenuating emotional responses in stressful situations. More specifically, the affective distress linked to high negative affect and low positive affect would have greater magnitude and longer duration in an individual with a low functioning 5-HT system.

CENTRAL NERVOUS SYSTEM MECHANISMS UNDERLYING SYMPTOMS OF DEPRESSION

Overview of Biobehavioral Control Systems Perspective

Measures of current mood state are highly correlated with trait measures of emotionality (Tellegen & Walker, 1992). This suggests that there are stable individual differences in the tendency to experience a specific mood state. Indeed, there is rather compelling evidence that the broad mood factors of positive affect and negative affect have a strong dispositional component. Positive and negative affect scores for an individual are extremely stable over time (Diener & Larsen, 1984; Ormel & Schaufeli, 1991; Watson & Slack, 1993) and across life situations, such as socializing versus being alone and work versus recreational setting (Diener & Larsen, 1984).

The observation that individual scores on measures of current mood state are so stable over time and across situations strongly suggests that the neural processes that underlie mood states exhibit homeostasis. More specifically, it seems reasonable to hypothesize that measures of current mood state are markers for the sensitivity of CNS systems underlying affect, such as those activated by reward and punishment, the one involved in the mediation of goal-directed behaviors in response to conditioned incentive stimuli (i.e., the APMS), and the one that responds to threat (i.e., the AVS). Moreover, the stability of self-reported mood scores indicates that the level of neural activity in these emotional systems is regulated by homeostatic mechanisms. Following this line of thinking, the symptoms of depression result from either (a) stressful life circumstances that alter the reference level (set point) for signal flow in an emotional system; or (b) changes in neural activity that reflect an attempt to defend homeostasis within an emotional system in response to a life stressor.

In our view, the symptom profile and time course of a depressive episode are also dependent on the nature of the stressor that led to the depression. Accordingly, in the remainder of this chapter, the regulation of affect is discussed in terms of three types of stressors: (a) *loss* is defined as the removal of positive reinforcement, as would occur when success is followed by failure, or when a major source of reward has been removed (e.g., a job loss or death of a significant other); (b) *punishment* is used to refer to physical pain or psychosocial distress (e.g., criticism and other forms of negative feedback); (c) *threat* is used to refer to situations in which there are signals that punishment or loss may occur in the future.

A major thesis of this chapter is that life events that have emotional significance are processed by homeostasis-promoting neural systems designed to regulate positive affect and negative affect when challenged by environmental stressors. This is accomplished, in part, by altering the gain of emotional systems such as the APMS. Low positive affect is a form of affective distress shared by most depressed patients. Accordingly, the discussion that follows focuses on the regulation of neural activity within the emotional system whose neural activity is most closely linked to positive affect, the APMS, although it is clear that rewarding experiences (i.e., reaching the goal) also impact positive affect (Clark & Watson, 1988). We propose, as a working hypothesis, that the stress of loss often produces a reduction in the set point for signal flow through the APMS (i.e., the strength of the motivational signal sent to CNS regions that control the motor programs involved in goal directed behavior—motor programs in Fig. 9.1) and thereby many of the symptoms of depression associated with low positive affect. The neural substrate for this path to depression is proposed to be a reduction in the gain of the APMS that is mediated by a decrease in the sensitivity of VTA DA neurons to incentive stimuli. The symptoms associated with this pathway to depression are the same as those described for the sadness affective dimension in the companion chapter (chap. 8, this volume). A second pathway to depression, in our view, is the sustained negative affect that is associated with prolonged punishment or threat, but not loss. Specifically, we present evidence that supports the view that the reduction in APMS activity linked to a depressive episode may result from a homeostasis-promoting enhancement of 5-HT activity that regulates negative affect during prolonged stress. The attempt to regulate negative affect during prolonged stress is thought to lead to a reduction in positive affect due to a 5-HT mediated decrease in the gain of the APMS. The symptoms linked to this pathway to depression correspond to those described for the anxious affective dimension in chapter 8 (this volume). Finally, we propose that symptoms of depression may also result from a homeostasis-promoting reduction in 5-HT activity that helps to regulate positive affect in response to loss. The symptoms displayed by these patients are those described for the hostile affective dimension as described in chapter 8 (this volume).

Reduced Activity in VTA DA Neurons Accounts for Symptoms of Depression That Are Coupled With Low Positive Affect

Symptoms of Reduced Energy Level (Fatigue), Psychomotor Retardation, Reports of Hypersomnia, and Low Positive Affect Result From a Reduction in Signal Flow Through the APMS. The reduction of positive affect and the disruption of appetitive motivation are core features of depression. In depressed patients in which the feeling of sadness or emptiness is the predominant mood, there is a general loss of the capacity to experience pleasure or respond to conditioned incentive stimuli that evoke behaviors leading to reward. Cognitive theorists emphasize a sense of hopelessness in which the depressed patient has an expectancy that goal-directed behaviors (either reward-seeking or active avoidance of aversive stimuli) will be ineffective. Because these characteristics are linked to activity in the APMS, our discussion focuses on research findings that advance our understanding of the role of the APMS in the symptoms of depression.

Many of the symptoms of depression appear to result from reduced signal flow through the APMS, particularly the nucleus accumbens. In order to activate the motor programs that lead to goal-directed behavior, an external or internal stimulus must be capable of producing an incentive motivational state (Fig. 9.1). An essential neural event linked to augmented incentive motivation is an increase in activity in the nucleus accumbens, a nodal structure in the APMS. Thus, low levels of activity in the nucleus accumbens would be associated with a general reduction in everyday activities that lead to reward. The low level of incentive motivation resulting from reduced signal flow in the nucleus accumbens would also be linked to lower energy levels, psychomotor retardation, sluggishness, and a general loss of interest in the environment, and hence, low positive affect on self-report measures of current mood state. It is not unreasonable to speculate that the inability to obtain rewards could contribute to the low self-efficacy and low self-esteem seen in depressed patients.

Decreased APMS activity and low positive affect might be expected to lead to hypersomnia if the set point for APMS activity (i.e., strength of motivational signal) has been lowered. Nevertheless, the clinician must be cautious when interpreting reports of excessive sleep by depressed patients. A careful analysis of the sleep–waking patterns of depressed patients, using standardized polysomnographic procedures, provide evidence that a substantial proportion of patients who report hypersomnia do not in fact show increased sleep time (Billiard, Dolenc, Aldaz, Ondze, & Besset, 1994). The complaint of excessive sleep in these patients probably reflects a decreased energy level and loss of incentive motivation (Nofzinger et al., 1991).

A Reduction in Signal Flow Through the APMS in Depressed Patients May Result From a Reduction in the Activity of VTA DA Neurons. Signal flow through the nucleus accumbens is facilitated by VTA DA neurons (see Fig. 9.1) and thus, a decrease in the secretion of DA by VTA neurons would lead to a reduction in goal-directed behavior and incentive motivation. An extensive multicenter study of NE, 5-HT, and DA variations in depressed patients revealed that reduced DA activity was the only consistent marker for depression (Davis et al., 1988). The results of animal studies are consistent with this finding and provide strong evidence for the view that diminished incentive motivation in depressed patients is linked to a reduction in the activity of VTA DA neurons. In animal studies, VTA DA lesions, or DA antagonists that reduce DA secretion by VTA neurons at the nucleus accumbens, produce behavioral changes associated with reduced incentive motivation, including reduced locomotor activity, sexual behavior, social interactions, and the learning of approach and active avoidance responses. In contrast, the enhancement of VTA DA activity by DA agonists facilitates locomotor behavior and a variety of goal-directed behaviors, including instrumental aggression, sexual and social behaviors, and those involved in the learning of goal-directed behaviors through instrumental conditioning (see reviews by Bozarth, 1987; Deutch et al., 1993; Fibiger & Phillips, 1987; Le Moal & Simon, 1991; Oades, 1985).

Why Do VTA DA Neurons Become Less Active in the Depressed Patient? It is certainly reasonable to hypothesize, as other investigators have (Beck, 1987; Clark & Watson, 1994), that depression is often an adaptive response to severe life stressors, particularly loss, and conserves energy. This conservation–withdrawal response (Selye, 1976) is only considered to be dysfunctional if prolonged. Viewed from a biobehavioral control system perspective, *a conservation–withdrawal response* designed to conserve energy would be linked to a reduction in the gain of the emotional system most directly related to appetitive motivation, the APMS. Indeed, there is evidence that is consistent with the view that the gain of the APMS can be modulated by endogenous mechanisms. The broad mood factor proposed to be a marker for signal flow through the APMS, positive affect, shows both a diurnal (Clark, Watson, & Leeka, 1989) and a seasonal variation (Smith, 1979). In view of the observation that DA activity is reduced in depressed patients (Davis et al., 1988), it seems reasonable to propose that a reduction in the gain of the APMS is mediated, at least in part, by a reduction in the sensitivity of VTA DA neurons to incentive stimuli.

An individual showing low trait positive affectivity manifests a strong tendency to experience the mood state of low positive affect. If low positive affect is a core symptom of depression, people who display low positive affectivity as a trait may be at a greater risk for a depressive episode. Viewed from a biobehavioral control systems perspective, this disposition is due in large part to an APMS with a low gain, which results from a reduction in the sensitivity of VTA DA neurons to incentive stimuli. An individual with a low set point for positive affect (i.e., low APMS gain) would be at greater risk for depression because his or her regulated level of positive affect is closer to the threshold for the low level of positive affect that characterizes depression. In this *biological diathesis model,* a stressor that leads to a substantial reduction in positive affect would lead to a depressive episode. There is indirect experimental evidence that supports this view. The tendency to experience differing levels of positive and negative mood states is reflected in EEG measures of baseline activity in anterior cerebral regions (e.g., prefrontal area and anterior temporal lobes). When the levels of left and right anterior activity are compared, individuals with higher levels of left anterior activity (relative to right side) report higher levels of positive affect and lower levels of negative affect than their more right-side activated counterparts (Tomarken, Davidson, Wheeler, & Doss, 1992). If these baseline measures of anterior asymmetries can be taken as markers for dispositional mood, individuals with low left anterior activity should be at greater risk for depression. Indeed, there is evidence for reduced left anterior cerebral activity in depressed patients (Davidson, Schaffer, & Saron, 1985) and in remitted, euthymic individuals who were previously depressed (Henriques & Davidson, 1990).

Many Cognitive Symptoms of Depression Can Be Accounted for by Reduced Activity in VTA DA Neurons That Project to the Cerebral Cortex. These symptoms include reduced cognitive flexibility, limitations in memory retrieval, excessive rumination, and difficulties in decision-making. The results of several studies provide evidence that current mood state affects an individual's cognitive processing mode (Clore, Schwartz, & Conway, 1994; Gotlib & Neubauer, chap. 7, this volume; Schwartz, 1990). Individuals in a positive affective state engage in an unconstrained heuristic processing style with less attention to detail (Bodenhausen, 1993; Forgas & Moylan, 1991; Isen, 1984, 1987); they show greater cognitive flexibility that results in more creative responses and the utilization of more remote associations (Isen, 1987). In contrast, people with low positive affect are more likely to use a more controlled systematic form of information processing with a greater focus on details (Bless, Bohner, Schwarz & Strack, 1990; Sinclair & Mark, 1992).

Animal studies test cognitive flexibility by utilizing tasks in which reinforcement contingencies change (e.g., extinction paradigms, reinforcement reversal tasks, and delayed alternation tasks) or in which goal attainment is dependent on changing behavioral strategies. VTA DA projections to the cerebral cortex, referred to as the *mesocortical dopaminergic system*, are thought to be critical to cognitive flexibility because performance is dependent on signal flow between neocortical areas and the ability of the prefrontal cortex (PFC) to orchestrate the cortical and subcortical activity that underlies adaptive behavioral changes in the face of changing reward contingencies. The PFC contains the neuronal circuitry that is involved in working memory, and the utilization of working memory is essential to the adaptive behavioral modifications that occur when changes in environmental circumstances alter the contingencies for reward. The PFC holds online, in working memory, representations of contemporaneous sensory information, the current emotional and motivational states, and retrieved memories regarding past reinforcement histories that are relevant to the current goal-directed behavior. The PFC constantly updates this information and regulates response selection by it connections to structures such as the basal ganglia and the thalamus. Importantly, in regard to the symptoms of depression, VTA DA projections to the PFC facilitate mechanisms such as working memory that underlie the higher order cognitive functioning that is necessary for behavioral flexibility. DA concentration in the prefrontal cortex is among the highest in neocortical areas (Brown, Crane, & Goldman, 1979) and increases in VTA DA functioning induced by DA agonists, such as amphetamines, enhance performance on reversal and spontaneous alternation tasks, and in an extinction paradigm (Brozoski, Brown, Rosvold, & Goldman, 1979; Cools, 1980; Louilot, Taghzouti, Deminiere, Simon, & LeMoal, 1987; Oades, 1985). Decreases in VTA DA activity by chemical lesions in the VTA or the prefrontal cortex lead to severe decrements in performance in these types of tasks. Similarly, increases in VTA DA functioning produced by DA agonists increase, whereas DA antagonists decrease, the number of cognitive strategies used in experimental paradigms that require behavioral flexibility to reach a goal (Cools, 1980; Le Moal & Simon, 1991).

According to Oades (1985), the reason increased VTA DA activity enhances performance on tasks that depend on behavioral flexibility is that DA activity promotes switching among various sources of information in different brain regions. Thus, animals with low VTA DA activity would tend to lock onto one program for a cognitive strategy, whereas animals with high DA activity would switch among the various available programs. Similarly, VTA DA activity would affect response selection by its impact on the variety of information that may be brought online in working memory in the PFC.

The role of DA in switching between alternative sources of information in the CNS may be important to the understanding of several symptoms shown by depressed patients. Depressed patients show limitations in the variety of declarative memories retrieved (see Scott, Winters, & Beevers, chap. 8, this volume). Access to various memory traces would be limited by a reduction in switching rate associated with low VTA DA activity, although this does not account for why depressed patients show a bias toward negative memories. Similarly, low switching rates may account for the excessive rumination and decision making difficulty seen in depressed patients. Rumination implies that the person is locked onto one thought pattern online in working memory, and decision making requires that numerous sources of information be brought online in working memory, and that others are removed.

The Role of Negative Affect in Depression

Although the core feature of depression is the disruption of appetitive motivation and low positive affect, depression often includes high negative affect as well; this is evidenced by the high rates of anxiety disorders among depressed individuals (Clark & Watson, 1991). As pointed out elsewhere (Akiskal, 1990; Fowles, 1994), a depressive episode often results from a natural sequence of emotional reactions to chronic psychosocial stressors. Initially, negative affect, particularly anxiety and frustration, predominate, and if coping is prolonged, negative affect is replaced by, or combined with, low positive affect and other symptoms of depression. Stressors involving threat or punishment elicit increases in negative affect. This response is attenuated by a homeostasis-promoting increase in 5-HT activity, which brings the level of negative affect back to its set point. One way it accomplishes this is by decreasing the gain of the AVS (i.e., sensitivity to threat). Not only does 5-HT activity increase in response to these types of stressors, but prolonged stressful periods increase the 5-HT response to additional stressors, that is, sensitization occurs (Adell, Garcia-Marquez, Armario, & Gelpi, 1988; Boadle-Biber, Corley, Graves, Phan, & Rosencrans, 1989). The *sensitized 5-HT response* that occurs during prolonged stress may, however, result in a substantial reduction in signal flow in the APMS, particularly the nucleus accumbens. 5-HT injections into the nucleus accumbens lead to a significant attenuation or the total abolishment of DA-facilitated behaviors and there is evidence that 5-HT directly inhibits (via presynaptic inhibition) DA release and synthesis at DA axonal terminals at the nucleus accumbens (Hetey et al., 1985). Thus, the *sensitized 5-HT response* evoked during prolonged stress reduces VTA DA steady-state activity, which would decrease the gain of the APMS (and reduce positive affect). Stated differently, APMS gain (and positive affect) are reduced as a consequence of the 5-HT system's attempt to regulate negative affect. It is proposed here that these changes account for the loss of incentive motivation, the low positive affect, and the reduced levels of DA observed in depressed patients with a history of prolonged stress in which negative affect predominates. The stressors that evoke this type of depression are punishment and threat, rather than loss.

The symptom profile of a depressed patient showing high negative affect coupled with low positive affect, would differ from the one associated with a conservation–withdrawal response because the heightened AVS activity would lead to increases in arousal, hypervigilance, and a reallocation of attentional resources. Based on the results of studies using an animal model of depression, prolonged stress leads to decreased food consumption, weight loss, loss of grooming behaviors, disturbances in sleep, and loss of aggressiveness (Weiss & Simson, 1985). These symptoms are best explained in Aston-Jones' (1985) description of the impact of a high level of activity in the LC (and increased AVS activity) on an animal's orientation toward the external environment:

> Increased locus coeruleus activity [or AVS activity] enhances the reliability and efficiency of feature extraction from sensory input and the suppression of CNS events that have little value in regards to coping or feature extraction associated with unexpected, potentially threatening external events. The locus coeruleus accentuates incoming information that is most likely to be relevant to immediately-needed coping response [i.e., coping with stress]. This leads to an interruption of internally driven vegetative behaviors such as sleep, food, sex, grooming, and other motivational and emotionally significant internally driven behaviors (p. 123).

Heightened Sensitivity to Threat Is a Risk Factor for Depression. The temporal sequence involving environmental challenge, high negative affect, followed by low positive affect and depression, would likely be accelerated in individuals who show high trait sensitivity to threat (Clark et al., 1994). The frequency of affectively distressing episodes would be expected to be elevated in an individual with high trait sensitivity to threat. As a consequence, he or she would be at a greater risk for reaching the high level of negative affect that triggers withdrawal and symptoms of depression.

Most antidepressant medications reduce the sensitivity of forebrain neurons to NE by down-regulation of beta-adrenergic receptors (Sulser & Sanders-Bush, 1989). This change would alter the tuned appraisal mechanism by decreasing the saliency of affective stimuli linked to threat of punishment or loss. The decrease in the saliency of threatening stimuli would be particularly beneficial for depressed patients who, due to heightened sensitivity of NE-secreting LC neurons or a hyperexcitable AVS, show high anxiety.

The Role of Serotonin in the Symptoms of Depression

Homeostatic systems vary in their ability to regulate a controlled variable when the system is challenged by changes in environmental circumstances. This characteristic of a control system is referred to as *regulatory strength*

(Depue & Zald, 1993). The monoamine most closely tied to the regulatory strength of the CNS mechanisms involved in the control of positive and negative affect is 5-HT. An increase in negative affect elicited by threat or punishment should lead to an increase in 5-HT activity, whereas a decrease in positive affect due to the loss of reinforcement should lead to a decrease in 5-HT activity (decrease in constraint of signal flow through the APMS) so as to bring positive affect back to its set point. In our view, many of the symptoms of depression are due to a reduced level of 5-HT activity. The reduction in 5-HT activity may be a homeostasis-promoting attempt to regulate positive affect following loss or it may be a reflection of a control system with low regulatory strength.

5-HT Buffers Emotional Responses to Threat and to Punishment. There is substantial evidence that 5-HT activity increases in response to environmental stressors that would increase negative affect. As an example, punishment from an uncontrollable physical stressor such as foot shock, which is often used as a stressor in animal studies, leads to an increase in 5-HT secretion (e.g., Dunn, 1988; Skurygin, 1995). Similarly, there is increased 5-HT activity in response to environmental stressors involving threat in which the organism is able to actively cope with the aversive stimulus (e.g., Petkov, Stoyanova, & Popova, 1989). Medications for depression that enhance 5-HT functioning, such as the selective 5-HT reuptake inhibitors (SSRIs), should be helpful in attenuating emotional reactions to a variety of stressful stimuli. As an example, there is evidence that SSRIs reduce the magnitude of threat-induced freezing behaviors in a conditioned fear experimental paradigm (Hashimoto, Inoue, & Koyama, 1996).

Decreases in 5-HT Activity Are Thought to Buffer the Reduction in Positive Affect Produced by the Stress of Loss. When an individual is rewarded for his or her efforts, there is an increase in positive affect due to the activation of the emotional system linked to positive reinforcement. Viewed from a biobehavioral control systems perspective, an increase in positive affect due to reward should lead to a compensatory homeostasis-promoting increase in 5-HT activity. Indeed, as discussed earlier, the reward associated with the taste and smell of food leads to an increase in 5-HT activity. Reduced 5-HT activity may account for binge eating, and an overfunctioning 5-HT system may lead to anorexia.

Although rewarding experiences increase positive affect, in our view, positive affect is primarily dependent on the level of activity in the emotional system that leads to reward, the APMS. 5-HT's role in the regulation of signal flow through the focal structure of the APMS, the nucleus accumbens, is particularly important to the understanding of the connection between CNS homeostatic mechanisms and symptoms of depression. If there is an increase in signal flow due an increase in the number of incentive stimuli (e.g., a new significant other or a new rewarding job), there should be an increase in 5-HT activity so as to regulate positive affect (by decreasing the gain of the APMS). Similarly, if signal flow is diminished due to a reduction in the cues for a source of reward (e.g., a loss of a loved one), there should be compensatory homeostasis-promoting decrease in 5-HT constraint of signal flow (i.e., an increase in the gain of the APMS) so as to return positive affect to its set point.

There is an empirical basis for these predicted changes in 5-HT activity. There is an increase in DA secretion and signal flow in the nucleus accumbens when an animal is engaged in intracranial self-stimulation of the medial forebrain bundle. There is also an increase in 5-HT activity in this intensely motivating experimental paradigm, but the time course of this response is quite different from the one shown by DA (Nakahara, Ozaki, Miura, Miura, & Nagatsu, 1989). DA secretion and turnover begin at the onset of intracranial self-stimulation and end at the termination of stimulation. In contrast, the 5-HT response has a longer latency and continues after the offset of the intracranial self-stimulation (Nakahara et al., 1989). The 5-HT pattern is consistent with the idea that its secretion is a compensatory homeostatic reaction to the increase in signal flow through the nucleus accumbens (Spoont, 1992). Viewed from a biobehavioral control systems perspective, the increase in neural activity in the nucleus accumbens evoked by reward-seeking behaviors is a challenge to the regulation of positive affect and would be expected to engage a negative feedback mechanism. An increase in nucleus accumbens activity and a compensatory increase in 5-HT activity would also be expected to occur when an individual is actively coping (active avoidance) with an environmental stressor. This type of behavior is also goal-directed and the goal is the safety that comes with avoiding punishment. Although the level of APMS activity in the reward seeker and the individual engaged in active coping may be quite similar, their emotional states would differ. They both would experience the positive affect linked to desire and hope, but the positive affect experienced by an individual who is coping with a stressor would be coupled with the negative affect from the threat-induced activation of the AVS.

There is also evidence for decreased 5-HT activity (decreased constraint of signal flow and an increase in the gain of the APMS) in response to a reduction in signal flow in the APMS, although this aspect of 5-HT's putative role in neural homeostasis has not been investigated extensively. One way to study this aspect of 5-HT's role in the regulation of positive affect is to measure changes in 5-HT activity when a major source of reward is removed from the environment. Prolonged social isolation would be expected to remove a major source of incentive stimuli in social animals and thus a reduction in the signal flow in the APMS. Many rodents subjected to prolonged social isolation show a decrease in 5-HT activity (Kempf, Puglisi-Allegra, Cabib, Schleef, & Mandel, 1984; Valzelli, 1981, 1982; Valzelli & Bernasconi, 1979) as would be predicted by a homeostatic model. Interestingly, those animals who showed a reduction in 5-HT activity also showed a symptom observed in many depressed patients, irritable aggression; animals who did not show a reduction in 5-HT activity to social isolation showed no increases in aggressive behavior.

Reduced 5-HT-Mediated Buffering Associated With Low 5-HT Activity Accounts for the Heightened Sensitivity to Pain Observed in Many Depressed Patients. One CNS change that is known to engage the 5-HT mechanism is an increase in nonspecific arousal (Auerbach, Fornal, & Jacobs, 1985). An increase in nonspecific arousal would be expected to be evoked by punishment such as a pain-producing stimulus, or the anticipation of punishment as would occur when the AVS is activated by threat (i.e., predictive homeostasis). An increase in 5-HT activity would be expected to occur at the earliest stages of sensory processing (Fig. 9.1). The impact of 5-HT's regulatory function at the initial stage of sensory processing becomes clear when one observes the impact of a pain-producing noxious stimuli in animals in which 5-HT functioning is low. As would be expected, low 5-HT activity increases the sensitivity of the nociceptive reflex involved in pain perception (Anderson & Dafny, 1982; Lakos & Basbaum, 1988; Roberts, 1984). High 5-HT activity is known to inhibit the nociceptive reflex (i.e., increases the threshold for pain) during a state of high arousal (Auerbach et al., 1985). Low 5-HT activity, therefore, may account for the finding that a significant number of depressed patients show a heightened sensitivity to pain (Meltzer & Lowy, 1987).

Low 5-HT Activity Accounts for the Irritable Affect and Outwardly Directed Hostility Observed in Many Depressed Patients. Decreased 5-HT activity would contribute to a number of symptoms of depression. 5-HT is involved in the initial stage of sensory processing and animals with low 5-HT activity show an elevated sensitivity to stimulation in several sensory modalities including the visual, tactile, and auditory systems, and this sensitivity is thought to underlie the apparent irritability seen in these animals. The results of human studies are consistent with these findings. Individuals showing low 5-HT activity also show a heightened sensitivity to a variety of sensory stimuli and this heightened sensitivity is reported as aversive (Depue & Zald, 1993). Moreover, numerous studies have shown a strong negative correlation between irritable aggression, outwardly directed hostility, and levels of 5-HIAA (a metabolite of 5-HT) in the cerebral spinal fluid of healthy human volunteers (Asberg, Schalling, & Traskman-Bendy, 1987; Roy, Adinoff, & Linnoila, 1988).

In general, 5-HT activity has a substantial impact on social behaviors. Rats with chemically-induced depletions of 5-HT show significantly fewer social interactions than controls (File, James, & Macleod, 1981), whereas chemical enhancement of 5-HT leads to the facilitation of social behaviors (Vergnes, Depaulis, & Boehrer, 1986). Chemical enhancement of 5-HT in primates also leads to the facilitation of social behaviors including increases in socially oriented approach behaviors, reductions in conspecific anxiety-driven hypervigilance and social solitude (Raleigh, Brammer, & McGuire, 1983). One possible explanation of these findings is that low 5-HT activity in tuned appraisal or the AVS may increase the saliency of social cues involving threat and thus avoidance of social interactions.

There is abundant evidence that animals with low 5-HT activity make social responses that are inappropriate to a particular situation (Gardner, 1985; Treit, 1985; Winslow & Insel, 1990). A critical aspect of social interactions is knowing when to inhibit social behaviors, such as aggression, whose consequence is punishment. Low 5-HT activity releases behavioral suppression in response to cues of punishment (Gray, 1982; Soubrie, 1986; Stein, 1981), so many antisocial behaviors, including affective aggression, may be linked to the disinhibition associated with low 5-HT activity.

The neural mechanisms underlying disinhibition of behaviors that lead to punishment are not known, but there are several possibilities. Low 5-HT activity would disfacilitate goal-directed behaviors by decreasing the amount of presynaptic inhibition of VTA DA neurons exerted at the nucleus accumbens. Interestingly, some forms of affective aggression are thought to be mediated by the APMS. A second possible mechanism of disinhibition involves the PFC circuitry discussed earlier. It is recalled that the *PFC circuitry*, which includes sites in the basal ganglia and thalamus, regulates response selection in the face of changing reinforcement contingencies. 5-HT-secreting raphe neurons modulate activity in the PFC circuitry that alters response set when reinforcement contingencies change (e.g., Haber, 1986; Limberger, Spath, & Starke, 1986). One consequence of disregulation in this circuitry is reduced inhibitory modulation of behavior. A third possible mechanism for reduced behavioral inhibition is offered by Gray (1979) in his neurobiological model of anxiety. According to this view, behavioral inhibition in response to cues of punishment (i.e., passive avoidance) is mediated by 5-HT connections to motor circuits.

Suicide and 5-HT. Suicide is considered to be a form of active avoidance, as opposed to passive avoidance, because the action (as opposed to inhibition of behavior) leads to the removal of intolerable life circumstances (Depue & Zald, 1993). Individuals showing low 5-HT functioning would be at a greater risk for suicide because DA-facilitated signal flow through the APMS would be unconstrained by 5-HT. Indeed, there is substantial evidence that low 5-HIAA (a metabolite of 5-HT) levels in the cerebral spinal fluid is inversely related to suicidal behaviors, including both successful and unsuccessful attempts (Asberg et al., 1987; Meltzer & Lowey, 1987).

Other Functions Related to 5-HT Activity. As discussed in the first section of this chapter, the mechanisms that mediate predictive homeostasis are engaged prior to the onset of a regulatory challenge. These mechanisms, which mitigate the impact of the challenge (or totally nullify it), are cued by a stimulus that predicts the event that would disrupt homeostasis. For example, a tonal stimulus is often used in an instrumental learning paradigm or in Pavlovian conditioning as a conditioned stimulus that predicts an impending pain-producing aversive stimulus. CNS mechanisms (e.g., the AVS) would be engaged by the tone, and the impact of the aversive stimulus would be attenuated or nullified by behavioral changes (i.e., active avoidance or inhibition of behavior) and/or physiological changes, such as the release of endogenous opiates (to mitigate the pain in the Pavlovian conditioning paradigm).

One of the most salient cues for the engagement of predictive homeostatic mechanisms is the sunrise. Indeed, most physiological, biochemical, and behavioral processes display a circadian rhythm, and many of these variations promote predictive homeostasis. For example, the secretion of the stress hormone cortisol shows a circadian variation in which it is elevated in the early hours of the day in anticipation of impending stressors. There is good reason to believe that 5-HT plays an important role in circadian rhythms that are controlled by internal biological clocks and entrained to zeitgebers such as light. The suprachiasmatic nucleus of the hypothalamus, which provides the primary control over the timing of sleep–wake cycles and other functions that show diurnal variations, is considered to be the primary biological clock responsible for organizing the body's circadian rhythms. The suprachiasmatic nucleus is richly innervated by 5-HT neurons so disturbances in circadian rhythms may result from altered 5-HT functioning, as would occur during prolonged stress (the sensitized 5-HT response) or loss (decreased 5-HT activity). Indeed, one of the most prominent symptoms of depression is disordered sleep. Perhaps abnormalities in 5-HT functioning account for the distortion in the circadian pattern for cortisol that is observed in depressed patients (e.g., Akiskal, Maskal, & Lemmi, 1983).

5-HT functioning is also related to food intake. More specifically, it is a component of the negative feedback mechanism (satiety) involved in the regulation of caloric intake. Injections of 5-HT into the hypothalamic regions involved in the regulation of caloric intake lead to decreased food consumption (Leibowitz, Weiss, & Suh, 1990) and pharmacological agents that inhibit the synthesis of 5-HT or block 5-HT receptors lead to increased food intake, especially carbohydrates (e.g., Stallone & Nicolaidis, 1989).

Thus, individuals with low 5-HT activity may also show increased food intake. In view of 5-HT's important role in the regulation of affect, it comes as no surprise that many patients with seasonal affective disorder show an increased appetite, particularly for carbohydrates (Meltzer & Lowy, 1987).

The Emotional Instability and Mood Swings Shown by Many Patients With Bipolar Disorder Are Thought to Reflect the Low Regulatory Strength Associated With Low 5-HT Functioning. A manic episode in bipolar disorder is thought to reflect an extremely high sensitivity of VTA DA neurons to incentive stimuli (Depue & Iacono, 1989). High VTA DA activity promotes switching between various signal sources in the CNS (Oades, 1985). These signal sources include various CNS representations of stimuli that have incentive value, thoughts, and memory traces. The high VTA DA activity associated with a manic episode would increase emotional reactivity, emotional lability, impulsivity, and positive affect. The high rate of switching between signal sources would limit the ability of the bipolar patient in a manic phase to maintain the focus necessary for sustaining goal-directed behavior because a new signal such as an incentive stimulus, a retrieved memory, or thought would gain access to the APMS thereby redirecting behavior.

5-HT functioning is also important to the understanding of bipolar disorder (Goodnick, 1998). Many bipolar patients show frequent mood swings, signifying low regulatory strength within CNS emotional systems (Depue & Zald, 1993). In regards to the APMS, low 5-HT functioning would lead to a deficit in gain control. Reduced ability to make appropriate APMS gain adjustments in response to changes in environmental circumstances (both internal and external) would underlie manic episodes in which the APMS gain is extremely high, and bouts with depression where APMS activity is low. Interestingly, it would be predicted that mood elevations due to intense rewarding or reward-seeking experiences should trigger manic episodes in a low 5-HT functioning bipolar patient who is prone to manic episodes. The challenge of these experiences should lead to a homeostasis-promoting increase in 5-HT activity and as a consequence, a reduction in APMS gain. Thus, there would an increase in the risk of a manic episode in a bipolar patient showing low 5-HT functioning due to the slow engagement of this negative feedback mechanism. As a consequence, APMS gain would become extremely high.

Following this line of thinking, Wehr, Sack, and Rosenthal (1987) suggested that sleep reduction is a final common pathway to a manic episode in bipolar patients. Sleep deprivation often elevates mood and leads to a temporary remission of symptoms in many depressed patients (e.g., Albert, Merz, & Schubert, 1998); it may induce a manic episode in a bipolar patient even if the patient is depressed when deprived of sleep (Wehr et al., 1987). Symptoms of depression return after recovery sleep. As discussed by Wehr et al. (1987), many events such as administration of (or withdrawal from) psychoactive drugs, separation, loss, common sleep-disturbing experiences (e.g., work, travel, social activities, shift work, and newborn infant), and emotional distress, can lead to sleep deprivation. One possibility is that mood elevation is due to a DA-mediated increase in APMS gain. Mood elevation from sleep reduction can be considered to be a challenge to the regulation of positive affect, and a bipolar patient showing low regulatory strength in emotional systems due to low 5-HT functioning would be expected to be at a greater risk for a manic episode.

Low 5-HT Activity Leads to Sleep Disturbances. One key to understanding the role of 5-HT in depression may come from the study of sleep disturbances in depression. The sleep pattern of healthy individuals is typically characterized by a continuous series of 90-minute cycles. Each cycle begins with a period of non-Rapid Eye Movements (non-REM) sleep, followed by REM and dreaming. The typical latency to REM during the first sleep cycle is around 85 to 90 minutes, with very little dreaming. The cycle is repeated several times during the course of the night with a progressive increase in the proportion of the cycle filled with REM and dreaming; most dreaming occurs during the last half of a night of sleep. 5-HT plays a key role in the cycle because it inhibits the acetylcholine-secreting neurons in the peribrachial region that generate the various components of REM sleep (Jacobs, Asher, & Dement, 1973; Lydic, McCarley, & Hobson, 1983). Thus, dreaming is linked to a reduction of 5-HT activity and the latency to REM can be taken as a marker for low 5-HT activity. This disruption of a normal ultradian rhythm would be expected to be associated with a number of disturbances in sleep, such as disrupted sleep and early awakenings.

Compared to healthy individuals, many depressed patients show a short latency to REM and in the first half of the night, a greater proportion of REM (Kupfer, 1976; Vogel, Vogel, McAbee, & Thurmond, 1980), thereby suggesting reduced 5-HT activity. Relatives of people with depression also show sleep abnormalities indicative of low 5-HT activity, even prior to their first depressive episode. First-degree relatives of people with depression show a short REM sleep latency (Giles, Roffwarg, & Rush, 1987) and those with the shortest REM latency are found to be at highest risk for a subsequent bout with depression (Giles, Biggs, Rush, & Roffwarg, 1988). Many antidepressant medications increase 5-HT functioning and depress REM sleep. If these characteristics of REM are premorbid markers for a low functioning 5-HT system, these individuals may be at greater risk for depression due to a diminished ability to regulate affect when faced with environmental stressors.

Implications for Pharmacological Treatment of Depression. There is good reason to believe that many antidepressant medications, particularly the SSRIs, enhance 5-HT functioning. Initially, antidepressant medications that inhibit 5-HT reuptake at synapses cause a decrease in the activity of raphe neurons that secrete 5-HT. When raphe neurons secrete 5-HT at forebrain structures such as the amygdala they also release 5-HT on their own dendrites and cell bodies. This leads to the activation of 5-HT_{1A} autoreceptors that are located at somatodendritic sites. Autoreceptor activation leads to the inhibition of firing of raphe neurons (Blier, de Montigny, & Chaput, 1987). Thus, raphe neurons regulate their own firing by a negative feedback mechanism, thereby preventing their own firing levels from becoming too high. Initially, the inhibition of 5-HT reuptake after its secretion at raphe axon terminals and somatodendritic sites leads to a decrease in firing due to enhanced stimulation of 5-HT_{1A} autoreceptors. After 2 to 3 weeks, however, the 5-HT_{1A} autoreceptors become desensitized (down-regulated) and raphe neurons become more reactive because of reduced autoreceptor-mediated negative feedback regulation. This enhancement in 5-HT functioning is reflected in more 5-HT released per nerve impulse (e.g., Chaput, de Montigny, & Blier, 1986).

Enhanced 5-HT functioning would promote emotional stability by facilitating the regulation of negative affect in response to threat, so it is not surprising that antidepressant medications that preferentially inhibit 5-HT reuptake are particularly beneficial for depressed patients in which anxiety is a prominent symptom (Rampello, Nicoletti, Raffaele, & Drago, 1995). Similarly, the increase in negative affect generated by punishment, and the decrease in positive affect evoked by loss would be expected to have shorter durations if 5-HT functioning is enhanced. Stated in the language of a biobehavioral control systems approach, there would be an enhancement of the negative feedback mechanism involved in the regulation of affect. There are potential drawbacks to improved 5-HT functioning, however. If 5-HT activity becomes too high, affect, incentive motivation, and responses to positive reinforcers would be blunted (Fig. 9.1). Also, the use of 5-HT reuptake inhibitors to treat bipolar disorder is ill-advised. The reduction in 5-HT activity during the first 2 to 3 weeks would render the bipolar patient more vulnerable to a manic episode (triggered by an elevation in mood) due to an increase in the gain of the APMS.

Summary: Symptoms of Depression Associated With the Stress of Loss. Viewed from a biobehavioral control systems perspective, there are several symptoms of depression that would be related to a homeostasis-promoting reduction in 5-HT activity in response to loss. These symptoms include irritable affect, increased sensitivity to pain, increased appetite, sleep disturbances resulting from decreased REM sleep latency and increased

REM density, externalized hostility, and compromised circadian rhythms (e.g., change in the circadian pattern associated with cortisol secretion). Thus, the affective distress of this type of depressed patient would be very different from the one involving a conservation–withdrawal response in which sadness (or feelings of emptiness) is the predominate affective state. The conservation–withdrawal response may signify that attempts to defend homeostasis by reduced 5-HT activity have failed. Symptoms associated with low 5-HT activity may also appear during the recovery phase of a conservation–withdrawal response because there should be reduced 5-HT activity when the set point for positive affect and APMS activity has been reset (elevated to its original level).

Summary

A major thesis of this chapter is that life events that have affective significance are processed by homeostasis-promoting neural systems designed to regulate positive and negative affect when challenged by environmental stressors. The symptoms of depression are viewed as coming from three sources: (a) a reduction in the set point for positive affect in response to loss; (b) an attempt by CNS neural systems to regulate positive affect in response to loss; and (c) a significant reduction in positive affect in an attempt of CNS neural systems to regulate negative affect during prolonged stress.

In many individuals, the affective distress associated with the loss of a major source of reward evokes a conservation–withdrawal response that serves the function of resource conservation. We propose that one neurobiological substrate of this conservation–withdrawal response is a reduction in the set point for APMS activity and that this change in set point is mediated by a reduction in the sensitivity of VTA DA neurons to incentive stimuli (i.e., the gain of the APMS is lowered). Positive affect is regulated during a conservation–withdrawal response, but at a lower set point. The engagement of a conservation–withdrawal response is linked to several symptoms of depression including, reduced energy level, psychomotor retardation, loss of incentive motivation, reports of hypersomnia, low positive affect, excessive rumination, cognitive inflexibility, limitations in memory retrieval, and difficulties in making decisions. This symptom pattern corresponds to the one described for the sad affective dimension in the companion chapter (chap. 8, this volume).

A reduction in APMS signal flow following loss would be expected to evoke a compensatory homeostasis-promoting decrease in 5-HT activity. This attempt of the CNS to regulate positive affect in response to loss underlies the symptoms of depression associated with low 5-HT activity, including irritable affect, increased sensitivity to pain, sleep disturbances resulting from decreased REM sleep latency and increased REM density, increased appetite, compromised circadian rhythms (e.g., change in the circadian pattern associated with cortisol secretion), and inappropriate social behaviors such as externalized hostility. These symptoms may also result from the increase in the set point for APMS activity and positive affect that occurs during the recovery phase of a conservation–withdrawal response to loss. The symptom pattern corresponds to the one described for the hostile affective dimension in chapter 8 (this volume).

A depressive episode may also result from the attempt of the CNS to regulate negative affect during prolonged periods of stress. The stress associated with threat and punishment elicits increases in 5-HT activity. Not only does 5-HT activity increase in response to these types of stressors, but also prolonged stressful periods increase the 5-HT response to additional stressors (i.e., sensitization of the 5-HT response occurs). A sensitized 5-HT system attenuates the emotional impact of stressors that evoke negative affect, but it also leads to the reduction in VTA DA activity and the depression-associated low positive affect. In addition to low positive affect, the symptom profile of this type of depressed patient would include signs of heightened activity in the AVS including reduced appetite, insomnia, hypervigilance, and heightened arousal; enhanced 5-HT activity may also lead to compromised circadian rhythms. This symptom pattern corresponds to the one described for the anxious affective dimension in chapter 8 (this volume).

REFERENCES

Adell, A., Garcia-Marquez, C., Armario, A., & Gelpi, E. (1988). Chronic stress increases serotonin and noradrenaline in rat brain and sensitizes their responses to a further acute stress. *Journal of Neurochemistry, 50*, 1678–1681.

Akiskal, H. S. (1990). Toward a clinical understanding of the relationship between anxiety and depressive disorders. In J. D. Maser & C. R. Cloniger (Eds.), *Comorbidity of anxiety and mood disorders* (pp. 597–607). Washington, DC: American Psychiatric Press.

Akiskal, H. S., Maskal, T. R., & Lemmi, H. (1983). Clinical, neuroendocrine, and sleep EEG diagnosis of "unusual" affective presentations: A practical review. *Psychiatric Clinics of North America, 6*(1), 69–83.

Albert, R., Merz, A., & Schubert, J. (1998). Sleep deprivation and subsequent sleep phase advance stabilizes the positive effect of sleep deprivation in depressive episodes. *Nervenarzt, 69*(1), 66–69.

Andersen, E., & Dafny, N. (1982). Microiontophoretically applied 5-HT reduces responses to noxious stimulation in the thalamus. *Brain Research, 241*, 176–178.

Asberg, M., Schalling, D., & Traskman-Bendy, L. (1987). Psychobiology of suicide, impulsivity, and related phenomena. In H. Meltzer (Ed.), *Psychopharmacology of the third generation of progress* (pp. 665–668.). New York: Raven.

Aston-Jones, G., Akoaka, H., Charl'ety, P., & Chouvet, G. (1991). Serotonin selectively attenuates glutamate-evoked activation of noradrenergic locus coeruleus neurons. *Journal of Neuroscience, 11*(3), 760–769.

Aston-Jones, G., Rajkowski, J., & Kubiak, P. (1997). Conditioned responses of monkey locus coeruleus neurons anticipate acquisition of discriminative behavior in a vigilance task. *Neuroscience, 80*(3), 697–715.

Aston-Jones, G. A. (1985). The locus ceoruleus: Behavioral functions of locus coeruleus derived from cellular attributes. *Physiological Psychology, 13*(3), 118–126.

Auerbach, S., Fornal, C., & Jacobs, B. L. (1985). Response of serotonin containing neurons in nucleus raphe magnus to morphine, noxic stimuli, and periaqueductal gray stimulation in freely moving. *Experimental Neurology, 88*, 609–628.

Azmitia, E. C., & Gannon, P. J. (1986). The primate serotonergic system: A review of human and animal studies and a report on macaca fascicularis. In S. Fahn (Ed.), *Advances in neurology, Vol. 43, Myoclonus* (pp. 407–468). New York: Raven.

Beck, A. T. (1987). Cognitive models of depression. *Journal of Cognitive Psychotherapy, An International Quarterly, 1*, 5–37.

Beninger, R. J. (1983). The role of dopamine in locomotor activity and learning. *Brain Research Reviews, 6*, 173–196.

Billiard, M., Dolenc, L., Aldaz, C., Ondze, B., & Besset, A. (1994). Hypersomnia associated with mood disorders: A new perspective. *Journal of Psychosomatic Research, 18*(1), 41–47.

Blackburn, J. R., Phillips, A. G., Jakubovic, A., & Fibiger, H. C. (1989). Dopamine and preparatory behavior: II. A neurochemical analysis. *Behavioral Neuroscience, 103*, 15–23.

Bless, H., Bohner, G., Schwarz, N., & Strack, F. (1990). Mood and persuasion: A cognitive response analysis. *Personality and Social Psychology Bulletin, 16*, 331–345.

Blier, P., de Montigny, C., & Chaput, Y. (1987). Modifications of the serotonin system by antidepressant treatments: Implications for the therapeutic response in major depression. *Journal of Clinical Psychopharmacology, 6*(Suppl.), 24S–35S.

Boadle-Biber, M. C., Corley, K. C., Graves, L. Phan, T. H., & Rosencrans, J. (1989). Increase in the activity of tryptophan hydroxylase from cortex and midbrain of male Fischer 344 rats in response to acute or repeated sound stress. *Brain Research, 482*, 306–316.

Bodenhausen, G. V. (1993). Emotions, arousal, and stereotypic judgments: A heuristic model of affect and stereotyping. In D. M. Mackie & D. L. Hamilton (Eds.), *Affect, cognition, and stereotyping: Interactive processes in group perception* (pp. 13–37). San Diego, CA: Academic Press.

Bozarth, M. (1987). Ventral tegmental reward system. In J. Engel & L. Oreland (Eds.), *Brain reward systrems and abuse* (pp. 204–222). New York: Raven.

Brown, R. M., Crane, A. M., & Goldman, P. S. (1979). Regional distribution of monoamines in the cerebral cortex and subcortical structures of the rhesus monkey: Concentrations and in vitro synthesis rates. *Brain Research*, 133–150.

Brozoski, T., Brown, R., Rosvold, H., & Goldman, P. (1979). Cognitive deficit caused by regional depletion of dopamine in prefrontal cortex of rhesus monkey. *Science, 205*, 929–931.

Cahill, L., & McGaugh, J. L. (1998). Mechanisms of emotional arousal and lasting declarative memory. *Trends in Neuroscience, 21*, 294–299.

Chaput, Y., de Montigny, C., & Blier, P. (1986). Effects of a selective 5-HT reuptake blocker, citalopram, on the sensitivity of 5-HT autoreceptors: Electrophysiological studies in the rat brain. *Naunyn Schmiedebergs Archives of Pharmacology, 333*, 342–348.

Clark, L. A., & Watson, D. (1988). Mood and the mundane: Relations between daily life events and self-reported mood. *Journal of Personality and Social Psychology, 54*, 296–308.

Clark, L. A., & Watson, D. (1991). Tripartie model of anxiety and depression: Psychometric considerations and taxonomic implications. *Journal of Abnormal Psychology, 100*, 316–336.

Clark, L. A., & Watson, D. (1994). Distinguishing functional from dysfunctional affective responses. In P. Ekman & R. J. Davidson (Eds.), *The nature of emotion: Fundamental questions* (pp. 131–136). New York: Oxford University Press.

Clark, L. A., Watson, D., & Leeka, J. (1989). Diurnal variation in the positive affects. *Motivation and Emotion, 13*, 205–234.

Clark, L. A., Watson, D., & Mineka, S. (1994). Temperament, personality, and the mood and anxiety disorder. *Journal of Abnormal Psychology, 103*(1), 103–116.

Clore, G. L., Schwartz, N., & Conway, M. (1994). Emotion and information processing. In R. S. Wyer & T. K. Srull (Eds.), *Handbook of social cognition* (2nd ed.; pp. 323–417). Hillsdale, NJ: Lawrence Erlbaum Associates.

Collins, P., & Depue, R. A. (1992). A neurobehavioral systems approach to developmental psychopathology. In D. Cicchetti & S. Toth (Eds.), *Developmental perspectives on depression* (Vol. 4, pp. 29–105). Rochester, NY: University of Rochester Press.

Cools, A. R. (1980). The role of neostriatal dopaminergic activity in sequencing and selecting behavioral strategies: Facilitation of processes involved in selecting the best strategy in a stressful situation. *Behavioral Brain Research, 1,* 361–374.

Damasio, A. R. (1994). *Descartes' error: Emotion, reason, and the human brain.* New York: Grosset & Dunlap.

Davidson, R. J., Schaffer, C. E., & Saron, C. (1985). Effects of laterilized presentations of faces on self-reports or emotion and EEG asymmetry in depressed and non-depressed subjects. *Psychophysiology, 22,* 353–364.

Davis, J., Koslow, S., Gibbons, R., Maas, J., Bowden, C., Casper, R., Hanin, I. Javaid, J., Chang, S., & Stokes, P. (1988). Cerebrospinal fluid and urinary amines in depressed patients and healthy controls. *Archives of General Psychiatry, 45,* 705–717.

Davis, M., Astrachan, D. I., & Kass, E. (1980). Excitatory and inhibitory effects of serotonin on sensorimotor reactivity measured with acoustic startle. *Science, 209,* 521–523.

Depue, R., Luciana, M., Arbisi, P., Collins, P., & Leon, A. (1994). Dopamine and the structure of personality: Relation of agonist-induced dopamine activity to positive emotionality. *Journal of Personality and Social Psychology, 67,* 485–498.

Depue, R., & Spoont, M. (1986). Conceptualizing a serotonin trait: A behavioral dimension of constraint. *Annals of the New York Academy of Sciences, 487,* 47–62.

Depue, R. A., & Iacono, W. G. (1989). Neurobehavioral aspects of affective disorders. *Annual Review of Psychology, 40,* 457–492.

Depue, R. A., & Zald, D. (1993). Biological and environmental processes in nonpsychotic psychopathology: A neurobehavioral system perspective. In C. Costello (Ed.), *Basic issues in psychopathology* (pp. 127–237). New York: Guilford.

Deutch, A., Bourdelais, A., & Zahm, D. (1993). The nucleus accumbens core and shell: Accumbal compartments and their functional attributes. In P. Kalivas & C. Barnes (Eds.), *Limbic motor circuits and neuropsychiatry* (pp. 114–153). Boca Raton, FL: CRC Press.

Diener, E., & Larsen, R. J. (1984). Temporal stability and cross-situational consistency of affective, behavioral, and cognitive responses. *Journal of Personality and Social Psychology, 47,* 871–883.

Dunn, A. J. (1988). Changes in plasma and brain tryptophan and brain serotonin and 5-hydroxyindoleacetic acid after footshock stress. *Life Sciences, 42*(19), 1847–1853.

Dworkin, B. R. (1993). *Learning and physiological regulation.* Chicago: The University of Chicago Press.

Everitt, B., & Robbins, T. (1992). Amygdala-ventral striatal interactions and reward-related processes. In J. Aggleton (Ed.), *The amygdala: Neurobiological aspects of emotion, memory, and mental dysfunction* (pp. 93–121). New York: Wiley.

Fibiger, H., & Phillips, A. (1987). Role of catecholamine transmitters in brain reward systems: Implications for the neurobiology of affect. In J. Engel & L. Oreland (Eds.), *Brain reward systems and abuse* (pp. 61–74). New York: Raven.

File, S., James, T. A., & Macleod, N. K. (1981). Depletion in amygdaloid 5-hydroxtryptamine concentration and changes in social and aggressive behavior. *Journal of Neural Transmission, 50,* 1–12.

Foote, S. L., Bloom, F. E., & Aston-Jones, G. (1983). Nucleus locus ceruleus: New evidence of anatomical and physiological specificity. *Physiological Reviews, 63,* 844–914.

Forgas, J. P., & Moylan, S. (1991). Affective influences on stereotype judgments. *Cognition and Emotion, 5,* 379–397.

Fowles, D. C. (1994). A motivational theory of psychopathology. In W. Spaulding (Ed.), *Nebraska symposium on motivation: Integrated views of motivation, cognition and emotion* (Vol. 41, pp. 1–33). Lincoln, NE: University of Nebraska Press.

Gardner, C. R. (1985). Pharmacological studies of the role of serotonin in animal models of anxiety. In A. R. Green (Ed.), *Neuropharmacology of serotonin* (pp. 222–248). New York: Oxford University Press.

Gerson, S. C., & Baldessarini, R. J. (1980). Motor effects of serotonin in the central nervous system. *Life Sciences, 27,* 1435–1451.

Giles, D. E., Biggs, M. M., Rush, A. J., & Roffwarg, H. P. (1988). Risk factors in families of unipolar depression. I. Psychiatric illness and reduced REM latency. *Journal of Affective Disorders, 14,* 51–59.

Giles, D. E., Roffwarg, H. P., & Rush, A. J. (1987). REM latency concordance in depressed family members. *Biological Psychiatry, 22,* 910–924.

Goldman-Rakic, P. (1995). Toward a circuit model of working memory and the guidance of voluntary motor action. In J. Houk, J. J. Davis, & D. Beiser (Eds.), *Models of information processing in the basal ganglia* (pp. 85–103). Cambridge, MA: MIT Press.

Goldman-Rakic, P. S. (1990). Cellular and circuit basis of working memory in prefrontal cortex of nonhuman primates. In H. B. M. Uylings, C. G. Van Eden, J. P. C. DeBruin, M. A. Corner, & M. G. P. Feenstra (Eds.), *Progress in Brain Research, 85,* 325–336.

Goodnick, P. J. (1998). Serotonin. In P. J. Goodnick (Ed.), *Mania: Clinical and research perspectives* (pp. 103–118). Washington, DC: American Psychiatric Press.

Gormezano, I., & Harvey, J. A. (1980). Sensory and associative effects of LSD in classical conditioning of rabbit (Oryctolagus cuniculus nicititating membrane response. *Journal of Comparative and Physiological Psychology, 94,* 641–649.

Grabowska, M. (1974). Influence of midbrain raphe lesions on some pharmacological and biochemical effects of apomorphine in rats. *Psychopharmacologia, 39,* 315–322.

Grant, S. J., & Redmond, D. E. (1981). The neuroanatomy and pharmacology of the nucleus locus coeruleus. In H. Lal & S. Fielding (Eds.), *The psychopharmacology of clonidine* (pp. 221–258). New York: Alan R. Liss.

Gray, J. A. (1979). A neuropsychological theory of anxiety. In C. E. Isard (Ed.), *Emotions and personality* (pp. 303–335). New York: Plenum.

Gray, J. A. (1982). *The neuropsychology of anxiety: An enquiry into the functions of the septo-hippocampal system.* New York: Oxford University Press.

Gray, J. A. (1987). *The psychology of fear and stress* (2nd ed.). Cambridge, England: Cambridge University Press.

Gupta, M. A. (1986). Is chronic pain a variant of depressive illness? A critical review. *Canadian Journal of Psychiatry, 31*(3), 241–248.

Haber, S. M. (1986). Neurotransmitters in the human an nonhuman primate basal ganglia. *Human Neurobiology, 5,* 159–168.

Haddjeri, N., de Montigny, C., & Blier, P. (1997). Modulation of the firing activity of noradrenergic neurons in the rat locus coeruleus by the 5-hydroxtryptamine system. *British Journal of Pharmacology, 120*(5), 865–875.

Hahn, R. A., Hynes, M. D., & Fuller, R. W. (1982). Apomorphine induced aggression in rats chronically treated with oral clonidine. Modulation by central serotonergic mechanisms. *Journal of Pharmacology and Experimental Therapeutics, 220,* 389–393.

Hashimoto, S., Inoue, T., & Koyama, T. (1996). Serotonin reuptake inhibitors reduce conditioned fear stress-induced freezing behavior in rats. *Psychopharmacology, 123*(2), 182–186.

Heninger, G. R., & Charney, D. S. (1988). Monoamine receptor systems and anxiety disorders. In G. Winokur & W. Coryell (Eds.), *Psychiatric clinics of North America* (pp. 309–326). London: W. B. Sanders.

Henriques, J. B., & Davidson, R. J. (1990). Regional brain electrical asymmetries discriminate between previously depressed and healthy control subjects. *Journal of Abnormal Psychology, 99*(1), 22–31.

Hestenes, D. (1992). A neural network theory of manic-depressive illness. In D. S. Levine & S. J. Leven (Eds.), *Motivation, emotion, and goal direction in neural networks* (pp. 209–257). Hillsdale, NJ: Lawrence Erlbaum Associates.

Hetey, L., Kudrin, F. S., Shemanow, A. Y., Reyevsky, K. S., & Oelssner, W. (1985). Presynaptic dopamine and serotonin receptors modulating tyrosine hydroxylase activity in synaptosomes of the nucleus accubens of rats. *European Journal of Pharmacology, 113,* 1–10.

Houk, J., Adams, J., & Barto, A. (1995). A model of how the basal gaglia generate and use neural signals that predict reinforcement. In J. Houk, J. J. Davis, & D. Beiser (Eds.), *Models of information processing in the basal ganglia* (pp. 204–239). Cambridge, MA: MIT Press.

Isen, A. M. (1984). Toward understanding the role of affection cognition. In R. S. Wyer, Jr., & T. K. Srull (Eds.), *Handbook of social cognition* (Vol. 3, pp. 111–123). Hillsdale, NJ: Lawrence Erlbaum Associates.

Isen, A. M. (1987). Positive affect, cognitive processes and social behavior. In L. Berkowitz (Ed.), *Advances in experimental social psychology* (Vol. 20, pp. 203–253). New York: Academic Press.

Jacobs, B. L. (1986). Single unit activity of locus coeruleus neurons in behaving animals. *Progress in Neurobiology, 27,* 183–194.

Jacobs, B. L., Asher, R., & Dement, W. C. (1973). Electrophysiological and behavioral effects of electrical stimulation of the raphe nuclei in cats. *Physiology and Behavior, 11,* 489–496.

Kalivas, P., Churchill, L., & Klitenick, M. (1993). The circuitry mediating the translating of motivational stimuli into adaptive motor responses. In P. Kalivas & C. Barnes (Eds.), *Limbic motor circuits and neuropsychiatry* (pp. 310–354). Boca Raton, FL: CRC Press.

Kayama, Y., Shimada, S., Hishikawa, Y., & Ogawa, T. (1989). Effects of stimulating the dorsal raphe nucleus of the rat on neuronal activity in the dorsal lateral geniculate nucleus. *Brain Research, 489,* 1–11.

Kaye, W. H., & Weltzin, T. E. (1991). Serotonin activity in anorexia and bulimia nervosa: Relationship to the modulation of feeding and mood. *Journal of Clinical Psychiatry, 52,* 41–48.

Kempf, E., Puglisi-Allegra, S., Cabib, S., Schleef, C., & Mandel, P. (1984). Serotonin levels and turnover in different brain areas of isolated aggressive or non-aggressive strains of mice. *Progress in Neuropsychopharmacology & Biological Psychiatry, 8,* 365–371.

Kupfer, D. J. (1976). REM latency: A psychobiologic marker for primary depressive disease. *Biological Psychiatry, 11,* 159–174.

Lakos, S., & Basbaum, A. I. (1988). An ultrastructural study of the projections from the midbrain periaqueductal gray to spinally projecting, serotonin-immunoreactive neurons of the medullary nucleus raphe magnus in the rat. *Brain Research, 443,* 383–388.

Lazarus, R. S. (1991). *Emotion and adaption.* Oxford, England: Oxford University Press.

LeDoux, J. E. (1993). Emotional memory systems in the brain. *Behavioural Brain Research, 58,* 69–79.

LeDoux, J. E. (1995). Emotion: Clues from the brain. *Annual Review in Psychology, 46,* 209–235.

Leibowitz, S. F., Weiss, G. F., & Suh, J. S. (1990). Medial hypothalamic nuclei mediate serotonin's inhibitory effect on feeding behavior. *Pharmacology, Biochemistry, and Behavior, 37,* 735–742.

Le Moal, M., & Simon, H. (1991). Mesocorticolimbic dopaminergic network: Functional and regulatory roles. *Physiological Reviews, 71,* 155–234.

Limberger, N., Spath, L., & Starke, K. (1986). A search for receptors modulating the release of g-[^{3}H] aminobutyric acid in rabbit caudate nucleus slices. *Journal of Neurochemistry, 46,* 1109–1117.

Louilot, A., Taghzouti, K., Deminiere, J. M., Simon, H., & Le Moal, M. (1987). Dopamine and behavior: Functional and theoretical considerations. In M. Sandler (Ed.), *Neurotransmitter interactions in the basal ganglia* (pp. 193–204). New York: Raven.

Lydic, R., McCarley, R. W., & Hobson, J. A. (1983). The time-course of dorsal raphe discharge, PGO waves and muscle tone averaged across multiple sleep cycles. *Brain Research, 274,* 365–370.

Marks, G. A., Speciale, S. G., Cobbey, K., & Roffwarg, H. P. (1987). Serotonergic inhibition of the dorsal lateral geniculate nucleus. *Brain Research, 418,* 76–84.

McKenzie, G. M. (1981). Dissociation of the antiaggression and serotonin-depleting effects of fenfluramine. *Canadian Journal of Physiology and Pharmacology, 59,* 830–836.

Meltzer, H. Y., & Lowy, M. T. (1987). The serotonin hypothesis of depression. In H. Y. Meltzer (Ed.), *Psychopharmacology: The third generation of progress* (pp. 513–537). New York: Raven.

Miller, N. E. (1951). Learnable drives and rewards. In S. S. Stevens (Ed.), *Handbook of experimental psychology* (pp. 435–472). New York: Wiley.

Mirenowicz, J., & Schultz, W. (1996). Preferential activation of midbrain dopamine neurons by appetitive rather than aversive stimuli. *Nature, 379,* 449–451.

Mowrer, O. H. (1947). On the dual nature of learning: Reinterpretation on conditioning and problem solving. *Harvard Educational Review, 17,* 102–148.

Nakahara, D., Ozaki, N., Miura, Y., Miura, H., & Nagatsu, T. (1989). Increased dopamine and serotonin metabolism in rat nucleus accumbens produced by intracranial self-stimulation of medial forebrain bundle as measured by in vivo microdialysis. *Brain Research, 495,* 178–181.

Nofzinger, E. A., Thase, M. E., Reynolds, C. F., Himmelhoch, J. M., Malling, A., Houck, P., & Kupper, D. J. (1991). Hypersomnia in bipolar depression: A comparison with narcolepsy using the multiple sleep latency method. *American Journal of Psychiatry, 148,* 1177–1181.

Oades, R. D. (1985). The role of noradrenaline in tuning and dopamine in switching between signals in the CNS. *Neuroscience and Biobehavioral Reviews, 9,* 261–282.

Ormel, J., & Schaufeli, W.B. (1991). Stability and change in psychological distress and their relationship with self-esteem and locus of control: A dynamic equilibrium model. *Journal of Personality and Social Psychology, 60,* 288–299.

Petkov, V. V., Stoyanova, F., & Popova, Y. (1989). Changes in the serotonin, dopamine and noradrenaline levels in the cerebral cortex of rats trained for active and passive avoidance. *Acta Physiol Pharmacol Bulg, 15*(2), 28–32.

Pycock, C. J., Horton, R. W., & Carter, C. J. (1978). Interactions of 5-hydroxytryptamine and aminobutyric acid with dopamine. *Advances in Biochemical Psychopharmacology, 19,* 323–341.

Raleigh, M. J., Brammer, G. L., & McGuire, M. T. (1983). Male dominance, serotonergic systems and the behavioral and physiological effects of drugs in vervet monkeys (Cercopithecus aethiops sabaeus). In K. A. Miczek (Ed.), *Ethnopharmacology: Primate models of neuropsychiatric disorders* (pp. 185–197). New York: Alan R. Liss.

Rampello, L., Nicoletti, G., Raffaele, R., & Drago, F. (1995). Comparative effects of amitriptyline and amineptine in patients affected by anxious depression. *Neuropsychobiology, 31*(3), 130–134.

Redmond, D. E. (1977). Alterations in the function of the nucleus locus coeruleus: A possible model for studies of anxiety. In I. Hanin & E. Usdin (Eds.), *Animal models in psychiatry and neurology* (pp. 278–295). New York: Pergamon.

Redmond, D. E. (1979). New and old evidence for the involvement of a brain norepinephrine system in anxiety. In W. E. Fann, I. Karacan, A. D. Pokorny, & R. L. Williams (Eds.), *Phenomenology and treatment of anxiety* (pp. 89–111). New York: Spectrum.

Redmond, D. E., & Huang, Y. H. (1979). Current concepts: 2. New evidence for a locus coeruleus-norepinephrine connection with anxiety. *Life Sciences, 25,* 2149–2162.

Roberts, M. H. (1984). 5-Hydroxytryptamine and antinociception. *Neuropharmacology, 23,* 1529–1536.

Rosen, R. B., & Schulkin, J. (1998). From normal fear to pathological anxiety. *Psychological Review, 105*(2), 325–350.

Rothbart, M. K., & Ahadi, S. A. (1994). Temperament and the development of personality. *Journal of Abnormal Psychology, 103*(1), 55–66.

Roy, A., Adinoff, B., & Linnoila, M. (1988). Acting our hostility in normal volunteers: Negative correlation with CSF 5-HIAA levels. *Psychiatry Research, 24,* 187–194.

Ruiz-Ortega, J. A., Ugedo, L., Pineda, J., & Garcia-Sevilla, J. A. (1995). The stimulatory effect of clonidine through imidazoline receptors on locus coeruleus noradrenergic neurones in mediated by excitatory amino acids and modulated by serotonin. *Naunyn Schmiedebergs Archives of Pharmacology, 352*(2), 121–126.

Schwartz, N. (1990). Happy but mindless? Mood effects on problem solving and persuasion. In R. M. Sorrentino & E. T. Higgins (Eds.), *Handbook of motivation and cognition* (Vol. 2, pp. 527–561). New York: Guilford.

Selye, H. (1976). *The stress of life.* New York: McGraw-Hill.

Sinclair, R. C., & Mark, M. M. (1992). The influence of mood state on judgment and action: Effects on persuasion, categorization, social justice, person perception, and judgmental accuracy. In A. Tesser & L. L. Martin (Eds.), *The construction of social judgments* (pp. 118–145). Hillsdale, NJ: Lawrence Erlbaum Associates.

Skurygin, V. P. (1995). Reverse absorption of serotonin by synaptosomes and its level in the rat cerebral cortex in acute and chronic stress. *Vpr Med Khim, 41*(3), 39–41.

Smith, T. W. (1979). Happiness: Time trends, seasonal variations, intersurvey differences, and other mysteries. *Social Psychology Quarterly, 42,* 18–30.

Soubrie, P. (1986). Reconciling the role of central serotonin neurons in human and animal behavior. *Behavioral and Brain Sciences, 9,* 319–364.

Spoont, M. (1992). Modulatory role of serotonin in neural information processing: Implications for human psychopathology. *Psychological Bulletin, 112,* 330–350.

Stallone, D., & Nicolaïdis, S. (1989). Increased food intake and carbohydrate preference in the rat following treatment with the serotonin antagonist metergoline. *Neuroscience Letters, 102,* 319–324.

Stein, L. (1981). Behavioral pharmacology of benzodiazepines. In D. F. Klein & J. Rabkin (Eds.), *Anxiety: New research and changing concepts* (pp. 201–213). New York: Raven.

Struss, D. T., & Benson, D. F. (1986). *The frontal lobes.* New York: Raven.

Sulser, E., & Sanders-Bush, E. (1989). From neurochemical to molecular pharmacology of antidepressants. In E. Costa (Ed.), *Tribute to B. B. Brodie* (pp. 309–331). New York: Raven.

Tellegen, A. (1985). Structures of mood and personality and their relevance to assessing anxiety, with an emphasis on self-report. In A. H. Tuma & J. D. Maser (Eds.), *Anxiety and the anxiety disorders* (pp. 681–706). Hillsdale, NJ: Lawrence Erlbaum Associates.

Tellegen, A., & Walker, N. G. (1992). Exploring personality through test construction: Development of the multidimensional personality questionnaire. In S. R. Briggs & J. M. Cheek (Eds.), *Personality measures: Development and evaluation* (Vol. 1, pp. 80–110). Greenwich, CT: JAI.

Tomarken, A. J., Davidson, R. J., Wheeler, R. E., & Doss, R. (1992). Individual differences in anterior brain asymmetry and fundamental dimensions of emotion. *Journal of Personality and Social Psychology, 62*(4), 676–687.

Treit, D. (1985). Animal models for the study of anti-anxiety agent: A review. *Neuroscience and Biobehavioral Reviews, 9,* 203–222.

Valzelli, L. (1981). *Psychobiology of aggression and violence.* New York: Raven.

Valzelli, L. (1982). Serotonergic inhibitory control of experimental aggression. *Pharmacological Research Communications, 14,* 1–13.

Valzelli, L., & Bernasconi, S. (1979). Aggressiveness by isolation and brain serotonin turnover changes in different strains of mice. *Neuropsychobiology, 3,* 35–41.

Vergnes, M., Depaulis, A., & Boehrer, A. (1986). Parachlorophenylalanine-induced serotonin depletion increases offensive but not defensive aggression in male rats. *Physiology and Behavior, 36,* 653–658.

Vogel, G. W., Vogel, F., McAbee, R. S., & Thurmond, A. J. (1980). Improvement of depression by REM sleep deprivation: New findings and a theory. *Archives of General Psychiatry, 37,* 247–253.

Watson, D., Clark, L. A., & Tellegen, A. (1988). Development and validation of brief measures of positive and negative affect: The PANAS scales. *Journal of Personality and Social Psychology, 54,* 1063–1070.

Watson, D., & Slack, A. K. (1993). General factors of affective temperament and their relation to job satisfaction over time. *Organizational Behavior and Human Decision Processes, 54,* 181–202.

Wehr, T. A., Sack, D. A., & Rosenthal, N. E. (1987). Sleep reduction as a final common pathway in the genesis of mania. *American Journal of Psychiatry, 144*(2), 201–204.

Weiss, J. M., & Simson, P. G. (1985). Neurochemical mechanisms underlying stress-induced depression. In T. M. Field, P. M. McCabe, & N. Schneiderman, *Stress and coping* (pp. 93–116). Hillsdale, NJ: Lawrence Erlbaum Associates.

Whybrow, P. C. (1997). *A mood apart: The thinker's guide to emotion and its disorders.* New York: Harper Perennial.

Wilkinson, L. O., & Jacobs, B. L. (1988). Lack of response of serotonergic neurons in the dorsal raphe nucleus of freely moving cats to stressful stimuli. *Experimental Neurology, 101,* 445–457.

Winslow, J. T., & Insel, T. R. (1990). Serotonergic and catecholaminergic reuptake inhibitors have opposite effects on the ultrasonic isolation calls of rat pups. *Neuropsychopharmacology, 3,* 51–59.

Winters, R. W., Ironson, G. H., & Schneiderman, N. (1990). The neurobiology of anxiety. In D. G. Byrne & R. H. Rosenman (Eds.), *Anxiety and the heart* (pp. 187–202). New York: Hemisphere.

Wolfe, B. E., Metzger, E., & Jamerson, D. C. (1997). Research update on serotonin function in bulimia nervosa and anorexia nervosa. *Psychopharmacological Bulletin, 33*(3), 345–354.

Zemlan, F. P. (1978). Influence of p-chloramphetamine and p-chloraphenylalanine on female mating behavior. *Annals of the New York Academy of Sciences, 305,* 621–626.

Part III

TREATMENT

Chapter **10**

Recent Findings Concerning the Processes and Outcomes of Cognitive Therapy for Depression

Robert J. DeRubeis
Tony Z. Tang
Lois A. Gelfand
Michael Feeley
University of Pennsylvania

In this chapter, we report recent findings from our laboratory that shed light on how cognitive therapy (CT) for depression (see Beck, Rush, Shaw, & Emery, 1979) achieves its beneficial effects. Our work borrows from traditions and methods found in the psychotherapy process literature. We assess therapist and patient behaviors that we believe are connected in some way to the symptomatic relief engendered by CT. Psychotherapy process research begins with the assumption that the intervention under investigation is effective on average, thus justifying the examination of its active processes. Until recently, the general effectiveness of CT was a widely held assumption (see, e.g., Dobson, 1989). Because this assumption has been challenged recently with regard to the treatment of severe depression, it is important first to visit the question of whether CT for depression is indeed a potent treatment for depression, whose processes warrant examination. We present new analyses of existing sets of outcome data that we believe justify our continued interest in CT as an effective form of therapy for depression. We then describe two different lines of research that we have conducted to investigate the processes of change in CT.

COGNITIVE THERAPY IS AS EFFECTIVE AS ANTIDEPRESSANT MEDICATIONS FOR SEVERE DEPRESSION

In 1977, Rush, Beck, Kovacs, and Hollon reported the first evidence from a controlled study that a psychological treatment is as effective as antidepressant medications (ADMs) in the treatment of patients with major depressive disorder. Between 1977 and 1989, CT for depression was widely considered the prime example of an effective psychological treatment for a serious mental disorder. In 1989, Elkin and colleagues reported findings that challenged the prevailing view. In the Treatment of Depression Collaborative Research Program (TDCRP; Elkin et al., 1989), CT did not outperform a pill–placebo condition, whereas, at least among the more severely depressed patients, the ADM imipramine did. In subsequent, more sensitive analyses (Elkin et al., 1995), imipramine's effects were shown to exceed those of CT in the more severely depressed subsample (but not in the less severely depressed subsample).

The impact of these findings can be seen in several published treatment guidelines. For example, the American Psychiatric Association's 1993 "Practice Guidelines for Major Depressive Disorder in Adults" included the following statement: "There is some evidence that cognitive therapy reduces depressive symptoms during the acute phase of less severe, non-melancholic forms of major depression, but not significantly differently from pill-placebo coupled with clinical management." The Agency for Health Care Policy and Research guidelines (1993) stated, "For severe and psychotic depressions, there is strong evidence for the efficacy of medication and little or none for the efficacy of psychotherapy alone."

The conclusions embedded in these guidelines about the relative benefits of cognitive therapy and ADMs, particularly those regarding the severely depressed, appear to derive completely from the TDCRP findings. The impact of the TDCRP findings has been due, in part, to the fact that the TDCRP was a large (total number of patients who entered treatment was 239), multisite trial that included a control condition (see Jacobson & Hollon, 1996a, 1996b; Klein, 1996; McNally, 1996 for a debate about the importance of a control condition in psychotherapy vs. medication outcome studies). Yet, less than 25% of the TDCRP total sample is relevant for the comparison of CT versus ADM in severe depression; only 27 severely depressed patients received CT and 26 received ADM.

Aside from the TDCRP, three other studies conducted in the United States (including the previously mentioned Rush et al., 1977 study) have examined the relative effects of ADMs and CT, and each of the studies included in its sample a number of more severely depressed patients. In all three studies' total samples, the outcomes produced by CT were at least as good as those produced by the respective ADM conditions (see Hollon et al., 1992; Murphy, Simons, Wetzel, & Lustman, 1984; Rush et al., 1977). These three studies were similar to each other and to the TDCRP in most respects; in all four studies, depressed patients were randomly assigned to an ADM condition or to CT (or to other conditions in some of the studies). In addition, in all four studies, similar criteria were used to diagnose depression, and the Hamilton Rating Scale for Depression (HRSD; Hamilton,

1967) was used to assess symptom levels before and after treatment. The study protocols were also similar with respect to duration of treatment, number of sessions, and management of dropout data. In three of the four studies, imipramine served as the ADM, whereas in one study (Murphy et al., 1984), nortriptyline was the ADM.

Findings from the severe subsample of one of the studies (Hollon et al., 1992) have already been published; they used the primary symptom severity cut-off employed by the TDCRP. Imipramine did not outperform CT in the more severely depressed patients in that study, leading Jacobson and Hollon (1996a; 1996b; see also Persons, Thase, & Crits-Christoph, 1996) to question the generalizability of the TDCRP findings, as well as the appropriateness of the treatment guideline recommendations. Given the discrepancy between the findings of the TDCRP and the Hollon et al. study, evidence from additional sources would help to resolve the question of whether CT is as effective as ADM for more severely depressed outpatients. Because neither Rush et al. (1977) nor Murphy et al. (1984) reported separate findings for their more severe subsamples, we enlisted the cooperation of the investigators, and obtained the data required to perform subset analyses. (We also were able to obtain raw data from the Hollon et al. 1992 study and from the TDCRP.) This allowed us to compare the efficacy of ADM and CT for the more severely depressed patients in each of the four studies (see DeRubeis, Gelfand, Tang, & Simons, 1999, for a more detailed report).

The results for the more severely depressed subsamples from each of the four studies are shown in Figure 10.1. For each study, endpoint analyses of covariance were conducted comparing CT versus ADM. The termination HRSD score (or the last score prior to dropout) served as the dependent variable; the pretreatment HRSD score was the covariate. In Rush et al. (1977), CT significantly outperformed ADM; in Murphy et al. (1984) and Hollon et al. (1992), CT did slightly, but not significantly, better than ADM; in the TDCRP, ADM did better than CT, but the difference was not significant. Thus, in the severely depressed subsamples of these four studies, there was a (nonsignificant) advantage to ADM only in the TDCRP. Because we had access to the data of all individual participants from all four studies, we also calculated the weighted average by treating each patient as if he or she were a subject in a single large study (CT sample size = 68; ADM sample size = 105). The average effect on symptoms was slightly better in CT than in ADM (effect size = 0.1), but the difference was not significant.

Elkin, Gibbons, Shea, and Shaw (1996) suggested that the equivalence of the CT and ADM conditions in Hollon et al. (1992) was due to poor results in the ADM condition in that study. However, as can be seen in Figure 10.1, the ADM conditions in both Rush et al. (1977) and Murphy et al. (1984) yielded end-of-treatment HRSD scores that are quite similar

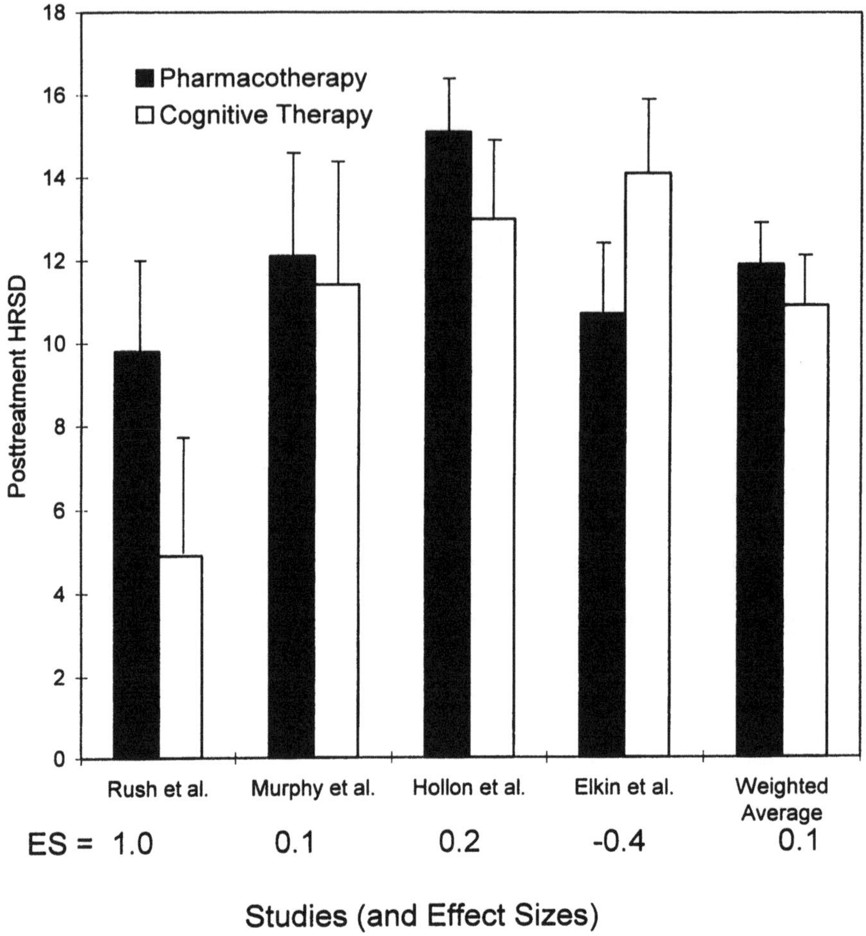

FIG. 10.1. Outcome comparisons of CT vs. ADM in the severely depressed subsamples (intake HRSD > 20) of four outcome studies. The weighted average is calculated by combining all participants' data together as if they were from a single study. The effect size (ES) is labeled positive when CT outperformed ADM.

to those obtained in the TDCRP. Clearly, then, CT can yield results equivalent to ADMs in more severely depressed patients, even when the ADMs achieve good results. Any explanation that focuses on the relatively poor showing of ADM in the Hollon et al. study must also account for the poor showing of the CT condition in the TDCRP, relative to the CT conditions in Rush et al. and Murphy et al.

Thus, the available data do not support the claim that ADMs are to be preferred to CT in the treatment of more severely depressed outpatients.

The pattern that favors ADMs occurred in only one study, the TDCRP. Collectively, the data strongly suggest that CT and ADMs are comparable in their effects on acute symptoms of depression among severely depressed outpatients. Moreover, because of the suggestion from several studies that CT provides protection against relapse (see Hollon, Shelton, & Loosen, 1991), CT should be considered a viable treatment for severely depressed outpatients. Treatment guidelines, insofar as they claim to have an empirical basis, must reflect this state of affairs more accurately than some have done thus far.

Fortunately, the field will not have to rely solely on the existing data for long. Along with Steven Hollon and Richard Shelton's group at Vanderbilt University, Robert DeRubeis and Jay Amsterdam's group at the University of Pennsylvania are engaged in a relatively large sample study (240 patients overall) that compares the short-term and long-term effects of CT, an ADM (paroxetine), and placebo in the treatment of severely depressed outpatients. We anticipate having completed acute phase data collection by the year 2000.

In the meantime, given the state of available evidence, we assume that CT is a potent method of treatment for depressed outpatients, including the more severely depressed. It thus makes sense to explore the means by which CT may achieve its effects.

THERAPIST FOCUS ON THE CONCRETE METHODS OF CT PREDICTS GOOD OUTCOME

One research paradigm that can be used to address questions about CT processes involves relating naturally occurring variations in therapist behaviors to variations in symptom change. Although such naturalistic investigations are vulnerable to threats to internal validity, we have been careful in our work to rule out a temporal confound that is common in process research. In most investigations of therapist or patient behavior, or of therapist–patient relationship variables, the in-session behavior of interest is measured after a substantial amount of symptom change has already occurred (see Barber, Crits-Christoph, & Luborsky, 1996, for an exception). For example, Burns and Nolen-Hoeksema (1992) reported that patients' ratings of therapist empathy were positively related to outcome in cognitive therapy, and they interpreted their causal modeling analysis as indicating that greater therapist empathy caused greater symptom change. Yet, their causal modeling analyses could not distinguish between two very different causal scenarios because patients' ratings of their therapists' empathy were collected at the end of therapy. Did empathic therapists engender greater change in their patients? Did patients who felt better by the end of therapy become positively disposed toward their therapists, so that at the end of therapy they rated them as having been empathic?

In our work, we rule out this temporal confound by measuring a therapist or patient behavior (or attitude) at a given point in time. If we wish to investigate the effects of these behaviors, we examine the course of symptom change that occurs after the behavior(s) of interest. We can also ask questions about whether a therapist or patient behavior might have been caused by symptom change. To do this, we relate symptom change up until a given session with behavior (or in the quality of the relationship) observed in that session.

Of course one can measure a vast number of constructs in this kind of work. We focused on a small set of constructs that either have shown promise in past research or are related specifically to the theory of change assumed in CT (see DeRubeis & Beck, 1988). Therapists' adherence to the methods of CT are worthy of study, on the face of it. If CT is a potent therapy for the reasons assumed by its practitioners, therapists who adhere more to its methods should produce more relief than those who engage in less CT-relevant behavior. It becomes important, then, to employ a valid set of measures of the construct of adherence. In our research (DeRubeis & Feeley, 1990; Feeley, DeRubeis, & Gelfand, 1999), we have used the CT scale from the Collaborative Study Psychotherapy Rating Scale (CSPRS; Hollon et al., 1988; see also Hill, O'Grady, & Elkin, 1992) to assess adherence. (The CSPRS comprises a set of items that are rated on a 1 to 7 scale by a rater who has listened to an entire session of therapy; see Table 10.1 later for exemplar items.)

In our earlier study (DeRubeis & Feeley, 1990), the CT scale separated into two factors in a factor analysis; we use these two factors when we address process or outcome relations. One factor, *CT-Concrete,* represents the symptom-focused, active methods of CT. A prototypic item from this factor asks the rater to indicate the extent to which the therapist "asked the patient to record (his/her) thoughts." The other factor, *CT-Abstract,* represents less focused discussions about therapy processes and the like (e.g., "Did the therapist explain the cognitive therapy rationale . . . ?" and "Did the therapist explore underlying assumptions . . . ?").

We also investigated two sets of variables that are not specific to CT of depression but that occupy an important position in the therapy process literature: Rogerian facilitative conditions (Rogers, 1957) and the therapeutic alliance (cf. Tichenor and Hill, 1989). *Facilitative conditions* refer to therapist behaviors such as warmth and empathy. Rogers' hypothesis was that the presence of these behaviors is both necessary and sufficient to produce symptom change. Initial research supported the hypothesis (cf. Truax & Mitchell, 1971), but more recent research has not (cf. Beutler, Crago, & Arizmendi, 1986).

The *therapeutic alliance* is a Freudian concept, which was further developed by Bordin (1979). It refers to the collaboration between the therapist and patient on the tasks of therapy and the warmth of the relationship that is established between them. Research in the early 1980's showed the therapeutic alliance to be positively related to outcome (cf. Morgan, Luborsky, Crits-Christoph, Curtis, & Solomon, 1982). Recent research (Gaston, Marmar, Gallagher, & Thompson, 1991; Krupnick et al., 1994) continues to show a positive relation between therapeutic alliance and outcome.

In two separate studies, we examined the role of the aforementioned therapist behaviors and the therapeutic relationship in CT for depression (DeRubeis & Feeley, 1990; Feeley, DeRubeis, & Gelfand, in press). In each investigation, we studied the therapeutic processes in 25 outpatients with major depressive disorder. Variability in treatment outcome within each of the samples allowed us to examine factors that might covary with outcome. The earlier study involved patients who sought treatment at the Center for Cognitive Therapy at the University of Pennsylvania; the second study was an examination of patients from the Hollon et al. (1992) outcome study.

Patients in both studies completed the Beck Depression Inventory (BDI; Beck & Steer, 1987), a widely used measure of depression symptom severity, prior to each therapy session. This allowed us to calculate two different kinds of temporally sensitive symptom change scores for each session. The *subsequent change* score is the difference between the rated session BDI and the 12-week (or final) BDI score. Relations between the subsequent change score and in-session behavior cannot reflect the effect of symptom change on therapy processes because the subsequent change score reflects only those symptom changes that occur after the session. The *prior change* measure for a rated session is the difference between the first session BDI and the rated session BDI. We examined the prior change score in relation to in-session phenomena that might result from symptom change because these phenomena are observed after the symptom change that is indexed by the prior change score.

We focused on three sessions from each patient–therapist dyad: Session 2; one randomly selected session from Weeks 7 through 9 (termed Quadrant 3); and another randomly selected session from Weeks 10 through 12 (Quadrant 4). We have been most interested in the relation of behavior in Session 2 to subsequent change. Conversely, we examined the behavior in Quadrants 3 and 4 in relation to prior change.

Two findings were rather consistent across the two samples. First, the more CT-Concrete methods observed in Session 2, the greater the subsequent change in BDI score. (In neither sample did levels of facilitative conditions, the Helping Alliance, or the CT-Abstract factor in Session 2 predict subsequent change.) Second, higher Helping Alliance scores in Quadrants 3 and 4 tended to be associated with greater prior change in

BDI score. (This pattern was not observed for any of the other three in-session constructs.)

These findings suggest that in CT for depression, it is critical that therapists focus on the problem-focused, pragmatic aspects of CT early in therapy. Table 10.1 displays the relations between CT-Concrete items and subsequent change in each of the two studies. As can be seen, in both investigations, positive correlations with subsequent change were obtained with items that assessed the degree to which therapists asked patients: (a) to record their thoughts; (b) to engage in self-monitoring; (c) to report cognitions verbatim; and (d) to review their homework efforts.

It is also our clinical impression that early emphasis on the change-oriented behavioral and cognitive techniques of CT is critical for success. Yet, we have not yet been able to isolate the determinants of adherence to the application of these methods. It is likely that patient characteristics, such as readiness or willingness to cooperate with therapists' attempts to engage these change-oriented methods, determines the extent of therapist adherence, at least to some degree. However, it is also apparent in our observations of CT, in research contexts and in clinical supervision, that opportunities for such interventions are frequently missed, with little justification. In future research, we plan to explore the determinants of adherence to CT-Concrete methods more thoroughly.

The finding that Helping Alliance in Quadrants 3 and 4 tends to be predicted by prior change, but that early Helping Alliance is not predictive of subsequent change, would seem to go against the findings in the Helping

TABLE 10.1
Cognitive Therapy–Concrete at Session 2—Correlations of Items to Subsequent Change in Study I[a] and Study II[b]

CT–Concrete Items[c]	*Study I*	*Study II*	*Mean*[d]
Asked patient to record thoughts	.49*	.37[t]	.43
Assigned/reviewed self-monitoring	.40[t]	.39[t]	.39
Asked patient to report cognitions verbatim	.30	.32	.31
Reviewed homework	.38*	.22	.30
Practiced rational responses with patient	.52**	.04	.28
Asked for specific examples of beliefs	.40*	.15	.27
Examined evidence re beliefs	.39*	.15	.27
Set and followed agenda	-.01	.34[t]	.17
Homework assigned	.06	.21	.13
Labeled cognitive errors	.18	-.08	.05

Note. [a]DeRubeis & Feeley, 1990; [b]Feeley & DeRubeis, 1998; Gelfand, in press; [c]From the CT subscale of the CSPRS (Hollon et al., 1988), ordered according to the magnitude of the mean correlation for both studies; [d]mean correlation for both studies; [t]$p < .10$; *$p < .05$; **$p < .01$; A positive correlation is associated with more improvement in depression.

Alliance literature. To the best of our knowledge, however, no other research group has employed a research method that avoids the temporal confound introduced when the Helping Alliance is assessed either in the midst of—or at the end of—the period of symptom change that the Helping Alliance is meant to predict. Especially with a construct like the Helping Alliance, which quite plausibly could reflect—rather than predict—the benefits of therapy, researchers should be cautious in their interpretations of an association between the Helping Alliance and outcome.

IMPROVEMENT IN CT OFTEN IS NOT GRADUAL: THE STUDY OF SUDDEN GAINS

In outcome research on CT for depression, patients—on average—improve considerably. In most studies, the mean pretreatment BDI score is between 25 and 30. During the course of CT, which comprises approximately 15 to 20 sessions, the mean BDI score decreases gradually and rather consistently—about one point per session—until by the end of treatment it is approximately 15 points lower. Yet, changes in group means can obscure interesting and potentially informative courses of change in individual patients. We became interested in session-to-session symptom changes and what they might tell us about the processes that individual patients experience in CT. The question we asked was: Are there special patterns of change that can reveal new insights about CT's mechanisms of change?

When we examined time-course data from individual patients in the TDCRP study and in the Hollon et al. (1992) study, we were struck by the frequent occurrence of a phenomenon we have come to refer to as the *sudden gain* (Tang & DeRubeis, in press). A *sudden gain* is a large improvement in symptoms that is observed in a single between-session interval. The sudden gains we observed often involved a 12-point to 18-point drop in BDI score, which is much larger than the average between-session BDI score change of less than 1. For many patients, the sudden gain accounted for more than half of their total change in BDI score.

The existence of these sudden gains raised a number of questions. Do they represent transient noise or stable therapeutic gains? Are they related to eventual outcome, or are they inconsequential mood swings? What triggers them? How do they influence subsequent therapy sessions? Using data and therapy session recordings from the TDCRP sample and the Hollon et al. (1992) sample, we investigated these questions, the preliminary answers to which are summarized in the following text.

We refer to the therapy session that immediately precedes the sudden gain as the *pregain session* (or N), and the therapy session immediately after the gain as the *after-gain session* (or $N+1$). The therapy session that precedes

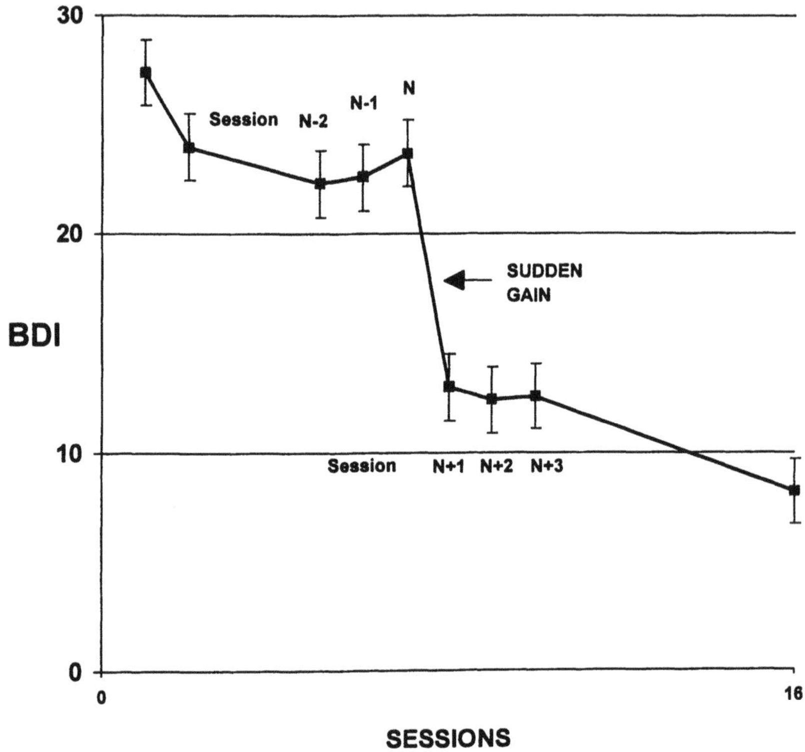

FIG. 10.2. The average sudden gain. Mean BDI scores are shown for sessions $N-2$, $N-1$, N, $N+1$, $N+2$, $N+3$. To provide context, also shown are the average BDI scores of the first, second, and last sessions of all patients who experienced sudden gains.

the pregain session is referred to as the *pre-pregain session* (or $N-1$; see Fig. 10.2). (In all cases, the BDI was completed by the patient before the session.)

We designed a set of objective, quantitative criteria to identify the sudden gains. They are as follows:

1. The magnitude of the gain is at least 7 BDI points:
   $BDI_N - BDI_{N+1} \geq 7$.
2. The magnitude of the gain is at least 25% of the pregain session's BDI score:
   $BDI_N - BDI_{N+1} \geq .25 \times BDI_N$.
3. The mean of the three session BDIs following the gain is significantly lower than the mean of the three session BDIs preceding the gain:
   $\text{Mean}(BDI_{N-2}, BDI_{N-1}, BDI_N) > \text{Mean}(BDI_{N+1}, BDI_{N+2}, BDI_{N+3})$, t-test at the $p < .05$ level.

Criterion 1 ensures that the absolute magnitude of the gain is large. Criterion 2 ensures that the magnitude of the gain is large relative to the patient's pregain depression severity. Criterion 3 ensures that the magnitude of the gain is large relative to the magnitude of symptom fluctuations preceding and following the gain.

The criteria's cut-off values were arbitrarily chosen, but there are some empirical justifications. In both the Hollon et al. (1992) sample and the TDCRP sample, the frequency distribution plots of between-session BDI score changes showed, as expected, a large peak centered at 1. Yet, they also contained a secondary peak that began at 7 BDI points and peaked at 9 BDI points. We have observed similar secondary peaks in the data sets of other CT outcome studies (Jacobson et al., 1996; Murphy et al., 1984). Thus, some of the between-session BDI changes greater than 6 BDI points might be qualitatively different from the smaller ones, and they might very well be the sudden gains that we wanted to identify.

Out of 927 between-session intervals observed in the 61 CT patients in our sample, our criteria selected 29 sudden gains, experienced by 23 patients. To check how well our criteria worked, we computed the average sudden gain (shown in Fig. 10.2). The BDI scores of the average sudden gainers' first session, second session, sessions N–2 through N+3, and last session are also displayed.

The mean magnitude of the sudden gains in our sample was 11.2 BDI points. In contrast, the mean of the total depression severity improvement accomplished by the entire CT treatment—from the Session 1 score to the posttreatment score—was 13.0 BDI points for all patients and 21.8 BDI points for the patients who experienced sudden gains. Thus, for patients with sudden gains, the mean magnitude of the sudden gains was more than 50% of the mean change experienced during the entire 15 to 20 sessions of therapy.

Our analyses suggested that sudden gains do not represent transient noise. Rather, they seem to have a longlasting impact on the patient's depression severity (Tang & DeRubeis, in press). From the sudden gain to the end of therapy, very few patients' depression severity level returned to the pregain level. We define a *reversal of a sudden gain* as a loss of at least half of the BDI improvement that occurred during a sudden gain. For example, if a patient's pregain session BDI score was 30 and the after-gain session BDI score was 20, then a rise in his or her BDI score to 25 or higher would be counted as a reversal of a sudden gain. Out of the 23 patients who experienced sudden gains, only 5 patients experienced a reversal. Moreover, these reversals were almost always transient; by the end of therapy, only one of these patient's BDI scores still met the reversal of gain criterion.

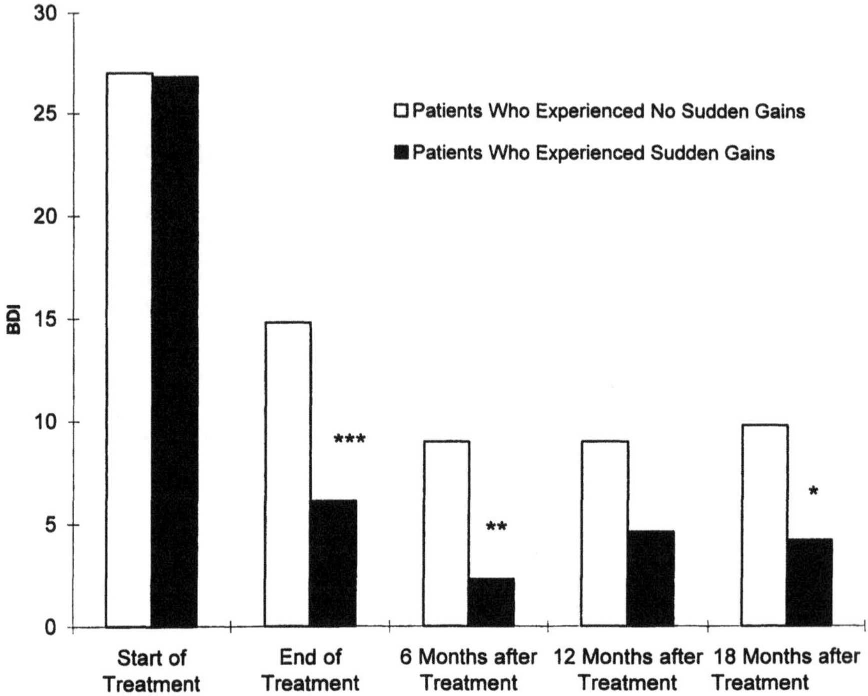

FIG. 10.3. The outcome comparison of patients who experienced sudden gains versus patients who did not experience sudden gains, at the end of treatment and at three points during the follow-up. Note: $*p < .05$; $**p < .01$; $***p < .001$.

Patients who experienced sudden gains evidenced especially good outcome. We compared patients who had sudden gains with those who did not. At the beginning of the first session, patients who subsequently did and did not experience sudden gains were essentially equally depressed (see Fig. 10.3). At the end of treatment, however, the sudden-gain patients were experiencing substantially fewer depressive symptoms. Furthermore, 6 months and 18 months after treatment, the sudden-gain patients remained significantly less depressed than the other patients, as shown in Fig. 10.3. We also noted that 53% of all treatment responders experienced at least one sudden gain. Together, this evidence suggests that the occurrence of a sudden gain portends excellent outcome in both the short run and the long run.

It may not be surprising that patients who evidenced a substantial between-session improvement benefitted more overall than those who did not. Yet, remarkably, treatment responders who experience sudden gains may benefit more in the long run than treatment responders who improve more gradually. (We define treatment response as a posttreatment BDI score of 9 or less.) At the end of therapy, the median BDI score for both

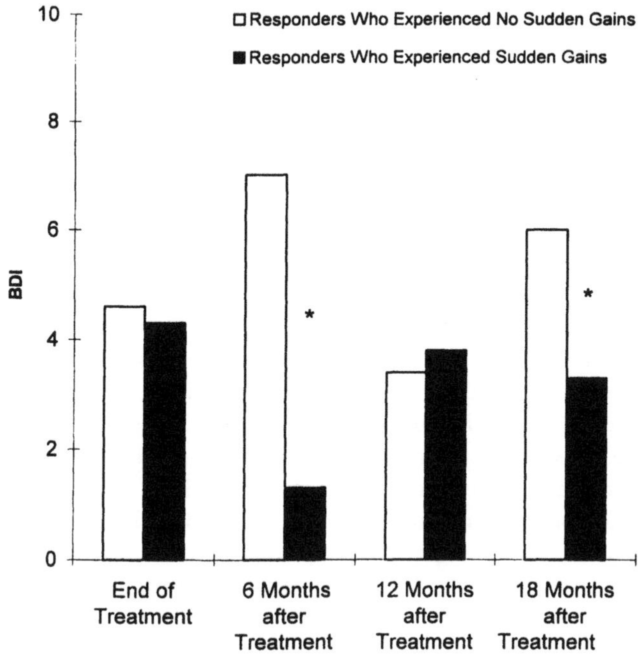

FIG. 10.4. The outcome comparison of sudden-gain responders versus no-sudden-gain responders 6, 12, and 18 months after end of treatment. *Note:* $*p < .05$.

the sudden-gain responders and the no-sudden-gain responders was approximately 4. As Figure 10.4 shows, 6 and 18 months after the end of the therapy, the median BDI score of the sudden-gain responders was significantly lower than that of the no-sudden-gain responders. (At 12 months after the end of treatment, median depression scores for the two groups were nearly equal.)

THERAPY PROCESS VARIABLES ASSOCIATED WITH TREATMENT GAINS

Impressed by the magnitude and the long-lasting impact of these sudden gains, we embarked on a search for their causes. Following previous therapy process research and considering the theory of change assumed in CT (Barber & DeRubeis, 1989; DeRubeis & Beck, 1988), we assessed therapist-offered facilitative conditions, the helping alliance, therapist adherence to CT techniques, and changes in patients' beliefs. The assessments were conducted by raters who listened to therapy sessions blind as to whether they were pregain, pre-pregain, or postgain sessions.

To assess changes in patients' beliefs, we designed a coding instrument specifically for this purpose. Whenever a patient explicitly acknowledged a cognitive change, the raters rated the importance of the cognitive change on a 1 through 4 scale, where *1* is *possible/potential change*; 2 is *definite change*; 3 is *important change*; 4 is *extraordinarily important change*. We summed the scores for all of the cognitive changes in each session as the session's cognitive change score, which reflects both the number and importance of the cognitive changes in that session. We rated only the cognitive changes that were explicitly acknowledged by the patients; raters noted each instance of cognitive change as soon as they heard it. If the same cognitive change was acknowledged twice, it was given only one score. (For more details regarding the rating method, please consult Tang & DeRubeis, in press.)

Our preliminary results suggest that the sudden gains are triggered by patients' cognitive changes in the pregain sessions. The main evidence for this comes from a comparison of the pregain sessions versus the pre-pregain sessions for all of the patients who experienced sudden gains. According to our measurement, most patients experienced very few cognitive changes in the pre-pregain sessions, but substantial amounts of cognitive changes in the pregain sessions. (The median score for all pre-pregain sessions was 1.5, whereas the median score for all pregain sessions was 5.0, which was significantly higher.)

Another piece of evidence comes from an analysis of the patients' discussions with the therapists in the after-gain session. Our ratings of these discussions showed that in 70% of the cases, the patients themselves attributed their recent sudden gains, at least in part, to cognitive changes. In addition, when we compared the pregain sessions with the pre-pregain sessions vis-à-vis therapeutic alliance, therapist competence, therapist-offered facilitative conditions, and therapist adherence to cognitive techniques, we did not find any significant differences (Tang & DeRubeis, in press).

We should caution that our results are based on the relatively small sample of 16 sudden gainers for whom we had access to recordings of sessions, and the method we used for measuring cognitive changes has not been extensively validated. Thus, the replication of these findings is crucial before we can draw firm conclusions about the relationship between cognitive changes and sudden gains.

The sudden gains, in conjunction with the cognitive changes in the pregain sessions, also might influence the nature of therapy conducted afterward. For example, they might lead to a stronger therapeutic alliance. After a rapid and sizable symptom decrease, a patient might feel grateful toward the therapist or the therapy, so that both the patient and the therapist are more confident about working together. In addition, the patient might observe that important cognitive changes occurred right before the sudden gain and conclude that the stated treatment rationale of CT is valid. This should enhance the patient's belief in CT's efficacy and encourage him or her to collaborate more fully with his or her therapist.

In addition, the sudden gains and the cognitive changes in the pregain sessions might make further cognitive change more likely to occur. The substantial amount of cognitive changes in the pregain sessions could prime the patients for additional cognitive changes in several ways. Mastered cognitive techniques might be applied to other beliefs; modification of one particular belief can be generalized to similar beliefs; and changes in less central beliefs may set the stage for the change of core beliefs and schemata. In addition, because patients are less depressed after the sudden gains, they also might become more active cognitively, and the negative bias caused by the depressed mood might decrease. Furthermore, if therapeutic alliance improved as we just hypothesized, it might also facilitate the accomplishment of more cognitive changes. All these factors might work together and bring forth extensive cognitive changes in the therapy sessions following the sudden gains.

As a first step in examining these possibilities, we measured the level of therapeutic alliance and cognitive changes in the after-gain sessions. We found that ratings of the therapeutic alliance in the after-gain session were higher than those of both the pre-pregain session and the pregain session. We also found that the amount of cognitive change in the after-gain sessions was comparable to that observed in the pregain session, and significantly higher than that in the pre-pregain sessions. These results support our speculation that the sudden gains and the cognitive changes in the pregain sessions strongly influence the nature of therapy conducted after them.

A brief summary of our observations concerning sudden gains during CT for depression is as follows:

- They are large, sudden symptom changes that occur during one between-session interval.
- They are experienced by about 50% of therapy responders and, on average, account for more than 50% of the sudden-gain responders' total symptom improvement in therapy.
- They appear to represent a stable decrease in depression severity—relatively few of these patients' depression severity scores reverse after the sudden gains.
- They strongly predict better outcome, both at the end of therapy and after the termination of therapy.
- They appear to be triggered by cognitive changes in the pregain session.
- After a sudden gain, the therapy seems to move to a different stage, characterized by higher therapeutic alliance and even further cognitive changes.

SUMMARY AND SYNTHESIS

We continue to find CT for depression to be a fruitful venue for studying the processes of therapeutic change. Even for more severe forms of depression, CT appears both to reduce symptoms and to offer protection against the return of symptoms. Beyond that, the fact that depression is a common human experience, and that it can be conceptualized as occurring along a continuum with nonpathological sad mood, means that inquiries about symptom relief during CT offer a window into the relation of thoughts and emotions more generally. We are especially interested in how people can come to control their moods. CT is, at least in part, about learning how to reverse dysfunctional or unpleasant moods (Barber & DeRubeis, 1989).

Our findings concerning sudden gains in CT lend support to a cognitive model of depression. During CT, mood change appears to be far more likely following changes in beliefs than following periods of static beliefs. Moreover, we obtained preliminary evidence that the belief changes that precede the sudden gains are more likely if the therapist used CT-Concrete methods early in therapy (Tang, Gelfand, & DeRubeis, 1998), bolstering the view that such methods are critical for the promotion of rapid, effective symptom relief. The finding that an improved helping alliance follows, rather than precedes, the sudden gain, causes us to be even more skeptical of the view that the helping alliance is an agent, rather than a product, of therapeutic progress.

Many of the questions we have touched on in this chapter are most fruitfully posed in the context of a controlled outcome study. Several groups, including our own, are engaged in just such research comparing CT with medication treatments. We anticipate the results of the next wave of CT for depression studies, which collectively will bring us closer to an understanding of the effectiveness of CT and to an appreciation of the reasons for its effectiveness.

ACKNOWLEDGMENTS

The preparation of this manuscript was funded in part by National Institute of Mental Health grants P30-MH-45178 and R10-MH55877.

REFERENCES

Agency for Health Care Policy and Research. (1993). *Depression in primary care: Volume 2. Treatment of major depression clinical practice guideline number 5* (AHCPR Publication No. 93-0551). Washington, DC: National Library of Medicine.

Barber, J. P., Crits-Christoph P., & Luborsky, L. (1996). Effects of therapist adherence and competence on patient outcome in brief dynamic therapy. *Journal of Consulting and Clinical Psychology, 64,* 619–622.

Barber, J. P., & DeRubeis, R. J. (1989). On second thought: Where the action is in cognitive therapy for depression. *Cognitive Therapy and Research, 13,* 441–457.

Beck, A. T., Rush, A. J., Shaw, B. F., & Emery, G. (1979). *Cognitive therapy of depression.* New York: Guilford.

Beck, A. T., & Steer, R. A., (1987). *Beck Depression Inventory manual.* San Antonio, TX: Harcourt Brace.

Beutler, L. E., Crago, M., & Arizmendi, T. G. (1986). Therapist variables in psychotherapy process and outcome. In S. L. Garfield & A. E. Bergin (Eds.), *Handbook of psychotherapy and behavior change* (3rd ed., pp. 257–310). New York: Wiley.

Bordin, E. (1979). The generalizability of the psychoanalytic concept of the working alliance. *Psychotherapy: Theory, Research and Practice, 16,* 252–260.

Burns, D. D., & Nolen-Hoeksema, S. (1992). Therapeutic empathy and recovery from depression in cognitive-behavioral therapy: A structural equation model. *Journal of Consulting and Clinical Psychology, 60,* 441–449.

DeRubeis, R. J., & Beck, A. T. (1988). Cognitive therapy. In K. S. Dobson (Ed.), *Handbook of cognitive-behavioral therapies* (pp. 273–306). New York: Guilford.

DeRubeis, R. J., & Feeley, M. (1990). Determinants of change in cognitive therapy for depression. *Cognitive Therapy and Research, 14,* 469–482.

DeRubeis, R. J., Gelfand, L. A., Tang, T. Z., & Simons, A. (1999). Medications versus cognitive behavioral therapy for severely depressed outpatients: Mega-analysis of four randomized comparisons. *American Journal of Psychiatry, 156,* 1007–1013.

Dobson, K. S. (1989). A meta-analysis of the efficacy of cognitive therapy for depression. *Journal of Consulting and Clinical Psychology, 57,* 414–419.

Elkin, I., Shea, M. T., Watkins, J. T., Imber, S. D., Sotsky, S. M., Collins, J. F., Glass, D. R., Pilkonis, P. A., Leber, W. R., Docherty, J. P., Fiester, S. J., & Parloff, M. B. (1989). National Institute of Mental Health Treatment of Depression Collaborative Research Program: General effectiveness of treatments. *Archives of General Psychiatry, 46,* 971–982.

Elkin, I., Gibbons, R. D., Shea, M. T., Sotsky, S. M., Watkins, J. T., Pilkonis, P. A., & Hedeker, D. (1995). Initial severity and differential treatment outcome in the National Institute of Mental Health Treatment of Depression Collaborative Research Program. *Journal of Consulting and Clinical Psychology, 63,* 841–847.

Elkin, I., Gibbons, R. D., Shea, M. T., & Shaw, B. F. (1996). Science is not a trial (But it can sometimes be a tribulation). *Journal of Consulting and Clinical Psychology, 64,* 92–103.

Feeley, M., DeRubeis, R. J., & Gelfand, L. A. (1999). The temporal relation of adherence and alliance to symptom change in cognitive therapy for depression. *Journal of Consulting and Clinical Psychology, 67,* 578–582.

Gaston, L., Marmar, C., Gallagher, D., & Thompson, L. (1991). Alliance prediction of outcome beyond in-treatment symptomatic change as psychotherapy processes. *Psychotherapy Research, 1*(2), 104–112.

Hamilton, M. (1967). Development of a rating scale for primary depressive illness. *British Journal of Social and Clinical Psychology, 6,* 276–296.

Hill, C. E., O'Grady, K. E., & Elkin, I. (1992). Applying the collaborative study psychotherapy rating scale to rate therapist adherence in cognitive-behavior therapy, interpersonal, and clinical management. *Journal of Consulting and Clinical Psychology, 60,* 73–79.

Hollon, S. D., DeRubeis, R. J., Evans, M. D., Wiemer, M. J., Garvey, M. J., Grove, W. M., & Tuason, V. B. (1992). Cognitive therapy and pharmacotherapy for depression: singly and in combination. *Archives of General Psychiatry, 49,* 774–781.

Hollon, S. D., Evans, M. D., Auerbach, A., DeRubeis, R. J., Elkin, I., Lowery, A., Kriss, M. R., Grove, W. M., Tuason, V. B., & Piasecki, J. M. (1988). *Development of a system for rating therapies for depression: Differentiating cognitive therapy, interpersonal psychotherapy and clinical management pharmacotherapy.* Unpublished manuscript, Vanderbilt University, Nashville.

Hollon, S. D. Shelton, R. C., & Loosen, P. T. (1991). Cognitive therapy and pharmacotherapy for depression. *Journal of Consulting and Clinical Psychology, 59,* 88–99.

Jacobson, N. S., Dobson, K. S., Truax, P. A., Addis, M. E., Koerner, K., Gollan, J. K., Gortner, E. G., & Prince, S. E. (1996). A component analysis of cognitive-behavioral treatment for depression. *Journal of Consulting and Clinical Psychology, 64,* 295–304.

Jacobson, N. S., & Hollon, S. D. (1996a). Cognitive-behavior therapy versus pharmacotherapy: Now that the jury's returned its verdict, it's time to present the rest of the evidence. *Journal of Consulting and Clinical Psychology, 64,* 74–80.

Jacobson, N. S., & Hollon, S. D. (1996b). Prospects for future comparisons between drugs and psychotherapy: Lessons from the CBT vs. pharmacotherapy exchange. *Journal of Consulting and Clinical Psychology, 64,* 104–108.

Klein, D. F. (1996). Preventing hung juries about therapy studies. *Journal of Consulting and Clinical Psychology, 64,* 81–87.

Krupnick, J., Collins, J., Pilkonis, P. A., Elkin, I., Simmens, S., Sotsky, S. M., & Watkins, J. T. (1994). Therapeutic alliance and clinical outcome in the NIMH Treatment of Depression Collaborative Research Program: Preliminary findings. *Psychotherapy, 31,* 28–35.

McNally, R. (1996). Methodological controversies in the treatment of panic disorder. *Journal of Consulting and Clinical Psychology, 64,* 88–91.

Morgan, R., Luborsky, L., Crits-Christoph, P., Curtis, H., & Solomon, J. (1982) Predicting the outcomes of psychotherapy by the Penn Helping Alliance Rating Method. *Archives of General Psychiatry, 19,* 397–402.

Murphy, G., Simons, A. D., Wetzel, R. D., & Lustman, P. J. (1984) Cognitive therapy and pharmacotherapy. *Archives of General Psychiatry, 441,* 33–41.

Persons, J. B., Thase, M. E., & Crits-Cristoph, P. (1996). The role of psychotherapy in the treatment of depression: Review of two practice guidelines. *Archives of General Psychiatry, 53,* 283–290.

Rogers, C. R. (1957). The necessary and sufficient conditions of therapeutic personality change. *Journal of Consulting Psychology, 21,* 95–103.

Rush, A. J., Beck, A. T., Kovacs, M., & Hollon, S. D. (1977). Comparative efficacy of cognitive therapy and pharmacotherapy in the treatment of depressed outpatients. *Cognitive Therapy and Research, 1,* 17–37.

Tang, T. Z., & DeRubeis, R. J. (in press). Sudden gains and critical sessions in cognitive behavioral therapy for depression. *Journal of Consulting and Clinical Psychology.*

Tang, T. Z., Gelfand, L. A., & DeRubeis, R. J. (1998). *Predictors of sudden gains in an early therapy session.* Unpublished manuscript, University of Pennsylvania, Philadelphia.

Tichenor, V., & Hill, C. E. (1989). A comparison of six measures of working alliance. *Psychotherapy, 26,* 195–199.

Truax, C. B., & Mitchell, K. M. (1971). Research on certain therapist interpersonal skills in relation to process and outcome. In A. E. Bergin & S. L. Garfield (Eds.), *Handbook of psychotherapy and behavior change* (1st ed., pp. 299–344). New York: Wiley.

Chapter 11

Effects of Cognitive Behavioral Stress Management Intervention on Depressed Mood, Distress Levels, and Immune Status in HIV Infection

Michael H. Antoni
University of Miami

HIV INFECTION IS A CHRONIC DESEASE

The Human Immunodeficiency Virus (HIV), a retrovirus of the human T-cell leukemia–lymphoma line, is the causative agent of the acquired immunodeficiency syndrome (AIDS). A unique feature of HIV spectrum disease, which includes AIDS, is that it can have an asymptomatic phase that may last as long as 10 to 15 years (Munoz et al., 1988). People with HIV infection become ill or die from the complications of their chronic disease not from the disease itself. Those people who are unable to maintain adequate immune system functioning for surveillance of pathogens develop the life-threatening infections and neoplasias that characterize full-blown AIDS (Kaplan, Wofsky, & Volberding, 1987). Newly emerging antiretroviral therapies and appropriate patient management help some patients to remain free of clinical symptoms for a prolonged period of time. Thus, it may be useful to view HIV as a chronic disease.

Homosexual men comprise a large majority of HIV-infected individuals in the United States. Today, however, an increasingly large percentage of HIV-infected people are heterosexual male drug users and women (Centers for Disease Control, 1997). Because there is no cure for AIDS, prevention is the major tool for limiting the spread of the disease. Primary prevention efforts focus on behavioral change techniques, increasing availability and use of condoms, and substance abuse management and treatment (Schneiderman, Antoni, Ironson, LaPerriere, & Fletcher, 1992). Secondary prevention programs have been developed to slow HIV spectrum disease progression.

During the past several years, a number of medications have been introduced to manage symptoms and to slow HIV progression. Agents such as pentamidine (to combat *pneumocystis cariini* pneumonia, PCP) have helped to make huge strides in medical management (Longini, Clark, & Karon, 1993). Medications such as azidothymidine (AZT), used to block the replication of HIV, were greeted with high expectations for being able to eradicate the virus entirely, although the benefits of antiviral therapies made up of AZT, dideoxyinosine (ddI), and dideoxycytidine (ddC) appear to be more controversial and less effective than initially projected. We now know that using a single antiretroviral agent may lead to the development of drug-resistant strains of HIV, which are ultimately harder to treat (Lewin, 1996). Thus, contemporary treatment approaches often focus on combination therapies (e.g., AZT + ddC). Newly emerging treatments, such as protease inhibitors used in combination with other antiretrovirals (i.e., triple combination therapy), offer some hope that viral replication can be slowed even more efficiently. Strict adherence is necessary, however, or the infected person can quickly develop resistance to these and crossresistance to other similar agents (Lewin, 1996; Schneiderman, Antoni, & Ironson, 1997). Clearly, these types of regimens place a great deal of stress on HIV-infected persons, who find themselves in the middle of regimens that can include up to 18 pills daily. This sort of psychological burden is one of a number of stressors with which HIV-infected persons must deal each day.

Because more effective medical treatment for HIV infection is becoming available, there is now a fast-growing population of infected individuals coping with the complex and multiple psychosocial demands of a chronic life-threatening illness (Antoni, 1991). Perhaps the first and certainly one of the most significant life events for the infected person is the initial news of seropositivity (Ironson et al., 1990). Subsequently, infected persons experience the direct burdens of the disease, as well as a number of lifestyle-associated social stigmas. These major life events include overt signs of progressive physical and neurological deterioration (Redfield & Burke, 1988), chronic legal and societal stigmas (Blendon & Donelan, 1988; Ginzburg & Gostin, 1986; Walkey, Taylor, & Green, 1990), overwhelming medical costs (Bloom & Carliner, 1988), and multiple bereavements (Martin, 1988)—all of which can be characterized as severe, chronic, unpredictable, and uncontrollable stressors.

Over time, these individuals may become overwhelmed and employ maladaptive coping strategies, such as denial and avoidance. These coping strategies can result in an increased likelihood of depression and distress, sexual risk behaviors, and substance use (Antoni, 1991). These phenomena may have direct health relevance for infected persons because they have been associated with decrements in immune system functioning, even in healthy populations. We proposed that external life stressors and disease do not operate independently and that success at managing stressors and emotional distress can influence one's quality of life and the course of the disease (Antoni et al., 1990; Schneiderman et al., 1994).

For years, researchers in behavioral medicine have examined the associations between the occurrence of stressful life events and alterations in mood states, which in turn, relate to resiliency or susceptibility to pathogenic processes underlying chronic diseases, such as coronary heart disease, diabetes mellitus, rheumatoid arthritis, several types of cancer, and more recently, HIV infection (Antoni, Schneiderman, & Ironson, 1998). Over the past 10 years, this line of inquiry has evolved into investigations of stress management interventions that might reduce the negative health influences of stressors in medically vulnerable populations. This chapter describes our research program on the development and evaluation of time-limited psychosocial interventions that are designed to improve psychosocial adjustment in HIV-infected populations at different critical points across the disease spectrum. Before describing the interventions, we review the incidence of distress and depression in HIV-infected persons, as well as the effects of psychosocial adjustment on health behaviors and on HIV disease progression.

INCIDENCE OF DISTRESS AND DEPRESSION IN HIV-INFECTED PERSONS

Emotional adjustment is one major facet of quality of life that is relevant to HIV-infected persons. Because of the debilitating nature of this disease, its uncertain course, and the tendency for infected persons to either withdraw or be rejected from important means of support, there is a great risk for mood disturbances and protracted distress states (Perkins et al., 1995; Siegel, Karus, & Raveis, 1997). The incidence of DSM-based Axis I affective and adjustment disorders and sustained distress levels have been fairly well-documented for HIV-infected persons, following the initial news of a positive HIV-antibody test (Cleary et al., 1988; Jacobsen, Perry, & Hirsch, 1990). It appears from several studies that adjustment disorder with depressed mood may be the most common, with major depressive disorder being far less common (Perkins et al., 1994; Rabkin, Wagner, & Rabkin, 1996; Williams, Rabkin, Remien, Gorman, & Ehrhardt, 1991). Not suprisingly, though, those with a prior history of mood disorders are at elevated risk for displaying similar mood disorders at particularly stressful points during the HIV spectrum (e.g., at the point of diagnosis). Some work suggests that the suicide rate among HIV-1 infected men may be up to 36 times that of age-matched uninfected men (Marzuk et al., 1988; Rundell, Paolucci, & Beatty, 1988), which supports the view that marked depressive symptoms can occur in the wake of an HIV-1 diagnosis. Emotional reactions may be different at the various diagnostic junctures across the infection (initial seropositivity, the first HIV-related clinical symptoms, a diagnosis of AIDS). Although many HIV-infected persons do not develop diagnosable mood disorders, it is quite common that they do experience significant levels of anxiety and depressed mood.

These reactions suggest that psychosocial interventions that provide support, teach coping strategies, and offer the opportunity for mastery experiences may be beneficial (Antoni et al., 1998). Such interventions also may help these individuals to ventilate feelings, such as anger and depression (Miller, 1988), and to manage anticipatory grief over expected losses in physical and vocational functioning and the death of others in their social network (Cohen, 1990; Lutgendorf, Antoni, Schneiderman, & Fletcher, 1994; Pickrel, 1989).

DEPRESSION AND NEGATIVE HEALTH BEHAVIORS IN HIV

When outlining intervention goals for HIV-infected persons, it is important to consider that depressed people are often more likely to engage in risky (unprotected) sexual behaviors (Gold & Skinner, 1992; Kelly et al., 1993) and substance abuse (Latkin & Mandell, 1993; Walker, Howard, Lambert, & Suchinsky, 1994). In regard to the former, some alarming trends have appeared in previously completed surveys. Despite steady reductions in sexual risk behaviors among the population of aging urban gay men over the past 10 years, a significant number of young gay men continue to engage in unprotected anal intercourse (Martin, 1989), the sexual activity that carries the highest risk for HIV infection in gay men (Kingsley et al., 1987). Moreover, up to 15% of those middle-aged gay men who modified their sexual behaviors in the early years of the AIDS crisis have relapsed to unsafe sexual activities (Coates, 1991). One important factor that may influence such risk-taking behavior is the use of alcohol and drugs during sex (Martin, 1990a). The prevalence of alcohol abuse in the gay community is quite a bit higher (30%) than for the general population (5%–10%) because drinking is a key facet of the primary gathering places—gay bars (Fifield, 1975; Martin, 1990b; Lohrenz, Connelly, Coyne, & Spare, 1978). Finally, depressive symptoms may be more likely to occur in HIV-infected men and women who are substance abusers, especially those who are injection drug users (Rabkin et al., 1996). Thus, chronic depressive symptoms, substance abuse, and unprotected sexual behaviors may be part of a self-perpetuating loop that characterizes poor psychosocial adjustment to HIV infection.

Although it is very likely that this same loop operates in women who are dealing with HIV, little empirical evidence is available to support this contention. At risk and infected women are disproportionately represented among minority populations, especially Blacks (Antoni, Schneiderman, Laperriere, et al., 1992). In addition to the burden of HIV seropositivity, young, Black American, low socioeconomic status (SES) women have been characterized as a group that experiences the multiple stigmas of race, class, and gender (Quinn, 1993), as well as major chronic daily stressors and hassles (Freudenberg, Lee, & Silver, 1989). Stressors include drug and alcohol dependency, poor social networks, medical problems, financial problems, overburdened public clinics, lack of transportation, and inaccessibility of child care (Quinn, 1993), all of which can amplify perceptions of helplessness and powerlessness. Therefore, this group of HIV-infected individuals may undergo many additional stressors beyond those experienced by HIV-positive gay men, thus placing them at increased risk for both mood disorders and related negative health behaviors that may create a vicious cycle. Unfortunately, very little research has explored the mechanisms that relate distress, depression, and these behaviors in this population. The bulk of the literature reviewed herein is based primarily on HIV-infected gay men and therefore is likely to be limited in its generality.

PSYCHOSOCIAL FACTORS PREDICTIVE OF DEPRESSION AND RISK BEHAVIORS IN HIV INFECTION

The risk factors for depression in HIV-infected persons are similar to those in the normal population: a prior history of depression (Rabkin et al., 1994), a family history of depression, and substance abuse (Rabkin, Wagner, & Rabkin, 1996). More specific to HIV-infected persons, factors that increase the risk of depression and distress, sexual risk behaviors, and substance abuse include: being faced with chronic, uncontrollable, and unpredictable stressors in the future (e.g., treatment responsiveness and side-effects, disease recurrence, stigmatizing behaviors, and medical costs; Blendon & Donelan, 1988; Bloom & Carliner, 1988; Ginzburg & Gostin, 1986; Redfield & Burke, 1988; Walkey et al., 1990); loss of familiar sources of social support due to deaths of close friends (Martin, 1988), desire for social insularity, and avoidance by acquaintances and significant others in response to disclosure of homosexual orientation (Beckett & Rutan, 1990).

We proposed that the combination of uncontrollable life stressors and diminishing social resources creates cognitive and emotional burdens

(Noh, Chondarana, Field, & Posthuma, 1990) that may overwhelm premorbid adaptive coping strategies (e.g., active coping, making plans, and focusing on the positive side of things) and result in the use of less adaptive coping strategies, such as denial and avoidance (Antoni, 1991). The perception of an inability to cope may bring about a loss of self-esteem and self-efficacy, feelings of helplessness and hopelessness, and depression, as well as increase maladaptive, potentially self-destructive behaviors, such as high-risk sex and substance use.

PSYCHOSOCIAL FACTORS AND THE COURSE OF HIV INFECTION

Among those individuals who are infected with HIV, there is wide variability in disease course. Some patients develop symptoms rapidly, whereas others remain free of AIDS symptoms for long periods of time (10 to 15 years). In addition to the biological factors that influence the length of survival (Friedland et al., 1991; Hardy & the Long-Term Survivor Collaborative Study Group, 1991), there is evidence that several psychosocial variables, such as depression, also contribute to individual differences in disease progression among asymptomatic HIV-infected individuals and to differences in survival time in those who already have developed AIDS.

Prospective studies attempting to relate depressive symptoms to faster rates of immunologic decline and disease progression in HIV-infected persons have produced mixed results. Burack et al. (1993) found that greater depressive symptoms predicted a faster decline in CD4 counts but did not predict time to AIDS or survival time in early-stage HIV-infected gay men followed over a 6-year period. Lyketsos et al. (1993) also found no prospective relationship between depression and either CD4 count slopes or clinical disease progression over a similar period. Studies employing shorter follow-up periods (1 to 2 years) also failed to document a prospective association between depressive symptoms and CD4 counts and clinical progression (e.g., Rabkin et al., 1991). More recently, however, Patterson et al. (1996) found that greater depressive symptoms predicted shorter survival time over a 5-year follow-up, even after controlling for baseline symptoms and CD4 counts. Differences across these studies could be due to differences in immune status and disease status at entry, variations in follow-up periods, and changes in medications or risk behaviors across the follow-up periods.

It is also plausible that other psychosocial factors may interact with distress levels or depressive symptoms to predict changes in immune status and health. For instance, longitudinal studies reveal that a mounting number of losses and grieving experiences constitute prevalent life stressors for HIV-infected individuals and that these events interact with distress levels to contribute to a faster rate of disease progression (Patterson et al., 1996). Further work suggests that maintaining a fatalistic–pessimistic attitude in the face of such repeated and uncontrollable stressors is a significant predictor of shorter survival time among men with AIDS (Blomkvist et al., 1994; Kemeny, 1994; Reed, Kemeny, Taylor, Wang, & Visscher, 1994). The use of coping strategies, such as extreme denial or extreme acceptance, have been associated with an accelerated disease course, whereas distraction (and perhaps low rumination about the disease) has been associated with a slower rate of progression (Ironson, Antoni, & Lutgendorf, 1995). Finally, people who remain socially isolated (and who may be the least comfortable in approaching their support network) appear to show the fastest progression of disease (Cole, Kemeny, Taylor, Visscher, & Fahey, 1996; Patterson et al., 1996; Solomon, Temoshok, O'Leary, & Zich, 1987; Theorell et al., 1995).

Another research strategy to provide evidence that psychosocial factors are associated with health course in HIV-infected individuals is to document the characteristics of those who substantially "outlive" their prognosis after a diagnosis of AIDS. This research has been reviewed by Ironson, Solomon, Cruess, Barroso, and Stivers (1995). Only a few studies of the psychosocial characteristics of long-term survivors of AIDS (defined by clinical symptoms) have been done, and as Ironson and colleagues noted, almost all of these have been crosssectional. These studies represent samples of persons with AIDS drawn from the Pacific (Solomon et al., 1987), Northeast (Remien, Rabkin, & Williams, 1992), and Southeast (Barroso, 1993) regions of this country. Ironson and her colleagues found a good deal of consensus on the existence of four psychosocial adjustment strategies: (a) healthy self-care behaviors; (b) a sense of connectedness; (c) a sense of meaning and purpose; and (d) maintaining perspective. It remains to be determined which psychological and biological mechanisms might explain the ways in which these four long-term survivor strategies relate to health outcomes in HIV-infected people. Ironson and colleagues hypothesized some of the possible mechanisms, including primary psychological mechanisms (e.g., distress and behavioral disenegagement) and several biological mechanisms, many of which tie in precisely with the rationale that we developed for the use of stress management interventions in HIV-infected individuals.

PSYCHONEUROIMMUNOLOGIC (PNI) RESEARCH AND HIV INFECTION

Because HIV infection has been shown to be associated with an increased risk for distress and depressive symptoms (Antoni et al., 1990; Kaisch & Anton-Culver, 1989; Viney, Henry, Walker, & Crooks, 1989), which in turn, have been shown to influence the immune system in a negative fashion (Calabrese, King, & Gold, 1987; Ironson et al., 1990; Irwin, Daniels, Smith, Bloom, & Weiner, 1987; Kiecolt-Glaser et al., 1987), it is conceivable that behavioral interventions that decrease distress may beneficially impact immune status. In the case of HIV infection, these interventions may affect the course of the disease by way of their effects on the immune system (Antoni et al., 1990). Because the degree of immunosuppression seems to be the strongest predictor of the progression to HIV-related symptoms and death, much research focused on ways to either slow the growth of the virus or slow the decline of the immune system by modulating the function of its cells.

We have been involved in PNI research that examines ways in which psychosocial influences, such as cognitive behavioral stress management (CBSM), can be used to modulate psychosocial and behavioral factors known to affect the immune system. We reasoned that as CBSM modifies psychosocial factors, such as emotional distress, cognitive–affective processing (i.e., stressor appraisals and emotional expression), maladaptive coping strategies, and social isolation, it might also modulate immune system components that could aggravate the course of the disease. By diminishing the impact of psychosocial and behavioral factors on the immune system, the individual might retard the onset of disease complications by maintaining immunologic status (e.g., by preserving an adequate number of T-helper cells and/or maintaining the functioning of surviving immune cells) within a range necessary to defend against certain pathogens.

Several neuroendocrines, such as cortisol and catecholamines, are known to be altered as a function of an individual's appraisal (i.e., controllable vs. uncontrollable) of and coping response (i.e., active vs. passive) to stressful stimuli. These neuroendocrines are capable of impairing certain components of the immune system (for extensive review, see Ader, Felten & Cohen, 1991). Some of these hormones, including those produced by the adrenal gland, also are dysregulated in depressed individuals (Calabrese et al., 1987). Because evidence has linked uncontrollable stressors, perceived loss of control, and social losses to alterations in some of these immunomodulatory hormones, we reasoned that the relations between psychosocial and behavioral events and immunologic changes might be partially mediated by the hormonal changes associated with an individual's appraisals of and coping responses to environmental burdens (for reviews, see Antoni et al., 1990; Schneiderman et al., 1994).

According to this model, stressful events that are interpreted by HIV-infected individuals as beyond their control might lead to social isolation, loneliness, anxiety, and depressed affect, which might accompany alterations in some neurohormones (e.g., peripheral catecholamine and cortisol elevations), due to sympathetic nervous system (SNS) activation and dysregulation of the hypothalamic pituitary adrenal (HPA) axis. These neuroendocrine changes also may be accompanied by changes in the immune system (e.g., redistribution of lymphocytes and decrements in functions concerning lymphocyte proliferation and cell killing) via interactions among neural and neuroendocrine signals at the immune cell membrane, intracellular cyclic nucleotide activation, and the production of cytokines (or immunohormone-like substances), such as interleukin (IL) I and II, and γ-interferon (γ-IFN). Because these structural (cell counts) and functional (proliferation and cytotoxicity) aspects of the immune system are known to decline progressively across the course of HIV-1 infection (Pantaleo, Graziosi, & Fauci, 1993), we hypothesized that additional stressor-induced changes in the functioning of the immune system may increase the rate at which infected people develop clinical symptoms, such as opportunistic infections and neoplasias. Thus, our theoretical model suggests at least two sets of related targets for intervention: psychosocial experiences and pathophysiological processes that involve the immune system. In the next section, we review the efficacy of psychosocial interventions for HIV-infected men and describe our treatment and research program.

THE EFFECTS OF STRESS MANAGEMENT INTERVENTIONS ON QUALITY OF LIFE, IMMUNE, AND HEALTH STATUS IN HIV INFECTION

Initial Studies of Psychosocial Interventions in HIV-Infected Men

Comprehensive reviews of the psychological effects (Chesney & Folkman, 1994) and immune and health effects (Ironson, Antoni, & Lutgendorf, 1995) of a range of psychosocial interventions in HIV populations are now available. We focus here on those interventions that employ cognitive behavioral techniques and/or operate in a group-based format, as these are most relevant to the CBSM intervention that is being developed and evaluated by our group.

In studies that specifically recruited HIV-positive men who were either experiencing ongoing mood problems (i.e., depressive symptoms; Chesney, Folkman, & Chambers, 1996; Kelly et al., 1993) or who were dealing with strong emotionally laden stressors (bereavement; Goodkin et al., 1996), investigators have been able to show that group-based, stress-reduction interventions are successful at decreasing perceived stress, affective distress, or depressive symptoms. Typically, these interventions involve groups of 6 to 8 participants led by two coleaders and met weekly over 2 to 3 months. One study found that a 10-week bereavement support group decreased distress levels and grief among 56 asymptomatic or early symptomatic HIV-positive gay men (Goodkin et al., 1996). Two studies focused specifically on HIV-positive gay men who were experiencing at least some symptoms of depression at entry. Chesney et al. (1996) found that men randomized to a 3-month Coping Effectiveness Training (CET) group revealed increases in self-efficacy and decreases in perceived stress and burnout, when compared to those men assigned to either an HIV-information group or a wait-list control. Kelly et al. (1993) compared HIV-positive gay men assigned to either a cognitive behavioral therapy group, a social support group, or a standard-of-care control group. Men assigned to the cognitive behavioral group showed significant reductions in distress compared to controls, although these changes were not different from those reported by men in the social support group. The authors suggested that men in the social support condition may have benefitted from the opportunity to ventilate their frustrations and emotions in a supportive environment and that this was as therapeutic as the cognitive behavioral group therapy.

The role of treatment orientation in psychosocial interventions for HIV-infected persons was addressed more systematically by Mulder and colleagues (1994). Specifically, they compared the effects of a group-based cognitive behavioral intervention to an existential–experiential group in HIV-infected gay men recruited from a large cohort study being conducted through the Amsterdam Municipal Health Center. Despite the differences in theoretical orientation, both interventions were of equal session length and frequency, total duration and group size, and each was designed to reduce stress, improve coping, build social support, and encourage emotional expression. Both of the psychosocial interventions (CBT, ET) produced significant and roughly equivalent decreases in Profile of Mood States (POMS) total mood disturbance and Beck Depression Inventory (BDI) scores, compared to the controls.

This collection of work suggests that group-based psychosocial interventions are capable of reducing distress levels in HIV-infected gay men, who are either currently experiencing mood problems or are dealing with major life events, such as partner loss. It seems important that interventions address certain specific goals, such as reducing stress, improving coping, building social support, and providing a healthy environment for expressing feelings. The degree to which one theoretical orientation may be superior to another among HIV-infected gay men may be dependent on the personal qualities of the participants, the severity of ongoing life events and their ongoing mood reactions to these, and the stage of disease. Our laboratory is evaluating the efficacy of a cognitive behavioral stress management intervention in HIV-positive gay men across different stressful periods and at different stages of the HIV spectrum.

COGNITIVE BEHAVIORAL STRESS MANAGEMENT (CBSM) EFFECTS ON MOOD AND IMMUNE FUNCTIONING AT DIFFERENT CRITICAL POINTS IN HIV INFECTION

The rationale that we followed in developing a stress management intervention for HIV infection was based on the psychosocial sequelae that have been well-documented for this chronic disease. HIV-infected people are faced with a wide variety of chronic, uncontrollable, and unpredictable stressors, such as changes in health, job status, health insurance, and medical costs. Because HIV infection is a chronic, progressive disease with an uncertain course, infected individuals must develop lifestyle changes, effective coping strategies, and often, new social networks to meet new challenges each day. Certain types of resources may be more or less important for dealing with the challenges that emerge at different points along the course of the disease (Lutgendorf et al., 1994). Even for those who are successful at mustering personal and interpersonal resources for managing most of these burdens, there still remain critical stressor events—emergence of new symptoms, development of resistance to a successful drug regime, loss of health-insurance benefits, deaths of friends, rejection from family members—which can trigger lapses into depression, anxiety, and other distress reactions, as well as negative health behaviors, such as substance abuse. Such lapses, if severe and unremitting, may contribute to an acceleration of disease progression through PNI processes (Antoni et al., 1990). Stress management interventions, such as the one we have developed, may be capable of reducing the frequency and severity of these lapses, reducing immunologic perturbations, and slowing the progression of the infection.

Our work over the past 10 years has tested the efficacy of group-based CBSM across several specific critical points of disease progression. The rationale underlying this approach is that HIV infection comprises not only a spectrum of diseases, but also a spectrum of psychosocial challenges that change over time. We proposed four somewhat artificial critical points that can be used to characterize these challenges: (a) response to the initial diagnosis of seropositivity; (b) adjustment to being infected during the early asymptomatic period when individuals are still healthy; (c) adjustment to the experience of HIV-related symptoms that are not life-threatening but do impact the quality of life; and (d) adjustment to a diagnosis of AIDS. We have completed or are in the process of examining the impact of a group-based CBSM program that addresses the needs and issues of HIV-infected men at each of these critical points along the path of this disease.

The Initial HIV-Seropositive Diagnosis

In our first study evaluating the effects of CBSM, 65 gay men who did not know their HIV serostatus were randomly assigned to either a CBSM intervention, a group-based aerobic exercise intervention (matched contact time), or a control group. After 5 weeks of participation in one of these conditions, blood was drawn for antibody testing and the men received news of their serostatus 3 days later. The intervention continued for another 5 weeks, thus enabling us to follow the men through the initial adjustment period.

The CBSM intervention consisted of 10 structured modules that focused on providing basic health, education material about safer sex, HIV, and the immune system; increasing awareness of emotional and physical stress responses and negative thoughts that accompany these; teaching cognitive restructuring techniques; providing coping-skills training; teaching interpersonal skills through assertion training and anger management; demonstrating relaxation techniques, such as progressive muscle relaxation, guided imagery, autogenics, and mindfulness meditation; and focusing on ways to enhance the men's social support resources.

Across the notification period the HIV-positive control group showed significant increases in anxiety and depressed mood, whereas the HIV-positive CBSM participants showed no significant changes in anxiety or depressed mood (Antoni et al., 1991). The same buffering effect was found for the HIV-positive exercisers (LaPerriere et al., 1990). With respect to immune findings, both HIV-positive control groups showed slight drops in lymphoproliferative responses to phytohemagglutinin (PHA), natural killer cell cytotoxicity (NKCC) and NK cell counts prenotification to postnotification (with no change in CD4 counts). In contrast, the HIV-positive CBSM subjects had significant increases in CD4 and NK cells and slight increases in PHA responsivity and NKCC, thus showing a buffering of the stress of notification (Antoni et al., 1991). It should be noted that despite the fact that the men were quite distressed during the postnotification period, they did not develop depressive syndromes, and the severity of their depressed mood elevations were not in the clinical range.

We also observed that there was considerable variability in the degree to which participants practiced techniques such as relaxation outside of the sessions as indicated in daily self-monitoring cards completed over the duration of the 10-week group. The frequency of home practice revealed on these cards ranged from 0 to 14 episodes per week. Importantly, Antoni et al. (1991) found that more home practice during the initial 5 weeks of the CBSM intervention was associated with larger decreases in distress and larger increases in NK cells and CD4 cell counts over the pre to postnotification period (after controlling for initial levels).

There also were several consistent immune changes noted over the total 10-week period of intervention. Men in the CBSM intervention showed significant decreases in antibody titers (putatively reflecting better cell-mediated immunologic control) to Epstein Barr Virus–Viral Capsid Antigen (EBV–VCA) and to Human Herpes Virus–Type 6 (HHV–6), as compared to controls, whose antibody titers remained constant over the 10-week intervention period and elevated relative to healthy male laboratory controls (Esterling et al., 1992). Stress-induced impairments in NKCC may facilitate herpes virus reactivation in HIV-infected individuals (Glaser & Kiecolt-Glaser, 1987) with subsequent effects of HIV replication and progression to AIDS (Carbonari, Fiorilli, Mezzaroma, Cherchi, & Aiuti, 1989; Rosenberg & Fauci, 1991). Because several herpes viruses prevalent in HIV infection are known to have independent immunosuppressive effects, reactivation of these viruses could have implications for clinical disease progression (Griffiths & Grundy, 1987).

An analysis of other psychosocial changes in this cohort showed that men in the control group showed significant decrements in social support during the notification period, whereas those in the CBSM group maintained their social support levels (Friedman et al., 1991). Interestingly, pre–post intervention decrements in social support reliable alliance scores (degree to which men were able to rely on and place more trust in members of their social network) were associated with declines in NKCC and with increases in antibody titers to EBV–VCA over a similar period (Antoni, Ironson, Helder, et al., 1992). This suggests that one of the ways in which this intervention buffers individuals from the stress of serostatus notification is by improving the ways in which they utilize available social supports. Indeed, one entire module of the CBSM program focuses on changing negative cognitive appraisals regarding the use of social support resources, and two other modules teach interpersonal skills (anger management and assertion training) that may be key for enhancing the quality of interpersonal relationships.

We followed the HIV-positive men randomized to either CBSM or exercise for 2 years to determine psychological predictors of disease progression (Ironson et al., 1994). We found that distress at the time of diagnosis, HIV-specific denial coping (pre–post diagnosis change), and low treatment adherence (attendance for either CBSM or exercise groups, frequency of relaxation practice during the 10 weeks for those in CBSM, and doing homework for those in CBSM) all predicted faster disease progression. Increases in denial and poorer treatment adherence remained significant, even after controlling for initial disease severity (CD4 cell counts). Furthermore, decreases in denial and a greater frequency of relaxation home practice during the 10-week intervention period were predictive of higher

CD4 cell counts and of greater lymphoproliferative responses to PHA at 1-year follow-up (Ironson et al., 1994).

In an expanded set of analyses of this data, we prospectively related coping strategies and immunologic measures in the HIV-positive men as compared to their HIV-counterparts over the first year following notification of their antibody test results (Antoni et al., 1995). We found that HIV-positive men scoring above the median on postnotification disengagement coping strategies (denial, behavioral disengagement, mental disengagement) had significantly lower concurrently measured T-helper–suppressor (CD4–CD8) cell ratios, T-inducer subset (CD4+CD45RA+) percentage values, and proliferative responses to PHA than did subjects scoring below the median on these scales. More disengagement coping responses also predicted poorer lymphocyte responsivity to PHA at 1-year follow-up. It should be noted that other work has indicated that greater reductions in depressed mood among HIV-positive gay men who completed a 15-week psychosocial intervention that uses many of the same techniques used in our CBSM groups predicted a slower decline in immune status over a 2-year follow-up period (Mulder et al., 1995).

The Asymptomatic Stage of HIV Infection

One of the most challenging aspects of asymptomatic HIV disease is the many uncertainties concerning one's future health and the availability of external resources such as health insurance. Some of these arise due to the unpredictable physical course of the HIV infection and some as a function of external and uncontrollable stressors, such as impaired occupational and social functioning, decreased earning power, high costs of medical care, complex medical treatments, difficulties with self care, multiple bereavements, and declining social supports (Blendon & Donelan, 1988; Ginzburg & Gostin, 1986; Redfield & Burke, 1988; Walkey et al., 1990). To address the efficacy of CBSM during this stage of the disease, we examined the effects of CBSM intervention with gay men who knew of their HIV-positive status, but who were still asymptomatic. Although their physical functioning had not yet been affected by the virus, knowledge of their positive serostatus and its eventual implications had affected their lifestyle and related behaviors (Lutgendorf, Antoni, Schneiderman, & Fletcher, 1994). Many had not yet disclosed their status to their family, acquaintances, or work associates. For several, this led to a sense of living a double life in which some people knew the truth about them and some did not. These men had all known their HIV status from 6 months to 5 years. Some were still dealing with residual anger regarding the manner in which they had been told they were positive. Others were concerned about whether and how to disclose HIV status to family members who did not know that they were gay. Vocational issues included concerns about making job transitions to maximize professional pursuits while they could, but also not wanting to jeopardize their health insurance.

In a pilot study of a few cohorts of men completing the CBSM program, we found that participants significantly reduced their anxiety, depressed mood, anger, fatigue, and confusion levels, and also increased their vigor (Antoni, Ironson, Helder, et al., 1992). In response to the threat of AIDS in their life, participants also reported increases in adaptive coping strategies (e.g., acceptance, planning, and active coping) and decreases in maladaptive coping strategies(e.g., mental disengagement and denial). These individuals also revealed significant increases in blastogenic responses to PHA and various indices of NKCC. Thus, among HIV-positive men dealing with all of the uncertainties of this period, CBSM was associated with reductions in distress and with increases in some indices of immune system functioning.

The Pre-AIDS Symptomatic Stage of HIV Infection

Another critical point in the course of HIV infection is the time at which overt symptoms begin to appear. These symptoms, including fatigue, diarrhea, and other constitutional symptoms, many of which are tied to viral and yeast infections, have a major impact on quality of life, but are rarely life-threatening. To evaluate the usefulness of CBSM during this stage of the disease, we examined the effects of the intervention in HIV-positive gay men who were dealing with similar types of symptoms, but who had not yet progressed to full-blown AIDS. Forty HIV-infected gay men who had mild symptoms (Category B of the 1993 CDC definition) were randomly assigned to either the 10-week CBSM intervention or to a modified wait-list control group in which they completed a 10-week waiting period and were provided a 1-day CBSM seminar. Across the 10 weeks, the CBSM group participants showed a significant decrease in BDI (Beck, Ward, Mendelson, Mock, & Erbaugh, 1961) scores as well as POMS depressed affect and anxiety and a significant decrease in antibody titers to herpes simplex virus–Type 2 (HSV–2; Lutgendorf et al., 1997). Moreover, the 10-week decreases in HSV–2 antibody titers were strongly associated with the degree to which participants lowered their BDI scores over this period. Subsequently conducted analyses revealed that the effects of CBSM on HSV–2 antibody reductions appeared to be mediated by the intervention-associated depression changes (Antoni, Lutgendorf, Ironson, Fletcher, & Schneiderman, 1997).

As in the earlier notification study, the degree to which the men practiced their stress-reduction techniques outside of the sessions ranged from 0 to 14 times per week (Lutgendorf et al., 1997). We also noted that a greater frequency of home practice was associated with greater reductions in depressed mood and anxiety over the 10-week period. In addition, cognitive coping changes, specifically acceptance of the HIV infection and social support attachment, reliable alliance, and guidance, were each strongly related to lower dysphoria, anxiety, and total mood disturbance in this sample. Multiple regression analyses suggested that changes in social support and in cognitive coping strategies appeared to mediate, in part, the effects of the CBSM intervention on the changes in distress and depressed mood noted during the intervention (Lutgendorf et al., 1998). Our ongoing work is exploring whether these same intervention-related changes are also predictive of changes in immune-system status and longer term health changes.

Full-Blown AIDS

Although there is a growing literature documenting psychosocial factors that predict psychological adjustment and physical health in AIDS patients (e.g., long-term survivor literature reviewed in Ironson, Solomon et al., 1995), little or no research tests the effects of various psychosocial interventions with patients who have progressed to AIDS. Adjusting to a long-term progressive lethal illness may entail addressing changes in self-expectations and vocational plans (Hoffman, 1991). A very tangible issue is that employment status often changes dramatically at this point in the disease. A majority of men diagnosed with AIDS in the samples studied to date had become unemployed by the time of the study (Chuang, Devins, Hunsley, & Gill, 1989; Dilley, Ochitil, Perl, & Volberding, 1985). One study reported that the monthly income of patients with AIDS had fallen by an average of $1,000 per month since their diagnosis (Ellerman, 1989). Intermittent episodes of *pneumocystis carinii* pneumonia are highly associated with diminished abilities to maintain employment (Wachtel et al., 1992). From a psychosocial standpoint, it is important to note that loss of one's source of employment can pervade many areas of life—loss of sources of social support, identity, income, and medical insurance—that, in turn, can hamper one's ability to adjust to the demands of the illness possibly increasing the risk for distress reactions and possibly, depressive episodes (Lutgendorf, Antoni, Schneiderman, & Fletcher, 1994).

With the steady progression to increasingly more serious and life-threatening symptoms, individuals with AIDS go through a continual process of emotional crises, recycling through the stages that Kubler-Ross (1969) originally noted as comprising the dying process: denial, anger, bargaining, depression, and acceptance (Hoffman, 1991). Some have proposed that HIV-infected patients may have emotional reactions that are more intense and labile than those described by Kubler-Ross and that this may be due to the fact that these challenges are at a much younger age among AIDS patients than in those with other types of terminal diseases (Hoffman, 1991). It is clear that these individuals are in need of psychosocial services, although one must be cautious in attempting to apply what has been learned from asymptomatic and early stage populations. It is plausible that persons with AIDS may find CBSM techniques useful for managing daily stressors, making treatment-related decisions that involve repeated communications with their physician, and balancing what can be a very demanding medication schedule (Schneiderman et al., 1997). The use of a group-based psychosocial intervention may also provide emotional support as individuals deal with loneliness in the wake of multiple losses in their social support network. Persons with AIDS may benefit from a therapeutic plan that combines a group-based stress reduction intervention together with individual-based therapy directed at confronting existential issues. With the greater likelihood of psychiatric diagnoses in later stage cases, the therapy plan may also involve pharmacologic treatment blended with the psychosocial intervention.

CONCLUSIONS

Work completed in this country by our group and others, and that done in Europe, demonstrates the efficacy of stress management interventions in HIV-infected individuals at various points along the HIV spectrum. This, along with the growing evidence that psychological characteristics, such as a sense of meaning, purpose, and connectedness may be predictive of long-term nonprogression and survival, highlights areas that should be targeted in psychosocial interventions. Relaxation and cognitive restructuring help to reduce distress and depressed mood. Coping-skills training can provide alternatives to avoidance, denial, and rumination as methods of dealing with the chronic stress of the infection. Assertion training and anger management can help individuals to seek out and utilize available social support as a stress buffer. Our CBSM intervention combines all of these techniques in the context of a supportive group environment.

The next frontier in our research program is to test the generality of this intervention in emerging, yet understudied populations of HIV-infected persons, including gay men with AIDS struggling with the daily challenge of an incredibly complex, demanding and delicately balanced set of medications to keep them healthy; HIV-infected persons combating addictions (e.g., injection drug use), a lifestyle that places them at increased risk for accelerated disease progression and viral transmission; and HIV-infected women, especially those from inner-city minority groups, who are faced with a wide range of additional interpersonal, economic, and social challenges. Tailoring these interventions to address the emotional adjustment issues of these different populations will be a critical research agenda in the coming years.

REFERENCES

Ader, R., Felten, D., & Cohen, N. (1991). *Psychoneuroimmunology* (2nd ed.). New York: Academic Press.

Antoni, M. H. (1991). Psychosocial stressors and stress management with HIV-1 seropositive and seronegative gay men. *International Reviews in Psychiatry, 3,* 385–402.

Antoni, M. H., Baggett, L., Ironson, G., August, S., LaPerriere, A., Klimas, N., Schneiderman, N., & Fletcher, M. A. (1991). Cognitive behavioral stress management intervention buffers distress responses and immunologic changes following notification of HIV-1 seropositivity. *Journal of Consulting and Clinical Psychology, 59,* 906–915.

Antoni, M. H., Goldstein, D., Ironson, G., LaPerriere, A., Fletcher, M. A., & Schneiderman, N. (1995). Coping responses to HIV-1 serostatus notification predict concurrent and prospective immunologic status. *Clinical Psychology and Psychotherapy,* 2(4), 234–248.

Antoni, M. H., Ironson, G., Helder, L., Lutgendorf, S., Friedman, A., LaPerriere, A., Fletcher, M. A., & Schneiderman, N. (1992, April). *Stress management intervention reduces social isolation and maladaptive coping behaviors in gay men adjusting to an HIV-1 seropositive diagnosis.* Paper presented at the scientific meeting of the Society of Behavioral Medicine, New York.

Antoni, M., Lutgendorf, S., Ironson, G., Fletcher, M. A., & Schneiderman, N. (1997). CBSM intervention effects on mood and immunity in HIV+ gay men: The role of relaxation training, coping skills and social support. *Psychosomatic Medicine, 59,* 81.

Antoni, M. H., Schneiderman, N., Fletcher, M. A., Goldstein, D., Ironson, G., & LaPerriere, A. (1990). Psychoneuroimmunology and HIV-1. *Journal of Consulting and Clincal Psychology, 58,* 38–49.

Antoni, M. H., Schneiderman, N., & Ironson, G. (1998). *Stress management for HIV-infection.* Unpublished manuscript, University of Miami.

Antoni, M. H., Schneiderman, N., LaPerriere, A., O'Sullivan, M. J., Marks, J., Efantis, J., Skyler, J., & Fletcher, M. A. (1992). Mothers with AIDS. In P. Ahmed (Ed.), *Living and dying with AIDS.* New York: Plenum.

Barroso, J. (1993). *Reconstructing a life: A nursing study of long term survivors of AIDS.* Unpublished dissertation, University of Texas at Austin.

Beck, A. T. , Ward, C. H., Mendelson, M., Mock, J., & Erbaugh, J. (1961). An inventory for measuring depression. *Archives of General Psychiatry, 4,* 561–571.

Beckett, A., & Rutan, J. S. (1990). Treating persons with ARC and AIDS in group psychotherapy. *International Journal of Group Psychotherapy, 40,* 19–29.

Blendon, R. J., & Donelan, K. (1988). Discrimination against people with AIDS: The public's perspective. *New England Journal of Medicine, 319,* 1022–1026.

Bloom, D., & Carliner, G. (1988). The economic impact of AIDS in the United States. *Science, 239,* 604–610.

Blomkvist, V., Theorell, T., Jonsson, H., Schulman, S., Berntorp, E., & Stiegendal, L. (1994). Psychosocial self-prognosis in relation to mortality and morbidity in hemophiliacs with HIV infection. *Psychotherapy and Psychosomatics, 62,* 185–192.

Burack, J. H., Barrett, D. C., Stall, R. D., Chesney, M. A., Ekstrand, M. L., & Coates, T. J. (1993). Depressive symptoms and CD4 lymphocyte decline among HIV-infected men. *Journal of the American Medical Association, 270,* 2567–2573.

Calabrese, J., King, M., & Gold, P. (1987). Alterations in immunocompetence during stress, bereavement, and depression: Focus on neuroendocrine regulation. *American Journal of Psychiatry, 144,* 1123–1134.

Carbonari, M., Fiorilli, M., Mezzaroma, I., Cherchi, M., & Aiuti, F. (1989). CD4 as the receptor for retroviruses of the HTLV family: Immunopathogenetic implications. *Advances in Experimental Medicine and Biology, 257,* 3–7.

Chesney, M. A., & Folkman, S. (1994). Psychological impact of HIV disease and implications for intervention. *Psychiatric Clinics of North America, 17,* 163–182.

Chesney, M. A., Folkman, S., & Chambers, D. (1996). Coping effectiveness training for men living with HIV: Preliminary findings. *International Journal of STDs and AIDS,* 7 (Suppl. 2), 75–82.

Chuang, H. T., Devins, G. M., Hunsley, J., & Gill, M. J. (1989). Psychosocial distress and well-being among gay and bisexual men with human immunodeficiency virus infection. *American Journal of Psychiatry, 146,* 876–880.

Cleary, P., Singer, E., Rogers, T., Avorn, J., VanDevanter, N., Soumerai, S., Perry, S., & Pindyck, J. (1988). Sociodemographic and behavioral characteristics of HIV antibody-positive blood donors. *American Journal of Public Health, 78,* 953–857.

Coates, T. (1991, August). *Who has been tested for HIV antibodies in the United States? The National AIDS Behavioral Survey (NABS).* Paper presented at the American Psychological Association, San Francisco, CA.

Cohen, E. D. (1990). Confidentiality, counseling, and clients who have AIDS: Ethical foundations of a model rule. *Journal of Counseling and Development, 68,* 282–286.

Cole, S., Kemeny, M., Taylor, S., Visscher, B., & Fahey, J. (1996) Accelerated course of HIV infection in gay men who conceal their homosexuality. *Psychosomatic Medicine, 58,* 219–231.

Dilley, J. W., Ochitil, H. N., Perl, M., & Volberding, P. A. (1985). Findings in psychiatric consultations with patients with acquired immune deficiency syndrome. *American Journal of Psychiatry, 142,* 82–86.

Ellerman, D. (1989). *Quality of life of persons with AIDS/ARC.* Proceedings of the Vth International Conference on AIDS, TDP62, Montreal.

Esterling, B., Antoni, M., Schneiderman, N., Ironson, G., LaPerriere, A., Klimas, N., & Fletcher, M. A. (1992). Psychosocial modulation of antibody to Epstein-Barr viral capsid antigen and herpes virus type-6 in HIV-1 infected and at-risk gay men. *Psychosomatic Medicine, 54,* 354–371.

Fifield, L. (1975). *On my way to nowhere: An analysis of gay alcohol abuse and an evaluation of alcoholism rehabilitation services.* Los Angeles Gay Community Services Center and Department of Health Services.

Freudenberg, N., Lee, J, & Silver, D. (1989). How Black and Latino community organizaations respond to the AIDS epidemic: A case study in one New York City neighborhood. *AIDS Eduction and Prevention, 1*(1), 12–21.

Friedland, G. H., Saltzman, B., Vileno, J., Freeman, K., Schrager, L. K., & Klein, R. S. (1991). Survival differences in patients with AIDS. *Journal of Acquired Immune Deficiency Syndromes, 4,* 144–153.

Friedman, A., Antoni, M. H., Ironson, G., LaPerriere, A., Schneiderman, N., & Fletcher, M. A. (1991, March). *Behavioral interventions, changes in perceived social support and depression following notification of HIV-1 seropositivity.* Presented at Society of Behavioral Medicine Annual Meeting, Washington, DC.

Ginzburg, H. M., & Gostin, L. (1986). Legal and ethical issues associated with HTLV-III diseases. *Psychiatric Annals, 16,* 180–185.

Glaser, R., & Kiecolt-Glaser, J. (1987). Stress-associated depression in cellular immunity: implications for acquired immune deficiency syndrome (AIDS). *Brain, behavior and immunity, 1,* 107–112.

Gold, R., & Skinner, M. (1992). Situational factors and thought processes associated with unprotected intercourse in young gay men. *AIDS, 6*, 1021–1030.

Goodkin, K., Tuttle, R., Blaney, N., Feaster, D., Shapshak, P., Burkhalter, J., Leeds, B., Baldewicz, T., Kumar, M., & Fletcher, M. (1996). A bereavment support group intervention is associated with immunological changes in HIV-1+ and HIV-1- homosexual men. *Psychosomatic Medicine, 58*, 83.

Griffiths, P. D., & Grundy, J. E. (1987). Molecular biology and immunology of cytomegalovirus. *Journal of Biochemistry, 241*, 313–324.

Hardy, A. M., & the Long-Term Survivor Collaborative Study Group. (1991). Characterization of long-term survivors of Acquired Immunodeficiency Syndrome. *Journal of Acquired Immune Deficiency Syndromes, 4*, 386–391.

Hoffman, M. A. (1991). Counseling the seropositive client: A psychosocial model for assessment and intervention. *The Counseling Psychologist, 19*, 467–542.

Ironson, G., Antoni, M., & Lutgendorf, S. (1995). Can psychological interventions affect immunity and survival? Present findings and suggested targets with a focus on cancer and human immunodeficiency virus. *Mind/Body Medicine, 1*(2), 85–110.

Ironson, G., Friedman, A., Klimas, N., Antoni, M., Fletcher, M. A., LaPerriere, A., Simoneau, J., & Schneiderman, N. (1994). Distress, denial and low adherence to behavioral interventions predict faster disease progression in gay men infected with Human Immunodeficiency Virus. *International Journal of Behavioral Medicine, 1*(1), 90–105.

Ironson, G., LaPerriere, A., Antoni, M. H., Klimas, N., Schneiderman, N., & Fletcher, M. A. (1990). Changes in immune and psychological measures as a function of anticipation and reaction to news of HIV-1 antibody status. *Psychosomatic Medicine, 52*, 247–270.

Ironson, G., Solomon, G., Cruess, D., Barroso, J., & Stivers, M. (1995). Psychosocial factors related to long-term survival in HIV/AIDS. *Clinical Psychology and Psychotherapy, 2*, 249–266.

Irwin, M., Daniels, M., Smith, T., Bloom, E., & Weiner, H. (1987). Impaired natural killer cell activity during bereavement. *Brain, Behavior, and Immunity, 1*(1), 98–104.

Jacobsen, P., Perry, S., & Hirsch, D. (1990). Behavioral and psychological responses to HIV antibody testing. *Journal of Consulting and Clinical Psychology, 58*(1), 31–37.

Kaisch, K., & Anton-Culver, H. (1989). Psychological and social consequences of HIV exposure: Homosexuals in Southern California. *Psychology and Health, 3*, 63–75.

Kaplan, L. D., Wofsky, C. B., & Volberding, P. A. (1987). Treatment of patients with acquired immunodeficiency syndrome and associated manifestations. *Journal of the American Medical Association, 257*, 1367–1376.

Kelly, J., Murphy, D., Bahr, G., Koob, J., Morgan, M., Kalichman, S., Stevenson, L., Brashfield, T., Bernstein, B., & St. Lawrence, J. (1993). Factors associated with severity of depression and high-risk sexual behavior among persons diagnosed with human immunodeficiency virus (HIV) infection. *Health Psychology, 12*, 215–219.

Kemeny, M. E. (1994). Stressful events, psychological responses and progression of HIV infection. In R. Glaser & J. Kiecolt-Glaser (Eds.), *Handbook of human stress and immunity* (pp. 245–266). New York: Academic Press.

Kiecolt-Glaser, J. K., Fisher, L. D., Ogrocki, P., Stout, J. C., Speicher, C. E., & Glaser, R. (1987). Marital quality, marital disruption, and immune function. *Psychosomatic Medicine, 49*, 13–34.

Kingsley, L., Kaslow, R., Rinaldo, C., Detre, K., Odaka, N., VanRaden, M., Detels, R., Polk, B., Chmiel, J., Kelsey, S., Ostrow, D., & Visscher, B. (1987). Risk factors for sero-conversion to human immunodeficiency virus among male homosexuals. *Lancet, 1*, 345–349.

Kubler-Ross, E. (1969). *On death and dying.* New York: MacMillan.

LaPerriere, A., Antoni, M. H., Schneiderman, N., Ironson, G., Klimas, N., Caralis, P., & Fletcher, M. A. (1990). Exercise intervention attenuates emotional distress and natural killer cell decrements following notification of positive serologic status for HIV-1. *Biofeedback and Self-Regulation, 15*, 125–131.

Latkin, C., & Mandell, W. (1993). Depression as an antecedent of frequency of intravenous drug use in an urban, nontreatment sample. *International Journal of the Addictions, 28,* 1601–1612.

Lewin, D. (1996). Protease inhibitors: HIV-1 summons a darwinion defense. *Journal of NIH Research, 8,* 33–35.

Lohrenz, L., Connelly, L., Coyne, L., & Spare, K. (1978). Alcohol problems in several midwestern homosexual communities. *Journal of Studies of Alcohol, 39,* 1959–1963.

Longini, I. M. J., Clark, W. S., & Karon, J. M. (1993). The effect of routine use of therapy in slowing the course of HIV infection in a population-based cohort. *American Journal of Epidemiology, 137,* 1229–1240.

Lutgendorf, S., Antoni, M. H., Ironson, G., Klimas, N., Starr, K., McCabe, P., Cleven, K., Fletcher, M. A., & Schneiderman, N. (1997) Cognitive behavioral stress management decreases dysphoric mood and Herpes Simplex Virus-Type 2 antibody titers in symptomatic HIV-seropositive gay men. *Journal of Consulting and Clinical Psychology, 65,* 31–43.

Lutgendorf, S., Antoni, M. H., Ironson, G., Starr, K., Costello, N., Zuckerman, M., Klimas, N., Fletcher, M. A., & Schneiderman, N. (1998) Changes in cognitive coping skills and social support mediate distress outcomes in symptomatic HIV-seropositive gay men during a cognitive behavioral stress management intervention. *Psychosomatic Medicine, 60,* 204–214.

Lutgendorf, S., Antoni, M. H., Schneiderman, N., & Fletcher, M. A. (1994). Psychosocial counseling to improve quality of life in HIV-infected gay men. *Patient Education and Counseling, 24,* 217–235.

Lyketsos, C. G., Hoover, D. R., Guccione, M., Senterfitt, W., Dew, M. A., Wesch, J., VanRaden, M., Treisman, G. J., & Morganstem, H. (1993). Depressive symptoms as predictors of medical outcomes in HIV infection. *Journal of the American Medical Association, 270,* 2563–2567.

Martin, D. (1989). Human immunodeficiency virus infection and the gay community: Counseling and clinical issues. Special Issue: Gay, lesbian, and bisexual issues in counseling. *Journal of Counseling and Development, 68,* 67–72.

Martin, J. (1988). Psychological consequences of AIDS-related bereavement among gay men. *Journal of Consulting and Clinical Psychology, 56,* 856–862.

Martin, J. (1990a). Drinking patterns and drinking problems in a community sample of gay men. In D. Seminara, R. Watson, & A. Pawlowski (Eds.), *Alcohol, immunomodulation and AIDS* (pp. 27–34). New York: Liss.

Martin, J. (1990b). Drug use and unprotected anal intercourse among gay men. *Health Psychology, 9,* 450–465.

Marzuk, P. M., Tierney, H., Tardiff, K., Gross, E. M., Morgan, E. B., Hsu, M. A., & Mann, J. (1988). Increased risk of suicide in persons with AIDS. *Journal of the American Medical Association, 259,* 1333–1337.

Miller, D. (1988). HIV and social psychiatry. *British Medical Bulletin, 44,* 130–148.

Mulder, C. L., Emmelkamp, P., Antoni, M. H., Mulder, J., Sandfort, T., & de Vries, M. (1994). Cognitive-behavioral and experiential group psychotherapy for HIV-infected homosexual men: A comparative study. *Psychosomatic Medicine, 56,* 423–431.

Mulder, N., Antoni, M. H., Emmelkamp, P., Veugelers, P., Sandfort, T., van der Vijver, F., & de Vries, M. (1995). Psychosocial group intervention and the rate of decline of immunologc parameters in asymptomatic HIV-infected homosexual men. *Journal of Psychotherapy and Psychosomatics, 63,* 185–192.

Munoz, A., Wang, M. C., Good, R., Detels, H., Ginsberg, L., Kingsley, J., Phair, J., & Polk, B. F. (1988, June). *Estimation of the AIDS-free times after HIV-1 seroconversion.* Paper presented at the Fourth Annual Meeting of the International Conference on AIDS, Stockholm, Sweden.

Noh, S., Chondarana, P., Field, V., & Posthuma, B. (1990). AIDS epidemic, emotional strain, coping and psychological distress in homosexual men. *AIDS Education and Prevention, 2,* 272–283.

Pantaleo, G., Graziosi, C., & Fauci, A. S. (1993). The immunopathogenesis of human immunodeficiency virus infection. *The New England Journal of Medicine, 328,* 327–335.

Patterson, T., Shaw, W., Semple, S., Cherner, M., McCutchan, J., Atkinson, J., Grant, I., & Nannis, E. (1996). Relationship of psychosocial factors to HIV disease progression. *Annals of Behavioral Medicine, 18,* 30–39.

Perkins, D., Leserman, J., Stern, R., Baum, S., Liao, D., Golden, R., & Evans, D. (1995). Somatic symptoms and HIV infection: Relationship to depressive symptoms and indicators of HIV disease. *American Journal of Psychiatry, 152,* 1776–1781.

Perkins, D., Stern, R., Golden, R., Murphy, C., Naftolowitz, D., & Evans, D. (1994). Mood disturbances in HIV infection: Prevalence and risk factors in a nonepicenter of the AIDS epidemic. *American Journal of Psychiatry, 151,* 233–236.

Pickrel, J. (1989). "Tell me your story": Using life review in counseling the terminally ill. *Death Studies, 13,* 127–135.

Quinn, S. (1993). AIDS and the African American woman. The triple burden of race, class and gender. *Health Education Quarterly, 20,* 305–320.

Rabkin, J., Rabkin, R., Harrison, W., & Wagner, G. (1994). Effect of imipramine on mood and enumerative measures of immune status in depressed patients with HIV illness. *American Journal of Psychiatry, 270,* 2609–2610.

Rabkin, J., Wagner, G., & Rabkin, R. (1996). Treatment of depression in HIV+ men: Literature review and report of an ongoing study of testosterone replacement therapy. *Annals of Behavioral Medicine, 18,* 24–29.

Rabkin, J. G., Williams, J. B. W., Remien, R. H., Goetz, R. R., Kertzner, R., & Gorman, J. M. (1991). Depression, lymphocyte subsets, and human immunodeficiency virus symptoms on two occasions in HIV-positive homosexual men. *Archives of General Psychiatry, 48,* 111–119.

Redfield, R., & Burke, D. (1988). HIV infection: The clinical picture. *Scientific American, 259,* 90–98.

Reed, G. M., Kemeny, M. E., Taylor, S. E., Wang, H. J., & Visscher, B. (1994). Realistic acceptance as a predictor of decreased survival time in gay men with AIDS. *Health Psychology, 13,* 299–307.

Remien, R., Rabkin, J., & Williams, J. (1992). Coping strategies and health beliefs of AIDS longterm survivors. *Psychology and Health, 6,* 335–345.

Rosenberg, Z. F., & Fauci, A. S. (1991). Activation of latent HIV infection. *Journal of the National Institutes of Health Research, 2,* 41–45.

Rundell, J., Paolucci, S., & Beatty, D. (1988). Psychiatric illness at all stages of human immunodeficiency virus infection (letter). *American Journal of Psychiatry, 145,* 652–653.

Schneiderman, N., Antoni, M. H., & Ironson, G. (1997). Cognitive behavioral stress management and secondary prevention in HIV/AIDS. *Psychology & AIDS Exchange, 22,* 1–8.

Schneiderman, N., Antoni, M. H., Ironson, G., Fletcher, M. A., Klimas, N., & LaPerriere, A. (1994). HIV-1, immunity and behavior. In R. Glaser (Ed.), *Handbook of human stress and immunity* (pp. 267–300). New York: Academic Press.

Schneiderman, N., Antoni, M., Ironson, G., LaPerriere, A., & Fletcher, M. A. (1992). Applied psychosocial science and HIV-1 spectrum disease. *Journal of Applied and Preventative Psychology, 1,* 67–82.

Siegel, K., Karus, D., & Raveis, V. (1997). Correlates of change in depressive symptomatology among gay men with AIDS. *Health Psychology, 16,* 230–238.

Solomon, G., Temoshok, L., O'Leary, A., & Zich, J. (1987). An intensive psychoimmunologic study of long-surviving persons with AIDS. *Annals of the New York Academy of Sciences, 496,* 647–655.

Theorell, T., Blomkvist, V., Jonsson, H., Schulman, S., Berntorp, E., & Stigendal, L. (1995). Social support and the development of immune function in human immunodeficiency virus infection. *Psychosomatic Medicine, 57,* 32–36.

Viney, L., Henry, R., Walker, B., & Crooks, L. (1989). The emotional reactions of HIV antibody positive men. *British Journal Medical Psychology, 62,* 153–161.

Wachtel, T., Piette, M. S., Mor, V., Stein, M., Fleishman, J., & Carpenter, C. (1992). Quality of life in persons with Human Immunodeficiency Virus infection: Measurement by the Medical Outcomes Study instrument. *Annals of Internal Medicine, 116,* 129–137.

Walker, R., Howard, M., Lambert, M., & Suchinsky, R. (1994). Psychiatric and medical comorbidities of veterans with substance use disorders. *Hospital and Community Psychiatry, 45,* 232–237.

Walkey, F. H., Taylor, A. J., & Green, D. E. (1990). Attitudes to AIDS: A comparative analysis of a new and negative stereotype. *Social Science and Medicine, 30,* 549–552.

Williams, J., Rabkin, J., Remien, R., Gorman, J., & Ehrhardt, A. (1991). Multidisciplinary baseline assessment of homosexual men with and without human immunodeficiency virus infection II. Standardized clinical assessment of current and lifetime psychopathology. *Archives of General Psychiatry, 48,* 124–130.

Chapter 12

Depression and Negative Affect in Post-Myocardial Infarction Patients: Assessment and Treatment Implications

Kristin Kilbourn
Patrice Saab
Neil Schneiderman
University of Miami

Coronary heart disease (CHD) continues to be the leading cause of death and the third leading cause of disability for both men and women in the United States (Gillum, 1993; Higgins & Thom, 1989; Manson et al., 1992). Every year, approximately 1.5 million individuals suffer from myocardial infarction (MI), which results in half a million deaths and a cost of more than $100 billion (American Heart Association, 1994). Of those patients who experience a MI, 7% to 15% will die prior to discharge from the hospital, and an additional 5% to 10% will die in the first year following their MI (Gillum, 1993; Goldberg et al., 1993; Manson et al., 1992; McGovern et al., 1992; Moss & Benhorin, 1990).

Behavioral risk factors that contribute to the risk of heart disease include a diet high in saturated fat, low levels of aerobic exercise, and smoking. In addition, a number of psychosocial factors, such as depression (Carney et al., 1987), high levels of hostility (Barefoot et al., 1989; Matthews, 1988), and the inability to express emotions when under distress (Denollet & Brutsaert, 1998; Suls, Green, Rose, Lounsbury, & Gordon, 1997) have been found to be associated with CHD. The traditional behavioral risk factors associated with coronary artery disease (CAD) are moderately good at predicting those patients who are most at risk for suffering from MI (Moss & Benhorin, 1990), but physicians have a more difficult time determining which variables are most important in predicting post-MI recovery.

Some of the prognostic indicators associated with survival following a MI include the extent of myocardial damage, residual ischemia, electrical instability, and poor autonomic tone (DeBusk, 1989; Krone, 1992). Yet, these factors do not account for all of the variance in morbidity and mortality following MI. Recent evidence suggests that psychosocial factors play a significant role in the recovery from MI. Some of these variables include hostility (Barefoot, Dahlstrom, & Williams, 1983; Matthews, 1988; Shekelle, Vernon, & Ostfeld, 1991), Type A behavior pattern (Brand, Rosenman, Sholtz, & Friedman, 1976), distressed personality type (Denollet & Brutsaert, 1995, 1998), hopelessness (Anda et al., 1993; Everson et al., 1996), low socio-economic status (SES) (Williams, Barefoot, & Califf, 1992), vital exhaustion (Appels & Moulder, 1988; Falger & Schouten, 1992; Kop, Appels, Mendes de Leon, Swart, & Bar, 1994), social isolation (Case, Moss, Case, McDermott, & Eberly, 1992; Gorkin et al., 1993; House, Robbins, & Metzner, 1982; Reifman, 1995; Ruberman, 1992; Williams et al., 1992), and depression (Ahern et al., 1990; Frasure-Smith, Lesperance, Talajic, 1993). In CHD and MI, the psychosocial factor most clearly linked to morbidity and mortality is depression.

In this chapter, we review the literature on depression and negative affect in post-MI patients and on the interaction between depression and other psychosocial risk factors. We discuss possible physiological mechanisms by which depression may affect post-MI prognosis and then present a selected review of psychosocial interventions for depression in post-MI patients.

DEPRESSION AND NEGATIVE AFFECT IN POSTMI PATIENTS

The Incidence and Course of Depression and Negative Affect in Post-MI Patients

It is estimated that two thirds of MI patients have some type of mental disorder. Many researchers have noted an alarmingly high rate of mood disorders in post-MI patients (Cassem & Hackett, 1971; Garcia, Valdes, Jodar, Riesco, & de Flores, 1994, Hackett, 1985; Lesperance, Frasure-Smith, & Talajic, 1996; Schleifer, Marcari-Hinson, & Coyle, 1989). Approximately 18% of post-MI individuals suffer from major depression (Carney et al., 1987; Forrester, Lipsey, Teitelbaum, DePaulo, & Andrzejewski, 1992; Schleifer et al., 1989; Travella, Forrester, Schultz, & Robinson, 1994) and an additional 15% to 30% suffer from some degree of depression (Barefoot et al., 1983; Kurosawa, Shimizu, Hirose, & Takano, 1983; Schliefer et al., 1989).

A particular problem that we will discuss in greater detail later is that as many as one third to one half of medical patients with major depressive disorder (MDD) are not properly diagnosed or treated by medical practitioners (Gullick & King, 1979). In cardiac patients, it is estimated that less than 25% of those with MDD are accurately diagnosed, and of those who are diagnosed with depression, only 50% ever receive any form of treatment (Carney et al., 1987; Kurosawa et al., 1983; Mayou, Macmahon, Sleight, & Florencio, 1978).

If left untreated, depressive symptoms following MI may continue for many months following discharge from the hospital. Schliefer and colleagues (1989) reported that 44% of those patients originally diagnosed with major depression were still depressed when assessed 3 to 4 months following their MI. There is evidence that in some MI patients depressive symptoms may not begin to appear until after discharge from the hospital. For instance, one study reported that approximately one half of patients identified as depressed at the 3-month follow-up were not diagnosed with depression prior to their discharge from the hospital (Schliefer et al., 1989).

The course of depression following MI also appears to vary in relation to the severity and type of depressive symptoms. Unlike the post-MI patients identified as suffering from major depression, Schleifer and colleagues (1989) found that only a small percentage of the patients diagnosed with minor depression showed evidence of depression 3 months later. The authors speculated that minor depression following MI may represent a normal grieving process, whereas major depression after MI can lead to chronic mood problems and increased disability. Similarly, Travella and collaborators (1994) reported the median duration of major depression in post-MI patients as being 4.5 months. The quality of the depressive symptoms also appears to play a role in the duration of the depression. Travella and colleagues (1994) noted that patients who remained depressed longer than 6 months following their MI tended to have a greater number of anxiety symptoms, as compared to those patients in whom depression resolved prior to the 6-month follow-up. In comparison, within a community sample, those who are diagnosed with major depression and are not treated typically recover from their depressive episode within 6 to 24 months (Rush et al., 1991).

A history of depression may also serve as a risk factor in the development of CHD and MI. A number of researchers have found that the risk of developing depression following a heart attack was related to past episodes of major depression (Freedland, Carney, Lustman, Rich, & Jaffe, 1992; Lesperance et al., 1996; Lloyd & Cawley, 1983) or a family history of psychopathology (Gonzalez et al., 1996). A longitudinal study of 1,551 participants found that over a 13-year period, the risk of MI was increased as a function of depressive symptoms (Pratt et al., 1996). Patients with a history of dysphoria or minor depression were at double the risk of suffering an MI, whereas those with at least one lifetime episode of major depression had more than four times the risk of MI. Also, CHD patients exhibiting symptoms of MDD at the time of coronary angiography were found to be at twice the risk of having a major cardiac event within the next year (Carney et al., 1988).

Depression and Negative Affect as Risk Factors for Morbidity and Mortality

Recently, researchers have noted an association between psychological adjustment in MI patients and health outcome, independent of physical disease severity (Dwight & Stoudemire, 1997; Frasure-Smith et al., 1993; Shapiro, 1996). For example, individuals identified as depressed or having negative affect following an MI tend to report more cardiac symptoms, as compared to other post-MI patients (Costa et al., 1985). A prospective study by Levine and colleagues (1996) found that symptoms of depression predicted rehospitalization, independent of disease severity in a group of 210 MI patients.

Regardless of the severity of cardiac disease, post-MI depression is associated with an increased risk of future cardiac events such as reinfarction, cardiac arrest, and cardiac death (Ahern et al., 1990; Carney et al., 1988; Dwight & Stoudemire, 1997; Falger & Appels, 1982; Follick et al., 1988; Lesperance et al., 1996; Silverstone, 1987). A study of 522 male MI patients reported that over a 6-month period, those patients identified as suffering from severe depression following their MI were at greatest risk for future angina (Ladwig, Roll, Breithardt, Budde, & Borggrete, 1994). Frasure-Smith, Lesperance, and Talajic (1993) found that symptoms of depression, anxiety, and a history of major depression all were independent risk factors of cardiac events over a 12-month period.

A number of studies have reported significant differences in the death rates of depressed and nondepressed MI patients. For example, depression predicted mortality rates in post-MI patients with ventricular arrhythmias, after controlling for history of prior MI, ejection fraction, use of various cardiac medications, and presence of premature complexes on the 24-hour ECG at baseline (Ahern et al., 1990). Similarly, Frasure-Smith and colleagues (1993) reported significantly higher rates of cardiac-related death over a 5-year period in MI patients identified as suffering from high levels of post-MI depression, as compared to other MI patients.

Major depression in hospitalized MI patients has also been found to be an independent risk factor for mortality up to 18 months following the initial MI (Frasure-Smith et al., 1995; Lesperance et al., 1996). It was estimated that the impact of clinical depression as a risk factor was equal to or greater than other commonly identified risk factors, such as ventricular dysfunction or previous MI, after controlling for disease severity (Ahern et al., 1990; Frasure-Smith et al., 1993; Frasure-Smith et al., 1995; Lesperance et al., 1996). In addition, Leperance and collaborators (1996) reported that patients with a history of depression, who suffered a recurrence of depression shortly following their MI, had an even higher risk of mortality at the 18-month follow-up.

Although few studies have examined the independent symptoms of depression commonly observed in MI patients, there is evidence that suggests that some of the specific symptoms of depression are independently associated with post-MI recovery. For example, *hopelessness* is a common symptom of depression, which is defined by feelings of helplessness, low motivation, and apathy. In general, feelings of hopelessness and "giving up" have been linked to poor physical and mental well-being (Scheier & Bridges, 1992; Scheier & Carver, 1985). For cardiac patients, hopelessness has been identified as a risk factor for CHD morbidity and mortality (Anda et al., 1993; Everson et al., 1996). More recently, Everson et al. (1996) reported that over a 4-year period, hopelessness was associated with accelerated progression of carotid atherosclerosis in CHD patients.

Vital Exhaustion in Post-MI Patients

Not all CHD researchers believe that the behavioral symptoms frequently associated with MI reflect true clinical depression. A number of European researchers, for example, have described a common set of physical symptoms in post-MI patients, which they have defined as vital exhaustion. Vital exhaustion refers to excess fatigue and loss of energy commonly reported by patients prior to MI and sudden cardiac death. It is estimated that approximately 30% to 60% of CHD patients experience these symptoms (Crisp, Queenana, & D'Souza, 1984; Klaboe, Otterstad, Winsness, & Espeland, 1987; Rissanen, Romo, & Siltanen, 1978; Stowers & Short, 1970). Recently, vital exhaustion was cited as a possible risk factor for MI (Appels & Moulder, 1988; Falger & Schouten, 1992; Kop, Appels, Mendes de Leon, & Bar, 1996) and was found to predict restenosis, incidence of angina, and rates of nonfatal MIs in coranary artery bypass graft (CABG) patients (Kop et al., 1994; Kop et al., 1996).

There have been some suggestions that vital exhaustion actually reflects clinical or subclinical levels of disease. For example, patients suffering from coronary artery disease or poor left ventricular function may complain of high levels of fatigue and low energy, which are associated with their degree of disease (Schafer et al., 1996). Yet, there are a number of studies that have found no association between vital exhaustion and the severity of coronary artery disease and left ventricular function (Kop et al., 1996; Kop et al., 1997).

There is considerable debate as to whether vital exhaustion represents a variable that is independent of the somatic symptoms of depression. Comparison of questionnaires designed to measure depression and vital exhaustion have shown high correlations between the two measures (Kop et al., 1997). In support of the idea that vital exhaustion is linked to depression, Lesperance and colleagues (1996) found that symptoms of fatigue were three times more common in depressed patients following MI. Yet, research by Van Diest and Appels (1991) reported that participants identified as suffering from vital exhaustion differed from nonexhausted patients on the *fatigue* and *vigor* subscales of the Profiles of Moods States (POMS) but not on the *depressed mood* subscale. Reanalysis of previous work examining 4,000 healthy individuals found that after controlling for fatigue, depression did not predict risk of future cardiac events, yet after controlling for depression, fatigue was predictive of future problems (Appels, 1997). These findings suggest that depression and vital exhaustion are two distinct sets of symptoms that may or may not occur together.

Despite the ongoing debate as to how vital exhaustion differs from physical disease and/or the somatic symptoms of depression, it appears that high levels of fatigue, lack of energy, increased irritability, and feelings of demoralization, whether they are of physiological or psychological origin, are associated with increased risk of MI. The origin of these symptoms, along with the mechanism by which these variables impact post-MI recovery, remains to be determined.

Interaction of Depression With Other Identified Psychosocial Risk Factors for Post-MI Events

There are a number of ways in which negative affect may interact with other variables and lead to negative outcome in post-MI patients. For example, the symptoms of depression may lead to social isolation, which can impact the patients' ability to care for themselves and to make important lifestyle modifications. Other individual variables, such as personality, socioeconomic factors and gender may interact with mood and affect variables and lead to decreased adherence and poor medical outcomes. The following section describes a number of psychosocial variables associated with negative outcome in post-MI patients, with emphasis on the interaction between each of these variables and the symptoms of depression. The last section focuses on the impact of depression and other psychosocial risk factors on adherence and compliance rates in post-MI patients.

Social Isolation. Clinical research suggests a strong relation between social isolation and negative affect. Social isolation is often a symptom of depression (Stokes & McKirnan, 1989) and is one of the diagnostic criteria for the disorder (DSM–IV, 1994). A lack of social support appears to be associated with a number of negative outcome measures in MI patients. Social support is inversely associated with the severity of coronary artery disease (Blumenthal et al., 1987; Seeman, & Syme, 1987), ST segment depression (Hedblad et al., 1992) and plasma fibrinogen concentrations (Rosengren et al., 1990). Low levels of integration into social support networks (House et al., 1982) and social isolation (Case et al., 1992; Ruberman, 1992; Williams et al., 1992) are associated with higher rates of mortality following MI. In addition, CHD patients with low perceived social support show an increase in post-MI mortality (Gorkin et al., 1993; Orth-Gomer, Unden, & Edwards, 1988; Ruberman, Weinblatt, Goldberg, & Chaudhary, 1984) and are found to be less adherent to their medical regimen (Blumenthal, Williams, Wallace, Williams, & Needles, 1982; Carney, Freedland, Eisen, Rich, & Jaffe, 1995; Guiry, Conroy, Hickey, & Mulcahy, 1987). Berkman, Leo-Summers, and Horowitz (1992) found that lack of emotional support in MI patients was associated with higher mortality rates within the first 6 months following the MI. Similarly, Gorkin and researchers (1993) reported that perceived levels of social support were predictive of mortality, after controlling for other medical risk factors.

Unfortunately, very little of the psychosocial research with MI patients has simultaneously assessed social support and depression. Of the published studies that have examined this relation (Berkman et al., 1992; Frasure-Smith et al., 1993; Ruberman et al., 1984; Travella et al., 1994), only two (Frasure-Smith et al., 1993; Travella et al., 1994) found an association between major depression and low social support. In a study examining the course of depression following an MI, acute depression was found to be correlated with greater functional impairment, and prolonged depression was associated with inadequate social support (Travella et al., 1994).

Personality Factors. Much of the early psychosocial research in the area of CHD focused on specific dispositional characteristics and their association with heart disease. Initially, a cluster of behavioral traits identified as Type A behavior was found to be associated with greater risk of CHD, after adjusting for other risk factors (Brand et al., 1976). Upon further analysis of the behaviors making up the Type A personality pattern, hostility was found to be one of the best discriminators between a subset of cases and controls (Matthews, 1988). More recently, a number of studies have found an association between hostility scores and CHD mortality (Barefoot et al., 1983; Shekelle et al., 1991). Interestingly, hostility has also been associated with social isolation (Blumenthal et al., 1987; Dembroski & Costa, 1987). It is hypothesized that hostile people are more prone to social isolation because of their lack of social skills and their pervasive negative affect, which can drive others away. Research has shown that individuals rated as more hostile, anxious, and pessimistic had more conflictual and less supportive relationships (National Heart Lung and Blood Institute, NHLBI, 1998).

The cognitive components of hostility are similar to those observed in depressed individuals. High levels of hostility are typically associated with negative thoughts and attitudes (NHLBI, 1998). These thoughts can lead to higher levels of anxiety and an increase in anger, which is often directed toward others. This is similar to the low tolerance and high levels of irritability that are sometimes observed in those with depression and anxiety (DSM–IV, 1994). Thus, an individual who is vulnerable to hostility and aggression may be at greater risk for lashing out at others, if he or she is suffering from depression or high levels of anxiety. This behavior in turn, may lead to decreases in social support and greater levels of dissatisfaction with existing social relationships.

In addition to Type A behavior pattern and hostility, a 1995 study by Denollet and collaborators noted a significant association between a distressed personality (Type D personality) and mortality rates in MI patients. The researchers reported that MI patients identified as inhibiting emotional expression, while experiencing distress, showed higher mortality rates. More recently, the same research group found that Type D personality continued to predict higher mortality rates 6 to 10 years following initial MI (Denollet & Brutsaert, 1998). This association was independent of biomedical predictors, social alienation, and depression.

These findings are similar to the results described in research examining the impact of emotional expression on psychological and physiological health. Overall, the literature has demonstrated that individuals who hold back their thoughts and feelings about emotionally charged events show associated autonomic nervous system changes (Pennebaker, 1993). In terms of cardiac patients, Helgeson (1991) reported that disclosure had a positive impact on health variables in post-MI patients. Thus, it appears that the combination of high levels of distress and the inability to express one's feelings can lead to higher rates of morbidity and mortality in post-MI patients.

Stressful Life Events. High levels of life stress are known to be associated with an increased risk of MI (Chorot & Sandin, 1994; NHLBI, 1998). Depression can interact with life stress through two mechanisms: Those with high levels of stress may be more prone to depression and individuals who are already feeling somewhat depressed or anxious may feel even more helpless and hopeless when faced with greater levels of life stress. Social isolation can further add to the impact of major life events because individuals who are depressed and socially isolated may feel especially helpless and hopeless regarding their current situation.

Low Socioeconomic Status, Gender and Race. Low socioeconomic status (SES) and minority racial background have long been identified as significant risk factors for CHD, as well as poor prognostic indicators (Kaplan & Kiel, 1993; Williams et al., 1992; Winkleby, Jutulis, Frank, & Fortmann,

1992). Low education and working in blue-collar jobs are associated with increased risk of CHD (LaCroix, 1994), and the rate of depression is greater in those individuals with low SES (Adler et al., 1994, Frasure-Smith, Lesperance, & Talajic, 1993).

In addition, SES and minority racial background have also been found to be associated with levels of social support. Depression and low levels of perceived social support may act in combination to increase the risk of CHD or MI. These factors can also impact post-MI recovery variables. In support of this, Frasure-Smith and researchers (1993) noted higher rates of post-MI depression in individuals who were either socially isolated or from low-income households. In another study, 5-year mortality rates for CHD patients were 1.9 times higher in those with an income of less than $10,000 dollars per year, as compared to those with an income above $40,000 per year, independent of social isolation and disease severity (Williams et al., 1992). Ruberman and colleagues (1984) reported that low education level, combined with social isolation, is a significant predictor of post-MI mortality.

Gender also appears to impact levels of distress in post-MI patients. In a community sample, the prevalence rate for anxiety and depression was higher in women than in men (Murphy, 1986). Travella and colleagues (1994) reported higher rates of MDD following MI in women, as compared to men at the time of the initial interview. Similarly, Freedland and associates (1992) noted that more than 50% of depressed CAD patients who reported a history of major depression were women.

Adherence. Adherence is an important issue with cardiac patients. Most CHD patients receive complicated medical instructions following their MI. Medical regimens typically include a combination of multiple medications, along with stringent dietary restrictions and complicated exercise prescriptions. Results from clinical trials suggest that those patients who did not adhere to medical instructions had higher mortality rates, even after controlling for the severity of the initial MI, SES, smoking, and life stress (Horowitz et al., 1990).

Negative affect and depression following MI can have a deleterious impact on adherence and compliance to medical regimens. Research has shown that depressed MI patients are less adherent to medical advice and instructions (Blumenthal et al., 1982; Carney et al., 1995; Guiry et al., 1987; Ladwig et al., 1994). In addition, a number of studies have demonstrated that depressed MI patients are at greater risk of dropping out of cardiac rehabilitation programs and are less likely to modify risk factors (Blumenthal et al., 1982; Finnegan & Suler, 1985).

Lack of adherence in depressed MI patients may be related to some of the specific symptoms of depression. Patients with low rates of energy and overwhelming feelings of helplessness and hopelessness may be less able and motivated to care for themselves following an MI. Changes in concentration and memory commonly associated with depression can make it especially difficult to understand and comply with complex medication schedules.

Negative mood states and social isolation may also work together to affect clinical outcome following MI through alterations in adherence rates. Research has shown that post-MI patients who are depressed and/or socially isolated are less adherent to medical advice and instructions (Blumenthal et al., 1982; Carney et al., 1995; Guiry et al., 1987). On the other hand, having a strong social support network may help to increase one's adherence. Other individuals may act as role models and can assist patients in adopting new skills and behaviors associated with their medical regimens (Burg & Seeman, 1994; Cohen, Stokhof, van der Ploeg, & Visser, 1996).

In terms of socioeconomic variables, Brezinka and Kittel (1996) found that lower SES was associated with poorer psychosocial adjustment, decreased rates of returning to work, and poorer adherence to cardiac rehabilitation programs. On the positive side, they noted that those individuals with low SES who attended and completed a cardiac rehabilitation program showed equal or greater functional improvement than did those patients of higher SES.

METHODOLOGICAL ISSUES IN THE MEASUREMENT OF DEPRESSION IN CHD PATIENTS

The research in the area of depression and negative affect in post-MI patients suggests that patients should be identified and assessed for psychiatric symptoms at the time of their hospitalization. It is hypothesized that early intervention will help to improve both psychological and physiological recovery variables. Unfortunately, the majority of depressed post-MI patients are not properly diagnosed, or if diagnosed, they are undertreated (Carney et al., 1987; Kurosawa et al., 1983; Mayou et al., 1978; Schleifer et al., 1989). In general, psychological morbidity is frequently undetected by medical staff in hospital settings (Maguire, Tait, Brooke, Thomas, & Sellwood, 1980). One reason for the low rates of psychiatric diagnosis is the difficulty distinguishing between those symptoms commonly observed following a heart attack and the somatic symptoms of depression. For example, post-MI patients commonly report decreased energy, loss of appetite, and problems with sleep. These symptoms of depression are also commonly reported by CHD patients, as the result of the side effects of medication, the hospitalization experience, or physical symptoms of heart disease (Fielding, 1991; Freedland et al., 1992; House, Landis, & Umberson, 1988). Furthermore, long periods of time in a coronary care unit can produce changes in mental status and alterations in mood suggestive of psychiatric symptoms (Gardner & Worwood, 1997).

Despite some of these difficulties in distinguishing the symptoms of depression from physical disease, a recent study examining self-report measures of depression in 306 CHD patients found that somatic symptoms of depression were not strong contributors to depression scores, when compared to cognitive and affective symptoms (Doerfler, Pbert, & De-Cosimo, 1997). A longitudinal study by Lesperance et al. (1996) found that even after sleep and appetite symptoms were removed from the MDD criteria, approximately 89% of those post-MI patients previously identified as suffering from MDD continued to meet diagnostic criteria. Interestingly, the association between depression and mortality was strengthened with the removal of these two somatic variables.

Another factor that contributes to the lack of proper diagnosis of depression in MI patients is the use of inadequately validated questionnaires (Ruberman et al., 1984) or measures that are not designed to properly distinguish symptoms of depression from medical complaints (Carney et el., 1995). Medical personnel need to use accurate and consistent measures when assessing symptoms of depression and anxiety in CHD patients. This is especially important when using self-report measures, which are prone to methodological problems.

PHYSIOLOGICAL MECHANISMS

One of the potential physiological mechanisms by which depression may affect post-MI prognosis is through the alteration of neuroendocrine responses mediated via the central nervous system (Bovard, 1962; Williams, 1985). Distress and depression are associated with elevations in cortisol (Depue & Kleiman, 1979) and catecholamines (Lake et al., 1982; Roy, Pickar, Linnoila, & Potter, 1985), which can lead to changes in sympathetic nervous system (SNS) and parasympathetic nervous system (PNS) function (Carney et al., 1988; Vieth et al., 1994). In support of this, depressed psychiatric patients have been shown to have decreased vagal tone and abnormal hypothalamic-pituitary-adrenocortical axis (HPA) and SNS regulation (Esler et al., 1982; Roy, Pickar, De Jong, Karoum, & Linnoila, 1988; Siever & Davis, 1985). Additionally, increases in platelet aggregability (Hjemdahl, Larrson, & Wallen, 1991), as well as elevated metabolites associated with platelet activation (Grande, Grauholt, & Madsen, 1990), are associated with increased SNS tone and are observed in nonmedical depressed psychiatric patients. These findings are especially significant for cardiac patients because prolonged and/or excessive activation of the HPA axis and the SNS are associated with hypertension and heart disease (Krantz

& Manuck, 1984; Troxler, Sprague, Albanese, Fuchs, & Thompson, 1977). An elevation in catecholamines can also affect the balance between the SNS and PNS, which is important in the control of heart-rate variability (HRV). Effective PNS control of the heart rate is demonstrated by a normal sinus rhythm, characterized by distinctive HRV. Both the SNS and PNS innervate the sinoatrial node, which is responsible for heart rate and rhythm. An increase in sympathetic output tends to decrease HRV. Literature has reported that individuals with depression often have lower HRV and elevated resting heart rate (Forbes & Chaney, 1980). These findings have also been observed in depressed CHD patients (Carney et al., 1988), where this pattern is associated with higher mortality rates in post-MI patients (Bigger, Fleiss, Rolnitzky, & Steinman, 1992; Dyer et al., 1980; Kannel, Sorlie, & McNamara, 1979; Kleiger, Miller, Bigger, & Moss, 1987). Carney and associates (1995) found that depressed CHD patients had a higher prevalence of ventricular tachycardias that are associated with increased catecholamine levels and can lead to cardiac complications (Bigger et al., 1992; Kleiger et al., 1987) as well as sudden death (Verrier, 1990). Depression was a significant predictor of ventricular tachycardias, after controlling for a number of other risk factors, such as gender, smoking, nitrates, and beta blockade. In a recent review article, Carney and researchers (1995) proposed that changes observed in electrocardiograms of depressed patients are similar to the prolongation of the QT interval often observed in patients at risk for ventricular arrhythmias and sudden death (Moss, 1986). Unfortunately, there are no published studies to date that examined the prevalence of prolonged QT intervals in depressed CHD patients. Nevertheless, these findings suggest that there is a great need for additional research to examine the potential physiological effects of depression on cardiac function and outcome.

INTERVENTIONS AIMED AT DECREASING NEGATIVE AFFECT IN POST-MI PATIENTS

A number of studies have examined the effects of pharmacological and psychosocial interventions aimed at improving emotional health in CHD patients. The following section provides a brief overview of various forms of psychiatric and psychological interventions that are designed specifically to decrease depression and negative affect in post-MI patients.

Often the first treatment of choice for patients identified as suffering from major depression is antidepressant medication. Yet, of those CHD patients identified as depressed, less than 50% are started on antidepressant medications (Carney et al., 1987; Mayou et al., 1978). Many physicians are hesitant to use antidepressant medication for fear of cardiac-related side effects (Giardina et al., 1983). However, with careful monitoring, antidepressant medications can be used safely in the majority of cardiac patients (Pary, Tobias, & Lippmann, 1989; Warrington, Padgham, & Lader, 1989). The newer generation of antidepressants, the selective serotonin reuptake inhibitors (SSRIs) may be particularly effective for cardiac patients because of their efficacy in treating depression, their low side-effect profile (Shapiro, 1996, Sheline, Freedland, & Carney, 1997), and their impact on increasing serotonin outflow (Verrier, 1990). This can lead to decreased appetite and to necessary weight loss (Fuller et al., 1991), decreased anger and aggression (Rubey, Johnson, Emmanuel, & Lydiard, 1996), and improvement in patients' smoking cessation efforts (Bowen, Spring, & Fox, 1991; Shapiro, 1996; Sheline et al., 1997). In addition, there is some evidence that the SSRIs may favorably impact the pathogenic process of ischemic heart disease (Hills & Lang, 1991).

Following an MI, distressed patients may become involved in individual psychotherapy aimed specifically at decreasing negative affect and assisting patients in the recovery process. Individual counseling or psychotherapy not only helps to challenge the patient's negative thoughts and feelings, but also helps the patient learn to deal with recent losses and to make plans for the future. Involvement in psychotherapy following a life-threatening event, such as an MI, can be particularly productive because the patient may be ready to make changes in his or her life and to reevaluate values and goals (Burell, 1996). Pharmacotherapy, interpersonal therapy, and cognitive therapy all have been shown to be effective forms of treatment for depression (Barlow, 1996). Unfortunately, to date, there are no published reports of the efficacy of these types of interventions in the treatment of depression in post-MI patients.

In addition to pharmacological treatment and individual psychotherapy, a number of medical centers offer cardiac rehabilitation programs, which include a combination of health education, stress management, and psychological counseling. Health-education-based cardiac rehabilitation programs are generally aimed at increasing the level of information that patients have about their medical condition, while providing suggestions for improving physical and emotional health.

The Ischemic Heart Disease Monitoring study (Frasure-Smith & Prince 1985; Frasure-Smith & Prince, 1989) was an example of a nonspecific stress-management intervention. Male post-MI patients, identified as highly stressed (68 of 461 participants), were randomly assigned to a home-based, stress-reduction program administered by trained nurses. The individually tailored visits consisted of teaching stress-reduction strategies and providing patients with support and referrals when deemed necessary. The 1-year intervention resulted in significantly lower rates of cardiac mortality and recurrence over a 4-year period.

A number of studies have reported positive effects of group-based psychosocial programs on negative affect in post-MI or CABG patients. Trzcieniecka-Green and Steptoe (1994) found that a 12-week, relaxation-based intervention resulted in significant decrease in depressive affect and anxiety and an increase in activities of daily living for 78 patients who had undergone MI, CABG surgery, or coronary angioplasty. Similarly, in a study of 170 male CHD patients (matched by medical category), those who participated in the six-session, group rehabilitation program showed significantly greater improvements in emotional well-being and health and disability measures 3 months later (Denollet & Brutsaert, 1995). At the 6-month follow-up, the intervention resulted in less depressed affect, decreased tranquilizer use, and greater levels of self-reported activity. In contrast, the control patients reported an increase in negative affect and well-being over the 6-month follow-up period. Thus, the rehabilitation intervention not only enhanced mood and activity levels, but also protected patients from deterioration of emotional well-being.

In a randomized study of 100 post-MI and CABG patients, those who received a 10-week, group-based, relaxation, stress-management program showed greater improvements in emotional well-being, activities of daily living, satisfaction with health, and less disruption associated with chest pain, when compared to control groups. These improvements were maintained at the 6-month follow-up period. Comparison of the infarction and bypass patients showed no significant differences in response to the intervention (Trzcienieka-Green & Steptoe, 1996).

To date, a few studies have examined the effectiveness of group-based psychosocial interventions on medical outcome. These interventions are based on the premise that decreasing distress in post-MI patients will lead to improved medical outcome. An early study by Ibrahim et al. (1974) showed a 50% reduction in mortality rates over a 50-week period in 118 post-MI patients randomized to a group psychotherapy intervention. Kallio, Annunziato, and Amateau (1979) found a 37% reduction in cardiac mortality over a 3-year period, in a randomized trial of 375 post-MI patients who received a rehabilitation program that included health education, psychotherapy, and physical exercise. In a more recent study of 201 randomized post-MI patients, Oldridge et al. (1991) reported an improvement in health-related quality of life and exercise tolerance, following an 8-week exercise conditioning and behavioral counseling group. Unfortunately, these differences were no longer evident at the 1-year assessment period.

In another large trial, the Recurrent Coronary Prevention project, 1,035 consecutive post-MI patients, all identified as exhibiting Type A behavior, were randomly assigned to one of two groups: a combination of group cardiac counseling and Type A behavioral counseling or group cardiac counseling alone. The results showed that over a 3-year period, the combined Type A behavior and cardiac counseling group intervention led to a significant decrease in cardiac-related mortality, lower reinfarction rates, and a decrease in anxiety and depressive symptoms, when compared to the cardiac counseling only group (Friedman et al., 1986). Yet, further analysis revealed that the decrease in cardiac mortality was greatest for those with good cardiac functioning at baseline (Powell & Thoreson, 1987). An evaluation of the efficacy of the intervention showed that the combined counseling led to changes in anger and hostility, social support, depressive affect, and self-efficacy at managing stress (Mendes de Leon, Powell, & Kaplan, 1991). Reduction in Type A behaviors, improvement in self-efficacy scores related to stress management, and a decrease in depressed affect predicted lower mortality and cardiac recurrence rates, after controlling for other medical variables (Powell & Thoreson, 1987). This is not surprising, given that a meta-analysis of the literature pertaining to interventions aimed at changing Type A behavior patterns found that overall, these types of interventions lead to a 50% reduction in the incidence of cardiac events over a 3-year period, when compared to control groups (Nunes, Frank, & Kornfeld, 1987).

FUTURE DIRECTIONS FOR INTERVENTION STUDIES

Problems With Current Interventions

Overall, a number of studies have examined the medical and psychological effects of psychosocial intervention in post-MI patient. Of the studies that have focused on psychological endpoints, it appears that such interventions are effective in decreasing levels of distress (Denollet & Brutsaert, 1995; Frasure-Smith & Prince, 1989; Frasure-Smith et al., 1995; Friedman et al., 1986; Trzcienieka-Green & Steptoe, 1996), improving various quality of life measures (Oldridge et al., 1991; Trzcienieka-Green & Steptoe, 1994), decreasing the time it takes patients to return to work (Horlick, Cameron, Firor, Bhalero, & Baltzan, 1984; Oldenburg, Perkins, & Andrews, 1985; Stern, Gorman, & Kaslow, 1983; Thompson & Meddis, 1990), and improvements in cardiac-related morbidity and mortality (Denollet & Brutsaert, 1995; Frasure-Smith & Prince, 1989; Frasure-Smith et al., 1995; Ibrahim et al., 1974; Kallio et al., 1979; Nunes et al., 1987; Powell & Thorenson, 1987). In general, improvements in psychosocial variables seem to be most effective for those with high levels of distress (Hill, Kelleher, & Shumaker, 1992).

Although the majority of clinical intervention studies with CHD patients have reported positive results associated with psychosocial interventions, there are a few studies that found no effect with psychosocial intervention (Horlick et al., 1984; Jones & West, 1996; Stern et al., 1983). The lack of consistent findings may be related to a number of methodological problems, such as small sample sizes, flawed randomization, inadequate follow-up periods, unreliable clinical endpoints, lack of statistical control over other risk factors, and attrition over follow-up. In addition, researchers have used different outcome measures, as well as different assessment tools, thus making cross comparisons very difficult.

Although a reasonable number of intervention studies have reported positive changes in emotional and medical outcome variables in post-MI patients, there are a number of problems with these studies. First, the majority of these studies did not target patients identified as being at high psychosocial risk for further cardiac complications (i.e., those with high levels of depression, a history of psychopathology, social isolation, and low SES). Although these studies report significant changes in mood and emotional well-being, it is often unclear if these differences are clinically significant. Rather than include all cardiac patients, post-MI intervention studies need to target high-risk MI patients, with the goal of producing clinically relevant changes in psychological and physiological outcome measures.

Second, most intervention studies rarely mention quality-control procedures. For example, it is often unclear how the interventionists are trained and supervised. Lack of clear and concise quality-control procedures can have a tremendous impact on the outcome of a study because much of the variance in the findings can be attributed to therapist differences, as opposed to the intervention itself. Interventions aimed at reducing distress in post-MI patients need to pay particular attention to issues of quality control, which could have a dramatic impact on outcome variables.

In addition, the mix of topics covered in many of the post-MI group interventions (i.e., risk reduction, adherence to medical regimens, and methods of decreasing psychological distress) makes it difficult to understand the individual impact of each of these components on physiological outcome. Despite the reports of positive correlations between negative affect and morbidity and mortality in post-MI patients, the mechanisms by which psychosocial factors impact physical outcome remains somewhat of a mystery. The mix of health education and psychosocial variables within the content of the group intervention make it hard to identify the separate effects of these variables on long-term outcome. For example, are changes in medical outcome a result of lifestyle modification or mood alterations? To date, there is no published research examining the sole impact of a psychological intervention on medical outcome in clinically depressed post-MI patients.

Finally, there is a need for post-MI intervention studies that measure physiological endpoints, which may be associated with changes in psychosocial variables. Although there are very few published studies to date reporting specific physiological changes in post-MI patients following psychosocial intervention, Ornish and researchers (1990) found that CHD patients randomized to a stress-management–lifestyle-modification intervention showed a 40% average diameter regression of coronary lesions after 1 year, as compared to a 45% average diameter progression in the control group. This area of research would help to connect some of the psychosocial variables found to be associated with poor recovery with specific physiological processes.

The Enhancing Recovery in Coronary Artery Disease (ENRICHD) Trial

Our group is involved in a major multicenter study examining the effects of psychological intervention with post-MI patients, specifically identified as depressed and/or reporting low levels of perceived social support. The goal of this study is to answer some of the previously unanswered questions regarding the effects of a psychosocial intervention on post-MI patients identified as being at high risk for experiencing future complications. The study is funded by the NHLBI at the National Institute of Health and is expected to enroll a total of 3,000 patients over a 3-year period. The ENRICHD study was designed to address some of the problems observed in earlier research, such as small sample size, demographically homogeneous populations (e.g., White males), lack of well-structured interventions, and insufficient long-term follow-up of CHD patients. The ENRICHD program is aimed at recruiting demographically diverse individuals, including women and minorities, who are being randomized to either usual care or an intervention condition.

The randomized intervention involves a combination of cognitive behavioral therapy, social-skills training, and the development of social support networks. All patients receive assessment of psychosocial and biological measures (e.g., cardiac function, enzyme levels, and comorbidity). Patients randomized to treatment receive a combination of individual and group therapy because both forms of therapy have been shown to be effective in treating depression and helping to increase social support. Individual therapy begins immediately after the patient is randomized into the study. Patients join the group sessions after participating in at least three individual sessions. The group reinforces some of the topics covered in the individual sessions, while also increasing social interactions among the post-MI patients. All of the therapists were trained in cognitive therapy at the Beck Institute. The intervention is carefully monitored by the Beck Institute in order to ensure that all of the interventionists are consistent in their application of the program. All intervention patients must receive a specific number of intervention sessions or achieve a certain score on the Beck Depression Inventory, as well as a number of measures of perceived social support and cognitive behavioral performance, before they are considered successful completors of the program. Once they have reached these criteria, or they have reached the 6-month cut off, they are terminated from the individual portion of the program.

Most patients also participate in a structured 12-week group intervention, which covers such topics as identification and challenging of distorted thoughts, increasing social support, improving communication skills, problem solving, anger management, assertiveness training, relapse prevention, and life goals and values. SSRI antidepressants are prescribed for those patients who are identified as suffering from severe depression. The intervention phase lasts for approximately 6 months, and patients are followed for up to 3 years following their initial MI. Although the primary outcomes are MI recurrence and all cause mortality, other outcome measures include psychosocial adjustment (depressive symptoms, coping skills, self-efficacy, and social support measures). The study will be able to address the issue of whether an intervention specifically targeting depression can reduce cardiac morbidity and/or mortality in post-MI patients.

CONCLUSION

A number of potential risk factors have been identified as contributing to the development and exacerbation of CHD. Of these risk factors, depression appears to play a dominant role in post-MI recovery. Depression and negative affect in post-MI patients is associated with increased morbidity and mortality. This is of particular importance because it is estimated that up to 50% of post-MI patients suffer from some degree of clinical depression. Unfortunately, only a minority of these patients are adequately identified and treated for their depressive disorder. Nevertheless, studies examining the impact of psychosocial interventions in post-MI patients have reported some positive results and suggest that decreasing levels of distress in post-MI patients may impact medical outcome variables. Yet, a number of methodological problems, as well as limited study populations, have not enabled researchers to make a definitive statement regarding the efficacy of psychosocial interventions for depressed post-MI patients. The multicenter ENRICHD trial was designed to help answer some of the questions regarding the effects of a psychosocial intervention on post-MI patients identified as being at high risk for future complications. It is hypothesized that a cognitive-based, psychosocial intervention aimed at high-risk (i.e., depressed or socially isolated) post-MI patients will impact morbidity and mortality variables. If this study is successful in meeting its goals, it is hoped that interventions such as these will be implemented around the country in an effort to increase the identification and treatment of depression in cardiac patients.

REFERENCES

Adler, N. E., Boyce, T., Chesney, M. A., Cohen, S., Folkman, S., Kahn, R. L., & Syme, S. L. (1994). Socioeconomic status and health: The challenge of the gradient. *American Psychologist, 49,* 308–315.

Ahern, D. K., Gorkin, L., Anderson, J. L., Tierney, C., Hallstrom, A., Ewart, C., Capone, R. J., Schron, E., Kornfeld, D., Herd, J. A., Richardson, D. W., & Follick, M. J. (1990). Biobehavioral variables and mortality or cardiac arrest in the Cardiac Arrhythmia Pilot Study (CAPS). *American Journal of Cardiology, 66,* 59–62.

American Heart Association (1994). Medical/Scientific Statement. Cardiac Rehabilitation programs. *Circulation, 90,* 1602–1610.

Anda, R., Williamson, D., Jones, D., Macera, C., Eaker, E., Glassman, A., & Marks, J. (1993). Depressed affect, hopelessness, and the risk of ischemic heart disease in a cohort of U.S. adults. *Epidemiology; 4*(4), 285–294.

Appels, A. (1997). Why do imminent victims of a cardiac event feel so tired? *International Journal of Clinical Practice, 51*(7), 447–450.

Appels, A., & Moulder, P. (1988). Excess fatigue as a precursor of myocardial infarction. *European Heart Journal, 9,* 758–764.

Barefoot, J. C., Dahlstrom, W. G., & Williams, Jr., R. B. (1983). Hostility, CHD incidence, and total mortality: A 25-year follow-up study of 255 physicians. *Psychosomatic Medicine, 45,* 59–63.

Barefoot, J. C., Peterson, B. L., Harrell, F. E. Jr., Hlatky, M. A., Pryor, D. B., Haney, T. L., Blumenthal, J. A., Siegler, I. C., & Williams, R. B. (1989). Type A behavior and survival: a follow-up study of 1,467 patients with coronary artery disease. *American Journal of Cardiology, 64,* 427–432.

Barlow, D. H. (1996). Health care policy, psychotherapy research, and the future of psychotherapy. *American Psychologist, 51,* 1050–1058.

Berkman, L. F., Leo-Summers, L., & Horowitz, R. I. (1992). Emotional support and survival after myocardial infarction. A prospective population-based study of the elderly. *Annals of Internal Medicine, 117,* 1003–1009.

Bigger, J. T., Fleiss, J. L., Rolnitzky, L. M., & Steinman, R. C. (1992). Stability over time of heart period variability inpatients with previous myocardial infarction and ventricular arrhythmias. The CAPS and ESVEM investigators. *American Journal of Cardiology, 69*(8), 718–723.

Blumenthal, J. A., Burg, M. M., Barefoot, L., Williams, R. B., Haney, T., & Zimet, G. (1987). Social support, type A behaviour, and coronary artery disease. *Psychosomatic Medicine, 49,* 331–340.

Blumenthal, J. A., Williams, R. S., Wallace, A. G., Williams, R., & Needles, T. L. (1982). Physiological and psychological variables predict compliance to prescribed exercise therapy in patients recovering from myocardial infarction. *Psychosomatic Medicine, 44,* 519–527.

Bovard, E. W. (1962, Autumn). The balance between negative and positive brain system activity. *Perspectives in Biology and Medicine,* 116–127.

Bowen, D. J., Spring, B., & Fox, E. (1991). Trytophan and high-carbohydrate diets adjuncts to smoking cessation therapy. *Journal of Behavioral Medicine, 14,* 97–110.

Brand, R. J., Rosenman, R. H., Sholtz, R. I, & Friedman, M. (1976). Multivariate prediction of coronary heart disease in the Western Collaborative Group Study compared to the findings of the Framingham study. *Circulation, 53*(2), 348–355.

Brezinka, V., & Kittel, F. (1996). Psychosocial factors of coronary heart disease in women: a review. *Social Science Medicine, 42*(10), 1351–1365.

Burell, G. (1996). Behavioral medicine interventions in secondary prevention of coronary heart disease. In K. Orth-Gomér & N. Schneiderman (Eds.), *Behavioral medicine approaches to cardiovascular disease prevention.* Mahwah, NJ: Lawrence Erlbaum Associates.

Burg, M. M., & Seeman, T. E. (1994). Families and health: The negative side of social ties. *Annals of Behavioral Medicine, 16*, 109–115.

Carney, R. M., Freedland, K. E., Eisen, S. A., Rich, M. W., & Jaffe, A. S. (1995). Major depression and medication adherence in elderly patients with coronary artery disease. *Health Psychology, 14* (1), 88–90.

Carney, R. M., Rich, M. W., Freedland, K. E., Saini, J., Tevelde, A., Simeoe, C., & Clark, K. (1988). Major depressive disorder predicts cardiac events in patients with coronary artery disease. *Psychosomatic Medicine, 50*, 627–633.

Carney, R. M., Rich, M. W., Tevelde, A., Saini, J., Clark, K., & Jaffe, A. S. (1987). Major depressive disorder in coronary artery disease. *American Journal of Cardiology, 60*, 1273–1275.

Carney, R. M., Saunders, R. D., Freedland, K. E., Stein, P., Rich, M. W., & Jaffe, A. S. (1995). Association of depression with reduced heart rate variability in coronary artery disease. *American Journal of Cardiology, 76*, 562–564.

Case, R. B., Moss, A. J., Case, N., McDermott, M., & Eberly, S. (1992). Living alone after myocardial infarction: Impact on prognosis. *Journal of the American Medical Association, 267*, 515–519.

Cassem, H., & Hackett, T. P. (1971). Psychiatric consultation in a coronary care unit. *Annals of Internal Medicine, 75*, 9–14.

Chorot, P., & Sandin, B. (1994). Life events and stress reactivity as predictors of cancer, coronary heart disease and anxiety disorders. *International Journal of Psychosomatics, 41*(1–4), 34–40.

Cohen, L., Stokhof, L. H., van der Ploeg, H. M., & Visser, F. C. (1996). Identifying patients recovering from a recent myocardial infarction who require and accept psychological care. *Psychological Report, 79* (3 pt 2), 1371–1377.

Costa, P., Zonderman, A. E., Engel, B T., Baile, W. F., Brimlow, B. L., & Brinker J. (1985). The relation of chest pain symptoms to angiographic findings of coronary artery stenosis and neuroticism. *Psychosomatic Medicine, 47*, 285–293.

Crisp, A. H., Queenana, M., & D'Souza, M. F. (1984). Myocardial infarction and emotional climate. *Lancet, 1*, 616–619.

DeBusk, R. F. (1989). Specialized testing after recent acute myocardial infarction. *Annals of Internal Medicine, 110*, 470–481.

Dellipiani, A. W., Cay, E. L., Phillip, A. E. Vetter, N. J., Colling, W. A., Donaldson, R. J. & McCormick, P. (1976). Anxiety after a heart attack. *British Heart Journal, 38*, 752–757.

Dembroski, T. M., & Costa, P. T., Jr. (1987). Coronary prone behavior: components of the type A pattern of hostility. *Journal of Personality, 55*(2), 211–235.

Denollet, J., & Brutsaert, D. L. (1995). Enhancing emotional well-being by comprehensive rehabilitation in patients with coronary heart disease. *European Heart Journal, 16*, 1070–1078.

Denollet, J., & Brutsaert, D. L. (1998). Personality, disease severity, and the risk of long-term cardiac events in patients with a decreased ejection fraction after myocardial infarction. *Circulation, 97*(2), 167–173.

Depue, R. A., & Kleiman, R. M. (1979). Free cortisol as a peripheral index of control vulnerability to major forms of polar depressive disorders. In R. A. Depue, Ed., *The psychobiology of the depressive disorders.* New York: Academic Press.

Diagnostic and Statistical Manual of Mental Disorders (Fourth Edition). (1994). Washington DC: American Psychiatric Association.

Doerfler, L. A., Pbert, L., & DeCosimo, D. (1997). Self-reported depression inpatients with coronary heart disease. *Journal of Cardiopulmonary Rehabilitation, 17*(3), 163–170.

Dwight, M. M., & Stoudemire, A. (1997). Effects of depressive disorders on coronary artery disease: a review. *Harvard Review of Psychiatry, 5*(3), 115–122.

Dyer, A. R., Persky, V., Stamler, J. Paul, O., Shekelle R. B, Berkson, D. M., Lepper, M., Schoenberger, J. A. & Lindberg, H. A. (1980). Heart rate as a prognostic factor for coronary heart disease mortality: Findings in three Chicago epidemiological studies. *American Journal of Epidemiology, 112,* 736–749.

Esler, M., Turbott, J., Schwartz, R., Leonard, P., Bobik, A., Skews, H., & Jackman, G. (1982). The peripheral kinetics of norepinephrine in depressive illness. *Archives of General Psychiatry, 39,* 285–300.

Everson, S. A., Goldberg, D. E., Kaplan, G. A., Cohen, R D., Pukkala, E., Tuomilehto, J., Salonen, J. T. (1996). Hopelessness and risk of mortality and incidence of myocardial infarction and cancer. *Psychosomatic Medicine, 58*(2), 113–121.

Falger, P., & Appels, A. (1982). Psychological risk factors over the life course of myocardial infarction patients. *Advances in Cardiology, 29,* 132–139.

Falger, P., & Schouten, E. (1992). Exhaustion, psychological stressors in the work environment, and acute myocardial infarction in adult men. *Journal of Psychosomatic Research, 36,* 777–786.

Fielding, R. (1991). Depression and cute myocardial infarction: A review and reinterpretation. *Social Science and Medicine, 32,* 1017–1027.

Finnegan, D. L., & Suler, J. R. (1985). Psychological factors associated with maintenance of improved health behaviors in postcoronary patients. *Journal of Psychology, 119*(1), 87–94.

Follick, M. J., Gorkin, L., Smith, T. W., Capone, R. J., Smith, T. W., Ahern, D. K., Stablein, D., Niaura, R., & Visco, J. (1988). Psychological distress as a predictor of ventricular arrhythmias in a post-myocardial infarction population. *American Heart Journal, 116,* 32–36.

Forbes, L. M., & Chaney, R. H. (1980). Cardiovascular changes during acute depression. *Psychosomatics, 21,* 472–477.

Forrester, A. W., Lipsey, J. R., Teitelbaum, M. L., DePaulo, J. R., & Andrzejewski, P. L. (1992). Depression following myocardial infarction. *International Journal of Psychiatry in Medicine, 22,* 33–46.

Frasure-Smith, N., Lesperance, F., & Talajic, M. (1993). Depression following myocardial infarction: Impact on 6-month survival. *Journal of the American Medical Association, 270,* 1819–1825.

Frasure-Smith, N., Lesperance, F., & Talajic, M. (1995). Depression and 18-month prognosis after myocardial infarction. *Circulation, 91*(4), 999–1005.

Frasure-Smith, N., & Prince, R. (1985). The Ischemic Heart Disease Life Stress Monitoring Program: Impact on mortality. *Psychosomatic Medicine, 47,* 431–445.

Frasure-Smith, N., & Prince, R. (1989). Long-term follow-up of the Ischemic Heart Disease Life Stress Monitoring Program. *Psychosomatic Medicine, 51,* 485–513.

Freedland, K. E., Carney, R. M., Lustman, P. J., Rich, M. W., & Jaffe, A. S. (1992). Major depression in coronary artery disease patients with vs. without a prior history of depression. *Psychosomatic Medicine, 54,* 416–421.

Friedman, M., Thoresen C. E., Gill, J. J., Ulmer, D., Powell, L. H., Price, V. A., Brown, B., Thompson, L., Rabin, D. D., Breall, W. S., Bourg, E., Levy, R., & Dixon, T. (1986). Alteration of type A behavior and its effects on cardiac recurrence in post-myocardial infarction patients: Summary results of the recurrent coronary prevention project. *American Heart Journal, 112,* 65–66.

Fuller, R. W., Wong, D. T., & Robertson, D. W. (1991). Fluoxetine, a selective inhibitor of serotonin uptake. *Medical Research Review, 11*(1), 17–34.

Garcia, L., Valdes, M., Jodar, I., Riesco, N., & de Flores, T. (1994). Psychological factors and vulnerability to psychiatric morbidity after myocardial infarction. *Psychotherapy Psychosomatic, 61*(3–4), 187–194.

Gardner, F. V., & Worwood, E. V. (1997). Psychological effects of cardiac surgery: A review of the literature. *Journal of Research and Social Health, 117*(4), 245–249.

Giardina, E. G. V., Bigger, J. T., Glassman, A. H., Perel, J. M., Saroff, A. L., Roose, S. P., Siris, S. G., & Davis, J. C. (1983). Desmethylimipramine and imipramine on left ventrical function and the ECG: A randomized crossover design. *International Journal Cardiology, 2,* 375–385.

Gillum, R. F. (1993). Trend in acute myocardial infarction and coronary artery disease death in the United States. *Journal of American College of Cardiology, 23,* 1273–1277.

Goldberg, R. J., Gorak, E. J., Yarzebski, J., Hosmer, D. W., Dalen, P., Gore, J. M., Alpert, J. S., & Dalen, J. E. (1993). A community wide perspective of sex differences and temporal trends in the incidence and survival rates after acute myocardial infarction and out-of-hospital deaths caused by coronary heart disease. *Circulation, 87,* 1947–1953.

Gonzalez, E., Snyderman, T. B., Colket, J. T., Arias, R. M., Jiang, J. W., O'Conner, C. M., & Krishman, K. R. (1996). Depression in patients with coronary artery disease. *Depression, 4*(2), 57–62.

Gorkin, L., Schron, E. B., Brooks, M. M., Wiklund, I., Kellen, J., Verter, J., Schoenberger, J. A., Pawitan, Y., Morris, M., & Shumaker, S. (1993). Psychosocial predictors of mortality in the Cardiac Arrhythnia Suppression Trial-1 (CAST-1). *American Journal of Cardiology, 71,* 263–267.

Grande, P., Grauholt, A., & Madsen, J. (1990). Unstable angina pectoris: Platelet behavior and prognosis in progressive angina. *Circulation, 81,* 16.

Guiry, E., Conroy, R. M., Hickey, N., & Mulcahy, R. (1987). Psychological response to an acute coronary event and its effects on subsequent rehabilitation and lifestyle change. *Clinical Cardiology, 10,* 256–260.

Gullick, E. L., & King, L. J. (1979). Appropriateness of drugs prescribed by primary care physicians for depressed outpatients. *Journal of Affective Disorders, 1*(1), 55–58.

Hackett, T. P. (1985). Depression following myocardial infarction. *Psychosomatics, 26,* 23–28.

Hedblad, B., Ostergren, P. O., Hanson, B. S., Janzon, L., Johansson, B. W., & Juul-Moller, S. (1992). Influence of social support on cardiac event rate in men with ischaemic type ST segment depression during ambulatory 24-hour long-term ECG recordings. The prospective population study 'Men born in 1914', Malmo, Sweden. *European Heart, 13*(4), 433–439.

Helgeson, V. S. (1991). The effects of masculinity and social support on recovery from myocardial infarction. *Psychosomatic Medicine, 53,* 621–633.

Higgins, M., & Thom, T. (1989). Trends in CHD in the United States. *International Journal of Epidemiology, 18,* S58–S66.

Hill, D. R., Kelleher, K., & Shumaker, S. A. (1992). Psychosocial interventions in adult patients with coronary artery disease and cancer. A literature review. In *General Hospital Psychiatry* (pp. 28S–42S). NY: Elsevier.

Hills, L. D., & Lang, R. A. (1991). Seratonin and acute ischemic heart disease. *New England Journal of Medicine, 324,* 688–689.

Hjemdahl, P, Larrson, T., & Wallen, N. H. (1991). Effects of stress and B-blockade onplatelet function. *Circulation, 84,* 44–61.

Horlick, L., Cameron, R., Firor, W., Bhalero, U., & Baltzan, R. (1984). The effects of group education and group discussion in the post myocardial infarction patients. *Journal of Psychosomatic Research, 28,* 485–492.

Horowitz, R. I., Viscoli, C. M., Berkman, L., Donadson, R. M., Horwitz, S. M., Murray, C. J., Ransohoff, D. F., & Sindelar, J. (1990). Treatment adherence and risk of death after myocardial infarction. *Lancet, 336,* 542–545.

House, J. S., Landis, K. R., & Umberson, D. (1988). Social relationships and health. *Science, 241,* 540–544.

House, J. S., Robbins, C., & Metzner, H. L. (1982). The association of social relationships and activities with mortality: prospective evidence from the Tecumseh community health study. *American Journal of Epidemiology, 116*, 123–140.

Ibrahim, M. A., Feldman, J. G., Sultz, H. A., Staiman, M. G., Young, L. J., & Dean, D. (1974). Management after myocardial infarction: A controlled trial of the effect of group psychotherapy. *International Journal of Psychiatry Medicine, 5*, 253–268.

Jones, D. A., & West, R. R. (1996). Psychological rehabilitation after myocardial infarction: Multicentre randomised controlled trial. *BMJ, 313*(7071), 1517–1521.

Kallio, T. W., Annunziato, B., & Amateau, L. M. (1979). Affiliation moderates the effects of social threat on stress-related cardiovascular responses: Boundary conditions for a laboratory model of social support. *Psychosomatic Medicine, 57*, 183–194.

Kannel, W. B., Sorlie, P., & McNamara, P. M. (1979). Prognosis after initial myocardial infarction: The Framingham study. *American Journal of Cardiology, 44*, 53–59.

Kaplan, G. A., & Kiel, J. E. (1993). Socioeconomic factors and cardiovascular disease: A review of the literature. *Circulation, 88*, 1973–1793.

Klaboe, G., Otterstad, J. E., Winsness, T., & Espeland, N. (1987). Predicitive value of prodromal symptoms in myocardial infarction. *Acta Medica Scandinavica, 222*, 27–30.

Kleiger, R. E., Miller, J. P., Bigger, J. T., & Moss, A. J. (1987). Decreased heart rate variability and its association with mortality after myocardial infarction. *American Journal of Cardiology, 113*, 256–262.

Kop, W., Appels, A., Howell, R. H., Krantz, D. S., Bairey, Merz, C. N., Caravalho, J., Lundgren, N., Gottdiener, J. S., & TOMIS Investigators. (1997). Relationship between vital exhaustion and stress-induced myocardial ischemia. *Annals of Behavioral Medicine, 19*, 159 (abstract).

Kop, W. J., Appels, A., Mendes de Leon, C. F., Swart, H. B., & Bar, F. W. (1994). Vital exhaustion predicts new cardiac new cardiac events after successful coronary angioplasty. *Psychosomatic Medicine, 56*, 281–287.

Kop, W. W. J., Appels, A., Mendes de Leon, C. F., & Bar, F. W. (1996). The relationship between severity of coronary artery disease and vital exhaustion. *Journal of Psychosomatic Research, 40*, 397–405.

Krantz, D. S., & Manuck, S. B. (1984). Acute psychophysiologic reactivity and risk of cardiovascular disease: A review and methodologic critique. *Psychological Bulletin, 96*, 435–464.

Krone, R. J. (1992). The role of risk stratification in the early management of a myocardial infarction. *Annals of Internal Medicine, 116*, 223–237.

Kurosawa, H., Shimizu, Y., Hirose, S., & Takano, T. (1983). The relationship between mental disorders and physical severities in patients with acute myocardial infarction. *Japanese Circulation Journal, 47*, 723–728.

LaCroix, A. Z. (1994). Psychosocial factors and risk of coronary heart disease in women: An epidemiological perspective. *Fertility and Sterility, 62*(6 Suppl 2), 133S–139S.

Ladwig, K. H., Roll, G., Breithardt, G., Budde T., & Borggrete, M. (1994). Post-infarction depression, incomplete recovery 6 months after acute myocardial infarction. *Lancet, 343*, 20–23.

Lake, C. R., Pickar, D., Ziegler, M G., Lipper, S., Slater, S., & Murphy, D. L. (1982). High plasma catecholamine concentrations inpatients with depression and anxiety. *Archives of General Psychiatry, 42*, 1181–1185.

Lesperance, F., Frasure-Smith, N., & Talajic, M. (1996). Major depression before and after myocardial infarction: its nature and consequences. *Psychosomatic Medicine, 58*(2), 99–110.

Levine, J. B., Covini, N. A., Slack, W. V., Safran, C., Safran, D. B., Boro, J. E., Davis, R. B., Buchanan, G. M., & Gervino, E. V. (1996). Psychological predictors of subsequent medical care among patients hospitalized with cardiac disease. *Journal of Cardiopulmonary Rehabilitation. 16*(2), 109–116.

Lloyd, G. G., & Cawley, R. H. (1983). Distress or illness? A study of psychological symptoms after myocardial infarction. *British Journal of Psychiatry, 142*, 120–125.

Maguire, P., Tait, A., Brooke, M., Thomas, C., & Sellwood, R. (1980). Effect of counseling on the psychiatric morbididty associated with mastectomy. *British Medical Journal, 281*(6253), 1454–1456.

Manson, J. E., Tosteson, H., Ridker, P. M., Satterfield, S., Hebert, P., Oçonner, G. T., Buring, J. E., & Hennekens, C. H. (1992). The primary prevention of myocardial infarction. *New England Journal of Medicine, 326*, 1406–1416.

Matthews, K. A. (1988). CHD and Type A behaviors: Update on and alternatives to the Booth-Kewley and Friedman quantitative review. *Psychological Bulletin, 104*, 373–380.

Mayou, R., Macmahon, D., Sleight, P., & Florencio, M. J. (1978). Psychological adjustment inpatients one year after myocardial infarction. *Journal of Psychosomatic Research, 22*, 447–453.

McGovern, P. G., Folsom, A. R., Sprafka, J. M., Burke, G. L., Doliszny, K. M., Demirovic, J., Naylor, J. D., & Blackburn, H. (1992). Trends in survival of hospitalized myocardial infarction patients between 1970 and 1985. *Circulation, 85*, 172–179.

Mendes de Leon, C., Powell, L. H., & Kaplan, B. H. (1991). Changes in coronary-prone behaviors in the Recurrent Coronary Prevention Project. *Psychosomatic Medicine, 53*, 407–419.

Moss, A. J. (1986). Prolonged QT syndromes. *Journal of the American Medical Association, 256*, 2985–2987.

Moss, A. J., & Benhorin, J. (1990). Prognosis and management after a first myocardial infarction. *American Journal of Epidemiology, 128*, 786–795.

Murphy, J. M. (1986). Trends in depression and anxiety: men and women. *Acta Medica Scandinavica, 73*, 113–27.

National Heart Lung and Blood Institute. (1998). *National Heart, Ling and Blood Institute report of the task force on behavioral research in cardiovascular, lung and blood health and disease.* Rockville, MD: US Dept of Health and Human Services, Public Health Services, National Institute of Health.

Nunes, E. V., Frank, K. A., & Kornfeld, D. A. (1987). Psychosocial treatment for Type A behavior pattern and for coronary heart disease: A meta-analysis of the literature. *Psychosomatic Medicine, 48*, 159–173.

Oldenberg, B., Perkins, R. J., & Andrews, G. (1985). Controlled trial of psychological intervention in myocardial infarction. *Journal of Consulting and Clinical Psychology, 53*, 852–859.

Oldridge, N., Guyatt, G., Jones, N., Crowe, J., Singer, J., Feeny, D., McKelvie, R., Runions, J., Streiner, D., & Torrance, G. (1991). Effects on quality of life with comprehensive rehabilitation after acute myocardial infarction. *American Journal of Cardiology, 67*, 1084–1089.

Ornish, D., Brown, S. E., Scherwitz, L. W., Billings, J. H., Armstrong, W. T., Ports, T. A., McLanahan, S. M., Kirkeeide, R. L., Brand, R. J., & Gould, K. L. (1990). Can lifestyle change reverse coronary artery disease? *Lancet, 336*, 129–133.

Ortho-Gomer, K., Unden, A. L., & Edwards, M. E. (1988). Social isolation and mortality in ischemic heart disease. *Acta Medica Scandinavica, 224*, 205–215.

Pary, R. P., Tobias, C. R., & Lippmann, S. (1989). Antidepressants and the cardiac patient: Selecting an appropriate medication. *Postgraduate Medicine, 85*(1), 267–269.

Pennebaker, J. W. (1993). Putting stress into words: Health, linguistic, and therapeutic implications. *Behavioral Research Therapy 31*, 539–548.

Powell, L., & Thoreson, C. (1987). Modifying the type A behavior pattern: A small group treatment approach. In J. A. Blumenthal & D. M. McKee (Eds.), *Applications in behavioral medicine: A clinician's sourcebook* (Vol. 1). Sarasota, FL: Professional Resource Exchange.

Pratt, L. A., Ford, D. E., Crum, R. M., Armenian, H. K., Gallo, J. J., & Eaton, W. W. (1996). Depression, psychotropic medication, and risk of myocardial infarction. Prospective data from the Baltimore ECA follow-up. *Circulation, 94*(12), 3123–3129.

Reifman, A. (1995). Social relationships, recovery from illness, and survival: A literature review. *Annals of Behavioral Medicine, 17*(2), 124–131.

Rissanen, V., Romo, M., & Siltanen, P. (1978). Premonitory symptoms and stress factors preceding sudden death from ischaemic heart disease. *Acta Medica Scandinavica, 204,* 389–396.

Rosengren, A., Wilhelmsen, L., Welin, L., Tsipogianni, A., Teger-Nilsson, A. C., & Wedel, H. (1990). Social influences and cardiovascular risk factors as determinants of plasma fibrinogen concentration in a general population sample of middle aged men. *British Medical Journal, 300*(6725), 634–638.

Roy, A., Pickar, D., De Jong, J., Karoum, F., & Linnoila, M. (1988). Norepinephrine and its metabolites in cerebrospinal fluid, plasma, and urine. *Archives of General Psychiatry, 45,* 849–857.

Roy, A., Pickar, D., Linnoila, M., & Potter, W. Z. (1985). Plasma norepinephrine level in affective disorders: Relationship to melancholia. *Archives of General Psychiatry, 42,* 1181–1185.

Ruberman, W. (1992). Psychosocial influences on mortality of patients with coronary heart disease. *Journal of the American Medical Association, 267,* 559–560.

Ruberman, W., Weinblatt, E., Goldberg, J. D., & Chaudhary, B. S. (1984). Psychosocial influences on mortality after myocardial infarction. *New England Journal of Medicine, 311,* 552–559.

Rubey, R. W., Johnson, M. R., Emmanuel, N., & Lydiard, R. B. (1996). Fluoxetine in the treatment of anger: An open clinical trial. *Journal of Clinical Psychiatry, 57*(9), 398–401.

Rush, A. J., Cain, J. W., Raese, J., Stewart, R. S., Waller, D. A., & Debus, J. D. (1991). Neurobiological basis for psychiatric disorders (pp. 555–603). In R. N. Rosenberg (Ed.), *Comprehensive neurology.* New York: Raven Press.

Schafer, S., Schardt, C., Burkhard-Meier, U., Klein, R. M., Heintzen, M. P., & Strauer, B. E. (1996). Angina pectoris and progressive fatigue in a 61-year-old man. *Circulation, 94*(12), 3376–3381.

Scheier, M. F., & Bridges, M. S. (1992). Person variables and health: Personality predispositions and acute psychological states as shared determinants for disease. *Psychosomatic Medicine, 57,* 255–268.

Scheier, M. F., & Carver, C. (1985). Optimism, coping and health: Assessment and implications of generalized outcome expectancies. *Health Psychology, 4,* 219–247.

Schleifer, S. J., Marcari-Hinson, M. M., & Coyle, D. A. (1989). The nature and course of depression following myocardial infarction. *Archives of Internal Medicine, 149,* 1785–1789.

Seeman, T. E., & Syme, S. L. (1987). Social networks and coronary artery disease: A comparative analysis of network structural and support characteristics. *Psychosomatic Medicine, 49,* 341–354.

Shapiro, P. A. (1996). Psychiatric aspects of cardiovascular disease. *Psychiatric Clinics of North America, 19*(3), 613–629.

Shekelle, R. B., Vernon, S. W., & Ostfeld, A. M. (1991). Personality and coronary heart disease. *Psychosomatic Medicine, 53,* 176–184.

Sheline, Y. I., Freedland, K. E., & Carney, R. M. (1997). How safe are seratonin reuptake inhibitors for depression in patients with coronary heart disease. *American Journal of Medicine, 102*(1), 54–59.

Siever, L. J., & Davis, K. L. (1985). Overview: Toward a dysregulation hypothesis of depression. *American Journal of Psychiatry, 142,* 1017–1031.

Silverstone, P. H. (1987). Depression and outcome in acute myocardial infarction. *British Medical Journal, 294,* 219–220.

Stern, M. J., Gorman, P. A., & Kaslow, L. (1983). The group counseling vs. exercise therapy study: A controlled intervention with subjects following myocardial infarction. *Archives of Internal Medicine, 143,* 1719–1725.

Stokes, J. P., & McKirnan, D. J. (1989). Affect and the social environment: The role of social support in depression and anxiety. In P. C. Kendall & D. Watson (Eds.), *Anxiety and depression: Distinctive and overlapping features* (pp. 253–284). San Diego, CA: Academic Press.

Stowers, M., & Short, D. (1970). Warning symptoms before myocardial infarction. *British Heart Journal, 32,* 833–838.

Suls, J., Green, P., Rose, G., Lounsbury, P., & Gordon, E. (1997). Hiding worries from one's spouse: Associations between coping via protective buffering and distress in male post-myocardial infarction patients and their wives. *Journal of Behavioral Medicine, 20*(4), 333–349.

Thompson, D. R., & Meddis, R. (1990). A prospective evaluation of in-hospital counseling for first time myocardial infarction men. *Journal of Psychosomatic Research, 34,* 237–248.

Travella, J. I., Forrester, A. W., Schultz, S. K., & Robinson, R. G. (1994). Depression following myocardial infarction: A one year longitudinal study. *International Journal of Psychiatry in Medicine, 24*(4), 357–369.

Troxler, R. G., Sprague, E. A., Albanese, R. A., Fuchs, R., & Thompson, A. J. (1977). The association of elevated plasma cortisol and early coronary artery disease. *American Journal of Cardiology, 60,* 1003–1005.

Trzcieniecka-Green, A., & Steptoe, A. (1994). Stress management in cardiac patients: a preliminary study of the predictors of improvement in quality of life. *Journal of Psychosomatic Research, 38*(4), 267–280.

Trzcieniecka-Green, A., & Steptoe, A. (1996). The effects of stress management on the quality of life of patients following acute myocardial infarction or coronary bypass surgery. *European Heart Journal, 17*(11), 1663–1670.

Van Diest, R., & Appels, A. (1991). Vital exhaustion and depression, a conceptual study. *Journal of Psychosomatic Research, 35,* 355–364.

Verrier, R. L. (1990). Behavioral stress, myocardial ischemia, and arrhythmias. In D. P. Zipes & J. Jalife (Eds.), *Cardiac electrophysiology: From cell to bedside* (pp. 343–352). Philadelphia: Saunders.

Vieth, R. C., Lewis, N., Linares, Q. A., Barnes, R. R., Raskind, M. A., Villacres, E. C., Murburg, M. M., Ashleigh, E. A., Castillo, S., Peskind, E. R., Pascualy, M., & Halter, J. B. (1994). Sympathetic nervous system activity in major depression: Basal and desipramine-induced alterations in plasma norepinephrine kinetics. *Archives of General Psychiatry, 51,* 411–422.

Warrington, S. J., Padgham, C., & Lader, M. (1989). The cardiovascular effects of antidepressants. *Psychological Medicine, 16*(suppl.), 1–40.

Williams, R. B., Jr. (1985). Neuroendocrine response patterns and stress: Biobehavioral mechanisms of disease. In R. B. Williams, Jr. (Ed.), *Perspectives on behavioral medicine, Vol. 2. Neuroendocrine control and behavior* (pp. 71–101). Orlando, FL: Academic Press.

Williams, R. B., Jr., Barefoot, J. C., & Califf, R. M. (1992). Prognostic importance of social and economic resources among medically treated patients with angiographically documented coronary artery disease. *Journal of the American Medical Association, 267,* 520–524.

Winkleby, M. A., Jutulis, D. E., Frank, E., & Fortmann, S. P. (1992). Socioeconomic status and health: How education, income, and occupation contribute to risk factors for cardiovascular disease. *American Journal of Public Health, 82*(6), 816–820.

Chapter 13

The Development of an Integrative Therapy for Depression

Adele M. Hayes
Melanie S. Harris
University of Miami

Unipolar depression is a prevalent and debilitating disorder that is associated with substantial work and interpersonal impairment, high health-care expenditures (Simon, Ormel, VonKorff, & Barlow, 1995), increased susceptibility to physical diseases and mortality (Herbert & Cohen, 1993), and a significant risk of suicide (Weissman & Olfson, 1995). Depression has been demonstrated to be associated with increased cortisol productivity and decreased immunocompetence, both of which may contribute to physical health problems and increased mortality rates associated with the disorder (Herbert & Cohen, 1993).

A number of therapies have been developed to treat depression, including pharmacotherapy, cognitive therapy, interpersonal therapy, and behavior therapy. In a recent review, the Agency for Health Care Policy and Research (AHCPR) concluded that although current treatments for depression are promising, a significant percentage of patients do not respond to treatment, and the relapse rates are uncomfortably high (Barlow, 1996). These findings highlight the chronic and debilitating course of depression and the need to improve treatment efficacy.

In response to the AHCPR guidelines, Muñoz, Hollon, McGrath, Rehm, Vanden Bos (1994) designated the development of more effective and efficient therapies for depression as high-priority research. These authors recommend that new treatments focus not only on symptom reduction, but also on the prevention of relapse and on the promotion of wellness. In this chapter, we describe a broad-based, integrative psychotherapy that we are developing to address the multifaceted nature and chronic course of depression. Three theoretical models form the foundation of this therapy: Gotlib and Hammen's (1992) psychopathology model of depression, Hayes and Strauss' (in press) dynamic systems model of change in psychotherapy, and Ryff and Singer's (1996, 1998a) model of well-being. Each of these is reviewed briefly.

THEORETICAL FOUNDATIONS

Psychopathology of Depression

When developing a new psychotherapy, we believe it is important to be guided by knowledge on the nature of the disorder and the variables that influence its course (Hayes & Newman, 1993). Gotlib and Hammen (1992) presented one of the most comprehensive psychopathology models of depression (see also Gotlib & Neubauer, chap. 7, this volume; Hammen, chap. 5, this volume). These authors reviewed and integrated research on cognitive, interpersonal, life stress, and developmental factors in depression. They identified two central vulnerabilities that are thought to arise primarily from early impairments in the parent–child attachment process: dysfunctional thinking about the self and others and dysfunctional interactions with others. Over the course of development, these problematic schemata and interpersonal patterns, along with ineffective coping strategies, can shape one's responses to negative life events, contribute to the occurrence of more negative events, and increase the risk of depression and relapse.

Given that there is considerable empirical support to suggest that the developmental, cognitive, interpersonal, and behavioral components of this model influence the course of depression, Gotlib and Hammen (1992) contended that any comprehensive therapy must attend to each of these domains if it is to produce lasting change. However, current psychotherapies for depression focus primarily on one domain of functioning. For instance, the focus of cognitive therapy is on dysfunctional patterns of thinking, and the focus of interpersonal therapy is on social relationships and functioning. Behavioral therapies focus on areas such as coping and problem solving, assertiveness, communication skills, and increasing pleasant activities. The therapy that we are developing integrates components from cognitive, interpersonal, and behavioral therapies in an effort to address the full range of psychosocial factors that influence the course of depression.

Dynamic Systems Model of Change in Psychotherapy

Another influence on the development of this new therapy is our dynamic systems model of change in psychotherapy (Hayes & Strauss, 1998). This model is based on principles from dynamic systems theory, a theory that is revealing fundamental principles of pattern formation, stability, and change across a variety of systems from neurons and cells to entire ecosystems. Dynamic systems theory is being applied across scientific disciplines as diverse as physics, neuroscience, biology, political science, and economics. This convergence across systems and sciences is exciting and has interesting implications for understanding the process of change in psychotherapy. In addition to an understanding of the factors that influence the course of depression, an understanding of the interventions and processes that may be associated with change can also guide treatment development.

Hayes and Strauss' (1998) model of change in psychotherapy is based on an integration of dynamic systems theories in developmental psychology (Kelso, Ding, & Schöner, 1993; Thelen, 1995; Thelen & Smith, 1994) and in psychotherapy (Caspar, Rosthenfluh, & Segal, 1992; Greenberg, Rice, & Elliott, 1993; Mahoney, 1991; Schiepek, Fricke, & Kaimer, 1992). According to this model, psychological growth is a lifelong process that is characterized by periods of stability and variability. An *adaptive system* maintains a dynamic balance between *stability*, which maintains system coherence, and *variability*, which provides the flexibility necessary for change.

Psychopathology is a state of dynamic equilibrium where the individual has settled into well-organized patterns (attractors) of thinking, feeling, behaving, and somatic functioning that interfere with well-being and everyday functioning (Mahoney, 1991). These patterns have been reinforced over time and thus are particularly stable, are activated over a variety of conditions, and require a significant amount of energy to change. For instance, one of the depressed clients in our treatment program reported that she was taught in childhood that her emotions were not important or valid and that she was not "good enough." She developed a pervasive pattern of avoiding and inhibiting emotions, seeking perfection, and sacrificing herself to combat chronic feelings of worthlessness and incompetence. This pattern took a toll on her interpersonal, somatic, and occupational functioning, which in turn reinforced her sense of worthlessness and incompetence. Over time, she became locked in a self-perpetuating, depressive cycle (cf. Teasdale & Barnard, 1993).

Such well-organized patterns can become so established that they are considered lifestyles (Schiepek et al., 1992). Because these patterns are familiar and provide structure to the person's life, they are well protected, even if the person does not function optimally. These self-protective mechanisms can be viewed as rate-limiting factors in that change can occur only to the extent that these mechanisms do not block challenges to the existing patterns, and thereby inhibit variation and growth.

From a dynamic systems perspective, therapy is viewed as a way to induce change by "shaking up" or destabilizing the patterns that maintain psychopathology. However, it is first necessary to assess and enhance the client's readiness for change. Providing a secure and safe therapeutic environment and strengthening internal and external resources can prepare the client to undergo destabilization (cf. Hanna, 1996). In a course of cognitive therapy for depression (Beck, Rush, Shaw, & Emery, 1979), Hayes and Strauss (1998) found that more therapist support and stabilization interventions were associated with less client protection, which in turn predicted better outcomes. In a supportive context, the therapist can introduce novelty and challenge to increase the variability necessary for change.

According to dynamic systems theory across sciences, *change* is heralded by periods of systemwide variability (Thelen, 1995). In psychology, variability plays a central role in theories of change in developmental psychology (Thelen, 1995; Thelen & Smith, 1994), and on the dynamics of marital and family relationships (Bateson, 1979; Gottman, 1993; Haley, 1971), and social cognition and behavior (Vallacher & Nowak, 1994). Similarly, Carver and Scheier (1998) suggested that there are naturally occurring instances of destabilization that may be similar to what happens in therapy. For instance, there is evidence that traumatic events that are associated with significant emotional distress can shake up a person's worldview and facilitate major reorganization (Foa, 1997; McMillan, Smith, & Fisher, 1997; Tedeschi & Calhoun, 1995). Theoretically, destabilization increases variability and allows for new patterns to emerge, be learned, or to be discovered. In line with predictions from dynamic systems theory, Hayes and Strauss (1998) found that more client destabilization in cognitive therapy for depression predicted more improvement in both depression and global adjustment.

A shift to a new organization can follow destabilization; this is called a *phase shift* or *bifurcation*. After transition, old patterns compete with the new, and there is an ongoing process of trial and error, until the new patterns stabilize with repeated practice (Thelen, 1995).

Although destabilization may be only one route to change, there appears to be convergence across areas of psychology on its importance in the change process. From this point of view, variability and chaos are not viewed as "noise" in the system or disturbances to quell, but rather as opportunities for change when the person has the capacities and resources to undergo destabilization and sustain the transformation. It is important to keep this perspective in mind because the turbulence of destabilization can look like a worsening of symptoms and thus, the client and the therapist may unwittingly interfere with the change process. For example, as the depressive patterns began to destabilize in the client just discussed, she was flooded with intense emotions, felt out of control and imperfect, could not work efficiently, pulled away from others, experienced a variety of somatic problems, and had trouble sleeping and eating. The therapist and client viewed this period as a product of shaking up the old depressive patterns and as an opportunity to try new ways and for new patterns to emerge. Indeed, this destabilization across domains preceded an important shift in the patterns that maintained her depression. Destabilization may be an example of the assertion that change in therapy can involve "getting worse before getting better" (Hager, 1992; Mahoney, 1991; Reynolds et al., 1996; Thompson, Thompson, & Gallagher-Thompson, 1995). It is also possible that destabilization may precede the "sudden gains" in cognitive therapy documented by DeRubeis and his colleagues (chap. 10) in this volume.

Kelso and his colleagues (1993) recommended that points of destabilization can provide a window into the change process because they herald transition. From here, researchers can identify the mechanisms that underlie transition and the factors that move a system to transition. Using this strategy to study the process of change in cognitive therapy for depression, Hayes and Strauss (1998) identified three therapist interventions that were associated with destabilization: (a) identifying the historical roots of current problems, (b) exposing the client to corrective information from multiple sources (cognitive, affective, behavioral, somatic), and (c) encouraging the repeated practice of new skills between sessions. In addition, destabilization was associated with more affective intensity in the session.

Dynamic systems researchers in developmental psychology have described similar strategies to facilitate destabilization (e.g., Siegler & Ellis, 1996; Thelen, 1995; Thelen & Smith, 1994). The importance of these interventions is consistent with recent theoretical advances in cognitive therapy and with calls for the development of more broad-based and integrative therapies for depression (Gotlib & Hammen, 1992; Hayes, Castonguay, & Goldfried, 1996; Hayes & Newman, 1993; Robins & Hayes, 1993; Teasdale & Barnard, 1993). Moreover, these interventions are strikingly similar to those identified as central to change in the treatment of anxiety disorders (e.g., Foa, Riggs, Massie, & Yarczower, 1995; Kozak, Foa, & Steketee, 1988). It is also interesting to note that each of these strategies has been proposed as a more general common factor of therapy (e.g., Arkowitz & Hannah, 1989; Goldfried, 1991; Grencavage & Norcross, 1990; Weinberger, 1993).

The therapy that we are developing applies the principles of dynamic systems theory. The first phase of therapy focuses on stabilizing the client, identifying the patterns associated with the client's depression, and preparing for change (cf. Hanna, 1996). The second phase focuses on destabilizing the patterns central to depression. The therapy involves a focus on patterns of cognitive, affective, behavioral, and somatic functioning, rather than on only one specific domain of functioning. Core cognitive, interpersonal, and behavioral patterns that relate to the client's depression are addressed, as well as patterns of emotion regulation and self-care. The goal of therapy is to teach skills that can not only help reduce the symptoms of depression, but also promote psychological health, which we conceptualize as helping the person to function as an adaptive and dynamic system. An adaptive system is stable and coherent, but also when necessary, it can adapt to and incorporate new information from the environment. Thus, much of the therapy involves teaching healthy regulation skills that emphasize increasing flexibility, balance, and resilience. The last phase of therapy focuses on stabilizing new changes, and increasing self-acceptance, sense of purpose, and general wellness. Because a dynamic systems approach is naturally consistent with the promotion of growth and well-being, we turned to the literature on psychological well-being as another theoretical foundation of our treatment.

Psychological Well-Being

As part of a recent emphasis on prevention and well-being, Muñoz, Mrazek, and Haggerty (1996) recommended mental health promotion, which focuses on the reduction of risk factors and the enhancement of protective factors. This approach represents a movement away from the preoccupation with negative functioning, symptoms, and disorder and toward enhancement of positive functioning. This involves enhancing one's "sense of coherence, health, wellness, zest, resilience, self-efficacy, empowerment, energy, flexibility, order, balance, harmony, and integrity" (Muñoz et al. 1996, p. 1121), an approach that is wholly consistent with a dynamic systems approach to facilitating growth and change.

Ryff and Singer (1996, 1998a; Ryff, 1995) reviewed the literature on life-course development, clinical psychology, mental health, as well as philosophical accounts of the "good life" and presented a comprehensive model of well-being. This multidimensional model moves beyond definitions of mental health as the absence of disorder or disease and beyond viewing it as simply happiness or life satisfaction. We believe that this model can serve as an excellent guide for the development of interventions that promote wellness.

The centerpiece of this model of well-being is having a sense of meaning and purpose in life and maintaining quality connections to others. These qualities often are developed in the context of and can be deepened by confrontations with life's difficult challenges (Ryff & Singer, in press). These qualities are likely to build and maintain the other proposed components of *well-being*—a positive sense of self-regard and self-realization, personal growth, and the capacity to manage one's life and surrounding world—which in turn, are likely to enhance the pursuit of life goals and deep connection with others (Ryff, 1995). Ryff and Singer (1998a, 1998b) presented crosscultural empirical support for many of these proposed components of mental health (see also Ryff, Lee, & Na, 1997), and they documented the associations between these components of well-being and enhanced optimism and physiological functioning under challenge.

The components of this model are strikingly similar to the variables identified in a recent report on vulnerability and resilience by the Basic Behavioral Science Task Force of the National Advisory Mental Health Council (1996). In addition, it is particularly interesting that the components of Ryff and Singer's (1996, 1998a) model represent the flip side of the hopelessness, attachment difficulties, negative view of self and others, and maladaptive coping that characterize depression in Gotlib and Hammen's (1992) model.

Another component proposed as important to mental health is adaptive emotion regulation (Gross, 1998; Gross & Muñoz, 1995), which is related conceptually to environmental mastery and coping. These authors defined emotion regulation as a dynamic process by which individuals influence which emotions they have, when they have them, and how they experience and express these emotions. They contend that emotion regulation is a fundamental prerequisite of mental health and that problems with regulation underlie many forms of psychopathology. The key to adaptive emotion regulation is to experience and express a range of emotions and to process them actively rather than inhibit, block, or otherwise avoid them (cf. Litrell, 1998). Hayes and his colleagues proposed that many forms of psychopathology can be conceptualized as the opposite of this—experiential avoidance—which they define as unhealthy efforts to escape and avoid emotions, thoughts, memories, and other private experiences (Hayes, Wilson, Gifford, Follette, & Strosahl, 1996). Furthermore, the substantial psychological and physiological costs of emotional inhibition have been documented extensively (e.g., Basic Behavioral Science Task Force of the National Advisory Mental Health Council, 1996; Pennebaker, 1995).

A positive health agenda should also emphasize positive health behaviors and practices, such as diet, exercise, sleep, relaxation, and leisure, all of which are important to address in depression (Sherbourne, Hays, & Wells, 1995). We believe that addressing patterns of neglect in these areas can reverse the negative influence of this neglect on mood, energy, and activity level. In addition, improvement in these areas can increase the resources the client has to address current stressors and to facilitate change.

The literature on wellness has had a significant impact on the treatment that we developed. The therapy addresses each of the components of Ryff and Singer's (1998a) model of well-being, as well as emotion regulation and lifestyle behaviors. The therapy is integrative in that it pulls together a number of intervention strategies from existing psychotherapies for depression, and it promotes both symptom reduction and wellness. In addition, we assess the impact of the treatment on neuroendocrine and immune functioning to begin to shed light on the relations between depression, psychosocial changes, and physiological functioning.

INTEGRATIVE THERAPY FOR DEPRESSION

Overview

The integrative therapy for depression (ITD) that we are developing is a 20-week protocol that includes four phases: (a) stabilizing and preparing the client for change; (b) destabilizing the core cognitive, interpersonal, emotion regulation, and behavioral patterns that maintain depression; (c) stabilizing the new changes and addressing self-acceptance, meaning and purpose in life, and goals; and (d) monthly continuation therapy for 3 months. Again, the therapy focuses on symptom reduction, as well as mental health promotion, which we conceptualize as a relapse prevention strategy. Clients are followed for 1 year after therapy is completed.

We are in the pilot phase of treatment development. At this point, we have developed a treatment manual, trained a team of therapists to deliver the therapy, and have begun a pilot study that compares ITD with a support–empathy therapy condition. In this chapter, we describe this novel integrative therapy and some new approaches to the study of therapy process and outcome.

Assessment and Case Conceptualization

Clients are enrolled in the study if they meet criteria for major depression on the Structured Clinical Interview for DSM–IV (First, Gibbon, Spitzer, & Williams, 1996) and do not meet criteria for anxiety disorders, eating disorders, bipolar disorder, substance abuse, and psychotic disorders. The depression must not be due to an organic or medical condition. In addition to a careful history of the symptoms, course, and history of depression, clients' functioning in the following domains is assessed with a battery of questionnaires and in clinical interviews: (a) lifestyle behaviors (diet, exercise, sleep, relaxation, and leisure) and well-being; (b) emotion regulation; (c) attachment patterns and interpersonal functioning; and (d) beliefs about self and others, as well as personal goals.

The information from the questionnaires and interviews is compiled and presented to the therapy team. Together, the team reaches a consensus on the strengths and difficulties in each of the four domains. It is through this exercise that we identify the core patterns that relate to the client's depression. The therapist shares this conceptualization with the client and explains how the therapy is designed to address each of these domains of functioning. In our experience thus far, the conceptualizations have been well-received by the clients, as they receive a comprehensive and individualized profile of the strengths and vulnerabilities that influence the course of depression. After the presentation of the case conceptualization to the client, the first phase of therapy begins.

Phase One: Stabilization and Preparation for Change

The first phase of therapy is designed to stabilize the client and to increase the resources for change. For approximately the first eight sessions, therapy focuses on improving coping, problem solving, and general stress-management skills. In addition, the costs and benefits of current depressive patterns are discussed to increase motivation for change.

As part of the stress-management section, clients are started on a program to improve healthy lifestyle behaviors. This involves increasing behavioral activation, social support, and exposure to positive experiences, as well as education on healthy diet, exercise, sleep, relaxation, and leisure, and their influence on mood, energy, and resilience. The information gathered in the pretreatment assessment provides detailed information on each of these areas so that we can develop a change program tailored to the individual client. In this section, we also introduce mindfulness meditation (Kabat-Zinn, 1994) because it not only is a form of relaxation, but it also can be conceptualized as a form of attentional control (Teasdale, Segal, & Williams, 1995). It is introduced initially as a stress-reduction strategy. The principles of mindfulness and acceptance that are inherent to this meditation are emphasized later in the therapy as a way to teach clients to unhook from the depressive spiral that can ensue from the activation of negative thoughts. In preliminary studies, mindfulness meditation is showing promise as a relapse-prevention strategy in the treatment of depression (Segal, Williams, & Teasdale, 1998; Teasdale et al., 1995). The clients enrolled in the treatment thus far have experienced initial symptom reduction in this first phase, as well as increased motivation for change, and a strong alliance with the therapist, all of which prepare them for the destabilization phase of therapy.

Phase Two: Destabilization of Patterns Related to Depression

In the 8 to 10 sessions in the second phase of therapy, therapists challenge the core cognitive, interpersonal, emotion regulation, and behavioral patterns related to the client's depression. Most often clients have issues that need to be addressed in each of these domains, and interventions are designed to address several issues at once. For the cognitive work, hypothesis-testing skills are taught and used to examine hopelessness, attributions for negative and positive life events, and core schemata related to self worth and competence. Adapting Elliott and Lassen's (1998) schema-focused therapy, the historical roots of the self-worth and competence schemata are examined, and the current triggers are identified, as well as the behavioral, emotional, interpersonal, and somatic responses associated with these schemata. The client and therapist work on describing a less negative and more adaptive, balanced version of the relevant schemata to make the goals of schema change more clear. The client then reviews and gathers evidence for and against the negative schemata and also generates exercises to facilitate the development or strengthening of the more balanced schemata.

This approach to cognitive change is consistent with our emphases on the dynamic process of change and on wellness. Elliott and Lassen's (1998) approach is an extension of Beck et al.'s (1979) cognitive therapy for depression and Young's (1994) schema-focused therapy. This therapy focuses on core patterns and provides strategies to dismantle negative patterns and develop new, more flexible and adaptive ones. In line with our dynamic systems model (Hayes & Strauss, 1998), this approach emphasizes the historical roots of current patterns, exposure to corrective information from multiple data streams, and repeated practice of new ways of thinking, feeling, and behaving.

In addition, and often as part of the cognitive work, the client is made aware of problems in interpersonal skills or functioning, with particular attention to maladaptive attachment patterns (see Hammen, chap. 5, this volume). Skills that were not taught in the stabilization phase of therapy can be taught in this phase; if the person has maladaptive patterns of relating and connecting with others, those patterns are addressed. Most often this involves skills training and behavioral exercises and experiments. We also introduce exposure exercises to trigger the negative beliefs and emotions associated with insecure attachment styles and then have the client examine the validity of the beliefs and experiment with new ways of interacting.

Clients with a history of maladaptive emotion-regulation strategies often have old material that has not been processed actively and effectively, and so it tends to play over and over or to otherwise interfere with functioning. In this part of therapy, the therapist targets inhibited grieving, unprocessed trauma, or old wounds that may be contributing to the cognitive, interpersonal, and behavioral patterns that maintain depression. This is done only if the material is directly relevant to the client's depression, and if he or she has the resources necessary to tolerate this emotionally charged work. In some cases, experiences such as in childhood abuse are likely to require more client resources and a more intensive and long-term focus than can be provided in this relatively short-term therapy. In such cases, we identify the themes related to that experience but maintain a focus on current patterns.

In cases where emotionally blocked material can be addressed, therapists help clients to the experience, express, and process old material, as well as ongoing experiences (Litrell, 1998). This teaches clients healthier emotion-regulation skills, which in turn, can give them more resources with which to face life's difficulties, improve their interactions with their environments, and improve their processing of those interactions.

Most long-standing and maladaptive behavioral patterns are addressed in the cognitive, interpersonal, and emotion-regulation work. Those patterns that are not are similarly addressed by teaching new skills and designing behavioral experiments and challenges.

Phase Three: Stabilization of New Changes and Promotion of Wellness

In the third phase of therapy (last two to four sessions), treatment gains are reviewed and between-session exercises are given to facilitate the maintenance of these gains and the continuation of progress. In addition, the client is taught skills to facilitate self acceptance and a philosophy of continuing development and growth. It is in this stage of therapy that clients explicitly learn how to use the mindfulness part of the meditation exercises as a way to prevent themselves from getting consumed by what was once an almost automatic spiral from negative mood to negative thoughts, rumination, and depression (Segal et al., 1998; Teasdale et al., 1995). This strategy can be conceptualized as a way to short-circuit the "rebound" effects documented with experiential avoidance (Hayes et al., 1996) and thought suppression (Beevers, Wenzlaff, Hayes, & Scott, in press).

After the symptoms of depression have lessened and clients begin to change some of the core patterns associated with their depression, it is not uncommon for them start to look forward to regaining aspects of their old selves and their lives before the depressive episode. It is at this point that we help them look at their lives in a broader perspective, make some meaning of what they have been through, find some sense of purpose in their lives, and hope again. We also anticipate potential problems over the next month and begin to prepare them for those. Finally, we review the progress made, the areas to continue working on, and help clients to set reasonable and achievable life goals for the next year.

Continuation Phase

After therapy has ended, clients are seen every month for 3 months to check on and facilitate continued progress. Therapists review with them successes and problems that occur each month, as they experiment with their still new ways of thinking, feeling, and acting.

RESEARCH DESIGN ISSUES

Following the guidelines recommended by Chambless and Hollon (1998) on how to develop new, empirically supported treatments, we are conducting a pilot study to compare the efficacy of ITD with a therapy that provides facilitative conditions and the same therapist contact time, but none of the hypothesized active interventions of the integrative therapy. The inclusion of a support–empathy condition permits a comparison of a therapy that should not facilitate destabilization with one that is designed for that purpose. This comparison may shed light on different types of therapeutic change and perhaps different pathways to change. In the next stage of research, we compare ITD with a more established standard, such as cognitive therapy for depression (Beck et al., 1979).

Because we are particularly interested in the process of change, this outcome study is designed with process in mind. Clients in both groups monitor both maladaptive and more adaptive schemata every other session so that individual patterns of change can be tracked over time. In addition, clients write weekly essays on their depression (cf. Pennebaker, 1997a, 1997b) and monitor their cognitive, affective, behavioral, and somatic functioning, as well as their symptoms of depression. Cortisol is collected biweekly. Together, these assessments permit an examination of the types of cognitive and emotional changes that occur over the course of therapy, as well as how these changes relate to changes in neuroendocrine functioning. In addition, the pathways between these variables and immune functioning can be explored.

This intensive monitoring across the course of therapy is necessary in order to move beyond pretreatment to posttreatment analyses of change and toward more sophisticated modeling and comparisons of trajectories and patterns of change (Newman & Howard, 1991). This design is also suited to new methods of identifying change points, such as that advocated by dynamic systems theorists in developmental biology (e.g., Kelso et al., 1993) and by DeRubeis and his colleagues (chap. 10) in this volume. Careful attention to what happens over the course of therapy facilitates the study of temporal sequencing of variables and pathways of change.

In terms of the measurement of outcome, we assess not only symptom change, but also functioning in the four domains targeted in therapy: (a) lifestyle behaviors and well-being, (b) emotion regulation, (c) attachment patterns, and (d) cognitions. Change in each of these domains can be examined as predictors of functioning over the follow-up period. Because of the important relation between depression and physical health (Herbert & Cohen, 1993), we also assess neuroendocrine and immune functioning, as well as utilization of health and medical services. Together, this battery of process and outcome measures addresses recent concerns about an overemphasis on a disease model of mental illness and the need to promote and study wellness in the context of both psychological and physical functioning.

CONCLUSION

The integrative therapy that we are developing is conceptually similar to Linehan's (1993) therapy for borderline personality disorder in that it blends a number of components from different therapies, using a higher order unifying framework. The framework is psychological wellness in that we educate clients on the principles of well-being and teach them skills to promote this. At the same time, these skills help to reduce the symptoms of depression, and we hypothesize that they help to reduce the likelihood of relapse. Our goal is to consolidate the knowledge bases on the psychopathology of depression, the nature and process of change, and on well-being so that this information can be disseminated to our depressed clients. We integrate existing empirically supported intervention strategies and develop some new strategies within a coherent treatment package. It is particularly striking that integrative therapies in health psychology that were designed to address the special needs of individuals with HIV infection (Antoni, chap. 11, this volume) and coronary heart disease (Kilbourn, Saab, & Schneiderman, chap. 12, this volume) have independently identified similar treatment components. This convergence is exciting and may suggest that these are indeed key components of psychological adjustment or well-being.

Integration of this nature can be an important advance in science and in the application of that science. Although based on sound empirically grounded principles, our integrative therapy must undergo rigorous testing in a program of research to determine whether it can achieve the status of an empirically supported (Chambless & Hollon, 1998) therapy for depression.

REFERENCES

Arkowitz, H., & Hannah, M. T. (1989). Cognitive, behavioral, and psychodynamic therapies: Converging or diverging pathways to change. In A. Freeman, K. M. Simon, L. E. Beutler, & H. Arkowitz (Eds.), *Comprehensive handbook of cognitive therapy* (pp. 143–167). New York: Plenum.

Barlow, D. H. (1996). Health care policy, psychotherapy research, and the future of psychotherapy. *American Psychologist, 51*, 1050–1058.

Basic Behavioral Science Task Force of the National Advisory Mental Health Council (1996). Basic behavioral science research for mental health: Vulnerability and resilience. *American Psychologist, 51*, 22–28.

Bateson, G. (1979). *Mind and nature: A necessary unity.* New York: Bantam.

Beck, A. T., Rush, A. J., Shaw, B. F., & Emery, G. (1979). *Cognitive therapy of depression.* New York: Guilford.

Beevers, C. G., Wenzlaff, R. M., Hayes, A. M., & Scott, W. D. (in press). Depression and the ironic effects of thought suppression: Therapeutic strategies for improving mental control. *Clinical Psychology: Science and Practice.*

Carver, C. S., & Scheier, M. F. (1998). *On the self-regulation of behavior.* New York: Cambridge University Press.

Caspar, F., Rothenfluh, T., & Segal, Z. V. (1992). The appeal of connectionism for clinical psychology, *Clinical Psychology Review, 12,* 719–762.

Chambless, D. L., & Hollon, S. D. (1998). Defining empirically supported treatments. *Journal of Consulting and Clinical Psychology, 66,* 7–18.

Elliott, C. H., & Lassen, M. K. (1998). *Why can't I get what I want?* Palo Alto, CA: Davies-Black.

First, M. B., Gibbon, M., Spitzer, R. L., & Williams, J. B. W. (1996). *User's Guide for the Structured Clinical Interview for DSM–IV Axis I Disorders: Research Version.* New York: New York State Psychiatric Institute (Biometrics Research Department).

Foa, E. B. (1997). Psychological processes related to recovery from a trauma and an effective treatment for PTSD. In Yehuda, R. & McFarlane, A. C. (Eds.). *Psychobiology of posttraumatic stress disorder. Annals of the New York Academy of Sciences* (pp. 410–424). NY: New York Academy of Sciences.

Foa, E. B., Riggs, D. S., Massie, E. D., & Yarczower, M. (1995). The impact of fear activation and anger on the efficacy of exposure treatment for posttraumatic stress disorder. *Behavior Therapy, 26,* 487–499.

Goldfried, M. R. (1991). Transtheoretical ingredients in therapeutic change. In R. C. Curtis & G. Striker (Eds.), *How people change: Inside and outside of therapy.* New York: Plenum.

Gotlib, I. H., & Hammen, C. L. (1992). *Psychological aspects of depression: Toward a cognitive-interpersonal integration.* West Sussex, England: Wiley.

Gottman, J. M. (1993). A theory of marital dissolution and stability. *Journal of Family Psychology, 7,* 57–75.

Greenberg, L. S., Rice, L. N., & Elliott, R. (1993). *Facilitating emotional change: the moment-by-moment process.* New York: Guilford.

Grencavage, L. M., & Norcross, J. C. (1990). What are the commonalities among the therapeutic common factors? *Professional Psychology: Research and Practice, 21,* 372–378.

Gross, J. J. (1998). The emerging field of emotion regulation: An integrative review. *Review of General Psychology, 2,* 271–299.

Gross, J. J., & Muñoz, R. F. (1995). Emotion regulation and mental health. *Clinical Psychology: Science and Practice, 2,* 151–164.

Hager, D. (1992). Chaos and growth. *Psychotherapy, 29,* 378–384.

Haley, J. (1971). Family therapy: A radical change. In J. Haley (Ed.), *Changing families: A family therapy reader.* New York: Grune & Stratton.

Hanna, F. J. (1996). Precursors of change: Pivotal points of involvement and resistance in psychotherapy. *Journal of Psychotherapy Integration, 6,* 227–264.

Hayes, A. M., Castonguay, L. G., & Goldfried, M. R. (1996). The effectiveness of targeting the vulnerability factors of depression in cognitive therapy. *Journal of Consulting and Clinical Psychology, 64,* 623–627.

Hayes, A. M., & Newman, C. (1993). Depression: An integrative perspective. In G. Striker & J. Gold (Eds.), *Comprehensive handbook of psychotherapy integration* (pp. 303–321). New York: Plenum.

Hayes, A. M., & Strauss, J. (1998). Dynamic systems theory as a paradigm for the study of change in psychotherapy: An application to cognitive therapy for depression. *Journal of Consulting and Clinical Psychology, 66*(6), 939–947.

Hayes, S. C., Wilson, K. G., Gifford, E. V., Follette, V. M., & Strosahl, K. (1996). Experiential avoidance and behavioral disorders: A functional dimensional approach to diagnosis and treatment. *Journal of Consulting and Clinical Psychology, 64,* 1152–1168.

Herbert, T. B., & Cohen, S. (1993). Depression and immunity: A meta-analytic review. *Psychological Bulletin, 113, 3,* 472–486.

Kabat-Zinn, J. (1994). *Wherever you go, there you are: Mindfulness meditation in everyday life.* New York: Hyperion.

Kelso, J. A. S., Ding, M., & Schöner, G. (1993). Dynamic pattern formation: A primer. In L. B. Smith & E. Thelen (Eds.), *A dynamic systems approach to development: Applications.* Cambridge, MA: MIT Press.

Kozak, M. J., Foa, E. B., & Steketee, G. (1988). Process and outcome of exposure treatment with obsessive-compulsives: Psychophysiological indicators of emotional processing. *Behavior Therapy, 19,* 157–169.

Linehan, M. M. (1993). *Cognitive-behavioral treatment of borderline personality disorder.* New York: Guilford.

Litrell, J. (1998). Is the reexperience of painful emotion therapeutic? *Clinical Psychology Review, 18,* 71–102.

Mahoney, M. J. (1991). *Human change processes: The scientific foundations of psychotherapy.* New York: Basic Books.

McMillan, J. C., Smith, E. M., & Fisher, R. H. (1997). Perceived benefit and mental health after three types of disaster. *Journal of Consulting and Clinical Psychology, 65,* 733–739.

Muñoz, R. F., Hollon, S. D., McGrath, E., Rehm, L. P., & VandenBos, G. R. (1994). On the AHCPR Depression in Primary Care Guidelines: Further considerations for practitioners. *American Psychologist, 49,* 42–61.

Muñoz, R. F., Mrazek, P. J., & Haggerty, R. J. (1996). Institute of Medicine report on prevention of mental disorders: Summary and commentary. *American Psychologist, 51, 11,* 1116–1122.

Newman, F. L., & Howard, K. I. (1991). Introduction to the special section on seeking new clinical research methods. *Journal of Consulting and Clinical Psychology, 59,* 8–11.

Pennebaker, J. W. (1995). Emotion, disclosure, and health: An overview. In J. W. Pennebaker (Ed.), *Emotion, disclosure, and health* (pp. 3–10). Washington, DC: American Psychological Association.

Pennebaker, J. W. (1997a). *Opening up: The healing power of expressed emotions* (Rev. ed.). New York: Guilford.

Pennebaker, J. W. (1997b). Writing about emotional experience as a therapeutic process. *Psychological Science, 8,* 162–166.

Reynolds, S., Stiles, W. B., Barkham, M., Shapiro, D. A., Hardy, G. E., & Rees, A. (1996). Acceleration of changes in session impact during contrasting time-limited psychotherapies. *Journal of Consulting and Clinical Psychology, 64,* 577–586.

Robins, C. J., & Hayes, A. M. (1993). An appraisal of cognitive therapy. *Journal of Consulting and Clinical Psychology, 61,* 205–214.

Ryff, C. D. (1995). Psychological well-being in adult life. *Current Directions in Psychological Science, 4,* 99–104.

Ryff, C. D., Lee, Y. H., & Na, K. C. (1997). *Through the lens of culture: Psychological well-being at midlife.* Unpublished manuscript. University of Wisconsin-Madison.

Ryff, C. D., & Singer, B. (1996). Psychological well-being: Meaning, measurement, and implications for psychotherapy research. *Psychotherapy and psychosomatics, 65,* 14–23.

Ryff, C. D., & Singer, B. (1998a). The contours of positive human health. *Psychological Inquiry, 9,* 1–28.

Ryff, C. D., & Singer, B. (1998b). Human health: New directions for the next millennium, *Psychological Inquiry, 9,* 69–85.

Ryff, C. D., & Singer, B. (in press). The role of purpose in life and personal growth in positive human health. In T. P. Wong & P. S. Fry (Eds.), *The human quest for meaning: A handbook of psychological research and clinical application.* Mahwah, NJ: Lawrence Erlbaum Associates.

Schiepek, G., Fricke, B., & Kaimer, P. (1992). Synergetics of psychotherapy. In W. Tschacher, G. Schiepek, & E. J. Brunner (Eds.), *Self-organization and clinical psychology* (pp. 239–267). Berlin, Germany: Springer-Verlag.

Segal, Z. V., Williams, J. M., & Teasdale, J. D. (1998, November). *Attentional control training (ACT): An integrative approach to relapse prevention in depression.* Presentation at the annual convention of the Association for the Advancement of Behavior Therapy, Washington, DC.

Sherbourne, C. D., Hays, R. D., & Wells, K. B. (1995). Personal and psychosocial risk factors for physical and mental health outcomes and course of depression among depressed patients. *Journal of Consulting and Clinical Psychology, 63,* 345–355.

Siegler, R. S., & Ellis, S. (1996). Piaget on childhood. *Psychological Science, 7,* 211–215.

Simon, G., Ormel, J., VonKorff, M., & Barlow, W. (1995). Health care costs associated with depressive and anxiety disorders in primary care. *American Journal of Psychiatry, 152*(3), 352–357.

Teasdale, J. D., & Barnard, P. J. (1993). Psychological treatment for depression—The ICS [Interacting Cognitive Subsystems] perspective. In J. D. Teasdale & P. J. Barnard (Eds.), *Affect, cognition, and change* (pp. 225–245). Hillsdale, NJ: Lawrence Erlbaum Associates.

Teasdale, J. D., Segal, Z., & Williams, M.G. (1995). How does cognitive therapy prevent depressive relapse and why should attentional control (mindfulness) training help? *Behavior Research and Therapy, 33,* 25–39.

Tedeschi, R. G., & Calhoun, L. G. (1995). *Trauma and transformation.* Thousand Oaks, CA: Sage.

Thelen, E. (1995). Motor development: A new synthesis. *American Psychologist, 50,* 79–95.

Thelen, E., & Smith, L. B. (1994). *A dynamic systems approach to the development of cognition and action.* Cambridge, MA: MIT Press.

Thompson, M. G., Thompson, L., & Gallagher-Thompson, D. (1995). Linear and nonlinear changes in mood between psychotherapy sessions: Implications for treatment outcome and relapse risk. *Psychotherapy Research, 5,* 327–336.

Vallacher, R. R., & Nowak, A. (1994). *Dynamical systems in social psychology.* San Diego, CA: Academic Press.

Weinberger, J. (1993). Common factors on psychotherapy. In J. Gold & G. Stricker (Eds.), *Handbook of psychotherapy integration* (pp. 43–56). New York: Plenum.

Weissman, M. M., & Olfson, M. (1995, August). Depression in women: Implications for health care research. *Science, 269,* 799–801.

Young, J. E. (1994). *Cognitive therapy for personality disorders.* Sarasota, FL: Professional Resource Press.

Chapter 14

Integrated Family and Individual Therapy for Bipolar Disorder

Elizabeth L. George
Joanne C. Friedman
David J. Miklowitz
University of Colorado at Boulder

This chapter describes the research and clinical background for a new psychosocial treatment for bipolar affective (manic–depressive) illness: integrated family and individual therapy (IFIT). IFIT is a 1-year outpatient treatment delivered in conjunction with mood-regulating medications. We describe the syndrome of bipolar disorder, the manner in which it is affected by psychosocial stress, and the role of psychotherapy in its treatment. The bulk of the chapter is devoted to describing the IFIT treatment method. It is our hope that the reader will gain an appreciation for the difficult life course of bipolar disorder, the ways in which it affects and is affected by families, and the importance of psychosocial treatments—both individual and family-based—as adjuncts to medication for the outpatient maintenance of the disorder.

BIPOLAR DISORDER AND ITS TREATMENT

What Is Bipolar Disorder?

Bipolar (manic–depressive) disorder is a recurrent major affective disorder. Patients with *bipolar I disorder* alternate between high, elated or irritable periods (manias) and deep depressions, and/or they have mixed episodes (periods in which mania and depression are present concurrently). *Bipolar II patients*, who are more frequently women, have recurrent major depressions that alternate with hypomanic (mildly or moderately manic) episodes. About 13% to 20% of bipolar patients have rapid cycling courses that involve four or more episodes of mood disorder per year (Calabrese, Fatemi, Kujawa, & Woyshville, 1996).

Bipolar disorder is associated with high social costs. In the United States alone, about $45 billion was spent in 1991 on the direct and indirect costs of this disorder (Wyatt & Henter, 1995). In addition, it is associated with a host of social and occupational disturbances. As many as 1 of 3 bipolar patients cannot work at all in the 6 months following a manic episode and only 20% work at their expected level (Dion, Tohen, Anthony, & Waternaux, 1988). Over 50% show declines in their work functioning in the 5 years after an episode (Coryell, Anreasen, Endicott, & Keller, 1987; Coryell et al.,1993). Family members suffer emotionally, economically, and socially from the effects of the disorder (Miklowitz & Goldstein, 1997).

Bipolar disorder is treated primarily with pharmacotherapy. Currently, lithium carbonate, divalproex sodium (Depakote), and carbamazepine (Tegretol) are the primary agents used as mood stabilizers. These drugs may be combined with antipsychotics, antidepressants, or anti-anxiety agents, depending on the patient's presenting symptoms, the stage of the disorder, and the prior life course. However, even when patients take medications as prescribed, as many as 40% relapse in 1 year, 60% in 2 years, and 73% in 5 years (Gelenberg et al., 1989; Gitlin, Swendsen, Heller, & Hammen, 1995; Shapiro, Quitkin, & Fleiss, 1989; Small et al., 1988). Even when patients do not relapse, a significant proportion (46% to 56%) show lengthy periods of intermorbid symptoms, even with medication (Gitlin et al., 1995; Harrow, Goldberg, Grossman, & Meltzer, 1990). Moreover, the suicide rate among bipolar patients is estimated to be 30 times greater than that of the normal population (Goodwin & Jamison, 1990; Guze & Robins, 1970). Although pharmacotherapy is critical to the community maintenance of bipolar patients, it does not fully address the recurrent nature of this disorder and the accompanying disturbances in psychosocial functioning.

Psychosocial Factors in the Course of Bipolar Disorder

Implicit in the assumption that psychotherapy will aid bipolar patients is the belief that psychosocial stress must play a role in the course of the disorder. Is there evidence for this view? If so, what kinds of stress are prognostically important?

Life-Events Research. A review by Johnson and Roberts (1995) of the life-events–bipolar-disorder literature concluded that elevated rates of life events occur during the periods just before the onset of illness episodes (compared to other periods in patients' lives) and that bipolar patients probably experience more major life events prior to episodes than nonpsychiatric controls studied over comparable time periods. They do not, however, experience more major life events than comparison psychiatric patients.

Johnson and Roberts (1995) reviewed various models for understanding this stress–outcome relation. Particularly promising are models that implicate biobehavioral dysregulation and circadian rhythm disruption (e.g., Wehr, Sack, & Rosenthal, 1987). Relevant to the latter, Malkoff-Schwartz et al. (1998) found that in the 8 weeks prior to a manic episode, bipolar patients were disproportionately likely to experience life events that might have disrupted daily routines and particularly, sleep–wake cycles (e.g., transatlantic air travel). As is noted later, psychotherapy models that help patients to recognize and minimize the disorganizing effects of certain life stressors (particularly those stressors that affect sleep–wake cycles) may go far in helping patients to stabilize their mood states (Frank et al., 1994).

Family Stress. A separate literature, and one that we are mostly concerned with here, addresses the influences of family discord and distress on the course of bipolar affective disorder. Early clinical writings on the family environments of bipolar patients described highly driven, competitive, and conventional family milieus (Cohen, Baker, Cohen, Fromm-Reichmann, & Weigert, 1954; Gibson, 1958). However, most of these observations were based on psychoanalytic explorations of patients who already had the disorder, rather than on controlled research. Other writers focused on the increased prevalence of childhood loss among diagnosed patients (Brodie & Leff, 1971; Carlson, Kotin, Davenport, & Adland, 1974; Perris, 1966; Roy, 1980), but they did not clarify whether losses of parents, which were sometimes due to suicide, reflected the genetic predispositions to major affective disorder in these patients and families.

For some time our research team has been systematically examining the family environments of bipolar patients, particularly as they compare to the families of schizophrenic patients. We have drawn several conclusions. First, during or shortly after the manic episode, the family environments of bipolar patients become quite stressful and disorganized, and the family's interactional patterns become conflictual. Miklowitz, Goldstein, and Nuechterlein (1995) observed that families consisting of biological parents and their bipolar offspring showed a different pattern of interaction than did families consisting of parents and their schizophrenic offspring. Their transactional cycles involved critical and/or intrusive statements from parents and oppositional, feisty, highly verbal, and counterargumentative stances by bipolar patients. However, the relatives of bipolar patients were less critical than the relatives of schizophrenic patients. Interestingly, in the families of schizophrenic patients, criticism and intrusiveness from parents was more often paired with self-critical, self-denigrating, and withdrawn stances by patients.

Perhaps most crucial was the finding that high levels of expressed emotion (critical, hostile, and/or emotionally overinvolved attitudes by relatives) measured during the acute manic episode, and negative relative-to-patient transactions during the postepisode period, interacted to predict relapses of bipolar disorder. Specifically, in a study conducted at the University of California, Los Angeles (UCLA), Miklowitz and colleagues found that when manic patients returned to families marked by high expressed emotion and/or parents' negative verbal–interactional behavior (negative affective style), 94% (15 out of 16) of the patients relapsed at a 9-month follow-up (Miklowitz, Goldstein, Nuechterlein, Snyder, & Mintz, 1988). When patients returned to family environments marked by affective neutrality—either in parental expressed emotion or verbal–interactional behavior—only 17% (1 out of 6) relapsed by 9 months. These findings were independent of potentially confounding variables such as the number of prior episodes of the patient's disorder or his or her adherence to medications.

These findings regarding expressed emotion and poor clinical or psychosocial outcome have been replicated in other laboratories, one in the United States (O'Connell, Mayo, Flatow, Cuthbertson, & O'Brien, 1991) and one in Germany (Priebe, Wildgrube, & Muller-Oerlinghausen 1989). Thus, family stress appears to be an important prognostic indicator in the course of this disorder. By extension, family-treatment models that help families to cope during and shortly after the patient's mood-disorder episode are potentially efficacious adjuncts to medication regimes. Testing this assumption, however, involves developing manuals for family treatments and then evaluating their efficacy in randomized, controlled trials.

Family Treatment Research

Family psychoeducation is a model in which families and patients coping with a psychiatric disorder learn about the nature, origins, course, and treatment of the disorder. This promising treatment model for bipolar patients has its roots in schizophrenia research. Numerous controlled studies have documented the superiority of single-family or multifamily psychoeducational groups (together with neuroleptic medications) over standard outpatient medical care in delaying relapses of schizophrenia and improving social functioning (for a review, see Goldstein & Miklowitz, 1995; but also see Schooler et al., 1997).

The Cornell Studies. The literature on family psychoeducation for bipolar disorder is less advanced than that for schizophrenia, but a body of evidence is beginning to accumulate in support of its efficacy. A study at the Cornell University Medical College (Glick, Clarkin, Haas, Spencer, & Chen, 1991; Spencer et al., 1988) examined a brief inpatient family intervention for families of hospitalized psychiatric patients ($N = 186$). The goals of the treatment were to help participants adjust to the hospitalization period and to set goals for a successful posthospital adjustment, such as identifying and learning to cope with current and future stressors (e.g., family conflict). A controlled trial that compared this psychoeducation and pharmacotherapy with standard hospital care and pharmacotherapy revealed positive effects for the psychoeducational approach in the domains of global patient functioning and symptomatic outcome at 6-month and 18-month follow-up. The effects were seen primarily in female patients and within the affective disorder subgroup ($N= 50$), mostly among patients with bipolar disorder ($N= 21$). This well-designed study provides promising, but not conclusive, data on the long-term efficacy of family intervention for bipolar disorder.

Clarkin, Carpenter, Hull, Wilner, and Glick (1998) reported the results of their 1-year outpatient trial of mood-stabilizing medication plus psychoeducational marital therapy for bipolar patients and their spouses. This treatment was compared with a medication only group ($N = 33$). The combination of pharmacological and marital intervention was associated with better global functioning among patients and with better medication compliance, but not with better symptomatic functioning. Clarkin et al. did not report whether there was a mediational relation between treatment group assignment, medication compliance, and global functioning at follow-up. This is an important question to address in future research.

The UCLA and Colorado Studies. Miklowitz and Goldstein (1990, 1997) developed a psychoeducational family-focused treatment (FFT) for bipolar patients. This treatment consists of 21 outpatient sessions held over 9 months and involves several of the key treatment components that Falloon, Boyd, and McGill (1984) found successful in treating outpatients with schizophrenia. These components include: a functional assessment of the family or marital unit, education about bipolar disorder, communication training, and training in problem-solving skills. FFT has six additional objectives to address themes that Miklowitz and Goldstein found central to the treatment of recently episodic bipolar patients. These six goals include assisting the patient and his or her relatives in:

1. Integrating and making sense of the experiences associated with acute episodes of bipolar disorder.
2. Accepting the notion of vulnerability to future episodes.
3. Accepting the necessity of a drug treatment regime.
4. Distinguishing between the patient's personality and his or her disorder.

5. Recognizing and learning to cope with stressful life events that trigger recurrences of the disorder.
6. Reestablishing functional relationships after the mood-disorder episode.

In a pilot treatment trial at UCLA, 9 patients and family members were assigned to FFT with mood-stabilizing medications (usually lithium) and were compared with 23 historical control participants who had been followed over time without family treatment but with similar medication regimes. After 9 months of follow-up, only 1 of the 9 patients (11%) receiving FFT and medications relapsed, whereas 14 of the 23 historical control participants (61%) relapsed. However, larger, randomized clinical trials need to be conducted to determine the efficacy of this program. Two such trials are nearing completion, one at UCLA (M. Goldstein, Principal Investigator, D. Miklowitz, Coprincipal Investigator) and one at the University of Colorado (Miklowitz, Principal Investigator). Data from these trials are still being analyzed, but initial results suggest high rates of completion of the full FFT protocol (79% to 86%).

Why Combine Individual and Family Treatment?

It became clear while conducting the UCLA and Colorado studies that certain patients and families—even those who had positive outcomes—were quite difficult to treat. To identify these patients and families, we asked FFT clinicians at Colorado to fill out posttreatment questionnaires about their experiences of administering FFT to each project patient and family. The results indicated that the patients who were most difficult to treat were those with personality problems (e.g., long-standing interpersonal and emotional conflicts), social skill–communication deficits, and high levels of resistance to treatment (e.g., erractic attendance and refusing homework assignments). Not surprisingly, these patient attributes interfered with the acquisition of communication and problem-solving skills. We wondered whether an individual treatment might be more appropriate for these patients, either by itself or in combination with family treatment. Indeed, we were aware that FFT did not adequately address certain adverse life events with which patients were coping (e.g., job stress) nor did they address patients' characteristic ways of relating to persons outside of the family. We were concerned, however, that individual therapy by itself would not adequately address the communication problems and lack of shared perceptions about the disorder that characterized the family or marital environments of these patients.

In collaboration with Ellen Frank, Ph.D., at the University of Pittsburgh School of Medicine, we began to examine a treatment that combined family psychoeducation with interpersonal and social rhythm therapy (IPSRT; Frank et al., 1994). The *IPSRT model* is similar to the interpersonal psychotherapy of depression (Klerman, Weissman, Rounsaville, & Chevron, 1984) and focuses on helping patients renegotiate the interpersonal environment in the aftermath of a mood-disorder episode (i.e., learn how interpersonal difficulties influence the onset of mood-disorder episodes, and in turn, how mood episodes affect the patient's interpersonal functioning). To tailor this treatment to bipolar disorder, Frank et al. added an important component: a regular self-monitoring assignment in which patients were encouraged to track and regularize their daily social routines (i.e., social rhythms) and sleep–wake cycles, using a measure called the *Social Rhythm Metric* (Monk, Flaherty, Frank, Hoskinson, & Kupfer, 1990; Monk, Kupfer, Frank, & Ritenour, 1991). As mentioned earlier, bipolar patients are exquisitely sensitive to even minor changes in their daily routines, changes that in controlled research appear to precipitate episodes of mania (e.g., Malkoff-Schwartz et al., 1998).

We began by piloting this combined treatment with bipolar patients who had serious marital or family conflicts and/or had experienced major life events (e.g., dropping out of college). We assigned to each patient two therapists, one for the IPSRT therapy and the other for the FFT component. Clinicians met weekly to discuss and develop joint conceptualizations of each case. Clinicians also watched videotapes of each other's individual or family sessions and used this information to plan for their next session.

We were immediately impressed by the synergy that developed between the two approaches: The progress of the individual IPSRT component was informed by the family component and vice versa. For example, patients who admitted having difficulty communicating with their relatives in family sessions were able to discuss and begin to work through these resistances in individual sessions. In turn, many patients admitted to interpersonal difficulties in individual sessions, such as having to cope with the social stigma of their psychiatric disorder. These patients were able to discuss problems of stigma with their family members (parents or spouses) present and they often pointed out ways in which their family members were unknowingly stigmatizing them (e.g., treating him or her like a child). Family members would often counter that the patient seemed to solicit these kinds of family interactions. Finally, the patient's parents or marital partner provided important support for keeping the patient on a regular sleep–wake regime.

IFIT is still in its treatment development phases. The remainder of this chapter is devoted to briefly describing the individual and family components of this treatment and outlining what we learned so far from the 25 or more families whom we have treated with this combined approach.

IMPLEMENTING THE INTEGRATED FAMILY AND INDIVIDUAL THERAPY (IFIT) FOR BIPOLAR DISORDER

Overview

The IFIT treatment consists of 50 weekly clinic-based, individual IPSRT sessions and FFT couple or family sessions. Individual sessions alternate weekly with family sessions, with the exception that the first 3 to 5 weekly sessions are individual so that the patient can develop an alliance with the IPSRT therapist before participating in the potentially more stressful family component. After that point, patients receive individual and family sessions in alternating weeks, with the modal structure being one session every week for 1 year. All patients remain on their recommended pharmacotherapy regimes, which typically involve at least one mood-stabilizing (lithium or anticonvulsant) medication.

Initial Contact and Family Assessment

Ideally, contact with the patient and family is made when the patient is in the midst of either a depressive or manic episode. The family is quite often in a crisis state at this time and searching for information and coping strategies. This is often the best time for the clinician to forge an alliance with the family, offer support, and begin to provide education.

Through initial assessment procedures, the clinician begins to identify areas in which the family has displayed strengths and weaknesses. These areas include, but are not limited to, their understanding of bipolar disorder and management of the illness, communication skills, and problem-solving skills. The assessments serve as tools for developing a treatment strategy.

Initial individual interviews are conducted with the patient and each family member involved in the treatment (i.e., parents and spouse). Information from the patient about the presenting symptoms and history of the disorder can be obtained in part from a diagnostic interview such as the Structured Clinical Interview for DSM–IV (First, Spitzer, Gibbon, & Williams, 1995). Information from relatives can be obtained from the *Camberwell Family Interview* for rating expressed emotion (Vaughn & Leff, 1976). This interview clarifies the relative's relationship with the patient, attitudes about the illness and the patient's role in the family, and attributions about the causes of the patient's symptoms and behaviors.

A separate assessment is conducted to gather information about the patient and relatives in the family context. We ask all participating family members, including the patient, to discuss two problem issues during a laboratory assessment session (for reviews of this procedure, see Goldstein, Judd, Rodnick, Alkire, & Gould, 1968; Miklowitz et al., 1995). The clinician, while watching the family interactions, notes the clarity and efficiency of the family's communication and the effectiveness of its attempts at problem solving. Feedback is given to the family on the basis of the clinician's observations of the discussions. This assessment session is usually best done when the patient is out of the hospital (if hospitalized) and in at least a partial state of remission.

The Interpersonal and Social Rhythm Therapy (IPSRT) Component

The individual IPSRT component of IFIT usually begins shortly after the pretreatment assessments have been completed. IPSRT has a number of objectives that include helping the patient to regulate his or her social rhythms and sleep–wake cycles, understand the interpersonal context associated with the onset of mood symptoms, and learn how mood disorder symptoms affect the patient's work and social relationships. The initial phases of IPSRT involve encouraging the rapid stabilization of the patient's index episode. Later phases focus on prevention of relapse.

We begin with 3 to 5 weekly individual sessions. During this initial phase, the focus is on gathering information regarding the patient's illness history, initiating the weekly Social Rhythm Metric (SRM), conducting an interpersonal inventory to assess the patient's current relationships, and identifying one or more key problem areas for consideration.

The Social Rhythm Metric (SRM). While gathering a history of the illness, the clinician helps the patient see linkages between life events, periods of social rhythm disruption, and episodes of mania, hypomania, and depression. In doing so, he or she provides a rationale to the patient for the necessity of stable daily social rhythms. The SRM is a measure the patient uses to record daily activities, level of stimulation, and mood. The SRM enables the patient to see the relations among unstable or erratic daily routines, social stimulation, sleep–wake times, and mood states. Later, the focus changes to how the patient can stabilize his or her routines in the face of life events that threaten this stability (e.g., a change in job hours).

The Interpersonal Inventory. The next step in IPSRT is to identify the scope and quality of the patient's current social support network. Through this inventory, the clinician gains a sense of what kind of impact the illness has had on the patient's interpersonal functioning. During the interpersonal inventory the clinician identifies an area that is most descriptive of the patient's current interpersonal difficulties. Interpersonal problems among bipolar and unipolar patients generally fall into one of the following categories (after Klerman et al., 1984): unresolved grief (e.g., loss of a significant other), role transitions (e.g., a change in the patient's lifestyle), interpersonal disputes (e.g., conflicts with an employer or significant other), and interpersonal deficits (e.g., difficulty navigating mutually satisfying relationships).

Initial Family Education Sessions

Once the patient is well-engaged in IPSRT, family-focused psychoeducation sessions can begin. FFT is often best conducted by a cotherapy team, as each clinician can provide a check on the other's objectivity. Furthermore, the team can model communication skills for the family during sessions. However, FFT can certainly be delivered by a single-family therapist.

The most important goal of the initial sessions of FFT is to "join" with the family. The first sessions are supportive, flexible in structure, and stress reducing. If the clinician initially begins with a strict agenda, the family may feel "steamrolled" and may express resistance. It is often helpful to explore the patient's and family's experiences of working with the mental health system as well as how these experiences affect the family's views of the upcoming treatment. We generally provide the family with a handout summarizing the format, topics, expectations, and duration of the treatment.

Family education sessions (seven or more) provide the patient and family with a comprehensive understanding of bipolar disorder. The following list of issues in psychoeducation (adapted from Miklowitz and Goldstein, 1997) presents the core topics that are covered in the psychoeducational module. Each session builds on itself so that at the end of the education module all of the information provided aids the family in developing a realistic plan for reducing the risk of relapse.

The Symptoms and Course of the Disorder

- The signs and symptoms of bipolar disorder.
- The development of the most recent episode.
- Initial symptoms that present before an episode.
- Discussing the episode and/or hospitalization experience.
- Variations in prognosis: the course of the disorder.

The Etiology of Bipolar Disorder

- The vulnerability–stress model.
- The roles of stress and life events.
- Genetic and biological predispositions.
- Risk and protective factors.

Intervening Within the Vulnerability–Stress Model

- Types of medication and their uses.
- Psychosocial treatments.
- How the family can help.
- The self-management of the disorder.
- The relapse drill (Miklowitz & Goldstein, 1997).

During the education component several objectives are met. First, the patient and family identify the symptoms that the patient experienced during the most recent episode. Second, the *vulnerability–stress hypothesis* is presented as a model for understanding etiology. This hypothesis states that stress can activate a pre-existing vulnerability (i.e., a genetically based biochemical imbalance) to mood disorder. Family members are asked to identify sources of biological vulnerability relevant to the patient (i.e., family history of affective disorder). Likewise, they are asked to identify stressful events that may have contributed to the onset of the most recent manic or depressed episode. These discussions provide a rationale for maintaining a low stress home environment, a topic that becomes the focus of later communication and problem-solving segments of the treatment. Third, the family clinicians discuss the importance of maintaining a reasonable level of stimulation and structure within the family. Information regarding the role of circadian and social rhythm regulation in controlling episodes of mood disorder is presented, complementing what the patient is concurrently learning in IPSRT. Finally, the FFT clinician conducts a "relapse drill." The clinician begins by having the patient and family recall the previously identified symptoms that the patient displayed at the beginning of the most recent manic or depressive episode. Once the early warning signs are identified, then the relapse plan is put into place, including who should call the psychiatrist for an emergency session, how a hospital bed can be arranged (if necessary), and how the family or couple will communicate about these matters.

Intermediate and Later Phases of IPSRT Treatment

The patient has up to this point been engaged in biweekly sessions of IPSRT that alternate with family sessions. This structure may be retained throughout the course of treatment. However, as treatment progresses, some patients and family members prefer to titrate the family sessions to monthly or they prefer to emphasize the family sessions over the individual sessions. IFIT allows the clinicians to develop a flexible, individualized treatment contract.

During the intermediate and later phases of IPSRT, as patients become increasingly stable after their acute episode, the focus becomes the patient's interpersonal functioning and the prevention of relapse. There are two areas that the patient and clinician focus on. First, a symptom management plan is developed. By this point, the clinician and patient have begun to identify triggers for erratic or disruptive patterns in the patient's daily routine. The patient and clinician then take steps toward finding an optimal balance of social stimulation, rhythm regularity, and mood. Second, the key interpersonal areas (identified during the initial phase) are explored and potential resolutions discussed, with an emphasis on how these problem areas disrupt social rhythms and exacerbate symptoms. The problem areas—grief, interpersonal disputes, role transitions, and interpersonal deficits—each have associated treatment plans (Frank et al., 1994; Klerman et al., 1984).

The Intermediate Phase of FFT: Communication Enhancement Training. As the focus of IPSRT turns more toward the prevention of future interpersonal problems, the FFT component of IFIT likewise takes a preventative turn. Specifically, patients and family members are taught new ways to communicate about and solve problems regarding conflicts that may trigger future affective disorder episodes. The IPSRT therapist furthers the objectives of FFT by helping the patient to identify areas of family distress that could be remediated through better communication.

The FFT approach to communication skills training of bipolar patients and their families is based on the approach recommended by Falloon et al. (1984) for the families of schizophrenic patients. Four basic communication skills are taught: active listening, positive feedback, positive requests for change, and expressing negative feelings. Patients and families have varying levels of competence with these skills when they enter IFIT, and the clinician focuses the training as a function of which of these skills needs the most remediation.

Many families have commented that learning these communication tools in isolation from a specific problem seems artificial and irrelevant. In these cases, the FFT clinician may briefly model, for the family, each skill and then move into a combination of problem solving and communication training.

The Late Phase of FFT: Problem-Solving Skills Training. One of the assumptions of FFT is that learning the steps involved in effective problem solving and using these steps with good communication reduces the tension in the family (Falloon, Liberman, Lillie, & Vaughn, 1981; Falloon et al., 1984). At this stage of treatment (often more than 6 months after entry into the program), the patient has been working with his or her IPSRT therapist to identify unresolved family problems and their impact. The patient is encouraged to bring these problems up in family sessions. The FFT clinician likewise asks family members to identify unresolved problems (many of which will have already surfaced in the ongoing treatment or during the initial assessment phase) and to review their current strategies for solving problems. Then the clinician teaches the family specific steps used in problem solving and has them record their efforts on a problem-solving worksheet (Falloon et al., 1981; Falloon et al., 1984; Jacobson & Margolin, 1979; Miklowitz & Goldstein, 1997).

The first skill is defining the problem. When doing so, family members are reminded to use their new communication skills. Once the family has identified the problem as specifically and clearly as possible, the family or couple "brainstorms" possible solutions. The next step is to list the pros and cons of each solution. In this process, many solutions are eliminated as the family recognizes that there are many more cons than pros. Finally, the family chooses the solution that appears most effective and sets a plan for implementation. Often families find later that implementing the solution to the problem generates its own problems and that they must alter the original solution or choose another one. The family continues with this process until they find an effective set of solutions that works best for all family members involved.

Problems Experienced by the Families of Bipolar Patients

Families of bipolar patients often present with a specific set of illness-related problems. We have summarized these as: medication usage and compliance, "life trashing" (the damage done to the patient's and family's or couple's lives as a result of the illness), resumption of prior work and social roles, and relationship and/or living situation conflicts (Miklowitz & Goldstein, 1997). These problems are similar to those concurrently addressed in the intermediate and later phases of IPSRT (i.e., role transitions, role disputes, etc.). However, the FFT treatment complements the exploration of these same problems in IPSRT by breaking larger problems down into smaller ones, involving family members in the solution process, and taking a more structured approach to problem resolution. The combination of these two approaches is often powerful in bringing about resolutions to problems that at first may have seemed daunting to the family.

Termination of IFIT

Toward the end of treatment, the IPSRT and FFT clinicians review with the patient and family the areas of improvement and those that still need additional work. Sessions during the termination period concentrate on reviewing symptoms, recognizing signs of recurrence, and instituting a relapse prevention plan in the event of future episodes.

If the clinician feels that either the patient and/or family is still in need of treatment, referrals for family and/or individual therapy are made. Sometimes, self-help or support groups for families coping with major affective disorders are the best referral source. The clinician continues to be a source of support to the patient and family until a trusting relationship with a new therapist has developed. Often, patients and families who have been through the program prefer maintenance sessions (e.g., every 3 months) to beginning afresh with a new clinician.

CONCLUSIONS AND FUTURE DIRECTIONS

The IFIT treatment has undergone a series of treatment development and standardization steps (i.e., manual development, piloting with patients, and devising training and therapist monitoring protocols). We have now begun a controlled clinical trial at the University of Colorado, comparing standard medication protocols plus IFIT with similar medication protocols plus family-focused treatment, IPSRT, or individual case management. The objective of this research is first, to determine which of these programs is most effective for a broad population of patients, and second, to determine which subgroups of patients (defined by various high-risk criteria) respond to each of these treatments.

The larger question of the efficacy of psychotherapy in combination with pharmacotherapy for bipolar disorder requires more study. We do not have answers to basic questions such as: At what stage of the disorder will psychotherapies have their greatest impact? Which domains of outcome are most likely to be influenced by psychotherapy (symptoms, drug compliance, economic costs of the illness, quality of life)? Which subgroups of patients will benefit from adjunctive family therapy, and which might best be served by a self-help or multifamily group? Furthermore, in developing and testing new psychosocial approaches, investigators must develop ways to export their treatments from academically based laboratories to real-world settings (the "efficacy–effectiveness" gap). Yet, important first steps are taken when investigators clearly spell out the techniques that define their treatments, the degree to which the clinician can be flexible in implementing them, and the populations of psychiatric patients for which their treatments are intended.

ACKNOWLEDGMENTS

Preparation of this chapter was supported in part by National Institute of Mental Health Grants MH55101 and MH42556, a grant from the John D. and Catherine T. MacArthur Foundation Network on the Psychobiology of Depression and by a Faculty Fellowship to Dr. Miklowitz from the University of Colorado at Boulder.

REFERENCES

Brodie, H. K. H., & Leff, M. J. (1971). Bipolar depression: A comparative study of patient characteristics. *American Journal of Psychiatry, 127,* 1086–1090.

Calabrese, J. R., Fatemi, S. H., Kujawa, M., & Woyshville, M. J. (1996). Predictors of response to mood stabilizers. *Journal of Clinical Psychopharmacology, 16*(1), 24–31.

Carlson, G. A., Kotin, J., Davenport, Y. B., & Adland, M. (1974). Follow-up of 53 bipolar manic-depressive patients. *British Journal of Psychiatry, 124,* 134–139.

Clarkin, J. F., Carpenter, D., Hull, J., Wilner, P., & Glick, I. (1998). Effects of psychoeducational intervention for married patients with bipolar disorder and their spouses. *Psychiatric Services, 49,* 531–533.

Cohen, M., Baker, G., Cohen, R. A., Fromm-Reichmann, F., & Weigert, E. V. (1954). An intensive study of 12 cases of manic-depressive psychosis. *Psychiatry, 17,* 103–137.

Coryell, W., Anreasen, N. C., Endicott, J., & Keller, M. (1987). The significance of past mania or hypomania in the course and outcome of major depression. *American Journal of Psychiatry, 144,* 309–315.

Coryell, W., Scheftner, W., Keller, M., Endicott, J., Maser, J., & Klerman, G. L. (1993). The enduring psychosocial consequences of mania and depression. *American Journal of Psychiatry, 15,* 720–727.

Dion, G. L., Tohen, M., Anthony, W. A., & Waternaux, C. (1988). Symptoms and functioning of patients with bipolar disorder six months after hospitalization. *Hospital and Community Psychiatry, 39,* 652–656.

Falloon, I. R. H., Boyd, J. L., & McGill, C. W. (1984). *Family care of schizophrenia: A problem-solving approach to the treatment of mental illness.* New York: Guilford.

Falloon, I. R. H., Liberman, R. P., Lillie, F., & Vaughn, C. (1981). Family therapy of schizophrenics with high risk of relapse. *Family Process, 20,* 211–221.

First, M. B., Spitzer, R. L., Gibbon, M., & Williams, J. B. W. (1995). *Structured Clinical Interview for DSM–IV Axis I Disorders.* New York: New York State Psychiatric Institute.

Frank, E., Kupfer, D. J., Ehlers, C. L., Monk, T. H., Cornes, C., Carter, S., & Frankel, D. (1994). Interpersonal and social rhythm therapy for bipolar disorder: Integrating interpersonal and behavioral approaches. *Behavior Therapy, 17,* 143–149.

Gelenberg, A. J., Kane, J. N., Keller, M. B., Lavori, P., Rosenbaum, J. F., Cole, K., & Lavelle, J. (1989). Comparison of standard and low serum levels of lithium for maintenance treatment of bipolar disorders. *New England Journal of Medicine, 321,* 1489–1493.

Gibson, R. W. (1958). The family background and early life experience of the manic-depressive patient. *Psychiatry, 21,* 71–90.

Gitlin, M. J., Swendsen, J., Heller, T. L., & Hammen, C. (1995). Relapse and impairment in bipolar disorder. *American Journal of Psychiatry, 152,* 1635–1640.

Glick, I. D., Clarkin, J. F., Haas, G. L., Spencer, J. H., & Chen, C. L. (1991). A randomized clinical trial of inpatient family intervention: VI. Mediating variables and outcome. *Family Process, 30,* 85–99.

Goldstein, M. J., Judd, L. L., Rodnick, E. H., Alkire, A., & Gould, E. (1968). A method for studying social influence and coping patterns within families of disturbed adolescents. *Journal of Nervous and Mental Disease, 147,* 233–251.

Goldstein, M. J., & Miklowitz, D. J. (1995). The effectiveness of psychoeducational family therapy in the treatment of schizophrenic disorders. *Journal of Marital and Family Therapy, 21,* 361–376.

Goodwin, F. K., & Jamison, K. R. (1990). *Manic-depressive illness.* New York: Oxford University Press.

Guze, S. B., & Robins, E. (1970). Suicide and primary affective disorders. *British Journal of Psychiatry, 117,* 437–438.

Harrow, M., Goldberg, J. F., Grossman, L. S., & Meltzer, H. Y. (1990). Outcome in manic disorders: A naturalistic follow-up study. *Archives of General Psychiatry, 47,* 665–671.

Jacobson, N., & Margolin, G. (1979). *Marital therapy.* New York: Brunner/Mazel.

Johnson, S. L., & Roberts, J. E. (1995). Life events and bipolar disorder: Implications from biological theories. *Psychology Bulletin, 117,* 434–449.

Klerman, G. L., Weissman, M. M., Rounsaville, B. J., & Chevron, E. S. (1984). *Interpersonal psychotherapy of depression.* New York: Basic Books.

Malkoff-Schwartz, S., Frank, E., Anderson, B., Sherrill, J. T., Siegel, L., Patterson, D., & Kupfer, D. J. (1998). Stressful life events and social rhythm disruption in the onset of manic and depressive bipolar episodes: A preliminary investigation. *Archives of General Psychiatry, 55,* 702–707.

Miklowitz, D. J., & Goldstein, M. J. (1990). Behavioral family treatment for patients with bipolar affective disorder. *Behavior Modification, 14,* 457–489.

Miklowitz, D. J., & Goldstein, M. J. (1997). *Bipolar disorder: A family-focused treatment approach.* New York: Guilford.

Miklowitz, D. J., Goldstein, M. J., & Nuechterlein, K. H. (1995). Verbal interactions in the families of schizophrenic and bipolar affective patients. *Journal of Abnormal Psychology, 104,* 268–276.

Miklowitz, D. J., Goldstein, M. J., Nuechterlein, K. H., Snyder, K. S., & Mintz, J. (1988). Family factors and the course of bipolar affective disorder. *Archives of General Psychiatry, 45,* 225–231.

Monk, T. H., Flaherty, J. F., Frank, E., Hoskinson, K., & Kupfer, D. J. (1990). The social rhythm metric: An instrument to quantify daily rhythms of life. *Journal of Nervous and Mental Disease, 178,* 120–126.

Monk, T. H., Kupfer, D. J., Frank, E., & Ritenour, A. M. (1991). The social rhythm metric (SRM): Measuring daily social rhythms over two weeks. *Psychiatry Research, 36,* 195–207.

O'Connell, R. A., Mayo, J. A., Flatow, L., Cuthbertson, B., & O'Brien, B. E. (1991). Outcome of bipolar disorder on long-term treatment with lithium. *British Journal of Psychiatry, 159,* 132–139.

Perris, C. (1966). A study of bipolar (manic-depressive) and unipolar recurrent depressive psychoses: IV. Personality traits. *Acta Psychiatrica Scandinavica, 42*(194), 68–82.

Priebe, S., Wildgrube, C., & Muller-Oerlinghausen, B. (1989). Lithium prophylaxis and expressed emotion. *British Journal of Psychiatry, 154,* 396–399.

Roy, A. (1980). Parental loss in childhood and onset of manic-depressive illness. *British Journal of Psychiatry, 136,* 86–88.

Schooler, N. R., Keith, S. J., Severe, J. B., Matthews, S. M., Bellack, A. S., Glick, I. D., Hargreaves, W. A., Kane, J. M., Ninan, P. T., Frances, A., Jacobs, M., Lieberman, J. A., Mance, R., Simpson, G. M., & Woerner, M. G. (1997). Relapse and rehospitalization during maintenance treatment of schizophrenia: The effects of dose reduction and family treatment. *Archives of General Psychiatry, 54,* 453–463.

Shapiro, D. R., Quitkin, F. M., & Fleiss, J. L. (1989). Response to maintenance therapy in bipolar illness. *Archives of General Psychiatry, 46,* 401–405.

Small, J. G., Klapper, M. H., Kellams, J. J., Miller, M. J., Milstein, V., Sharpley, P. H., & Small, I. F. (1988). Electroconvulsive treatment compared with lithium in the management of manic states. *Archives of General Psychiatry, 45,* 727–732.

Spencer, J. H., Glick, I. D., Haas, G. L., Clarkin, J. F., Lewis, A. B., Peyser, J., DeMane, N., Good-Ellis, M., Harris, E., & Lestelle, V. (1988). A randomized clinical trial of inpatient family intervention, III: Effects at 6-month and 18-month follow-ups. *American Journal of Psychiatry, 145,* 1115–1121.

Vaughn, C. E., & Leff, J. P. (1976). The influence of family and social factors on the course of psychiatric illness: A comparison of schizophrenic and depressed neurotic patients. *British Journal of Psychiatry, 129,* 125–137.

Wehr, T. A., Sack, D. A., & Rosenthal, N. E. (1987). Sleep reduction as a final common pathway in the genesis of mania. *American Journal of Psychiatry, 144,* 210–214.

Wyatt, R. J., & Henter, I. (1995). An economic evaluation of manic-depressive illness. *Social Psychiatry and Psychiatric Epidemiology, 30,* 213–219.

Author Index

E

I

J

K

L

Subject Index

F

G

H